CAMPAIGNING WHILE BLACK

CAMPAIGNING WHILE BLACK

CAMPAIGNING WHILE BLACK

BLACK CANDIDATES,
WHITE MAJORITIES,
and the
QUEST FOR POLITICAL OFFICE

MATTHEW TOKESHI

Columbia University Press
New York

Columbia University Press
Publishers Since 1893
New York Chichester, West Sussex
cup.columbia.edu
Copyright © 2023 Columbia University Press
All rights reserved

Library of Congress Cataloging-in-Publication Data
Names: Tokeshi, Matthew, author.
Title: Campaigning while Black : Black candidates, white majorities, and the quest for political office / Matthew Tokeshi.
Description: New York : Columbia University Press, [2023] | Includes bibliographical references and index.
Identifiers: LCCN 2023011981 (print) | LCCN 2023011982 (ebook) | ISBN 9780231209267 (hardback) | ISBN 9780231209274 (trade paperback) | ISBN 9780231557856 (ebook)
Subjects: LCSH: Political campaigns—United States—Case studies. | African American politicians—United States—Public opinion. | White people—United States—Attitudes—History—21st century. | Race discrimination—Political aspects—United States. | Racism—Political aspects—United States. | United States—Race relations—Political aspects. | United States—Politics and government—21st century.
Classification: LCC JK2281 .T65 2023 (print) | LCC JK2281 (ebook) | DDC 324.7089/96073—dc23/eng/20230413
LC record available at https://lccn.loc.gov/2023011981
LC ebook record available at https://lccn.loc.gov/2023011982

Printed and bound by CPI Group (UK) Ltd, Croydon, CR0 4YY

Cover design: Elliott S. Cairns
Cover image: Kevin Lamarque / Reuters / Alamy Stock Photo

TO MY MOM AND DAD
AND TO CRISTINA, LUISA, AND CATALINA

CONTENTS

Acknowledgments ix

INTRODUCTION 1

1. WHY ARE BLACK GOVERNORS AND U.S. SENATORS SO RARE? RACIAL BIAS AGAINST BLACK CHALLENGERS, 2000–2020   16

2. THE RACIALIZATION OF BLACK CANDIDATES   35

3. THE RESPONSE OF BLACK CANDIDATES   53

4. THE DEVAL PATRICK AND HAROLD FORD JR. CAMPAIGNS OF 2006   71

5. THE 2013 CORY BOOKER AND 2014 ANTHONY BROWN CAMPAIGNS   99

6. WHEN BLACK WOMEN RUN: THE 2018 STACEY ABRAMS AND 2020 KAMALA HARRIS CAMPAIGNS   130

7. THE BOOKER EXPERIMENT 150

8. THE CRIMINAL PARDON EXPERIMENT 168

CONCLUSION 187

Appendixes 205
Notes 243
Index 277

ACKNOWLEDGMENTS

This book could not have been written without the help of many, many people. I am honored to be able to thank them for all they've done over the years to provide the emotional, practical, intellectual, and financial support necessary to write a book. First, I thank my parents, David and Yoko. Thank you for instilling in me the empathy and respect for the human condition, intellectual curiosity, hard work, and resilience that are the foundation for all of my life's endeavors. I had to draw upon all of those values to finish this project. My mother died in December 2021, so she did not get to see the finished product. Of course, she would be proud of my achievements, but what made her a wonderful mother is that she would be proud of me no matter what. I hope to live my life in a way that honors her memory.

Among my many intellectual debts, my greatest debt is to my primary mentor at Princeton, Tali Mendelberg. I thank her for her unwavering belief in me from my first semester in graduate school, which continues to this day. There are far too many things to thank her for than I can list here, but among them are introducing me to the literature on racial attitudes and political behavior, teaching me how to design surveys and experiments, taking me on as a coauthor early in graduate school and showing me how to produce political science scholarship, offering critical feedback on countless drafts of my work, helping me find a job, offering advice on how to deal with harsh criticism, and helping me find a home for this book. Among the big-picture lessons I learned from watching Tali are the commitment that it takes to succeed in this profession and that you should never settle for OK when you're capable of excellence. I thank Tali for her inspired example and the many kindnesses she has shown me over the years.

I also had the very good fortune to meet Chris Achen during my time at Princeton. Chris spent many hours listening to my musings (and offering his own!) on topics that were way beyond the scope of my research. The main thing those conversations conveyed to me is that I belong at Princeton and that I have something to contribute to political science. I thank him for that. Thanks also go to Marty Gilens and Omar Wasow, as well as other Princeton faculty who shaped my intellectual and professional growth: Paul Frymer, LaFleur Stephens-Dougan, Ali Valenzuela, and Ed Freeland. I am especially grateful to my Princeton classmate Mike Hoffman for being the kind of friend everyone needs to make it through graduate school.

After leaving Princeton, I found a new home at Williams College. I thank my colleagues in the political science department for their camaraderie and the many conversations that have enabled me to grow as a political scientist. The learning curve as an assistant professor is steep, but it has been eye-opening and rewarding to learn from such outstanding scholars and educators. The Oakley Center for the Humanities and Social Sciences at Williams provided a nurturing home during the year 2020, which suddenly became very quiet when the coronavirus pandemic broke out in March. Thankfully, I had the opportunity to present at the fellows seminar in May 2020 (over Zoom), where I received many helpful comments that made me rethink the conclusion of this book. I also thank the dozens of phenomenal students I have taught at Williams over the years who have taught me a lot about American politics.

Several of those wonderful Williams students provided excellent research assistance for this book. I thank Kaitlin Braband, Jose Manuel Corichi Gomez, Sam Mermin, Yannick Davidson, Grace Kim, Ondine Jevremov, Stephanie Teng, and Utsav Bahl for doing work that was absolutely critical to the book's completion. I also thank Princeton students Chaya Crowder and Sonya Chen for their research assistance and Michele Epstein for pointing them in my direction.

Generous financial support for this project was provided by Princeton's Center for the Study of Democratic Politics, Princeton's Bobst Center for Peace and Justice, Princeton's Industrial Relations Section, Princeton's Program in American Studies, and Princeton Research in Experimental Social Science. At Williams, I benefitted from the Class of 1957 Research Fund. I also thank Jay Leve and Ken Alper at SurveyUSA, Steve Raabe at the *Baltimore Sun*, David Redlawsk, and Michael Hanmer for generously providing data that I used in chapters 4 and 5. Stephen Wesley at Columbia University Press also deserves thanks for his enthusiastic support of this project.

On a personal note, I thank the many friends I've made in Williamstown through sports and games, dinners, little kids' birthday parties, and everyday parenting. I didn't know what to expect when I first moved to this small New England town with only one stoplight. But I quickly found Williamstown to be full of wonderful people. A very special thanks goes to Emilce Salas for invaluable help when I needed it most. Thanks also go to the Brooklyn gang. The challenges of graduate school were manageable because of the Christmakkuhs, New Year's Eves, Sunday dinners, birthdays, weddings, births, and all the other good times in between. I will always cherish those times, and I look forward to more in the years to come.

Thanks also go to Jun and Paul for being the best brothers anyone could ask for; my cousin Tai for always being my buddy; my late grandparents Edward and Yone for their example of perseverance, dignity, and tolerance in the face of bigotry and injustice; the Thompsons for being the East Coast version of my family; and Calvin for being my loyal companion during the many hours I spent sitting at the computer in the early days of this project. Finally, to my wonderful wife, Cristina: thank you for being my partner through all of the ups and downs we've experienced over the years. I am grateful for the many sacrifices you've made—including moving all over the place and listening to my worries and complaints about many inconsequential things—so that I could pursue a career I love. You and our amazing daughters, Luisa and Catalina, are the reason for everything in my life. Thanks for making all of my dreams come true.

CAMPAIGNING WHILE BLACK

CAMPAIGNING WHILE BLACK

INTRODUCTION

In late August 2022, Mandela Barnes's campaign to become Wisconsin's first Black U.S. senator looked promising. Barnes held a 5.5 percentage point lead over Republican Ron Johnson on August 18, according to *RealClearPolitics*' aggregation of polls. But then Johnson and allied super PACs unleashed an onslaught of ads attacking Barnes on crime. One ad criticized Barnes for opposing cash bail. It showed video clips of Darrell Brooks, a Black man, driving his car into a crowd at a 2021 Christmas parade in Waukesha, Wisconsin, followed by Brooks's mug shot and footage of him in police custody. The ad ended with Barnes's photo alongside three Democratic House members and women of color: Alexandria Ocasio-Cortez, Rashida Tlaib, and Ilhan Omar. The words "different" and "dangerous" appeared on screen. Another ad featured old footage of Barnes saying, "Reducing prison populations is now sexy." A third ad showed Barnes in front of a wall with the words "Defund the Police" written in spray paint. Both ads repeated the association with Ocasio-Cortez and Omar and the word "dangerous" at the end. According to the ad-tracking firm AdImpact, 70 percent of Republican ads airing in the Wisconsin Senate race from August 30 to October 31 mentioned crime.[1] The ads appear to have had an effect, as Johnson led the final *RealClearPolitics* polling average on November 8 by 3.6 percentage points and went on to win the election by a single percentage point.

The attack on Barnes was not unique. Across the country in 2022, Black candidates running competitively for the high-level statewide offices of governor or U.S. senator faced similar attacks on their stances on crime. In North Carolina, the Senate candidate Cheri Beasley was attacked for her legal representation of two Black men accused of killing a white police officer in 1998. The ad showed the Black men wearing orange jumpsuits. Another ad criticized her decision as a North Carolina Supreme Court justice to strike down a law that would require lifetime GPS tracking for child sex offenders. The ad featured the mug shot of a Black man who was accused of raping a seven-year-old boy and impregnating a fifteen-year-old girl. Beasley lost a hard-fought race to Republican Ted Budd by a narrow 3.2 percentage point margin. In Georgia, footage of the gubernatorial candidate Stacey Abrams saying she favored the reallocation of police resources was used to tie her to the "defund the police" movement. Abrams lost by 7.5 percentage points. In Florida, the Senate candidate Val Demings was accused of being antipolice, and her race, which was once expected to be competitive, ended up being a 16.4 percentage point blowout in favor of her opponent, Marco Rubio.

Political scientists have long understood the potency of these messages. Using George H. W. Bush's Willie Horton attack ads, which were aimed at painting his Democratic opponent Michael Dukakis as soft on crime in 1988, as a case study and in follow-up lab experiments, research has demonstrated that attacks on stereotypically anti-Black themes like crime activate racial attitudes among white voters, making these attitudes a stronger predictor of vote choice than they would otherwise be in the absence of such attacks.[2] In other words, attacks on racialized issues like crime are often understood in racial terms by many white Americans. But the full story on racial attacks cannot be known until we know more about how effective those attacks are after facing some form of contestation from the attacked candidate.

How do the attacked candidates respond? One strategy is to highlight the attacker's negativity, as Barnes did in a counter ad in which he said, "Look, we knew the other side would make up lies about me to scare you."[3] Barnes also tried to shift attention to a subject he thought his opponent was weaker on: Johnson's support for the January 6 insurrection. Barnes said, "When we talk about respect for law enforcement, let's talk about the 140 officers [Johnson] left behind because of the insurrection he supported."[4] Demings countered attacks that she was antipolice by saying, "I am the police," touting her pro-police credentials as the former police chief of Orlando, Florida.[5] Occasionally, Black candidates condemn an attack as racist, as the 2018 Florida gubernatorial candidate Andrew Gillum did in response to attacks from his opponent, Ron DeSantis, and from President Donald Trump, who both repeatedly accused Gillum of being corrupt and soft on crime. Gillum said that DeSantis and Trump "no longer do whistle calls. They're now using full bull horns."[6] A variety of strategies have been tried, but political scientists have largely overlooked this critical aspect of "campaigning while Black." This book systematically examines not only the broader message environment that Black candidates encounter when running for high-level statewide office but also how candidates respond, whether rebuttals are effective at all, and, if so, which ones and why.

Understanding the effects of racial messages is important because they play a central role in limiting the representation of Black Americans at the highest levels of American politics. Although President Barack Obama broke the presidential color barrier, a wider look at the highest rungs of power in American politics reveals that Blacks are still rarely elected to the most powerful and prestigious offices. One rung below the presidency are the high-level statewide offices of governor and senator. Only ten Blacks have ever been elected governor or senator since Reconstruction.[7] Blacks were 11 percent of the 2020 presidential electorate. If the number of Black officeholders was proportionate to the Black share of the electorate, there would be about eleven Black senators and five or six Black governors right now, rather than only ten Black governors or senators *ever.* Following the 2022 elections, only three out of the hundred senators (Cory Booker of New Jersey, Tim Scott of South Carolina, and Raphael Warnock of Georgia) and one governor out of fifty (Wes Moore of Maryland) were Black. Forty-two of the fifty states have never elected a Black governor or senator. So while Obama broke the presidential color barrier, the glass ceiling one level below the presidency is largely intact across the vast majority of American states.

This book's examination of the general election campaigns of every Black challenger for governor or senator from 2000 to 2020 points to the formidable hurdle posed by white voters in statewide electorates and the continuing relevance of racial appeals in campaigns as being a significant reason for the persistence of this racial barrier to high office. The emphasis on the role of racial appeals is especially relevant in an era in which former President Trump has demonstrated the viability of racial politics.[8] As the experiences of Black candidates in 2022 demonstrate, Black candidates are likely to confront challenging racialized campaign dynamics long after Trump's presidency. However, this does not necessarily spell doom for them. I show that Black candidates respond to negative racial messages and, in some circumstances, can neutralize their damaging effects. Thus, although Black candidates face unique obstacles, they can nonetheless find ways to respond to attacks they are likely to encounter when attempting to reach the highest offices in the United States.

WHY HIGH-LEVEL STATEWIDE CANDIDACIES?

The Obama presidency has dominated popular and scholarly interest on the question of how a candidate's race influences voting behavior.[9] Some observers viewed Obama's successful campaigns for the presidency as prima facie evidence that race is no longer a net negative factor in whites' voting decisions.[10] Careful empirical study, however, has demonstrated that racial attitudes powerfully shaped evaluations of Obama in ways that hurt him on balance.[11]

Although much is now known about how racial prejudice shaped evaluations of Obama, the exclusive focus on Obama has obscured a broader understanding of how race shapes electoral politics. For one, the focus on Obama makes it easy to forget the basic facts regarding the current state of underrepresentation at the gubernatorial and senate levels cited earlier. Focusing on a wider range of high-level offices calls into question the sanguine conclusion that race is no longer an obstacle to winning those offices. The studies that find evidence of racial prejudice in the Obama elections are also limited in the sense that Obama represents the only case at the presidential level. Obama is unique in ways that may amplify or somewhat reduce the impact of prejudice. Being the first viable Black candidate for the presidency amplifies the impact of prejudice, given that it represents a powerful symbolic challenge to the existing racial order.[12] On the other hand, his biracial heritage and light skin color are but two factors that probably mitigated the impact of prejudice.[13] Either way, an examination of the full range of cases at the statewide level will provide results that are more broadly generalizable than those found in the existing literature on the Obama presidential campaigns.

Another reason to focus on statewide candidacies is that existing research on Black candidacies for lower offices are likely to underestimate the effect of racism. Research on Black candidacies at the congressional or mayoral levels does not reach a consensus on the question of whether white voters demonstrate racial bias.[14] Two prominent studies say they do not,[15] with one study of U.S. House elections in 1996 and 1998 concluding that "the barrier presented by white voters in general elections does not appear especially daunting, especially in relation to the barrier it is often perceived to be."[16] But appraisals of prejudice at the congressional and mayoral levels may be too optimistic for two reasons. First, these offices are likely to be perceived as less powerful and more geographically limited than the offices of governor and senator and are therefore less likely to trigger racial anxiety.[17] Second, unlike in municipal or congressional elections, white voters outnumber Black voters in every U.S. state. The substantial power held by white voters over who gets elected governor or senator presents a hurdle facing any Black candidate seeking those offices. This is a significant hurdle as Black candidates rarely win elections in majority-white jurisdictions.[18] One recent illustration of this is the 2014 elections for the U.S. House, where only 5 percent of districts with white majorities elected Black representatives.[19] In sum, a study of statewide elections for powerful offices in which Black candidates must win substantial support from a predominantly white electorate are likely to detect racial effects that studies focused on local offices may miss.

For all of these reasons, this book advances scholarship on the impact of racism in electoral politics by providing a comprehensive examination of white voters' evaluations of Black candidates one level below the presidency. This is a better or at least complementary test of the effect of prejudice because these offices represent a broader set of cases. In any event, it is a novel test, as no previous study of Black high-level statewide candidates compiles the entire set of relevant cases.[20]

THE NATURE OF CAMPAIGNS

The book also presents new evidence on the nature of campaigns when Black candidates run for high-level statewide office. We know that Black candidates are careful in their self-presentation to white voters, usually opting for a "deracialized" presentation to predominantly white electorates.[21] But do their white opponents try to inject race into the campaign anyway? If so, under what conditions, and are they successful? From existing case studies, we know that Black statewide candidates face attacks on issues that evoke stereotypically anti-Black themes like crime and sexual misbehavior.[22] Consider a few memorable examples. In 2006, Democrat Deval Patrick became the second elected Black governor since Reconstruction when he won the Massachusetts gubernatorial election over Republican Kerry Healey. Patrick was elected despite facing racially tinged campaign attacks that resembled the Willie Horton ads used by George Bush in the 1988 presidential election.[23] One notable Healey ad known as the "parking-lot rape" ad began with a white woman walking alone in a dark parking garage and then cut to footage of Patrick describing a convicted rapist as "thoughtful" and "eloquent." Another Healey ad known as the "cop-killer" ad criticized Patrick's legal advocacy decades earlier on behalf of a man who killed a Florida police officer in the 1980s. The ad featured Patrick's photo paired with the killer's mug shot. Also in 2006, Harold Ford Jr., a Black Democrat running for a Tennessee U.S. Senate seat, was attacked in an ad run by the Republican National Committee that showed a blond woman who claimed to have met Ford at a Playboy party.[24] This ad generated national attention during the 2006 midterm elections and became known as the "call me" ad.

Although we know such attacks happen, we do not know whether they are exceptional or part of a broader strategy of attack against Black candidates. Similar attacks have been made against white candidates, most notably against Dukakis in 1988. But we have no hard evidence to date on the frequency of racialized attacks faced by Black and comparable white candidates. If Black candidates are more likely to encounter racialized attacks, this is likely to have negative consequences for their chances of winning, according to an influential body of research on the effects of racialized communication.[25] Existing research suggests that as the frequency of racialized attacks increases, so does the association between whites' racial attitudes and their vote, leading to diminished support for Black candidates among white voters with ambivalent or negative attitudes toward Blacks—a wide swath of voters in statewide elections.[26]

Although we know about the effects of racialized communication, we know little about how Black candidates respond to such messages. Previous studies of Black (and white) candidates facing racial attacks suggest that they often do not directly address racial attacks and instead choose to ignore them or change the subject to a topic more favorable to them.[27] But no study to date systematically identifies the full range of responses used by Black candidates, quantifies how often candidates use different response strategies, or tests which responses succeed and among which types of voters—questions that are vital to understanding how Black candidates navigate the statewide campaign environment.

THE ARGUMENT AND WHY IT MATTERS

The book sheds light on these unanswered questions by examining the campaigns of every Black challenger for governor or U.S. senator from 2000 to 2020. Given the historic scarcity of Blacks in these offices, the book focuses on candidates trying to win election to those offices for the first time. The analysis includes all available survey data for each campaign involving a viable Black candidate,[28] two original surveys, a content analysis of newspapers in all relevant states, and three original survey experiments.

One of my major claims is that Black candidates experience a heavily racialized campaign environment that poses a serious obstacle in their quest for high-level statewide office. When I systematically compare the attacks faced by viable statewide Black candidates to a comparable set of white candidates, I find that Black candidates face a greater number of attacks on themes that highlight negative stereotypes of Blacks such as crime, sexual misbehavior, and economic dependency. In fact, every viable Black challenger faced an unusually high number of attacks on at least one of these themes. One striking finding is that Deval Patrick faced about seven times as many crime attacks, and Cory Booker, a 2013 New Jersey U.S. Senate candidate, faced about eight times as many crime attacks compared to similar white Democratic candidates for Massachusetts governor and New Jersey senator, respectively. I also show that racial attacks activated white voters' racial attitudes (but not their nonracial attitudes, such as partisanship or ideology) in both laboratory and real-world settings.

My other major claim, however, is more optimistic: though the racialized campaign environment presents a formidable obstacle, it is not necessarily fatal. Some candidates, like Cory Booker in 2013 and Anthony Brown, who ran for governor of Maryland in 2014, made the mistake of allowing long stretches of their racialized campaigns to go by without a response, which led to the activation of racial resentment and the loss of white support. But others, like Deval Patrick, addressed negative racial attacks and mitigated their damage. The main conclusion to draw from these cases, which is also supported by my experimental findings, is that silence is a failed strategy, an important finding because the Booker and Brown examples demonstrate that silence is a strategy used by attacked candidates.

Although silence in the face of racial attacks is ineffective, there are some important caveats to how rebuttals work. First, I find that they are usually effective only among racially sympathetic whites. Second, I find that rebutting the message by explicitly pointing out its racial content is ineffective for Black candidates. This is true among all but the most racially sympathetic white respondents. Finally, in experimental tests of common real-world rebuttal strategies, I find that offering a credible justification for the attacked action restores the favorability of Black candidates. In sum, Black candidates face heavily racialized campaigns and are constrained in their rebuttal options, but they can still find effective ways to respond.

Before defending these claims, I elaborate on the broader importance of this argument. In the aftermath of the COVID-19 pandemic and the mass protests in response to the police killings of George Floyd, Breonna Taylor, and other Black Americans, the United States is once again grappling with the legacy of slavery and the ongoing effects of racism and structural inequality.

One consequence of the national reckoning on race has been a reexamination of how racism continues to shape representation in the most influential roles in American society. The underrepresentation of people of color at the top of American professional life had been a regular topic of public discussion for years leading up to the summer of 2020.[29]

For example, during the "Oscars So White" controversy of February 2016, in which the American Academy of Motion Picture Arts and Sciences was criticized for the lack of diversity among its major category nominees, the *New York Times* published a story showing "503 of the most powerful people in American culture, government, education, and business."[30] The luminaries shown in this story included the CEOs of the largest American companies; executives of news media and entertainment media organizations who hold considerable power over what Americans watch, listen to, and read; presidents of Ivy League universities; America's top military brass; owners of America's professional sports franchises, who almost all come from the corporate world; and America's political elite, including the president and his cabinet, senators, Supreme Court justices, governors of the fifty states, and mayors of America's twenty largest cities. While deciding which 503 leaders represent the "true" American elite is admittedly subjective, the results of the *New York Times* analysis are still telling. The graphic's title aptly sums up its findings: "The Faces of American Power, Nearly as White as the Oscar Nominees." Only forty-four of the 503 leaders—slightly under 9 percent—were nonwhite, compared to 36 percent of the country that was nonwhite according to the 2010 U.S. Census.[31] A follow-up study published by the *New York Times* in 2020 of 922 American leaders found that about 20 percent were people of color, though the analysis included big-city police chiefs and district attorneys as well as members of the U.S. House, positions that were not included in the 2016 analysis and are less visible and prestigious than the ones analyzed in that report.[32]

Though informative, the authors do not address why racial minorities experience such difficulty reaching the most powerful positions in American society. Scholars of inclusion in political offices have long been interested in the how social groups are represented in political institutions, but they have devoted more attention to explaining the underrepresentation of women and, recently, the working class.[33] This book attempts to understand the racial dynamics involved in determining who reaches the highest political offices in the United States. It is an account of how political competition and voter psychology intersect in ways that make Black leadership at the highest levels of American politics unlikely.[34]

In addition to addressing a critical issue of representation in a diverse society, the book also addresses a number of important theoretical questions in the study of American politics. First, I promote the general understanding of campaigns and political communication as iterative and dynamic, advancing a literature on campaign effects that largely focuses on the effects of messages without examining how those effects change when pitted against a countermessage.[35] Second, this book contributes to research on the political dynamics of racial attitudes, a topic that has become one of the most important areas of inquiry in political science during the Obama and Trump presidencies.[36] This book addresses not only the conditions that activate racial animosity but also strategies for neutralizing that activation. Finally, the book has normative implications for the quality of public opinion in American politics. Scholars of race and campaigns often paint a dim picture of the American public as being highly susceptible to manipulation by racial cues. However, my findings suggest that the American public is perhaps not as susceptible to these cues as they are often portrayed in the literature, depending on whether and how the other side responds.

WHAT LIES AHEAD

In chapter 1, I examine why Blacks are underrepresented in high-level statewide offices. First, I test the hypothesis that they are simply not running for these offices in numbers proportional to their share of the citizenry. I find some evidence for this in 2010, but none in 2020. In both 2010 and 2020, however, I find that Blacks are not winning the general election at rates we would expect given their proportion of the general election candidate pool. This suggests that the general election stage is where potential Black governors and senators are screened out, and so the rest of the chapter focuses on the performance of Black gubernatorial and senate candidates among white voters in general elections.

I introduce a new data set designed to test whether Black candidates are penalized because of their race. Existing studies of Black statewide candidates focus on only one or two elections. I assess the racial penalty across the full range of cases from 2000 to 2020. Furthermore, I test and rule out a host of alternative explanations to race. Comparing Black candidates to white candidates from the same party running in the same state for the same office around the same time, I find that white candidates are about twice as likely to win and receive about eight percentage points more support among white voters. These estimates hold when controlling for potential confounding factors such as ideology, previous officeholding, money raised, running for an open seat, and national economic conditions. Thus, I provide new evidence on a longstanding question in American racial politics, namely, whether Black candidates are penalized by white voters. I find clear evidence that in statewide elections, they are.

In chapter 2, I argue that in order to understand why Black candidates experience difficulty in their campaigns, we need to understand the amount of racialized communication they face and its effects. First, I turn to the literature on racial communication to identify a set of issues I expect to be the focus of campaigns against Black candidates: crime, sexual deviance, and taxes. Next, I test the hypothesis that Black candidates experience more attacks on these issues than comparable white candidates. To do so, I conduct a content analysis of news stories from the six Black versus white elections for governor or U.S. Senate from 2000–2018 in which the Black candidate was viable: Harold Ford Jr. for U.S. Senate in Tennessee in 2006, Deval Patrick for governor of Massachusetts in 2006, Cory Booker for U.S. Senate in New Jersey in 2013, Anthony Brown for governor of Maryland in 2014, Stacey Abrams for governor of Georgia in 2018, and Andrew Gillum for governor of Florida in 2018. I examine all news stories that ran in each state's highest-circulation newspaper in the last month of each campaign and calculate the percentage of stories in each contest in which the white opponent either discussed their own views or attacked the Black candidate on the three racialized issues. I repeated this for a comparison set of white candidates of the same party who ran for the same office in the same state around the same time as the Black candidate. The results show that each of the six campaigns featured an unusually high amount of campaign speech by the white opponent on at least one of the three racialized issues.

The findings in chapter 2 raise the question of how Black candidates respond to the tactics of their white opponents. In chapter 3, I argue that past research does not adequately consider the agency of Black candidates facing racial attacks. Little systematic evidence exists on what they do in response. I draw upon research in political communication to develop a typology of common types of rebuttals offered by Black candidates and show the frequency with which Patrick, Ford, Booker, Brown, Abrams, and Gillum used them. This content analysis was conducted using the same newspaper sources from chapter 2: all news stories that ran in each state's highest-circulation newspaper during the last month of each campaign. The results challenge the long-held assumption that Black candidates generally do not respond to racial attacks. I also find that Black candidates rarely challenge these attacks in racial terms, which goes against the conventional wisdom in the racial politics literature about what attacked candidates should do. Instead, Black candidates usually delegate racial rebuttals to surrogates or, more often, find other nonracial ways to respond. Overall, I find variation in how often, early, and directly racially attacked candidates respond, setting the stage to then analyze the effects of that variation on white response.

I explore in greater depth the relationship between the flow of campaign messages and white voters' attitudes in chapters 4 and 5 for four campaigns. The importance of rebuttals is highlighted in chapter 4 by comparing the 2006 Deval Patrick and Harold Ford Jr. campaigns. Both faced high-profile racial attacks: Patrick was attacked for advocating for the release of convicted criminals, and Ford was implicitly criticized for pursuing white women as sexual partners. Only Patrick, however, had a high-volume response to the attacks. To test the influence of attacks and rebuttals, I collected all available polling data on the two campaigns (including polls conducted by *USA Today* / Gallup, *Los Angeles Times* / Bloomberg, and SurveyUSA) to compare perceptions of the candidates before the attacks, after the attacks, and after the rebuttals. Using a validated measure of whites' racial attitudes, I show that racial resentment was activated following salient attacks on the themes of crime and sex. I also show that only Patrick managed to restore his favorability ratings after several days of well-publicized rebuttals. Another important finding is that neither Patrick's nor Ford's rebuttals helped them among whites with high levels of racial animus. This subgroup of white voters was about as supportive of both candidates after the rebuttals as they were before. The difference between Patrick and Ford is that Patrick gained support among racially sympathetic white voters while Ford actually lost support among this subgroup.

Chapter 5 begins with an examination of the 2013 New Jersey U.S. Senate campaign between Cory Booker and Republican Steve Lonegan. In the first part of the chapter, I analyze newspaper stories from New Jersey's most widely circulated daily newspaper (the *Star-Ledger*) and television ad buys based on reports filed with the Federal Communications Commission to determine the frequency of attacks made by Lonegan and rebuttals offered by Booker. I find that Lonegan engaged in over a month of sustained attack that Booker hardly contested. Next, I collected original survey data on white voters' racial attitudes and their views of the candidates from two telephone surveys conducted during the campaign, which provides the best test of the impact of white voters' racial attitudes in any recent statewide campaign involving a Black candidate. Together with polling data from Monmouth and Quinnipiac, I show that during the period of uncontested Lonegan attacks, Lonegan erased Booker's double-digit lead among whites and that whites' racial considerations were activated while nonracial considerations such as party identification and ideology were not. I also rule out a number of alternative explanations for this racial activation. Then I show that during the last two weeks of the campaign, Booker contested Lonegan's attacks with greater frequency, and Lonegan's gains among white voters stalled. Like Patrick, Booker's gains among white voters following his rebuttals are concentrated among racially sympathetic whites.

The second part of chapter 5 reports findings from Anthony Brown's 2014 campaign for governor of Maryland. The campaign was called Maryland's "tax revolt" by some in the media, with Brown's opponent Larry Hogan focusing primarily on the issue of high taxes driving people and businesses out of Maryland. Using polling data from CBS News / *New York Times* / YouGov, the *Washington Post*, and the *Baltimore Sun*, I show that the result of these attacks, as for the other three Black candidates, was the activation of whites' racial attitudes. Brown's response, however, was unusually weak even when compared to the less-than-robust responses offered by Ford and Booker, as Brown rarely defended the record of the administration he was a part of as lieutenant governor. Brown's rebuttal rate to attacks on taxes fell sharply over the course the campaign, mirroring the decline in his support among white voters overall.

The case studies of viable Black candidates in chapters 4 and 5 all feature Black men. In recent election cycles, however, viable Black women have run for high-level statewide and national offices, including Stacey Abrams for governor of Georgia in 2018 and Kamala Harris for vice president in 2020. In chapter 6, I go beyond existing work that examines only racial bias to assess the relative influences of race and gender when both were made salient by the candidates' embodiment of Black womanhood and a flurry of race- and gender-based attacks against both women. Using survey data from the Cooperative Congressional Election Study, the American National Election Study, an original national survey conducted in October 2020, and an original survey experiment conducted in 2021, I compare the effects of racism and sexism on evaluations of Abrams and Harris to their effects for comparable Black men and white women. I find that while racism and sexism uniquely contributed to opposition to Abrams, only racism did for Harris.

While the case studies are important for showing how white voters' opinions shift in real elections in response to racial attacks and rebuttals, it is difficult to disentangle the effect of specific attacks and rebuttals with survey data, as multiple attacks and multiple rebuttals often occur simultaneously during a campaign. Chapters 7 and 8 support the case studies by testing the effects of attacks and rebuttals in an experimental setting. Chapter 7 tests the effects of actual attacks used by Lonegan in an original survey experiment that isolates each attack in turn. In line with previous research on racial communication, attacks on racialized themes such as associating Booker with his minority constituency of Newark, attacking Booker for his online flirtation with a stripper, and attacking Booker for being the undeserving beneficiary of rural and suburban tax dollars as Newark's mayor activated white respondents' racial attitudes, but attacks on nonracial themes such as Booker not being patriotic enough did not. The innovation of the experiment, however, is that after reading the Lonegan attack, respondents read a description of Booker's actual rebuttal to that attack. The findings show that some of Booker's rebuttals, such as criticizing Lonegan's negativity and denying charges of incompetently running Newark as its mayor, improved his favorability rating and others, such as calling attacks racially motivated, did not.

Although the virtue of the experiment in chapter 7 is that it faithfully replicates attacks and rebuttals used in a real campaign, the effects of specific rebuttal types remain unclear because in actual campaigns, different rebuttals may address different attacks. That is, rebuttal types are not all responding to the same attack. Thus, in chapter 8, I report findings from a set of four survey experiments conducted from 2011 through 2014 that define and test seven different rebuttals to the same attack. An additional strength of these experiments is that they allow for tests of racial disadvantage for any given attack and any given rebuttal by comparing a Black candidate to an identical white candidate. The experiments simulated an attack-rebuttal episode in a fictitious U.S. Senate campaign. First, respondents read a fictitious news story about an attack ad in a Senate race. The story explains that the target of the ad was attacked for his ties to a disgraced Black politician who has been convicted of several crimes including assaulting a police officer. After evaluating the target and the attacker, respondents are randomly assigned to one of seven rebuttal types I define based on real-world examples. When I systematically analyze each strategy, I find that rebutting the attack by calling the attack racially motivated backfires against Black candidates but serves white candidates well, pointing to a racial disadvantage for Black candidates. However, a number of other rebuttal types restore the favorability ratings of Black and white candidates alike. The strategy that proved most effective was offering a credible justification for the attacked action, a strategy that was effective not only among racially sympathetic respondents but also among racially moderate and resentful respondents. In sum, the experimental chapters (7 and 8) and case study chapters (4 and 5) demonstrate that although Black candidates are constrained in their rebuttal options, they can nevertheless find effective ways to respond to racialized attacks in predominantly white jurisdictions.

Finally, I conclude by taking stock of the findings and offering thoughts on what they reveal about the current state of race and politics in America. The main conclusions I highlight are that candidate race still matters to white voters; racial attacks against Black candidates for high-level offices are common, potent, and likely to continue into the future; and rebuttals help counter the negative effects of racial attacks, but with important qualifications regarding which responses work (and don't work) and among which subgroups of white voters.

The empirical core of the book begins in the next chapter, where I test the hypothesis that Black candidates suffer a penalty because of their race. I do so by systematically analyzing all Black challenger (i.e., nonincumbent) campaigns for governor and U.S. senator from 2000–2020 and evaluating their performance among white voters in those elections. As we will see, the results suggest that statewide electorates evaluate Black challengers differently from comparable white challengers.

1

WHY ARE BLACK GOVERNORS AND U.S. SENATORS SO RARE?

Racial Bias Against Black Challengers, 2000–2020

In the introduction, we learned that only ten Black Americans have been elected governor or U.S. senator since Reconstruction and that the color barrier remains intact for these offices in forty-two out of the fifty states. In this chapter, I ask, what explains these low numbers? Scholars who study the underrepresentation of historically disadvantaged groups (such as women and the working class) suggest that the decision to run is one stage where potential candidates from these groups are screened out.[1] Because of resource gaps tied to inequality in society, historically disadvantaged groups may have fewer members who have the typical qualifications (e.g., money, connections, experience) of people who successfully run for office. Another possibility is that group members have the qualifications on paper but do not perceive themselves to be strong candidates. A third possibility is that they are not recruited to run by party and interest group leaders, either because those leaders know fewer members of the group or because leaders do not believe group members would make good candidates. All of these are reasons to suggest (among many others) that one explanation for the scarcity of Black governors and senators is that Black Americans are simply not running for these offices in large numbers.

Another potential explanation is that when Black candidates run, they face a unique hurdle: that white voters are less likely to vote for a Black candidate because of their race. If this is true, it has major implications for Black candidates because the electorate in a statewide contest differs from one in a U.S. House, state legislative, or mayoral election. While Blacks make up a large percentage of the population in many cities and legislative districts, Blacks make up no more than 15 percent of the population in any state outside of the South.[2] Thus, Black candidates must win a sizable share of white voters in order to win a statewide election. This is problematic because Black candidates typically fare poorly when running in majority-white jurisdictions.[3]

In this chapter, I examine the explanations for why so few Blacks have reached the high-level statewide offices of governor and senator. First, I test the idea that Black candidates are not running in large numbers and find mixed evidence—there's evidence that in 2010, Black candidates ran at levels below what we would expect given their share of the electorate. However, that disparity closes by 2020. And in both 2010 and 2020, there is a notable decline in the number of Black candidates who win compared to the number of Black candidates who run for these offices. In other words, when Black candidates run, they don't win, which suggests that something is happening at the general election level that eliminates potential Black governors and senators.

With that in mind, I turn to examining how well Blacks have performed among white voters in elections for these offices. I start by reviewing the modern history of Black gubernatorial and Senate candidacies. Then, I provide a brief review of the existing literature on white voting in contests involving a Black candidate, much of which focuses on elections below the level of governor or senator. After that, I introduce a new data set designed to answer the question of whether Black candidates are penalized by white voters in statewide elections and present new evidence suggesting that racial bias in the general election remains a significant factor. Finally, I conclude with a possible explanation for the underperformance of Black candidates, an explanation that I test in the next chapter.

DO BLACK CANDIDATES RUN?

The first possibility outlined earlier is that Black candidates simply do not run for governor and senator in large enough numbers. In order to answer the question of whether Black candidates run for office, we need to know the racial makeup of the entire pool of candidates for governor and senator in recent election cycles. The names of the candidates are easy to find on records of primary election results. To my knowledge, though, no data set exists that lists the candidate's name and race. However, if the candidates' names are known, it is possible to identify their race by examining photographs and biographical information available online.

I did this for every candidate who received votes in a Democratic or Republican primary election for governor or U.S. senator in 2010 and 2020. I chose 2020 because it was the most recently completed election cycle at the time this analysis was conducted, and I chose 2010 in order to see if the diversity of the candidate pool had changed since the start of the decade. In 2010, 506 candidates ran for those offices, while 325 candidates ran in 2020. The racial makeup of the candidate pools in both years is shown in figure 1.1. In both panels, I plotted the percentage of Black people in the electorate (labeled "Citizens") of the most recently completed presidential election (2008 for the 2010 data and 2020 for the 2020 data) to serve as a benchmark for the percentage of Black people in the primary candidate pool (labeled "Candidates"). I also plot the percentage of primary winners ("Winners (primary)") and general election winners ("Winners (general)") who were Black.

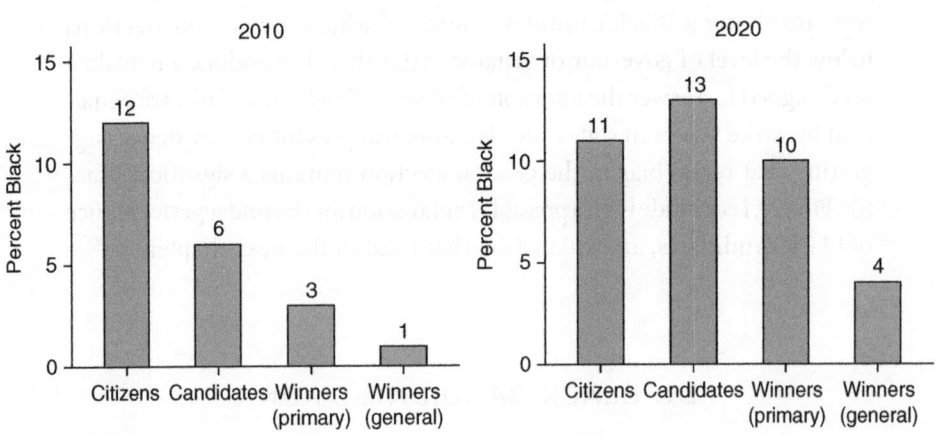

FIGURE 1.1 Percentage of Blacks running in gubernatorial and U.S. Senate elections, 2010 and 2020.

If the problem is that Blacks simply do not run for these offices, we should see a sharp drop-off from the Black percentage of the electorate to the Black percentage of the primary candidate pool. In figure 1.1, we see some evidence of this in 2010. About 12 percent of the 2008 presidential electorate was Black, compared to only 6 percent of the primary candidate pool. By 2020, however, about 13 percent of the primary candidate pool for governor and senator was Black, which slightly outpaces the Black percentage of the 2020 presidential electorate (11 percent). In other words, Blacks ran at rates we would expect given their share of the electorate in 2020. On the other hand, we observe a drop-off in both 2010 and 2020 from the percentage of primary winners who are Black compared to the percentage of general election winners who are Black. The percentages of primary winners who are Black in 2010 (3 percent) and 2020 (10 percent) are whittled down to 1 percent (in 2010) and 4 percent (in 2020) among general election winners. This decline in Black success across both years suggests that the general election stage is where a significant amount of attrition occurs. Thus, it is worth shining a brighter light on exactly what happens at that stage.

A BRIEF HISTORY OF MODERN BLACK HIGH-LEVEL STATEWIDE CANDIDACIES

I begin by providing historical perspective on Black gubernatorial and senate campaigns. The first post-Reconstruction election involving a Black challenger for one of these offices took place in 1966. Figure 1.2 shows the entire set of cases from 1966 to 2020. The analysis is limited to elections in which the Black candidate is the challenger rather than the incumbent. The book's focus on the scarcity of Black officeholders justifies the focus on candidates trying to win election to those offices for the first time.[4] In all, there have been sixty Black challenger candidacies since 1966.[5]

The first post-Reconstruction election in which a Black American ran featured Edward Brooke (R-MA), who defeated his white opponent, former Governor Endicott Peabody (D), and became the first Black American elected to the U.S. Senate.[6] Brooke's victory, however, did not immediately lead to more Black candidacies and victories. The next candidacy

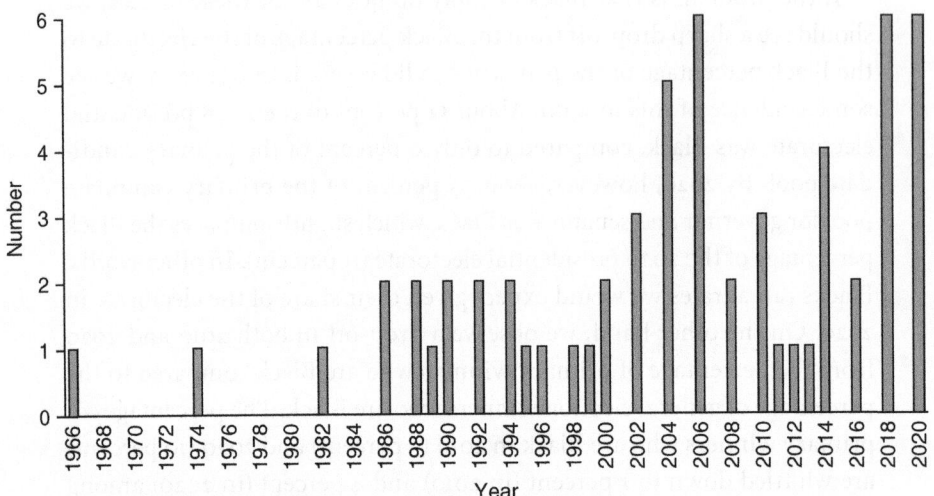

FIGURE 1.2 Number of Black challengers facing white opponents in gubernatorial or U.S. Senate elections, by year.

Source: The data in figure 1.2 for elections before 2006 comes from David Bositis, "Testing the Glass Ceiling: Mid-Term Prospects for Black Candidates," *Focus: The Magazine for the Joint Center for Political and Economic Studies* 34, no. 3 (2006): 6. Data for elections after 2006 are compiled from various issues of *Focus* magazine, newspaper articles, and internet resources.

was eight years later, when James Brannen (R-CT) lost a Connecticut U.S. Senate election in 1974. Another eight years passed until Tom Bradley (D) ran for governor of California in 1982. Bradley narrowly lost that election and lost again when running for governor in 1986.[7]

Despite Bradley's defeats in the 1982 and 1986 California gubernatorial elections, the 1980s marked the beginning of the rise in the number of statewide Black candidacies. In 1986, two Blacks ran for high-level statewide office, marking the first multicandidacy election cycle since Reconstruction. Since that year, at least one Black candidate has run for high-level statewide office in every presidential or midterm election year. The end of the 1980s also marked the next Black statewide victory when L. Douglas Wilder (D) was elected governor of Virginia in 1989, becoming the first elected Black governor in U.S. history.[8]

The next period of growth in the number of candidacies was the 2000s. The ten-year period from 2000–2009 saw the same number of candidacies (eighteen) as the previous four decades combined. A record six candidates ran in 2006, marking the high point in the number of Black candidacies in one cycle until six candidates ran in 2018. In all, only ten Blacks have ever been elected to a governorship or Senate seat as of the 2022 elections: Brooke, Wilder, Sen. Carol Moseley-Braun (D-IL) in 1994, Sen. Barack Obama (D-IL) in 2004, Gov. Deval Patrick (D-MA) in 2006, Sen. Cory Booker (D-NJ) in 2013, Sen. Tim Scott (R-SC) in 2014, Sen. Kamala Harris (D-CA) in 2016, Sen. Raphael Warnock (D-GA) in 2020, and Gov. Wes Moore (D-MD) in 2022.

RESEARCH ON THE IMPACT OF RACE FOR BLACK CANDIDACIES

For a nation with the bitter racial history and racially polarized present of the United States,[9] it is not surprising that racial bias among white voters is a prominent topic in the study of race and U.S. politics. Previous studies conducted on whether they demonstrate a bias against Black candidates do not reach a consensus, however. Some studies that examine the role of race in one campaign[10] or one or two election cycles[11] find that white voters do not evaluate Black candidates according to different criteria than they evaluate white candidates. While whites' racial predispositions play a prominent role in shaping the vote decision when a Black candidate is involved, those predispositions do not play a larger role than they ordinarily do when both candidates in the election are white. Others go further and argue that racial prejudice plays little to no role in contemporary U.S. politics in general.[12] Another set of studies argues that the role of racial prejudice in the evaluation of Black candidates is not fixed but instead varies depending on the circumstances surrounding a given campaign. These studies find that white prejudice against Black candidates declines in response to positive information about Blacks, such as citizens' positive experiences under Black political leadership[13] or counterstereotypical portrayals of Black candidates in the media.[14]

On the other hand, many scholars maintain that white voters penalize Black candidates because of their race. Experimental studies have shown that voters evaluate Black candidates more negatively than identical white candidates.[15] Several studies conducted following Obama's first presidential campaign in 2008 find that racial attitudes and stereotypes were stronger determinants of vote choice in 2008 than in previous all-white U.S. presidential contests and continued to play a major role in shaping attitudes about his presidency.[16] A few studies have estimated the net effect of Obama's race in 2008 and find that Obama received less support than he would have if he was white.[17] In sum, the literature on white voters' evaluation of Black candidates offers no widely agreed upon answer.

The inconsistency of the findings in the existing literature reflects the wide range of cases and methods used to examine the role of prejudice when Black candidates run. The analysis in this chapter aims to advance the literature by addressing the limitations related to case selection and methodology. As mentioned in the introduction, one limitation regarding case selection is that much of the existing research focuses on lower-level elections for mayor or U.S. House.[18] Focusing on elections for these offices may underestimate the impact of prejudice, since those offices are less visible and powerful than governor or senator. Studies cited earlier that found racial bias in evaluations of Obama are consistent with the idea that racism becomes more of a factor as the visibility and power of the office increases.

Another limitation related to case selection is that some studies focus on one or two campaigns, which leaves open the question of whether the findings are generalizable to a wider range of cases. For example, the political scientists Jack Citrin, Donald Green, and David Sears's null finding of a racial penalty for Tom Bradley may be attributable to the unique circumstances of Bradley's biography and messaging: his background in law enforcement, his moderate reputation on racial matters, and his fiscally conservative campaign message.[19] Studies of Obama's 2008 campaign also leave open the possibility that findings of racial bias are unique to the circumstances of Obama's campaign that year. As the first viable Black presidential candidate, it is likely that Obama evoked more profound racial anxieties than Black candidates running for governor or U.S. senator. On the other hand, Obama's 2008 campaign was unique in ways that may have dampened the influence of racial prejudice. For one, his biracial heritage and light skin color may have helped mitigate the negative impact of his race.[20] Also, the circumstances of the 2008 election probably somewhat reduced the role of prejudice. Obama ran against a deeply unpopular incumbent party in the middle of an economic crisis, which elevated the salience of nonracial considerations such as presidential approval and retrospective evaluations of the economy.[21] Either way, this chapter's evaluation of the full range of relevant cases at the statewide level helps address concerns about generalizability that remain in much of the existing literature.

With respect to methodology, experimental studies can confidently identify race as the reason for differences in the evaluation of Black versus white candidates. However, experimental studies are limited by concerns that their findings do not translate to the real world. By examining real-world candidacies, this chapter aims to address these external validity concerns. Of course, the downside of an observational study such as this one is that real-world candidates differ on countless dimensions besides race, which makes it difficult to conclude that race is the reason why Black candidates fare worse than white candidates. While any study that examines real-world candidates can never completely rule out alternative explanations, I argue that the methodology used in this chapter does more to test and rule out possible confounding factors than other observational studies in the literature.

In sum, my aim in this chapter is to revisit the basic question of racial bias in voting with a comprehensive analysis of Black gubernatorial and Senate candidates. I test the following hypothesis: *Black candidates for these offices earn less support among white voters and the electorate as a whole than comparable white candidates.* I test this hypothesis with a new data set of all Black gubernatorial and U.S. Senate candidates from 2000 to 2020 and a comparison set of white candidates who are similar on several key characteristics. My aim is to improve on studies cited earlier that examine the racial penalty in one or two (often lower-level) elections or experimental studies with questionable external validity by testing the racial penalty hypothesis for the entire set of real-world cases.

DATA AND APPROACH

To test whether Black statewide candidates face a racial penalty, I start by collecting data on voters' evaluations of all Black challengers for governor or U.S. senator from 2000 to 2020. The reason for considering candidates only going back to 2000 is that I am interested in measuring the effect of candidate race in the current political context. Including cases from the 1960s through the 1990s may increase the chances of finding racial bias against Black candidates.[22] Limiting the timeframe from 2000 to 2020 provides a hard test of the racial bias hypothesis, meaning that it is less likely that results will support the hypothesis if racial prejudice has been declining over time. Meanwhile the focus on challengers is justified by the historic scarcity of high-level Black officeholders.[23] I omit the two cases of Black candidates facing a Black opponent because white support for Black candidates is 100 percent in those contests, which tells us little about white support for Black candidates.[24] In all, the data set includes thirty-seven Black challengers who faced white opponents from 2000 to 2020.

In order to assess the performance of Black candidates, I need comparable white candidates to serve as a comparison group. My strategy is to take each Black candidate and find three white candidates of the same party who ran as challengers against a white opponent for the same office in the same state around the same time. To fulfill the last criterion of running around the same time, I select the three white candidates whose election took place most proximately to the Black candidate's election. For example, Deval Patrick's white comparison set consists of the three white Democratic challengers who ran for governor of Massachusetts in the years closest to 2006, the year when Patrick ran. Those three candidates were Martha Coakley in 2014, Shannon O'Brien in 2002, and Scott Harshbarger in 1998. As this example illustrates, white comparison candidates' elections can take place either before (as it did for Harshbarger and O'Brien) or after the Black candidate's election (as it did for Coakley). Repeating this procedure for each Black candidate yields a comparison group of 115 white candidates.[25] The complete list of Black candidates and white candidates in the data set is shown in appendix table 1.1.[26]

This method of finding white comparison candidates for each Black candidate worked well in all but one case: Kamala Harris's 2016 California U.S. Senate candidacy. In 2010, California adopted a nonpartisan primary system, in which the top two vote getters regardless of party affiliation advance to the general election. This allows for two members of the same party to square off in the general election, which is exactly what happened in 2016 when Harris faced fellow Democrat Loretta Sanchez. Two of Harris's three most recent white Democratic challengers (Barbara Boxer and Dianne Feinstein in 1992) ran before the adoption of the top-two primary system, which means they faced Republican opponents. Since the dynamics of an interparty general election are not directly comparable to those in an intraparty general election, Harris is omitted from the data set.

OUTCOME MEASURES

The main outcome measures I collected for both Black and white candidates are:

- *Election result* (did the candidate win or lose?)
- *Margin of victory among white voters.* This was obtained from three sources. Whenever available, I used exit polls. When exit polls were not available, I averaged surveys conducted no more than one month before Election Day. In the rare event that more than three surveys were conducted in the last month of the election, I averaged the three that were conducted closest to Election Day.[27] Finally, when neither exit polls nor survey data were available, I estimated the margin of victory among whites using the ecological inference (EI) procedure developed by the political scientist Gary King.[28] This procedure uses actual vote returns at the county level and U.S. Census data on county-level racial demographics to estimate the vote by race based on the actual outcome across all counties in the state.[29] Exit polls were used to estimate the white margin of victory for 70 percent of the 152 candidacies examined, while surveys and ecological regression were used for 20 percent and 10 percent, respectively.
- *Margin of victory among all voters.* This is simply the election result and is not estimated using polls of any kind.[30]

Of these three outcomes, I consider the margin of victory among white voters to be the best measure of white support for Black candidates for a straightforward reason: it is the one outcome that only accounts for the opinion of white voters. However, I also measure the election result and the margin of victory among all voters for two reasons: first, these outcomes are likely to be measured with less error because they do not rely on the various sampling and statistical techniques used to estimate the margin of victory among whites and, second, these outcomes are consequential in their own right, particularly the outcome of the election itself. At minimum, these outcomes provide additional tests of the effect of candidate race.

POTENTIAL CONFOUNDERS

In addition to these measures, I also need measures of confounding factors that might account for differences between Black and white candidates found on the outcome measures. One factor is candidate quality, which is a predictor of election outcomes at all levels of U.S. politics.[31] The data set contains two measures of candidate quality: political experience and campaign fundraising. For the political experience measure, I borrow from Jonathan Krasno and Donald Green and other earlier research and code candidate quality on a three-point scale: 3 = candidates who have held statewide office (such as state attorney general, U.S. senator, or governor) or federal office (such as U.S. representative); 2 = candidates who have held local elected office (such as state representative or mayor); 1 = candidates who have held local appointed office or are otherwise well known; 0 = candidates with no elected or appointed experience.[32] For the fundraising totals of U.S. Senate candidates, I use data from Federal Election Commission (FEC) reports. Fundraising totals for gubernatorial candidates are obtained from the National Institute on Money in State Politics (NIMSP), a nonpartisan organization that collects data from the disclosure agencies with which gubernatorial candidates must file their campaign finance reports. In the 11 percent of cases (sixteen out of 152) where FEC and NIMSP data was not available, I used newspaper reports.

A second factor is whether the challenger is running for an open seat or trying to unseat an incumbent. It is well established that incumbents dominate elections at all levels, and so challengers stand a much better chance in open-seat races.[33]

A third factor is candidate ideology. A candidate who is ideologically extreme may find it more difficult to win a statewide general election than a moderate candidate. For Black candidates, it may be that statewide candidates are more liberal than typical white candidates, which is a reasonable assumption, given that Black members of the U.S. House are more liberal than white members on average.[34] I measure ideological extremity using campaign finance (CF) scores developed by Adam Bonica based on a candidate's financial contributors.[35] Bonica's data set contains ideology estimates for most candidates for state and federal office from 1980 to 2020, which enables measuring the ideology of 129 out of the 152 (85 percent) candidates in my data set. The main benefit of using CF scores instead of other measures of ideology that rely on legislators' roll call behavior such as DW-NOMINATE or NPAT is that CF scores are measured for losing candidates,[36] which make up a majority (129 out of 152) of the observations. CF scores take on negative values for liberals and positive values for conservatives, with magnitudes representing the extremity of the candidate's ideology. Since I am interested in measuring ideological extremity, I use the absolute value of the candidate's CF score.

A fourth and fifth factor is the performance of the national and state economies. A significant body of research finds that national and state economic conditions shape gubernatorial and Senate election outcomes.[37] It is important to account for economic performance as a confounding factor because of the possibility of a "glass cliff" effect, which refers to the possibility that minority candidates tend to run during economic hard times, when the position may be less attractive to white candidates.[38] I measure national economic performance by calculating the change in per capita income growth from the year before to the year of the election. State economic performance is calculated the same way within each state. National and state per capita income data is obtained from the Bureau of Economic Affairs.

A sixth factor is the state's partisanship. Candidates are likely to get more votes in states where they represent the party favored by that state's voters.[39] State partisanship is measured by taking the share of the two-party presidential vote won by the Democratic presidential candidate above or below the share of the two-party presidential vote won by the Democratic presidential candidate nationwide in the most recently completed presidential election. Following the political scientist Daniel

Hopkins, this measure of state partisanship accounts for swings in the national vote.[40]

In addition to these six factors, I also collected data on the Black population in the state, the candidate's sex, the year of the election, party, and office sought (governor or Senate). These measures serve as additional controls in the multivariate analysis. The data for the Black population in each state comes from the American Community Survey (ACS) for all years after 2005. For all years before 2005, data is interpolated using the relevant decennial U.S. Census years.[41]

ARE BLACK CHALLENGERS PENALIZED BECAUSE OF THEIR RACE?

I start by showing the comparison between Black and white challengers on the three outcome measures (figure 1.3). On all three measures, white challengers enjoy greater levels of success. Their win percentage is more than double that of Black challengers (17.39 percent versus 8.11 percent). On average, their margin of defeat is 7.60 percentage points less than their Black counterparts among white voters and 4.61 percentage points among all voters. To address concerns that these effects are driven mostly by white candidacies that happened much earlier or later than the Black candidacy, I repeat this comparison using only the white candidacies that are closest in time to the Black candidacy (for example, only including Shannon O'Brien as Deval Patrick's comparison, since O'Brien's candidacy happened four years before Patrick's compared to eight years before for Harshbarger and eight years after for Coakley). When only considering the most recent white candidacies, the differences are even greater: an 8.11 percent victory rate for Blacks compared to 20.45 percent for whites ($p=0.03$, one-tailed); 36.43 percent margin of defeat among white voters for Blacks compared to 24.70 percent for whites ($p=0.02$, one-tailed); and 17.68 percent margin of defeat among all voters for Blacks compared to 10.86 percent for whites ($p=0.01$, one-tailed).

While interesting, the results in figure 1.3 could be driven more by confounding factors than by candidate race. For example, it could be that the average Black candidate is of lower quality than the average white

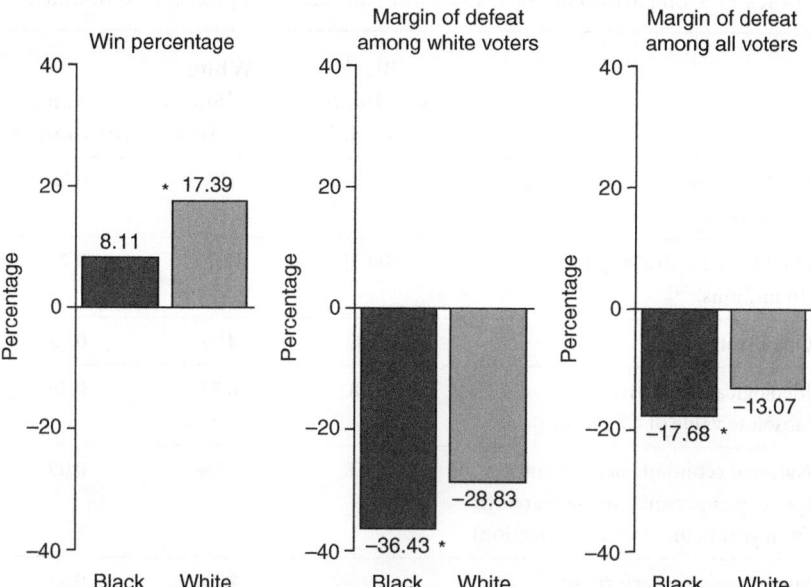

FIGURE 1.3 Comparison of Black and white challengers on outcome measures.
Note: Statistical significance at p < 0.1 level is denoted with *.

candidate, in which case it could not be ruled out that candidate quality rather than race is the explanation for the weaker performance of Black candidates. In table 1.1, I show a comparison of the Black and white candidates on all of the confounding factors for which I have measures for each candidate. The two groups are indistinguishable on most factors, lending some reassurance that the comparisons in figure 1.3 are not misleading. White candidates are not of higher quality on either quality measure (previous experience and fundraising), they are not running for open seats at a higher rate, they are not closer to the center ideologically, they are not running more often during times of strong state economic performance, and they are not more likely to be men. Since I constructed the white data set to match the Black data set on party, state, and office sought, it is no surprise that the two groups do not differ on party advantage, Black population in state, party, and office sought.[42] The only two factors on which the two groups differ are national economic performance

TABLE 1.1 Comparison of Black and white candidates on potential confounders

	Black candidates (n = 37)	White candidates (n = 115)	p-value (two-tailed)
Quality — previous experience (0–3 scale)	1.65	1.79	0.51
Quality — fundraising total (in millions)	$14.35	$8.25	0.23
Open seat	38%	41%	0.75
Ideological extremity (absolute value of CF score)	0.78	0.72	0.46
National economic performance (per capita personal income growth from year before to year of election)	2.9%	3.8%	0.09
State economic performance	3.9%	4.2%	0.52
Party advantage	−8.6%	−7.6%	0.74
Black population in state	21%	21%	0.90
Male	86%	83%	0.65
Year	2011	2008	0.02
Republican	27%	28%	0.93
Running for U.S. Senate	68%	68%	0.98

Note: Entries are mean values.

and year: the average white candidate ran longer ago and during marginally better times for the national economy.

To account for these differences, I estimate the effect of candidate race on the three outcome measures using ordinary least squares (OLS) regression. I include controls for both quality measures (previous experience and fundraising), open seat, ideological extremity, state economic performance, party advantage, Black population in state, male, and office sought. I also include state and party-year fixed effects to account for factors specific to each state and the fact that some years might be better for one of the political parties across the country. The confounders listed in table 1.1 that are not explicitly controlled for—national economic performance, year, and party—are captured by the party-year fixed effects.

The negative effect of being Black controlling for potential confounders is plotted in figure 1.4 for each of the outcomes.[43] For comparison, I show these effects next to the simple Black versus white differences from figure 1.3. The results indicate that the apparent relationship between candidate race and outcomes shown in figure 1.3 persists after the inclusion of controls. The regression models estimate that being Black reduces the chance of victory by almost 13 percentage points, reduces the share of the white vote by about 10.7 percentage points, and reduces the share of the total vote by about 6.9 percentage points. These estimates are similar in magnitude to the raw estimates derived from figure 1.3. By accounting for potential confounders, we can be more confident that the Black-white differences shown in figure 1.3 are not attributable to nonracial factors.

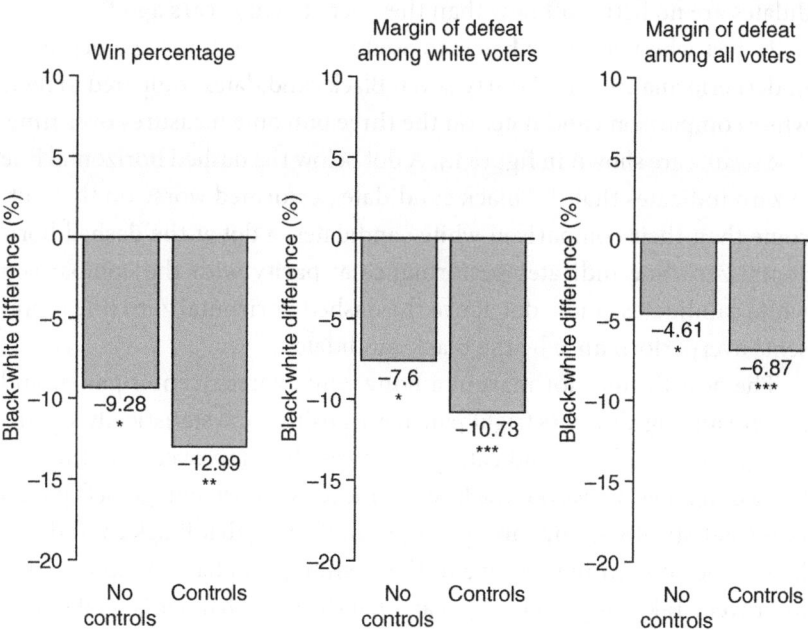

FIGURE 1.4 Being Black is associated with underperformance on three outcomes.

Note: Statistical significance is denoted as follows. ***p < 0.01, **p < 0.05, *p < 0.1, all one-tailed tests.

IS RACIAL BIAS GETTING BETTER?

Overall, it appears that Black candidates from 2000 to 2020 have fared worse than their white counterparts. But has this disadvantage changed over time? Dramatic events in racial politics occurred during the period from 2000 to 2020, such as the election of Barack Obama as the nation's first Black president in 2008, the rise of the Black Lives Matter movement in the mid-2010s, and the election of Donald Trump to the presidency in 2016. These events occurred against a backdrop of demographic change as the nonwhite share of the population grew rapidly from 2000 to 2020.[44] Also, as figure 1.2 shows, the number of Black candidates running for governor and senator went up over this twenty-year span. One possible outcome of this reshaping of America's racial landscape is that perhaps bias against Black candidates has decreased over time as (increasingly diverse) voters have gotten used to the prospect of Black leadership. On the other hand, the election of Trump and the declining power of norms against the explicit derogation of racial minorities suggest that perhaps Black candidates are no better off now than they were twenty years ago.[45]

To test whether parity has increased since 2000, I plot the degree of underperformance for all thirty-seven Black candidates compared to their white comparison candidates on the three outcome measures over time. The results are shown in figure 1.5. A dot below the dashed horizontal line at zero indicates that the Black candidate performed worse on that outcome than their comparison white candidates, a dot at the dashed horizontal zero line indicates performance at parity with the comparison white candidates, and a dot above the dashed horizontal zero line represents overperformance by the Black candidate.

The best-fit lines for margin among white voters (center panel) and margin among all voters (right panel) are positive and statistically significant ($p = 0.01$ for both), indicating that parity has improved over time for these outcomes. However, the best-fit line for win percentage (left panel) is not statistically significant ($p = 0.44$), indicating that Black candidates' likelihood of winning relative to their white peers has not appreciably improved. Taken together, it appears that the racial barrier is weakening, which comports with the finding from figure 1.2 that 2018 and 2020 saw the highest number of Black candidacies for governor and senator. It makes sense that more Black candidates have run in recent cycles as race

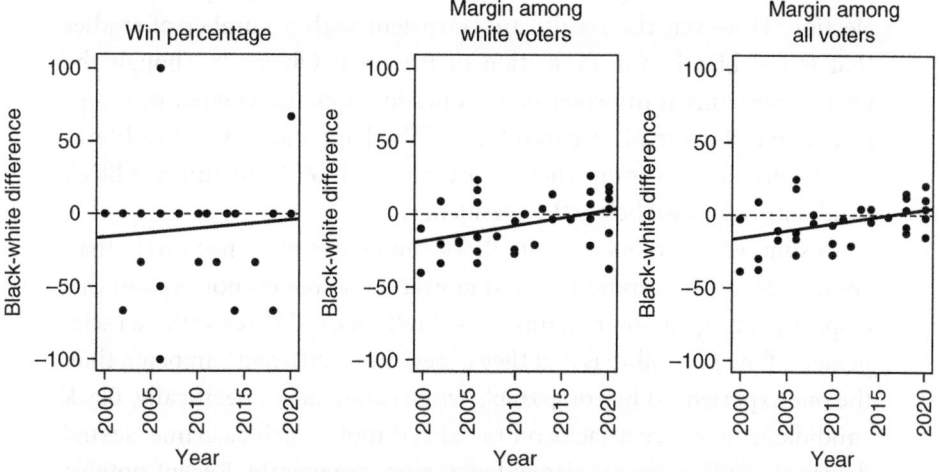

FIGURE 1.5 Black-white differences on three outcomes from 2000–2020.

Dots represent the difference between each Black candidate and the average of that candidate's white comparison group for each outcome. The best-fit line is statistically significant in the center and right panels (p = 0.01 for both) but not in the left panel (p = 0.44).

appears to be less of a barrier. But improvement in margins has not yet translated into improvement in Black win percentages, which suggests that the margin trends need to continue in order for Black candidates to actually win at parity with their white counterparts. Only time (and more Black candidacies) will allow us to know with more certainty whether these trends will hold up.

CONCLUSION

To summarize, Black challengers from 2000 to 2020 performed worse than a comparable set of white challengers on three key outcome measures. This is not due to differences in candidate quality, ideology, national or state economic performance, likelihood of running for an open seat, or other plausible alternative explanations. The results diverge from earlier studies focusing on U.S. House elections or a single gubernatorial election. However, the results are consistent with a number of studies that found bias in the evaluation of President Obama.[46] Though the Obama literature is informative, the question remains whether he is representative of other Black candidates. This chapter advances this literature by providing a comprehensive examination of the fortunes of Black candidates one level below the presidency.

In sum, white voters evaluate Black candidates more negatively than comparable white candidates, and nonracial factors do not explain this disparity. The question remains: why do Black candidates suffer a racial penalty? One possibility is that they experience a different campaign than the one experienced by comparable white candidates. Specifically, Black candidates may face attacks on racialized topics such as crime, sexual deviance, and economic dependency more frequently. Recent notable examples include an advertisement showing a young white woman hinting at Harold Ford Jr.'s pursuit of white women as sexual partners during the 2006 Tennessee U.S. Senate election, negative advertisements accusing Deval Patrick of supporting "cop killers" and rapists during the 2006 Massachusetts gubernatorial election, and numerous attacks linking Cory Booker to crime in his home city of Newark during the 2013 New Jersey U.S. Senate election. I address this possibility in the next chapter.

2

THE RACIALIZATION OF BLACK CANDIDATES

The finding from chapter 1 that Black candidates underperform relative to comparable white candidates raises the question of why this disparity exists. In chapter 2, I investigate the hypothesis that Black candidates experience a different campaign than the one experienced by comparable white candidates—a campaign that emphasizes attacks using racialized themes such as crime, sexual deviance, and economic dependency. Previous studies show that attacks that contain cues such as these that highlight negative stereotypes of Blacks reduce support for the attacked candidate among white voters.[1] Though white candidates also face attacks on these topics, the relative frequency of racialized attacks faced by Black and white candidates is unknown. If Black candidates are targeted by racialized attacks more often than white candidates, this could explain why white voters support them at lower rates. Existing studies find that the frequency of racialized attacks is related to how strongly racial considerations are brought to bear on vote choice and that racialized attacks are more damaging to Black candidates than comparable white candidates.[2]

To test the hypothesis that Black candidates face more of these attacks, I conduct a content analysis of news stories in every election involving a *viable* Black challenger facing a white opponent (challenger or incumbent) for governor or U.S. Senate from 2000 to 2018. My definition of viability and my reasons for focusing only on viable Black challengers will be explained shortly. But first, I explain how I define and measure racialized discourse in campaigns.

DEFINING RACIALIZATION

The "parking lot rape," "cop killer" and "call me" ads run against Deval Patrick and Harold Ford Jr. mentioned at the end of the previous chapter are all memorable examples of racially tinged campaign messages. But in order to go beyond anecdotal evidence and identify broader patterns, we need to systematically measure the level of racialized messaging in the campaign environment. The first step in doing this is to be clear about how I define racialized messages.

To do this, I turn to the existing literature on racial communication. The political scientist Tali Mendelberg traces the origin of modern racial campaign communication to the century before the founding of the nation, when slavery gave rise to widespread notions of Black inferiority. Whites' negative attitudes toward Blacks centered on three themes: criminality, sexual immorality, and economic dependency.[3] Though beliefs about Black inferiority were widespread during the early decades of the American nation, negative racial predispositions did not play a prominent role in electoral politics until the 1860s, when the parties took different positions on slavery. Since beliefs about Black inferiority were open and pervasive, racial campaign appeals during the 1860s were explicit. For example, a Democratic campaign pamphlet from 1860 accused Republican presidential candidate Abraham Lincoln of wanting to repeal "all laws which erect a barrier between you and the black man."[4]

By the 1960s, however, the norm of white supremacy gave way to a norm of nondiscrimination, thanks to sympathy generated by the civil rights movement, landmark legislation, court rulings, and the pronouncements of scientific and political elites beginning in the 1930s.[5] However, the change in norms did not eliminate racial conflict in the party system. Since the 1960s, the Democratic Party has supported policies aimed at improving the economic and social standing of Black Americans, such as affirmative action in government contracts, employment, and higher education; public school desegregation; criminal justice reform; and assistance to the poor, policies that often generate substantial white opposition. Thus, the Republican Party since the 1960s has had incentives to appeal to white voters' concerns on these matters. These concerns are rooted in cultural, rather than biological, notions of Black inferiority in order to remain consistent with the nondiscriminatory norms of the modern era.[6] But these cultural notions nonetheless recycle the familiar themes of criminality, lack of sexual restraint, and economic dependency that have been associated with Black Americans throughout U.S. history. According to the political scientist Donald Kinder, contemporary notions of racial inferiority are "seen in the customs and folkways of black life: idleness, violence, drug abuse, teenage mothers—the whole 'tangle of pathology' that many whites see as characteristics of life in black neighborhoods."[7]

The solution to the Republican dilemma of appealing to white racial resentment while not violating egalitarian norms is to communicate racial messages in an "implicit" way by invoking putatively nonracial issues that are nonetheless linked to Blacks in the minds of many whites, but avoiding any explicit reference to race. The most well-known and extensively studied examples of implicit racial appeals are the Willie Horton ads from the 1988 presidential campaign, in which Republican George Bush ran a series of ads featuring the mug shot of a Black convict named Willie Horton that were intended to paint Democrat Michael Dukakis as being soft on crime.[8] A more recent example is an anti-Obama welfare ad from the 2012 presidential campaign in which Mitt Romney accused President Obama of eliminating work requirements that accompany welfare benefits.[9]

From this reading of the racial communication literature, the set of issues I expect to be emphasized by the white opponents of Black candidates are crime, sexual deviance, and taxes. As I have mentioned, crime and sexual deviance are longstanding anti-Black themes that are likely to activate racial considerations. Though taxation is a multifaceted issue that raises a number of nonracial considerations, it still might activate racial thinking given its connection to the anti-Black theme of economic dependency. Taxes are often discussed by elites and citizens alike as a form of redistribution from hard-working, responsible Americans to pay for social programs (such as food stamps, health care, or housing) that benefit undeserving minorities and/or the poor. Recent high-profile examples of elites connecting minorities, particularly Blacks, to taxes are not hard to find. For example, 2012 Republican presidential candidate Mitt Romney expounded on the taxes-as-redistribution theme at an election fundraiser, saying that "there are 47 percent who are with [Obama], who are dependent upon government, who believe that they are victims, who believe that government has a responsibility to care for them, who believe that they are entitled to health care, to food, to housing, to you name it . . . These are people who pay no income tax . . . And so my job is not to worry about those people—I'll never convince them that they should take personal responsibility and care for their lives."[10] Romney made the same argument in explicitly racial terms after losing the election, explaining his defeat as the result of "gifts" that President Obama used to win the support of specific groups, "especially the African-American community, the Hispanic community and young people."[11] Fox News' Bill O'Reilly also attributed Romney's defeat to minority voters and their dependence on government programs. "It's a changing country, the demographics are changing," said O'Reilly, cable news' top-rated commentator at the time. "It's not a traditional America anymore. And there are 50 percent of the voting public who want stuff. They want things and who is going to give them things? . . . The white establishment is now the minority."[12]

The consequence of this discourse is that public opinion about taxes is shaped by citizens' attitudes toward the racial groups they perceive as being the beneficiaries of tax revenue. The most authoritative demonstration of this point is the political scientists David Sears and Jack Citrin's study of the California "tax revolt" of the late 1970s and early 1980s, a series of ballot measures aimed at reducing taxes and limiting their future growth.[13] The authors showed that attitudes toward Blacks were strongly associated with support for California's tax revolt propositions even after accounting for a host of other factors such as ideology, partisanship, preferences for smaller and less intrusive government, trust in government, the belief that government is inefficient and wastes money, homeownership, personal financial situation, perceived high tax burden, and non-public-sector employment. Other studies reach similar conclusions. The political scientists Donald Kinder and Lynn Sanders show that racial resentment powerfully shapes opinion on federal spending on food stamps and welfare even after controlling for other factors.[14] In sum, all three issues—crime, sex, and taxes—though not overtly racial issues, will nonetheless activate racial thinking because they have a long history of entanglement with race (as they are directly connected with the trio of longstanding anti-Black themes of criminality, sexuality, and economic dependency) and because the mass media and political elites reinforce the connection between Blacks and these issues.[15]

Though crime, sex, and taxes are the three issues that form the backbone of modern racialized campaigns, they are not the only topics that activate racial considerations. There are other racial themes that I will explore more selectively in the campaigns where they figure prominently. In Cory Booker's campaign, for example, his white opponent Steve Lonegan focused on three other types of attacks that draw on anti-Black sentiments. First, Lonegan associated Booker with Newark, the city that Booker served as mayor and that has a large Black population.[16] Scholars have long speculated that racially resentful whites punish candidates for their association with large numbers of Black voters, a hypothesis that is supported by recent research.[17] Second, Lonegan accused Booker of various acts of corruption, illegally using his position as Newark mayor for private gain. Black politicians' propensity for corruption was a widely held stereotype during the Reconstruction era, which was seen by many whites as the era of corrupt Black rule.[18] In modern times, corruption remains a concern among white voters evaluating Black candidates and is a common theme of political ads run against Black candidates.[19] Finally, Lonegan repeatedly used the phrase "rubber-stamp" to tie Booker to President Obama. The political scientist Michael Tesler convincingly demonstrates that the mere mention of President Obama acts as a racializing cue, as the racial animus evoked by President Obama "spills over" to policies and public figures associated with Obama that were not racialized before they were tied to him. In a clever experiment, Tesler shows that whites' health care policy preferences are associated with racial resentment only in an experimental condition framing health care reform as Obama's plan but not in an experimental condition framing it as Bill Clinton's plan.[20] Thus, tying Booker to Obama is likely to result in more racialized evaluations of Booker.

At this point, it is important to address a few possible objections to my definition of racialized issues. The first objection is, are taxes really a racialized issue? Of the three core issues I define as racialized, taxes are probably the least clearly racialized, as lowering taxes is a standard

Republican talking point used against all Democratic candidates. However, as I argue earlier, political elites often frame the issue of taxes as a form of unjust redistribution from hard-working Americans to the undeserving. Frequently, commentators (and occasionally politicians) spell out in explicit terms that they believe the hard-working are white and the undeserving are Blacks and other minorities. As a result of this framing, research has demonstrated that attitudes toward Blacks are a strong predictor of whites' attitudes on tax issues even after accounting for other plausible influences. Considering all of this, I expect Black candidates to be more likely to face attacks on this issue. However, given that the issue of taxes also raises many nonracial considerations, I expect the disparity between the number of attacks faced by Black versus white candidates to be greater on the issues of crime and sexual misbehavior than the Black-white disparity on taxes.

The second objection is, if crime, sex, and taxes are racialized issues, what would a nonracial attack against a Black candidate look like? Would a nonracial attack also be effective in diminishing white support similarly to a racial attack? My answer to the first question is that a nonracial attack would be on an issue that is less evocative of existing anti-Black stereotypes. An example of such an attack against, say, Cory Booker, would be that Booker failed to deliver results as mayor. In chapter 7, I experimentally test the racial effects of this type of attack versus stereotypically anti-Black attacks that Booker faced (such as violent crime rising in Newark under Booker's leadership) and find that the racial effects are stronger for the stereotypical attacks. This suggests that the answer to the second question is that racial attacks are more effective in diminishing white support compared to a nonracial attack. It should not be surprising, then, that Booker faced an unusually high number of attacks on racialized themes (see results from later in this chapter). His white opponent has an incentive to inject racial messages into the campaign because Booker (and many other Black candidates for high-level office) often pursue a strategy of deracialization, in which they avoid discussions of race in order to minimize the salience of racial attitudes. I will say more about this in chapter 7. For now, the important point is that the effects of racial attacks are unique. The findings in this book are based on racial attacks, not simply any attacks against a Black candidate.

A third objection might be that by calling attacks on these issues "racialized," am I implying that every promise to be tough on crime or every call to lower taxes is derogatory toward Blacks? The short answer is no: these issues are multifaceted and raise a number of nonracial considerations. I also do not make a strong claim that white opponents *intend* to refer to race when addressing these topics. It is possible that the intent of white opponents is to address nonracial aspects of these topics. However, the way these issues are often discussed has been shown to raise the salience of racial considerations in white voters' political judgments and diminish their support for Black candidates. Given the potency of attacks on these themes, we should expect that at least some white candidates will see a strategic advantage in opening these lines of attack in a campaign against a Black opponent. If that is true, then these are the topics that we will most likely see discrepancies in the number of attacks Black candidates face compared to similar white candidates, regardless of the intentions of any individual white opponent.

Now that I have defended my set of racialized themes, I test the following hypothesis in this chapter: *Black candidates face more attacks on racialized issues such as crime, sex, and taxes than a comparable set of white candidates.* By systematically counting how often racial attacks occur and providing a baseline measure of how often comparable white candidates face racial attacks, I improve upon work that does not systematically measure the frequency of attacks[21] or provide the critical white baseline measure.[22]

MEASURING RACIALIZATION

I start by focusing on the campaigns of the six viable Black challengers between 2000 and 2018: Deval Patrick for governor of Massachusetts in 2006, Harold Ford Jr. for U.S. senator from Tennessee in 2006, Cory Booker for U.S. senator from New Jersey in 2013, Anthony Brown for governor of Maryland in 2014, Andrew Gillum for governor of Florida in 2018, and Stacey Abrams for governor of Georgia in 2018. Viability is defined by either winning the election or losing by less than 5 percentage points. I justify this definition in the next section. Next, I examine all news stories that ran in the last month of each campaign in the state's highest-circulation newspaper whose articles are available in the ProQuest and NewsBank databases. Those newspapers are the *Boston Globe* (MA),

Memphis Commercial-Appeal (TN), *Star-Ledger* (NJ), *Baltimore Sun* (MD), *Tampa Bay Times* (FL), and *Atlanta Journal-Constitution* (GA).[23] For each search, I included the last names of the major party candidates to narrow the universe of articles to only include ones about the campaign. I coded each article for mentions of the three racialized issues outlined earlier—crime, sexual misbehavior, and taxes—in order to calculate the percentage of stories in which the white opponent either mentioned his own position or attacked the Black candidate on the three racialized issues.[24] Then, I identified comparable white candidates according to the same criteria described in chapter 1: the most recent white challengers of the same party for the same office in the same state around the same time who ran against a white opponent. Finally, I calculated the percentage of stories in which the white opponent either mentioned his own position or attacked the comparison white candidate on the three racialized issues. The percentage of racialized stories targeting Black candidates was then compared to the analogous percentage for the comparison white candidates.

To elaborate more on what constitutes the boundaries of the issues of "crime," "sexual misbehavior," or "taxes," I define crime rhetoric as being any discourse around policing or the operation of the criminal justice system, including the handling of criminal defendants, in order to capture the types of policies associated with "crime control" since the 1960s.[25] This includes statements about the death penalty, which I counted because it deals specifically with the treatment of criminal defendants. Other topics that are arguably related to crime such as gun control or marijuana legalization were not considered crime mentions, as they are likely to raise different types of considerations than the ones typically raised by policing and the criminal justice system. I also included accusations of personal criminal misconduct, given that such charges are consistent with longstanding anti-Black stereotypes and are therefore likely to raise the salience of racial considerations. By defining crime rhetoric to include both accusations of personal criminal misconduct and issue positions on criminal justice policies, my aim is to capture charges that the Black candidate is either sympathetic to criminals or a criminal himself.

The mentions could be either attacks on the Black candidate's position or record on the issue or a statement of the white opponent's position or record. For example, Kerry Healey's statement "I will not be looking out to release dangerous offenders into society prematurely" was counted as a crime mention because it was an attack on Deval Patrick's advocacy on behalf of a convicted rapist. Also counted as a crime mention was Healey's comment "There is no benefit to hiding someone's criminal history" because it was a statement of her position that employers should have greater access to the state's criminal records for the purpose of screening potential employees. I also counted when the newspaper writer paraphrased a Healey crime mention. In one such example, the writer wrote, "Republican candidate Kerry Healey says that his [Patrick's] assistance [of the rapist] was a mistake."[26]

Mentions could be made by either the white opponent or a surrogate. Surrogates were defined as people who could be considered as having an interest in supporting the candidate, such as the candidate's official spokespeople and staff, members of the same party in government, and activists who favor the candidate's positions. Academics and journalists, even when criticizing or praising a candidate, were not considered surrogates.

I defined sex mentions as references to one's opponent or one's own sexual conduct. This does not include references to positions on issues plausibly related to sex and sexuality such as same-sex marriage or abortion. Defined in this manner, sex mentions were rare, occurring in only two campaigns: Harold Ford's and Cory Booker's. Any statement related to these incidents were considered sex mentions: the attacks on Harold Ford for attending a *Playboy*-sponsored party and his acceptance of campaign donations from the porn industry, attacks on Cory Booker suggesting that he was gay, and attacks on Cory Booker for having a brief online flirtation with a stripper. Booker's association with the stripper was different from the other three in that it was information that was first brought to light by the media without any comment from the campaign of Booker's opponent, Steve Lonegan. Following the guideline that mentions should come from the opposing campaign, I only included comments that were made by Lonegan's campaign after Booker's connection with the stripper was revealed. Not surprisingly, white opponents never discussed their own sexual conduct, and so all of the stories that were coded as sex mentions were attacks on either Ford or Booker. The coding guidelines regarding paraphrasing and surrogates for crime also apply to sex.

Finally, tax mentions included any statements made by the white opponent that referenced his stance or attacked his opponent on various kinds of taxes: income, sales, business, etc. For example, a *Baltimore Sun* article referencing Republican Larry Hogan's attacks on tax increases levied by the Democratic administration of Martin O'Malley and Anthony Brown was counted as a tax mention. I did not include statements on topics that are tangentially related to taxes, such as economic performance, unemployment, or business relocation. For example, Hogan claimed that ten of Maryland's *Fortune* 500 companies left Maryland while Brown was lieutenant governor. In instances when Hogan did not explicitly mention taxes as the reason for the relocation, it was not counted as a tax mention. Coding rules for paraphrasing and surrogates explained earlier also apply to the coding of tax mentions.

WHY FOCUS ONLY ON VIABLE BLACK CHALLENGERS?

In this section, I defend my focus on viable Black challenger candidacies. Since I am interested in examining Black candidates who are attempting to break historic color barriers, the ones who really matter are the ones who actually have a decent chance to win. Including candidates who have little chance to win may result in underestimating the obstacle posed by racialized campaigns, as the degree of racialization is likely to be significantly higher when the Black candidate is viable. The logic behind this is that white opponents may be more willing to pursue a risky line of attack against a Black challenger who has a good chance to win but may see little need to do so when they are likely to win no matter what. This hypothesis is supported by the political scientists David Metz and Katherine Tate, who find that competitiveness is a predictor of racial appeals in Black-white mayoral elections from 1969 to 1991.[27]

To test this hypothesis with my data set, I define viability as the Black challenger either winning the election by any margin or losing the election by less than 5 percentage points. *Ex post* measures such as the actual margin of victory are used in roughly 70 percent of political science articles that study electoral competitiveness, according to the political scientists

Bernard Fraga and Eitan Hersh.[28] Though the cutoff point is admittedly arbitrary, extending the threshold to 10 percentage points does not change the results. In fact, the association between viability and volume of racialized attacks is stronger when the viability threshold is 10 percentage points instead of 5 percentage points.[29]

With this measure of viability in hand, I regressed the percentage of stories that mention racialized rhetoric (whether crime, sex, or taxes) used by a white opponent on a dummy variable indicating whether the Black candidate was viable or not. To account for confounding factors that might explain this viability effect, I collected data on the following:

Mayor of a city with a large Black or Hispanic population. Black candidates who lead heavily minority cities may be attacked more on crime, given public perceptions linking urban minorities to crime. Coded 1 if the candidate was the mayor of a city that is at least 25 percent Black or Latino and 0 if not.

Party. Democrats may be attacked more frequently on crime than Republicans given the Republican Party's reputation as the "tough-on-crime" party. Coded 1 for Republican and 0 for Democrat.

Year. Crime declined as the "most important problem" named by Gallup survey respondents from 6 percent in October 2000 to 1 percent in December 2020.[30] Thus, Black candidates in earlier years may face more crime attacks given the greater public concern about crime during those years. Beginning with 2000, coded 0 (for 2000) to 20 (for 2020), recoded to the 0–1 interval.

Office sought: Governors may face more attacks on crime given their law enforcement role as head of the state's executive branch. Coded 1 for governor and 0 for senator.

Results are displayed in table 2.1. The first column shows the bivariate correlation between viability and racialized campaign rhetoric. The significant and positive intercept coefficient of 0.10 indicates that white opponents employ racialized rhetoric even when the Black candidate is not viable. However, viability greatly enhances the volume of racialized rhetoric Black candidates can expect. The significant and positive coefficient on the viability dummy variable indicates that viable Black candidates' campaigns featured about 18 percent more discussion of racialized issues generated by their white opponents than nonviable Black candidates' campaigns. The second column of table 2.1 shows the relationship between

TABLE 2.1 Predicting the percentage of campaign stories in which a white opponent mentions racialized issues (crime, sex, or taxes) in Black challenger campaigns for governor or U.S. Senate from 2000 to 2020

	Model 1	Model 2
Viable (0–1)	0.18*** (0.05)	0.16** (0.05)
Mayor of city with large black population (0–1)		0.02 (0.06)
Republican (0–1)		−0.05 (0.04)
Year (variable ranging from 0 (2000) to 1 (2020))		−0.04 (0.06)
Office sought (0 = Sen, 1 = Gov)		0.11* (0.04)
(Intercept)	0.10*** (0.02)	0.11* (0.05)
Adjusted R^2	0.27	0.38
N	37	37

*p < 0.1; **p < 0.01; ***p < 0.001.

viability and racialized campaign rhetoric including controls for each of the potential confounders. Including these controls does not greatly diminish the association between viability and racialized issue focus for Black candidates. These results suggest that focusing on the racialization of campaigns against *viable* black challengers is justified.

RACIALIZATION OF SIX VIABLE BLACK CHALLENGERS

Returning to this chapter's core task of measuring the racialization of the campaign environment faced by Black versus comparable white challengers, I start with the six Black candidates from 2000 to 2018 who meet the viability criterion of losing by less than 5 percentage points or winning by any margin: Deval Patrick (MA), Harold Ford Jr. (TN), Cory Booker (NJ), Anthony Brown (MD), Andrew Gillum (FL), and Stacey Abrams (GA). For the white comparison group, I started with the three or four most recent white challengers of the same party for the same office in the same state around the same time who ran against a white opponent. However, in order to provide a better comparison of viable Black candidates to viable white candidates, I set aside all uncompetitive white Democratic candidates (defined as losing by more than 10 percentage points): Mark Clayton (2012 Tennessee U.S. Senate), Bob Tuke (2008 Tennessee U.S. Senate), Jeff Clark (2000 Tennessee U.S. Senate), Roy Barnes (2010 Georgia gubernatorial), and Mark Taylor (2006 Georgia gubernatorial). The exclusion of uncompetitive white Tennessee and Georgia Democrats leaves Ford and Abrams with one white comparison candidate each (Bob Clement in 2002 for Ford and Jason Carter in 2014 for Abrams).[31] I also set aside one of Booker's New Jersey comparison candidates, Bob Menendez (2006), who is Latino.[32] This leaves Booker with two white comparison candidates, while Patrick, Brown, and Gillum have three each.[33]

To clarify my expectations for the results, I expect that Black candidates will be attacked more often than comparable white candidates on at least one of the themes but not necessarily all three. Since a high volume of attacks on any of these themes will raise the salience of race, candidates are likely to pick the line of attack that makes the most sense based on their opponent's reputation. For example, if Deval Patrick represented criminal defendants early in his legal career, his opponent, Kerry Healey, can develop a line of attack against Patrick as being soft on crime more credibly than one that says Patrick is a sexual deviant when nothing in his past suggests this line of attack would be credible. Thus, we would expect to see Patrick attacked more on crime than comparable white Massachusetts Democratic gubernatorial candidates but not more often on sex. Since the circumstances of each campaign vary, we expect to see an emphasis on different issues depending on candidate reputations and other factors. But since racialization is the goal, the expectation is that Black candidates will face a larger number of attacks on at least one of the three issues.

In figure 2.1, I compare crime mentions for each Black candidate to their viable white comparison candidates. The Patrick, Booker, Gillum, and Abrams campaigns faced white opponents who mentioned crime significantly more often than they typically do when facing white Democratic opponents. For every one crime mention in a campaign against a white Florida Democrat, Gillum faced almost 2.5 crime mentions. Those numbers increase to almost seven for Patrick and a little more than eight

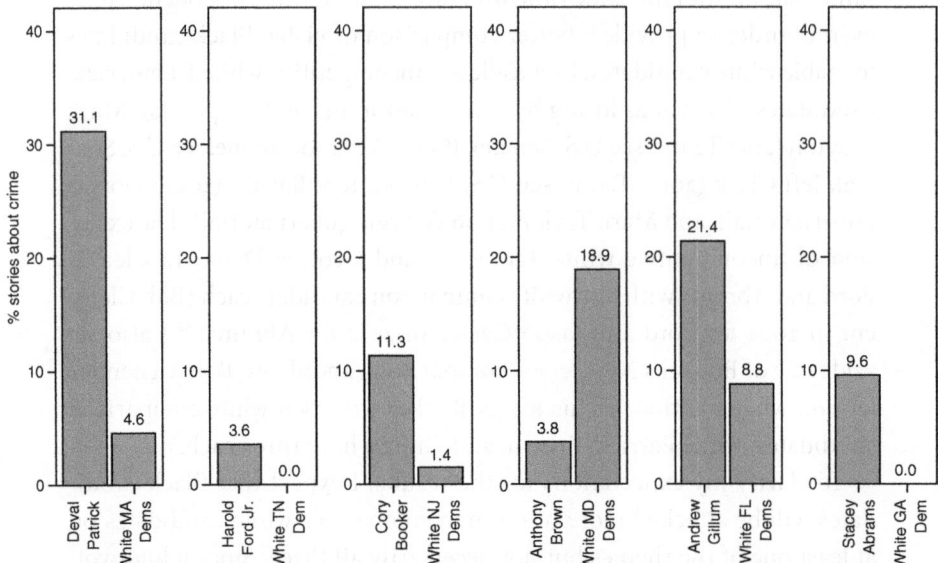

FIGURE 2.1 Crime focus of white opponents when facing viable Black challenger versus comparable viable white challenger.

for Booker. All of these differences are statistically significant (p < .01 for all comparisons). Also, 9.6 percent of stories included a crime mention in the Abrams campaign compared to zero for her white comparison candidate (p < .01).

The outliers in figure 2.1 are Ford and Brown. Ford's opponent, Bob Corker, did not focus much on crime (3.6 percent of articles), but much of the campaign was focused on another racialized theme: Ford's alleged sexual misbehavior—more on this later. As for Brown, the last three white Democratic gubernatorial challengers faced about six times as much crime coverage as Brown (p < .01). Part of the explanation is who those white Democratic gubernatorial challengers were and the circumstances of those elections. One Democratic challenger was Martin O'Malley in 2006, the mayor of Baltimore at the time. As suggested earlier, it is not surprising that mayors of cities with large minority populations and high crime rates will be attacked on crime. Another Democratic challenger, Kathleen Kennedy Townsend, ran in the midst of the October 2002 Washington, DC, sniper attacks. That unusual event made crime salient in Maryland that fall: Townsend's Republican opponent Robert Ehrlich used it to highlight his support for executing the sniper suspect. The final challenger was Parris Glendening in 1994, which was a year when crime was highly salient in the national conversation given the debate and passage of a major federal crime bill that year. As we will soon see, however, Brown's opponent Larry Hogan focused on the racialized theme of taxes.

Figure 2.2 shows the results for mentions of sexual conduct. Over 16 percent of articles that appeared in the last month of the Ford campaign and 9 percent of articles in the last month of the Booker campaign mentioned sex-themed attacks, both significantly different than 0 percent for their white comparison candidates (p < .01 for both Ford versus white TN Dem and Booker versus white NJ Dems).

The results for tax rhetoric are shown in figure 2.3. Overall, white opponents focus more of their attention on taxes than they do on crime and sex: the percentage of stories that include tax mentions by the white opponent is greater than 10 percent for ten out of the twelve bars in figure 2.3, compared to four out of twelve for crime mentions in figure 2.1 and one

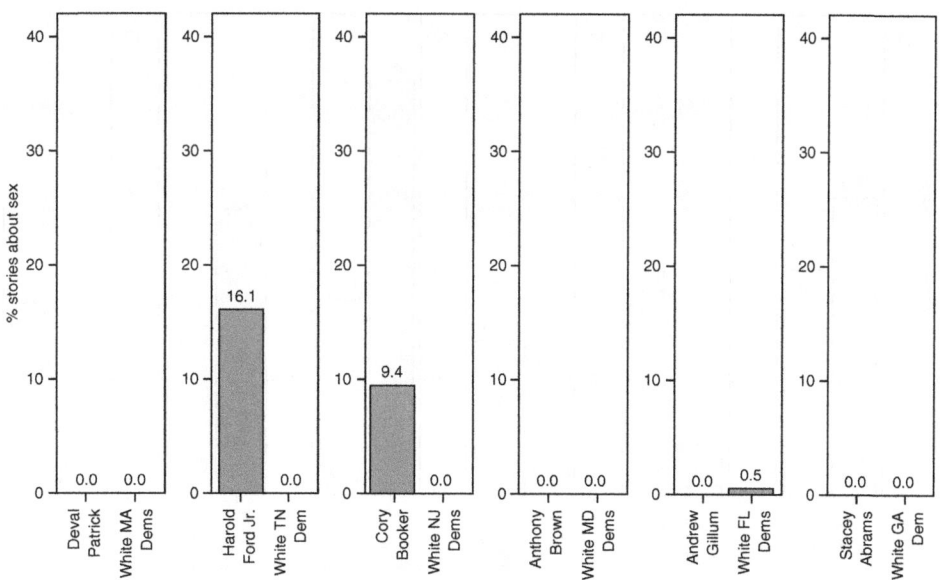

FIGURE 2.2 Sex focus of white opponents when facing viable Black challenger versus comparable viable white challenger.

out of twelve for sex mentions in figure 2.2. This makes sense in light of the earlier discussion of taxes being a central plank of the Republican platform. There is also a murkier pattern with respect to their frequency in Black candidate versus white comparison candidate elections. Though Brown, Patrick, and Gillum faced opponents who focused more of their campaigns on taxes than did opponents of comparable white candidates ($p < .01$ for Brown, $p = .07$ for Patrick, and $p = .06$ for Gillum), Booker's opponent focused on the issue about as much ($p = .95$), while Ford and Abrams' opponents focused on the issue much less than the opponent of his comparison white candidate ($p < .01$ for Ford and $p = .08$ for Abrams). However, the expectation was not that every Black candidate would face a high number of tax attacks. It was that they would face a high number of attacks on at least one of these issues. To that end, the key result in figure 2.3 is that taxes, not crime or sex, was the issue that Brown's opponent, Larry Hogan, focused an unusual amount of attention on. In chapter 5, I show that this focus during the campaign strengthened the connection between racial attitudes and white Marylanders' voting decisions.

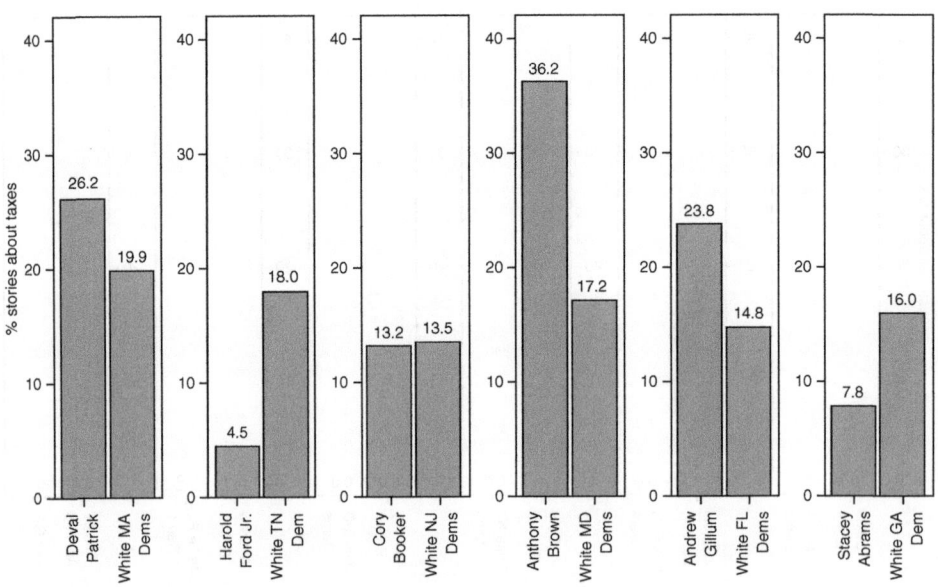

FIGURE 2.3 Tax focus of white opponents when facing viable Black challenger versus comparable viable white challenger.

TABLE 2.2 Did the Black candidate face more attacks than comparable white candidates in racialized issue domains?

	Crime	Sex	Taxes
Deval Patrick	✓		✓
Harold Ford Jr.		✓	
Cory Booker	✓	✓	
Anthony Brown			✓
Andrew Gillum	✓		✓
Stacey Abrams	✓		

Note: Summary of results from figures 2.1–2.3; statistically significant differences are indicated with a ✓.

In sum, the findings suggest that viable Black candidates face a different campaign with respect to the high frequency of attacks on racialized themes than the one they might experience if they were white. Table 2.2 is a summary table indicating which themes each candidate faced a significantly higher number of attacks on.

CONCLUSION

In this chapter, I identified a set of issues—crime, sex, and taxes—that I expect to see viable Black candidates attacked on with greater frequency than comparable white candidates. I collected data on the frequency of attacks on these topics for the six viable Black candidates between 2000 and 2018 and a set of thirteen white comparison candidates and found that each Black candidate faced a greater number of attacks on at least one of the three themes. As expected, the specific themes differed across candidates. Patrick and Gillum were heavily attacked on crime and taxes, Booker on crime and sex, Ford on sex, Brown on taxes, and Abrams on crime. But the key takeaway is that campaigning while Black during this period meant being defined by your opponent on themes with a longstanding connection to anti-Black stereotypes. Also, the findings in this chapter are a conservative estimate of the amount of racialization faced by Black candidates because I am not accounting for other attacks likely to raise the salience of race that only arose in individual campaigns, such as associating Cory Booker with the heavily Black city of Newark or criticizing Stacey Abrams's call to remove a Confederate monument. I will have more to say about the racializing effects of these attacks in later chapters. In the next chapter, I turn to the question of how Black candidates respond to racialized attacks.

3

THE RESPONSE OF BLACK CANDIDATES

In the previous chapter, I showed that Black candidates are targets of campaign discourse on racially themed issues at higher rates than comparable white candidates. This has implications for Black statewide electoral prospects because a body of existing research finds that messages on stereotypically anti-Black themes lead to the activation of racial attitudes among white voters.[1] In later chapters, I present new evidence from the campaigns of Deval Patrick, Harold Ford Jr., Cory Booker, and Anthony Brown that is consistent with these earlier findings: as attacks on racialized issues went up, support for the Black candidate went down among the many white voters with negative views of Blacks.

All of this raises the question of how Black candidates respond to these damaging attacks. According to the surprisingly sparse literature on this question, they usually do not. Studies of Black candidates in the 1980s find that they often pursue a strategy of "deracialization," in which they avoid any discussion of race in order to minimize its salience.[2] From this perspective, it is considered risky to directly confront racially tinged attacks. Other studies of white Democrats in the 1970s and 1980s find that they, too, usually tried to avoid confrontation with Republicans on racially inflected issues.[3]

In this chapter, I present findings that challenge the existing literature: attacked candidates sometimes respond to negative racial messages. First, I define a number of strategies that the six viable candidates from the previous chapter used when targeted by attacks on the three racialized issue areas of crime, sex, and taxes plus other racialized themes that came into play during the Ford, Booker, Gillum, and Abrams campaigns. Next, I show how frequently each candidate and their surrogates used each strategy in response to each type of attack. Finally, I show the candidates' overall level of response by comparing the percentage of stories containing a rebuttal to an opponent's mention of a racialized issue.

REBUTTAL TYPES

Before I classify rebuttals into different types, I begin by explaining how I defined a "rebuttal." I coded a rebuttal as any statement that explicitly argued against, refuted, or negatively referenced a racialized issue mention in the same article. For example, a *Boston Globe* article from the Patrick-Healey campaign included a crime attack by one of Healey's surrogates, who addressed Patrick in a letter, saying, "We challenge you to take a hard look at your own conduct in this case and ask yourself why at every opportunity you took the side of the violent offender over that of the victim." Later in the same article, the following passage argued against the crime attack and was coded as a rebuttal:

> Patrick's campaign yesterday said it had not received the letter and insisted the candidate has fought for victims throughout his career. Patrick was an assistant US Attorney General for civil rights under President Clinton. "Deval Patrick has dedicated his life toward working on issues of fairness and justice," said Doug Rubin, a senior adviser to Patrick. "He deeply sympathizes with the victims of any kind of violence and has in fact worked on behalf of victims his entire career. As head of the civil rights division and in private practice on a number of pro bono cases, Deval has aggressively fought for the rights of victims."[4]

As this example shows, statements made by surrogates were counted as rebuttals, with surrogates being defined the same way they were in the previous chapter: people who have an interest in supporting the candidate, including their campaign staff, fellow party members, and advocacy groups who favor their positions. Also consistent with the coding rules from the previous chapter, paraphrased statements were counted.

After identifying rebuttals, I coded them as different types according to the considerations raised by the rebuttal. I define several different rebuttal types with the help of the existing literature on rebuttals to racialized and general attacks.[5] For specific examples of each type, see appendix table 3.1.[6] More detail for each rebuttal type is provided here:

1. *Racial.* The key feature of this strategy is that the attacked candidate calls attention to the racial nature of the attack. President Obama used this strategy during the 2008 campaign in response to a John McCain ad that interspersed Obama images with irrelevant images of the blond female celebrities Paris Hilton and Britney Spears. Obama replied to the ad by saying that it was an attempt to remind voters that he "doesn't look like all those other presidents on the dollar bills."[7]

2. *Negative.* This strategy also denounces the attack but uses general, nonracial terms such as "negative" or "inappropriate." President Obama used this strategy in April 2011 following the release of his long-form birth certificate. In his attempt to put an end to the speculation about his birth place, Obama said he is "speaking to the vast majority of the American people as well as to the press—we do not have time for this kind of *silliness*."[8]

3. *Justify.* This strategy involves an explanation of the attacked action that accepts ownership of the action but argues that there are credible reasons for it. For example, Patrick responded to the controversy surrounding his past legal defense of criminal suspects by justifying his actions as a defense attorney, saying, "I'll tell you one thing. I have occasionally stood up in favor and in support of the unsavory defendant, and you should be glad somebody does. That's what makes the American legal system a just system."[9]

4. *Distract.* With this rebuttal, the attacked candidate pivots from the topic on which he is attacked to a topic more favorable to him. This is the type of strategy implied by deracialization—talk about issues other than race. For example, Obama usually avoided directly addressing any attacks or speculation that referenced his race during the 2008 campaign, instead choosing to focus on the economy.

5. *Counterimaging.* This strategy involves targeted candidates reframing the attack in a way that allows them to talk about their strengths on

the very topic on which they are being attacked. For example, Deval Patrick responded to the parking garage ad by emphasizing his experience as a tough-on-crime federal prosecutor.

6. *Counterattack.* An example of this is Patrick's charge that his opponent is in fact the one who is soft on crime because the crime rate had risen and the number of state police officers had decreased during her tenure as lieutenant governor. The key difference between this strategy and *counterimaging* is that *counterattack* focuses attention on negative aspects of the attacker, while *counterimaging* portrays the target in a positive light.

7. *Deny.* A candidate does this by saying that they did not do what their opponent accuses them of doing or that they are not what their opponent accuses them of being. One example is when Cory Booker responded to Steve Lonegan's charge that violent crime and murders have gone up for five years in row by saying that violent crime and murders had actually gone down during that period.

8. *Ignore.* This strategy involves not offering any type of response. One notable example of its use was Booker, who allowed a long stretch of the 2013 New Jersey U.S. Senate campaign to go by without addressing his opponent's attacks (see chapter 5).

In addition to coding rebuttals for all mentions of crime, sex, and taxes that occurred in the last month of the campaign, I also included rebuttals to attacks on other racialized themes that figured prominently in the Booker, Ford, Gillum, and Abrams campaigns. Booker was racialized by attacks on his association with the heavily Black city of Newark, New Jersey and his alleged corruption; Ford was the target of an explicitly racial attack: a radio ad claiming that Ford favored Blacks over whites; Gillum's opponent Ron DeSantis said that Florida voters shouldn't "monkey this up" by electing Gillum; and Abrams was criticized for burning a Confederate flag at a protest when she was a college student and for her support for removing Confederate imagery from state symbols.

Almost all rebuttals could be coded into one of the first seven categories, with no rebuttals coded as *ignore* because it is, by definition, a nonresponse.[10] I consider news stories that contain a mention without a rebuttal in the last part of the chapter. For now, I focus on the frequency of the first seven rebuttal types.

Several articles contain more than one rebuttal. In such cases, rebuttals were coded separately, which allows for an article to contain more than one rebuttal. An example of this is the *Boston Globe* article mentioned earlier that included quotations from a letter written by a Healey surrogate criticizing Deval Patrick's sympathy for criminal defendants. In addition to the rebuttal offered by Patrick's senior advisor Doug Rubin, the same article also contained this rebuttal offered by U.S. senator (and Patrick surrogate) Ted Kennedy:

> Before the letter surfaced yesterday, U.S. Senator Edward M. Kennedy said that Healey "has chosen the low road in her campaign." Repeating a line used by other Democrats over the last several days, Kennedy said in a statement that Republicans were "swift-boating" Patrick. The term refers to the attacks on U.S. Senator John F. Kerry's military record during his 2004 presidential bid. "The voters in Massachusetts are not going to allow Kerry Healey and the Republican Party to do the same thing to Deval Patrick."[11]

This Kennedy rebuttal was coded as *negative* (since its main theme emphasized Healey choosing the low road), while the Rubin rebuttal emphasizing Patrick's work on behalf of crime victims was coded as *counterimaging* (since it portrayed Patrick as being tough on crime).

FREQUENCY OF EACH REBUTTAL

Table 3.1 shows the percentage and frequency of each rebuttal's use by Deval Patrick and his surrogates for the two racialized issues that his opponent discussed: crime and taxes. Comparing across the two issues, it appears that Patrick had a different strategy for dealing with each attack. When confronted with the charge that he was soft on crime, Patrick mixed across three strategies: *negative* (33 percent of all rebuttals), *counterimaging* (23 percent), and *counterattack* (19 percent). In response to attacks on raising taxes, his preferred strategy was to *counterattack* (42 percent), charging his opponent Kerry Healey with being part of a free-spending

TABLE 3.1 Frequency of rebuttals used by Deval Patrick

	Racial	Negative	Justify	Distract	Counterimaging	Counterattack	Deny
Crime	0	33%	13%	12%	23%	19%	0
		17	7	6	12	10	
		(8P/9S)	(2P/5S)	(5P/1S)	(6P/6S)	(4P/6S)	
Taxes	0	5%	26%	5%	5%	42%	16%
		1	5	1	1	8	3
		(0P/1S)	(4P/1S)	(1P/0S)	(1P/0S)	(5P/3S)	(2P/1S)
Overall	0	25%	17%	10%	18%	25%	4%
		18	12	7	13	18	3
		(8P/10S)	(6P/6S)	(6P/1S)	(7P/6S)	(9P/9S)	(2P/1S)

Note: The top number in each cell represents the percentage of rebuttals to an attack type (indicated by the row) that were classified as falling into a particular rebuttal category. Percentages may not add to 100 percent because of rounding. The middle number indicates the frequency of each rebuttal. The bottom numbers indicate the frequency of each rebuttal used by the candidate versus a surrogate. P indicates that rebuttal was offered by Patrick; S indicates that rebuttal was offered by one of Patrick's surrogates.

administration as lieutenant governor of Massachusetts under Mitt Romney. He also used *justify* (26 percent), as exemplified by his response to Healey's charge that he would waste taxpayer money by arguing that there are socially useful purposes for spending taxpayer money, saying, "It's their money. It's also their broken roads and their overcrowded schools. It's their broken neighborhoods and broken neighbors."[12]

Two other patterns in table 3.1 are worth noting. First, the number of rebuttals offered by him versus his surrogates is relatively balanced for each of the four rebuttals he used frequently, indicating that there was no rebuttal type he preferred to use himself rather than to delegate to his surrogates. Second, Patrick never used *racial* in the last month of the campaign, perhaps after dealing with the fallout from an incident from earlier in the campaign in which he distanced himself from a racial remark made by state Democratic Party chairman Philip Johnston (who is white), who said Kerry Healey came "perilously close to race baiting" by promoting her positions against offering driver's licenses to illegal immigrants and in favor of voter identification laws.[13]

Table 3.2 shows Harold Ford's rebuttals to attacks he faced on sex, taxes, and the one explicitly racial attack he faced of favoring Blacks over whites.

TABLE 3.2 Frequency of rebuttals used by Harold Ford

	Racial	Negative	Justify	Distract	Counterimaging	Counterattack	Deny
Sex	20% 2 (0F/2S)	40% 4 (3F/1S)	20% 2 (2F/0S)	10% 1 (1F/0S)	0	0	10% 1 (1F/0S)
Taxes	0	0	0	0	0	100% 1 (1F/0S)	0
Favor Blacks over whites	100% 1 (0F/1S)	0	0	0	0	0	0
Overall	25% 3 (0F/3S)	33% 4 (3F/1S)	17% 2 (2F/0S)	8% 1 (1F/0S)	0	8% 1 (1F/0S)	8% 1 (1F/0S)

Note: The top number in each cell represents the percentage of rebuttals to an attack type (indicated by the row) that were classified as falling into a particular rebuttal category. Percentages may not add to 100 percent because of to rounding. The middle number indicates the frequency of each rebuttal. The bottom numbers indicate the frequency of each rebuttal used by the candidate versus a surrogate. F indicates that rebuttal was offered by Ford; S indicates that rebuttal was offered by one of Ford's surrogates.

Ford also faced attacks on crime, but the table does not contain a row for crime rebuttals because no rebuttals were recorded in the *Memphis Commercial Appeal*. The first row shows how Ford responded to charges that he attended a *Playboy* party and accepted money from the porn industry. This is the most informative row; it accounts for the vast majority of Ford's rebuttals overall. Ford's most common rebuttal to the sex attacks was *negative*, exemplified by his response, "I was a little surprised to see the smut and the slime coming into my living room during family time."[14] However, Ford surrogates (though not Ford himself) used *racial* twice in response to the sex attacks and once more in response to the explicitly racial attack Ford faced when a group called Tennesseeans for Truth ran this radio ad:

> His daddy handed him his seat in Congress and his seat in the Congressional Black Caucus, an all-black group of congressmen who represent the interests of black people above all others. Ford's Congressional

Black Caucus secretly prepares and presents their own alternative budget to Congress each year to fund aid to black Americans. Discrimination at its worst. Tennesseeans want a color-blind senator, a real Tennessean representing all of us without discrimination.[15]

Racial was used to respond to this attack, though only by surrogates. In contrast, Ford delegated all other types of rebuttals to surrogates far less frequently (one out of nine nonracial rebuttals).

Table 3.3 shows Cory Booker's rebuttals to attacks on five racialized issues. In addition to attacks on crime, sex, and taxes, another type of attack was to tie Booker to Newark, a city with a large Black population.

TABLE 3.3 Frequency of rebuttals used by Cory Booker

	Racial	Negative	Justify	Distract	Counterimaging	Counterattack	Deny
Crime	0	0	0	33% 1 (1B/0S)	0	33% 1 (0B/1S)	33% 1 (0B/1S)
Sex	0	100% 1 (0B/1S)	0	0	0	0	0
Taxes	0	50% 1 (1B/0S)	0	50% 1 (1B/0S)	0	0	0
Ties to Newark	0	11% 1 (1B/0S)	11% 1 (1B/0S)	11% 1 (1B/0S)	33% 3 (1B/2S)	11% 1 (0B/1S)	22% 2 (0B/2S)
Corruption	0	0	0	0	50% 1 (0B/1S)	50% 1 (0B/1S)	0
Overall	0	18% 3 (2B/1S)	6% 1 (1B/0S)	18% 3 (3B/0S)	24% 4 (1B/3S)	18% 3 (0B/3S)	18% 3 (0B/3S)

Note: The top number in each cell represents the percentage of rebuttals to an attack type (indicated by the row) that were classified as falling into a particular rebuttal category. Percentages may not add to 100 percent because of rounding. The middle number indicates the frequency of each rebuttal. The bottom numbers indicate the frequency of each rebuttal used by the candidate versus a surrogate. B indicates that rebuttal was offered by Booker; S indicates that rebuttal was offered by one of Booker's surrogates.

Lonegan painted Booker as unable to control Newark's rampant dysfunction. "Newark is worse off now than it was under Sharpe James," Lonegan said at a news conference on October 8, referring to Booker's predecessor. "Think about this. Under Sharpe James, unemployment was 8 percent. And things have actually gotten worse under Mayor Booker. It's hard to believe it, but Sharpe James—he was a criminal and went to jail, rightfully so—but he still did a better job running that city than Cory Booker does."[16] Lonegan also attacked Booker on another trait that has historically been linked to Black public officials: corruption.[17] Lonegan sued Booker for blocking requests for his expense records as Newark's mayor and also claimed that Booker received a large payout from his former law firm in exchange for city agency contracts when Booker became mayor.

One notable finding from table 3.3 is that Booker or his surrogates never responded the same way more than once to attacks on crime, sex, or taxes. Compare this to Patrick's response to attacks on crime and taxes and Ford's response to attacks on sex. Both emphasized at least one clear theme in their rebuttals. The fourth row shows that the most common reply to Lonegan's portrayal of him as the face of Newark's dysfunction was *counterimaging* (33 percent), using the attacks as an opportunity for surrogates to tout his record on urban revitalization. Booker also responded to attempts to tie him to Newark by using *deny* (22 percent). One example was when Lonegan held a press conference in front of an abandoned Newark property he called "Booker's abandoned crack house" and accused Booker of allowing the property to fall into disrepair.[18] A Booker surrogate denied the allegation by explaining that Booker had sold the property six months earlier. Overall, as shown in the bottom row, Booker's most commonly used rebuttals were *counterimaging* (24 percent), *negative* (18 percent), *counterattack* (18 percent), *deny* (18 percent), and *distract* (18 percent).

Table 3.4 shows Anthony Brown's rebuttals to attacks he faced on taxes. Brown also faced a few attacks on crime but did not respond. Thus, Brown's rebuttals on taxes represent all of his rebuttals to attacks on racialized issues. When faced with charges that he would raise taxes, he relied evenly on *distract* (33 percent), *counterimaging* (33 percent), and *deny* (33 percent). His reliance on these strategies at the expense of *justify* was criticized by fellow Democrats and some in the media. One *Baltimore Sun*

TABLE 3.4 Frequency of rebuttals used by Anthony Brown

	Racial	Negative	Justify	Distract	Counterimaging	Counterattack	Deny
Taxes/ Overall	0	0	0	33% 4 (3B/1S)	33% 4 (4B/0S)	0	33% 4 (4B/0S)

Note: The top number in each cell represents the percentage of rebuttals to an attack type (indicated by the row) that were classified as falling into a particular rebuttal category. Percentages may not add to 100 percent because of rounding. The middle number indicates the frequency of each rebuttal. The bottom numbers indicate the frequency of each rebuttal used by the candidate versus a surrogate. B indicates that rebuttal was offered by Brown; S indicates that rebuttal was offered by one of Brown's surrogates.

columnist argued that one reason why the election was closer than expected (in October) was that

> Brown does not offer sufficient defense of progressive policies. Just, once, I'd like to hear Brown stand without shame and say, "Taxes? Look, we don't like taxes, either. Who likes taxes? We'd cut them if we could, and we'll cut them if we can. But if you want a decent quality of life, good schools, good roads, public transportation, affordable colleges, clean rivers and a cleaner Chesapeake, and a vigilant public health system, then we need to pay for it."[19]

In chapter 5, I take a closer look at Brown's rebuttal strategy and his polling performance over the course of the campaign.

Table 3.5 shows Andrew Gillum's rebuttal pattern. Gillum stands out for his high usage of *racial*. He used that response four times himself and delegated it once to a surrogate in response to attacks on crime. In one of the debates, DeSantis accused Gillum of illegally accepting gifts (in this case, tickets to see the Broadway musical *Hamilton* in New York) from two undercover FBI agents. In response, Gillum replied, "I don't take free trips from anybody. I'm a hard-working person. *I know that may not fit your description of what you think people like me do*, but I've worked hard for everything that I've gotten in my life."[20] Aside from *racial* (which accounted for 29 percent of rebuttals to crime attacks), Gillum's other preferred response was *deny* (35 percent), which was used entirely by surrogates. After accounting for rebuttals to attacks on taxes and DeSantis's

THE RESPONSE OF BLACK CANDIDATES 63

TABLE 3.5 Frequency of rebuttals used by Andrew Gillum

	Racial	Negative	Justify	Distract	Counterimaging	Counterattack	Deny
Crime	29% 5 (4G/1S)	18% 3 (3G/0S)	6% 1 (1G/0S)	0	6% 1 (1G/0S)	6% 1 (1G/0S)	35% 6 (0G/6S)
Taxes	0	40% 2 (1G/1S)	0	20% 1 (1G/0S)	0	0	40% 2 (2G/0S)
"Monkey this up"	0	100% 1 (0G/1S)	0	0	0	0	0
Overall	22% 5 (4G/1S)	26% 6 (4G/2S)	4% 1 (1G/0S)	4% 1 (1G/0S)	4% 1 (1G/0S)	4% 1 (1G/0S)	35% 8 (2G/6S)

Note: The top number in each cell represents the percentage of rebuttals to an attack type (indicated by the row) that were classified as falling into a particular rebuttal category. Percentages may not add to 100 percent because of rounding. The middle number indicates the frequency of each rebuttal. The bottom numbers indicate the frequency of each rebuttal used by the candidate versus a surrogate. G indicates that rebuttal was offered by Gillum; S indicates that rebuttal was offered by one of Gillum's surrogates.

"monkey it up" comment, it appears that Gillum's strategy for dealing with racialized attacks was to label them *racial* or *negative* himself while deploying *deny* to his surrogates.

Finally, table 3.6 shows Stacey Abrams's rebuttals. The similarities between Abrams and Gillum—the fact that they ran in the same year for the same office in neighboring southern states against Republican provocateurs in the mold of Trump (DeSantis and Georgia's Brian Kemp)—suggest that comparisons of their rebuttal patterns may be illuminating. With respect to the use of *racial*, Abrams's nonusage of the rebuttal is in contrast to Gillum's frequent usage. Like Gillum, Abrams faced an accusation of personal criminal misconduct when Kemp said, "If that's not criminal, it should be," referring to Abrams's lending her campaign $50,000 despite owing taxes. While Gillum often responded with *racial*, Abrams responded with *justify*, explaining that her debt was the result of financially supporting her parents and grandparents after Hurricane Katrina and adopting her twelve-year-old niece. She added that the money

TABLE 3.6 Frequency of rebuttals used by Stacey Abrams

	Racial	Negative	Justify	Distract	Counterimaging	Counterattack	Deny
Crime	0	18% 2 (1A/1S)	36% 4 (4A/0S)	27% 3 (2A/1S)	9% 1 (0A/1S)	9% 1 (1A/0S)	0
Taxes	0	0	0	43% 3 (2A/1S)	14% 1 (1A/0S)	0	43% 3 (3A/0S)
Confederate symbols	0	0	100% 1 (1A/0S)	0	0	0	0
Overall	0	11% 2 (1A/1S)	26% 5 (5A/0S)	32% 6 (4A/2S)	11% 2 (1A/1S)	5% 1 (1A/0S)	16% 3 (3A/0S)

Note: The top number in each cell represents the percentage of rebuttals to an attack type (indicated by the row) that were classified as falling into a particular rebuttal category. Percentages may not add to 100 percent because of rounding. The middle number indicates the frequency of each rebuttal. The bottom numbers indicate the frequency of each rebuttal used by the candidate versus a surrogate. A indicates that rebuttal was offered by Abrams; S indicates that rebuttal was offered by one of Abrams's surrogates.

she loaned to her campaign came from the advance she got for her memoir and that she had paid the taxes she owed.[21] Abrams also used *justify* in response to criticism she'd received for burning a Confederate flag as a college student in 1992, saying that her actions were part of a "permitted, peaceful protest" at a time when Georgia was rightfully questioning whether it was appropriate for the state flag to have the Confederate battle emblem on it.[22] Overall, Abrams used *justify* more frequently than Gillum, as it accounted for 26 percent of Abrams's rebuttals compared to just 4 percent for Gillum. Aside from *justify,* Abrams's other preferred rebuttal was *distract* (32 percent of all rebuttals), which she often used in response to charges that she would raise taxes. She responded to this attack by trying to shift attention to the positive fiscal consequences that would come from addressing major social problems: "You spend less on criminal justice when you have people who are economically secure, you spend less on emergency room costs when people have better preventative care access, you spend less on trying to address the issue of homelessness when people have access to affordable housing."[23] Despite facing similar attacks in similar circumstances as Gillum, Abrams relied mostly on *distract* and *justify* instead of *racial* and *deny*.

OVERALL REBUTTAL LEVELS

Aside from looking at the type of rebuttal used, it is also possible to evaluate how frequently Black candidates rebutted their opponent's racialized frames. To be clear, the relationship between rebuttal frequency and likelihood of winning is complicated by several factors. One is the competitiveness of the campaign. Just as white candidates with large leads tend not to deploy racialized attacks because they perceive little to be gained from saying much of anything when they are way ahead, Black candidates with large leads may be less likely to respond to racialized attacks when they are way ahead.[24] Another complicating factor is the seriousness and credibility of the attack. Perhaps an attack on Booker for allowing his Newark property to become an "abandoned crack house" is so outlandish that it can be safely ignored, but a more serious and credible charge such as Patrick's connection to a convicted criminal needs to be addressed. Related to the seriousness and credibility of the attack is the reputation of the attacker. Charges from well-funded, experienced Republicans like Bob Corker, Ron DeSantis, or Brian Kemp might be harder to ignore than charges from long-shot eccentrics like Steve Lonegan. Considering that the candidates faced widely varying circumstances on all of these dimensions, it is unlikely that rebuttal frequency will be the same across all of the campaigns.

While recognizing the reality that some attacks are more damaging than others, however, my general expectation is that Black candidates are better served by rebutting racialized attacks because it gives them an opportunity to challenge the racialized narrative advanced by their opponent. Political communication research provides insight into how rebuttals might play an important role in combating racial attacks. The pioneering work on "counterframing" by Chong and Druckman and Sniderman and Theriault critiques earlier work on framing, which showed that how political arguments are "framed" can have dramatic effects on the types of considerations (such as group attachments, values, and interests) that citizens draw upon when making political evaluations.[25] Chong and Druckman criticize the early framing research for ignoring the reality of democratic competition among elites. They argue that in the real world, opposing elites offer competing frames to the public in an effort to persuade citizens to evaluate a political matter using their preferred set of criteria.

In their experiments, they find that framing effects dissipate when pitted against a counterframe that emphasizes a different consideration, assuming that the counterframe is a compelling argument. This occurs because the counterframe promotes deliberate evaluation of the original frame. Though race and racial attacks are not discussed in their work, the relevance of their findings for my examination of rebuttals is clear: while racial attacks are a type of frame that is meant to activate racial considerations, rebuttals are a type of counterframe that can potentially raise an alternative set of considerations, thus changing how citizens evaluate candidates and the considerations they draw upon when doing so.

In the upcoming case study chapters, I find support for the hypothesis that the overall volume of rebuttals offered by Black candidates targeted by racial attacks improves their evaluation among white voters, as white support is generally correlated with the level of Black candidates' contestation of racial attacks over the course of a campaign. But for now, my aim is to show how frequently the six candidates rebutted racial attacks. To do this, I first counted the number of stories about each campaign that mentioned a racialized theme: crime, sex, taxes, ties to Newark (for Booker), corruption (for Booker), explicit racial attacks (for Ford), the "monkey it up" comment (for Gillum), and Confederate symbols (for Abrams). I then calculated the percentage of those stories that also contained a rebuttal from the candidate or one of their surrogates.[26] The results are shown in the first column of table 3.7. Overall, Abrams had the highest rebuttal rate at 67 percent, followed by Gillum at 50 percent. No other candidate reached 40 percent, with Ford and Brown lagging behind at 32 percent and 31 percent, respectively. The second column of table 3.7 shows the percentage of racialized stories that contain a rebuttal from the candidate him- or herself (and not one of their surrogates). In this column, we see that Booker had the lowest rate of rebutting racialized attacks himself (19 percent). As we will see in chapter 6, Booker delegated rebuttals (and at times, all campaigning) to surrogates for much of the campaign.

TABLE 3.7 Percentage of stories with racialized frames that also included rebuttals

	Overall	Overall (candidate only)	Most prominent racialized theme	On most prominent racialized theme	On most prominent racialized theme (candidate only)
Deval Patrick	39	25	Crime	49	30
Harold Ford	32	21	Sex	39	28
Cory Booker	39	19	Ties to Newark	50	20
Anthony Brown	31	28	Taxes	34	31
Andrew Gillum	50	40	Crime	78	67
Stacey Abrams	67	52	Crime	82	64

Overall rebuttal levels, however, may not be the best indicator of how vigorously Black candidates challenged racialization. For example, Harold Ford's rebuttals on taxes, a secondary theme of his campaign, may not matter as much as his rebuttals on the one racialized theme that stood out in his campaign: sex. To account for this possibility, I examine rebuttal levels on only the most prominent racialized theme in each campaign. In the third column of table 3.7, I list each campaign's most prominent racialized theme: crime for Patrick, sex for Ford, Newark/failure for Booker, taxes for Brown, crime for Gillum, and crime for Abrams. I determined this by simply counting the number of opponent mentions of each theme and selecting the one that was mentioned most often.

In the fourth column, I calculated the percentage of stories about those themes that also included a rebuttal by either the candidate or a surrogate. The results are similar to the overall results shown in the first column: Abrams (82 percent) and Gillum (78 percent) had the highest rebuttal rates for their respective themes, with Ford (39 percent) and Brown (34 percent) having the lowest. In the fifth column, I show the percentage of stories that mentioned the most prominent racialized theme that also contain a rebuttal by the candidate him- or herself. Similar to what I found for rebuttals overall (second column), Booker lagged behind in using his own words to defend himself against attempts to paint him as a symbol of urban dysfunction: only 20 percent of stories with that frame included a Booker rebuttal. By comparison, Abrams's and Gillum's rates exceeded 60 percent.

CONCLUSION

The goal of this chapter is to present evidence that challenges the conventional wisdom that Black candidates facing racial attacks do not respond to them. Patrick used a variety of strategies to ward off crime attacks: criticizing the negativity of the Healey campaign, justifying his actions as a criminal defense attorney, touting his own tough-on-crime credentials, and counterattacking Healey on her crime policies. Ford highlighted the negativity of attacks portraying him as a sexual deviant, and a few of his surrogates pointed out the racial nature of the attack. Booker's approach to fending off attacks on a number of racialized topics was less clear, though he most often denied Lonegan's allegations that Booker represented urban decay and used them as an opportunity to tout his efforts to revitalize Newark. Brown responded to charges that he would raise taxes and hurt Maryland's business climate by using *distract, counterimaging,* and *deny,* but never *justify*. Gillum responded to crime attacks by denouncing them as *racial* or *negative* or having surrogates *deny* the charges against him, while Abrams responded to similar attacks by justifying her actions or trying to pivot to more favorable issues. In terms of the overall response levels, Abrams and Gillum defended themselves more vigorously than the others. Among the four who defended themselves less often, Booker was especially unlikely to counter attacks himself.

One key finding from this chapter is that Black candidates rarely respond by challenging an attack in racial terms. In fact, my analysis shows that only Gillum ever used the racial rebuttal himself, though a surrogate also used it on Ford's behalf.[27] The abandonment of the racial rebuttal is notable because it runs against the recommendation made by the existing literature. The political scientist Tali Mendelberg argues that confronting the attack in racial terms is an effective rebuttal strategy.[28] If so, then Black candidates may be adhering too closely to their deracialized presentation. On the other hand, it is important to remember that

Mendelberg's test of the racial rebuttal was for a white candidate—Democratic presidential nominee Michael Dukakis in 1988. This response may work quite differently for a Black candidate. Fortunately, I test this hypothesis in chapter 8 and find that it is significantly more effective for a white candidate. The findings presented in this chapter suggest that Black candidates understand the difficulty of raising race-based objections to racial attacks when running before a white electorate.

We also see evidence of how often candidates respond themselves and how often they delegate rebuttals to surrogates. Booker was the only candidate who delegated over half of his rebuttals to surrogates. At first glance, this does not appear to tell us much about whether a candidate's own voice is more effective than his surrogates: Booker delegated the most and yet still won, while Brown used his own voice almost exclusively and suffered an embarrassing defeat. However, the question of whether the candidate's voice is more effective is unlikely to yield a simple answer. It likely depends on a number of factors: are surrogates the only people spreading the candidate's message, or is the surrogate amplifying what the candidate is also saying? Timing is also likely to matter: are surrogates the first voice coming from the campaign in response to racial attacks, or does the candidate respond first and surrogates take over later? Fortunately, the case studies in the next three chapters all have enough variation in terms of the balance and timing of candidate/surrogate rebuttals to allow us to better answer these questions than we can with the data in this chapter.

Another notable finding is the perhaps surprisingly low overall rebuttal rates—below 40 percent for four out of the six candidates. These low rates reveal something substantively important about the challenges Black candidates face. The denominator is all of the articles that include a racialized issue *mention*, which could be either an attack on the Black candidate *or* a statement of the white candidate's own position on the issue. The numerator represents the number of those articles that include a rebuttal by the Black candidate. Since rebuttals are almost always a response to an attack, it is not surprising that the rebuttal percentages are usually low: it is hard to think of how Anthony Brown would rebut Larry Hogan merely stating that he would lower taxes. Some may argue that if you only look at the rebutted percentage of attacks, the rebuttal percentages would be much higher. However, I argue that defining racial mentions as both attacks *and* nonattacks is justified because nonattack statements still represent the white candidate's efforts to raise the salience of that issue. In fact, nonattacks can be thought of as a "softer" form of criticism, one less direct than an attack but harder for Black candidates to refute. Capturing this softer form of criticism is essential to measuring the true amount of racialized discourse faced by Black candidates, and so the low percentages found in this chapter reflect not only a reticence to respond to attacks but also the inherent difficulty in responding to various forms of racialized campaign discourse.

This chapter leaves open a number of questions. Does rebuttal volume actually help attacked candidates? Do certain strategies work better than others? I examine these questions in depth in the following chapters. I start in the next chapter with a case study of the Patrick and Ford campaigns.

4

THE DEVAL PATRICK AND HAROLD FORD JR. CAMPAIGNS OF 2006

In chapters 1 and 2, I argue that Black candidates for high-level statewide office have had worse electoral outcomes compared to comparable white candidates and that part of this could be attributed to the greater frequency of racialized attacks faced by Black candidates. This, in turn, suggests that rebuttals play an important role in the election outcome. Now, I turn to the effects of attacks and rebuttals. In this chapter, I compare the Deval Patrick and Harold Ford Jr. campaigns of 2006. Both faced high-profile racial attacks: Ford was accused of interracial sexual promiscuity, and Patrick was attacked for advocating for the release of convicted criminals. Only Patrick, however, offered a sustained response to the attacks. To examine how each candidate's prospects may have been influenced by attacks and rebuttals, I collected all available polling data on the two campaigns to compare vote choice before the attacks, after the attacks, and after the rebuttals. The results indicate that while both candidates experienced a decrease in support among white voters after the attacks, only Patrick managed to restore his favorability ratings, which may be the consequence of several days of well-publicized rebuttals. The results suggest that these rebuttals helped restore Patrick's ratings and enabled him to win the election.[1]

EXPECTATIONS

EXPECTED EFFECTS OF RACIALIZED ATTACKS

Before I describe the major events and polling of the two campaigns, I begin by laying out my expectations for the effects of racialized attacks and rebuttals to them. With respect to racialized attacks, a body of research demonstrates that these attacks—on issues commonly associated with Blacks (such as crime) and often accompanied by racial imagery but not explicitly mentioning race—lead to the activation of racial attitudes among white voters (or "racial priming," as it is often referred to in the literature). In other words, racialized attacks lead to racial attitudes becoming a central determinant of whites' opposition to policies perceived as benefiting Blacks and candidates who are perceived to represent Black interests.[2] Based on these findings, I expect that racial attacks will make racial attitudes a stronger determinant of white voters' evaluation of attacked Black candidates than before the attacks took place.

REBUTTAL CHARACTERISTICS AND THEIR EXPECTED EFFECTS

Turning to rebuttals, I start by describing the characteristics of rebuttals that may influence their effectiveness. Later, I will examine opinion shifts in each campaign with respect to these characteristics.

Volume

Volume refers to how often the attacked candidate responds to racialized attacks. As explained in the previous chapter, I expect that a high volume of rebuttals will improve evaluations of the attacked candidate by white voters. The counterframing literature finds that framing effects dissipate when pitted against a counterframe because counterframes promote reconsideration of the original frame. Thus, the more often an attacked candidate rebuts an attack, the more often he raises an alternative set of considerations, which is more likely to lead to favorable evaluations than if he stayed silent. Rebuttal volume will be measured in two ways: first, by simply counting the number of rebuttals, and second, by calculating the proportion of stories mentioning a racialized theme that also mention a rebuttal.

Timing

Timing refers to *when* rebuttals were offered, as in, were rebuttals offered within the first few days of a salient attack? A quick response may help the candidate recover from the attack. On the other hand, allowing a few days to go by without a response is likely to be a mistake. The political scientists James Druckman, Jordan Fein, and Thomas Leeper find that the timing of exposure to frames and counterframes makes a difference in how persuasive the frame is.[3] When a strong frame and strong counterframe are presented simultaneously, their effects cancel out. However, if a strong frame is presented first and a strong counterframe is not presented until much later, the effect of the initial strong frame can persist because it influences the information people seek out. By seeking out information that is consistent with the first frame, people are essentially repeating exposure to the first frame, leading to the endurance of the initial effect. The negative effects of the attack may be difficult to reverse once it takes hold.

Surrogacy

All else equal, rebuttals offered by the candidate himself are more likely to be effective than rebuttals offered by a surrogate. However, this does not mean that surrogates are never effective. Surrogates' effectiveness likely hinges on how their role complements the actions of the candidate. Surrogates are likely to be more effective when they are working in tandem with the candidate rather than acting as the candidate's only spokespeople.

Type

One final characteristic of rebuttals I examine is the type. In the previous chapter, I showed the distribution of rebuttal types used in six viable campaigns. I cannot isolate the effect of any one type in this chapter because many different types occur simultaneously. However, I can show how the mix of rebuttals changes across different periods of a campaign and how the mix of rebuttals differed between the two campaigns. I test the effects of different rebuttal types in controlled experiments in chapters 7 and 8.

EFFECTS OF REBUTTALS ON KEY SUBGROUPS

In addition to examining whether rebuttals have a positive effect among whites overall, I also test their effects on racially resentful and sympathetic subgroups. We might expect rebuttals to have an effect on groups that are already receptive to the message—in this case, racially sympathetic whites. But if they also have an effect on the racially resentful, this would suggest that rebuttals can actually deactivate racial attitudes—a normatively attractive result given the inherently manipulative aspect of racial priming. Even if they do not, however, this would still be informative to Black candidates as a practical matter. If the racially resentful generally do not respond to rebuttals but the racially sympathetic do, then Black candidates would know that rebuttals are really about keeping one's supporters in the fold and should concentrate their efforts on appealing to this subgroup's sensibilities.

PATRICK CAMPAIGN

Now that expectations have been established, I briefly describe key events of the 2006 Massachusetts gubernatorial campaign between Black Democrat Deval Patrick and Republican Kerry Healey. The campaign featured a number of controversial attacks focused on Patrick's handling of the issue of crime. These attacks reminded some of the Willie Horton ads that sunk the presidential aspirations of another Massachusetts Democrat, Michael Dukakis, in 1988. Dukakis himself called the 2006 Patrick-Healey contest "the dirtiest gubernatorial campaign in my memory" and in another interview said, "It's Willie Horton all over again."[4]

The first major crime controversy centered on Patrick's correspondence with Benjamin LaGuer, a Massachusetts man of Puerto Rican descent who was convicted of raping a fifty-nine-year-old woman in 1984. LaGuer's case gained public attention in the late 1980s after reports that members of the all-white jury in the case used anti-Hispanic slurs during deliberations. Patrick was among many prominent Massachusetts public figures who advocated for DNA testing to be conducted. The *Boston Globe* first reported his tie to LaGuer on September 29, and the Healey campaign soon seized on the controversy to paint Patrick as a coddler of criminals. In addition to attacking Patrick for his involvement with LaGuer, Healey opened another line of attack on crime. The *Globe* first mentioned Healey's "cop-killer" ad on October 5, which highlighted Patrick's legal defense in 1985 of Carl Ray Songer, a Florida man convicted of murdering a Florida state trooper. The ad featured Patrick's photo side by side with Songer's mug shot and ended with the narrator asking, "While lawyers have a right to defend admitted cop killers, do we really want one as governor?" The week of October 4–11 featured a steady stream of crime-focused anti-Patrick advertising with little response from Patrick. The *Globe* reported that Healey outspent Patrick by more than three to one during that week, noting that while Healey's advertising focused mostly on painting Patrick as soft on crime and likely to raise taxes, Patrick's ads focused on promoting him as the candidate who could change the state's political culture.[5]

Another controversy erupted on October 13, as the *Boston Herald* reported that Patrick's sister was raped by her husband in 1993. This incident, however, seemed to mark a turning point in Patrick's strategy for dealing with attempts to tie him to criminals. Instead of apologizing as he had to the previous attacks, he accused the Healey campaign of leaking the story and denounced the leak, saying:

> It's pathetic and it's wrong. By no rules of common decency should their private struggles become a public issue. But this is the politics of Kerry Healey. It disgusts me. And it must be stopped. . . . My sister and her husband went through a difficult time, and through hard work and prayer, they repaired their relationship and their lives. Now they and their children, who knew nothing of this, have had their family history laid out on the pages of a newspaper. Why? For no other reason than that they had the bad luck to have a relative who is running for governor. . . . We need a change. Gimmicks, slogans, and dirty politics is no substitute for progress. The politics of fear is not an acceptable alternative to

the politics of hope. That's the change we need. And if anybody in the Healey campaign or in the public thinks I am unwilling to fight for that, they have badly underestimated me.[6]

Soon after, Patrick began touting his experience as a federal prosecutor in the 1990s. He had rarely mentioned that aspect of his biography earlier in the campaign, instead focusing on his corporate experience. But as Healey continued with her assertion that Patrick was soft on crime in the week following the *Herald* story, Patrick contrasted his real-world experience as a federal prosecutor against Healey's academic credentials as a criminologist and unapologetically defended his actions as a defense attorney. At a rally in the Boston suburb of Melrose, he tied many of these themes together. First, he argued that Healey's attacks were an attempt to divert attention away from her record: "When you think about all of the attacks and all of the negative ads and all of the mean-spiritedness that you've been hearing on the airwaves and on talk radio and maybe at conversations at work, all of that is about changing the subject—anything but talk about their record. And, if I had their record, I'd want to change the subject, too."[7] He then pivoted to promote his tough-on-crime credentials directly: "You know what? Let's talk about crime; we ought to talk about crime. I'm the only one in this race who's actually ever sent anyone to prison. Let's talk about crime. I've been a victim of crime. You can't grow up in a place like the South Side of Chicago, with crime all around you, without understanding the impact—on families, on communities—of crime. I don't need to be lectured to about crime." Finally, he offered a justification of his actions as a defense attorney: "But I'll tell you one thing. I have occasionally stood up in favor and in support of the unsavory defendant, and you should be glad somebody does. That's what makes the American legal system a just system."[8]

RACIAL PRIMING DURING THE PATRICK CAMPAIGN

Was Patrick racialized as a result of the crime focus of the campaign? To test this, I need individual-level survey data before and after Patrick faced an onslaught of crime attacks. The Cooperative Congressional Election Study (CCES), a high-quality survey that has fairly large statewide samples, is inappropriate for this task, since most interviews for that survey are conducted in the last ten days of the campaign—well after the crime attacks became the focus of the campaign in early October.[9] Fortunately, I obtained data sets for two surveys conducted earlier in the campaign by SurveyUSA: one conducted from September 19–21, before the revelation of Patrick's ties to LaGuer and the first wave of anti-Patrick crime ads hit the airwaves, and one conducted on October 8–10, after the early crime attacks.

One limitation of the SurveyUSA surveys is that they do not contain any direct measures of racial attitudes such as the racial resentment scale or the racial stereotypes scale.[10] However, the surveys contain demographics that are correlated with racial resentment such as education, age, and sex that can be used to predict a racial resentment score for each respondent.[11] To address concerns regarding the validity of predicted racial resentment, I validate it in the next chapter by showing that it has a similar relationship to vote choice as measured racial resentment in two polls from the 2013 New Jersey U.S. Senate election for which I have both measured and predicted racial resentment.[12]

For now, the key test of whether the attacks had a racial effect is that predicted racial resentment should be a stronger predictor of vote choice after the attacks compared to before, similar to effects found in previous studies of racial priming.[13] The first step to obtaining predicted racial resentment scores is to identify a survey that measures racial resentment, education, age, and sex for a large sample of white Massachusetts respondents. I chose the 2010 Cooperative Congressional Election Study (CCES) because it has all four measures, plus a large sample of white Massachusetts respondents (n = 838). While the 2006 CCES would be ideal, 2010 was the first year the CCES measured racial resentment. Since 2010 is the closest year for which racial resentment can be predicted for Massachusetts whites, I use that year's CCES. Fortunately, I was able to obtain more contemporaneous estimates of racial resentment in later chapters on Cory Booker (2013) and Anthony Brown (2014) by using the 2014 CCES.

Next, I predicted racial resentment as a function of education, age, and sex using the 2010 CCES data for white Massachusetts respondents.

Specifically, the relationships among those variables are captured in the following equation (all variables coded 0–1)[14]:

Racial resentment = 0.64 − (0.28 × education) + (0.06 × age) + (0.10 × male)

Finally, I multiplied the education, age, and sex variables in the Survey-USA data (coded the same as they were in the CCES data) by the coefficients obtained from the CCES equation to calculate a predicted racial resentment score.

With this score in hand, I estimated the relationship between racial resentment and vote choice for the September 19–21 (preattack) and October 8–10 (postattack) surveys. If the attacks activated racial resentment, we would expect the relationship between racial resentment and the vote to be stronger in the postattack survey than in the preattack survey. Of course, it is possible that all predispositions, including nonracial ones, become more influential over the course of a campaign because voters learn how to match up their vote with their predispositions as they hear more information about the candidates. In order to show a specifically *racial* effect of the attacks, I need to show that a similar priming effect does not occur for nonracial predispositions. With that in mind, I also account for the influence of partisanship and ideology in both surveys to see if a similar priming effect occurs for them as well. Since vote choice is binary, the effects of racial resentment, partisanship, and ideology are estimated using logistic regression.[15]

The results, presented in table 4.1, indicate that while racial resentment was unrelated to vote choice before the highly publicized crime attacks, it was following those attacks. Though the difference between the racial resentment coefficients in the two surveys is not statistically significant (probably because of the greater amount of error inherent in estimating rather than measuring racial resentment), the magnitude of the difference (1.16) is larger than the comparable magnitudes for party identification (0.30) and ideology (0.61).

To facilitate the interpretation of the coefficients in table 4.1, I translate the coefficients into graphic form. In figure 4.1, I show the predicted probability of Republican vote intention as a function of racial resentment (left panel), partisanship (center panel), and ideology (right panel),

TABLE 4.1 Was racial resentment associated with Republican (Healey/Mihos) vote intention following crime attacks? (logistic regression)

	Preattack (Sept. 19–21)	Postattack (Oct. 8–10)	Difference
Predicted racial resentment	1.08 (0.75)	2.24** (0.71)	1.16 (1.04)
Party identification	2.40*** (0.24)	2.70*** (0.24)	0.30 (0.34)
Ideology	1.80*** (0.27)	2.41*** (0.26)	0.61 (0.38)
Intercept	−3.21*** (0.45)	−3.79*** (0.44)	−0.58 (0.64)
N	965	1063	

***$p < .001$; **$p < .01$.
Note: Predicted racial resentment ranges from 0 for the least resentful attitudes to 1 for the most resentful attitudes. Party identification is coded 0 for Democrat, .5 for Independent, and 1 for Republican. Ideology is coded 0 for liberal, .5 for moderate, and 1 for conservative.

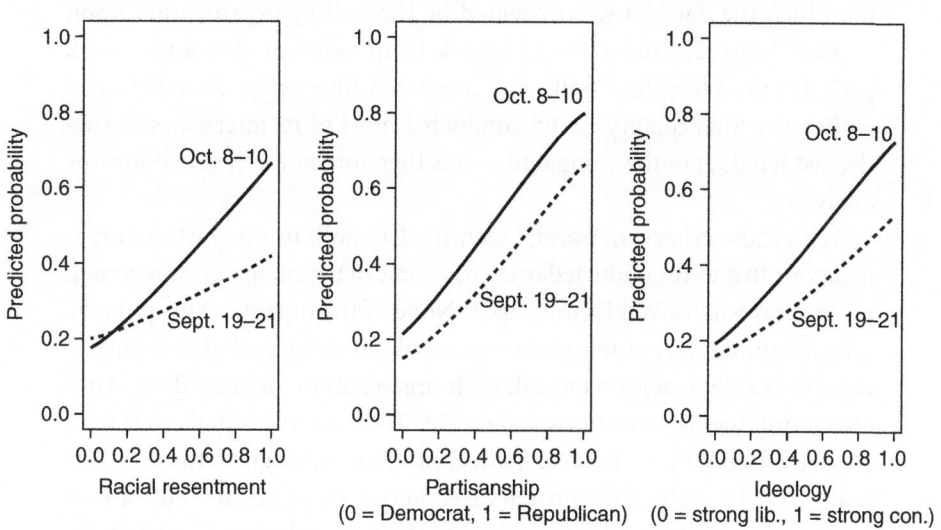

FIGURE 4.1 Predicted probability of Republican (Healey/Mihos) vote intention as a function of predicted racial resentment, partisanship, and ideology, September 19–21 versus October 8–10 SurveyUSA polls.

holding the other variables in the model constant at their mean level. As the figure shows, racial resentment's power as a predictor of the vote increases following the attacks more than the other two predispositions.

REBUTTALS AND WHITE OPINION DURING THE PATRICK CAMPAIGN

DATA

Next, I turn to the relationship between Patrick's handling of crime attacks and his white support. To examine this, I need measures of white support over the course of the campaign. I selected all polls that met two criteria. First, since I need measures of white support, I cannot rely on media reports of the polls, which often do not include results broken down by race. Thus, I selected polls that had cross-tabulations that included results by race, ones for which the data set was publicly available, or ones for which the data set was provided by the polling organization upon request. Second, since I need to track white opinion over a five-week period, I need to collect polls that cover that time range. As mentioned earlier, the high-quality CCES conducted most of its interviews during the last ten days of the campaign and is therefore not well suited for this analysis.

With those criteria in mind, I identified all polls by nonpartisan organizations that were conducted over the course of the campaign as recorded on the campaign's Wikipedia page.[16] None of the organizations publicly released the data set or released cross-tabulations that included results by race, so the next step was to ask each organization for their data. After contacting the organizations responsible for the sixteen polls that were conducted since the start of the general election campaign (defined as September 19, the night of the primary election), I obtained data sets for four surveys, all conducted by SurveyUSA: the September 19–21 and October 8–10 surveys discussed in the previous section, plus two additional surveys conducted on October 20–23 and October 31–November 1. While a complete set of polls would be ideal, I have enough polls conducted over a long enough span of time to see how white support for Patrick changed over the course of the campaign.

VOLUME

To examine the relationship between Patrick's handling of the crime attacks and his white support, I plot the number of Healey crime mentions and Patrick rebuttals along with polling among white voters over the course of the campaign in figure 4.2. Only stories that mention Healey or a Healey surrogate as the source of the crime mention are included, while stories that cast Patrick in a negative light on crime that originate from the news media are not included. A dashed vertical line marks September 29, the date that the LaGuer controversy was first mentioned by the *Boston Globe*. The dots represent reported vote choice. The dashed trend line represents the number of *Boston Globe* articles in the previous

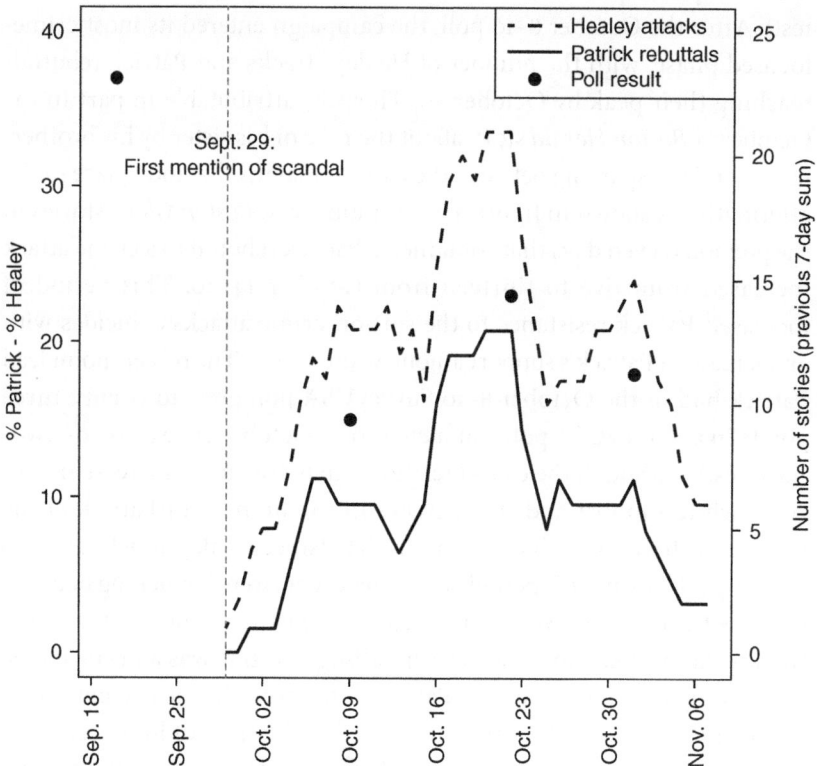

FIGURE 4.2 Polling in Massachusetts gubernatorial race (white voters only) versus campaign rhetoric on crime.

seven days that reference Healey or a surrogate either promoting her own crime stance or attacking Patrick on crime. The bold line represents the number of *Boston Globe* articles in the previous seven days that mention a rebuttal offered by either Patrick or one of his surrogates to a Healey campaign attack on crime. Only rebuttals to stories that identify the Healey campaign as the source are included. The articles are summed over the previous seven days in order to show a smooth trend that reduces the influence of idiosyncrasies in campaign coverage that can occur on any given day.

The LaGuer controversy and the increase in Healey crime attacks that followed, coupled with Patrick's infrequent response, took a toll on his support among white voters. The thirty-seven-point lead Patrick enjoyed in the September 19–21 SurveyUSA poll was whittled to just fifteen points in the SurveyUSA poll conducted from October 8–10 ($p < .01$, two-tailed test). After the October 8–10 poll, the campaign entered its most crime-focused phase, with the number of Healey attacks and Patrick rebuttals reaching their peak by October 20. This was attributable in part to the October 13 *Boston Herald* story about the rape of his sister by his brother-in-law and the sparring between the two campaigns that took place in the aftermath. As shown in figure 4.2, the number of *Boston Globe* stories in the previous seven days that contained a Patrick rebuttal to a crime attack increased from five to thirteen from October 14–20. This period of increased Patrick resistance to the soft-on-crime attacks coincides with an increase in Patrick's support among white voters. The fifteen-point lead Patrick had in the October 8–10 SurveyUSA poll grew to twenty-three points in a SurveyUSA poll conducted from October 20–23 ($p < .01$, two-sided test). Although the causal relationship between the increase in Patrick's white support and the increase in the number of Patrick crime rebuttals is hard to establish with this data (since Healey attacks are also at their peak during this period, and other events were happening between the time the two polls were conducted), it at least seems plausible that the two are connected. Since Patrick's handling of crime was a major theme of the campaign, it is likely that Patrick's efforts to change perceptions of his crime record would result in improved evaluations of him overall.

Another way to show Patrick's level of response is to show the *proportion* of stories mentioning a crime attack that also mentioned a rebuttal.

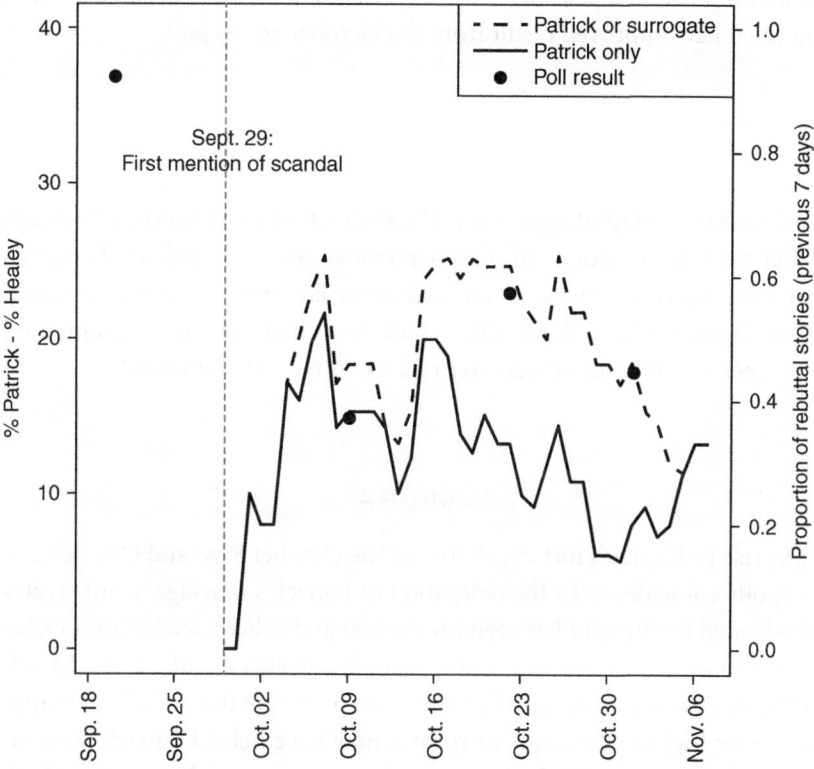

FIGURE 4.3 Polling in 2006 Massachusetts gubernatorial race (white voters only) versus proportion of rebuttal stories.

For example, if four stories appeared in the *Globe* over the previous seven days that mentioned a Healey attack and all four mentioned a rebuttal, the proportion would be 1. If none of those stories mentioned a rebuttal, the proportion would be 0. Figure 4.3 shows the proportion of Healey attack stories that mentioned either a rebuttal by Patrick or a surrogate (dashed line) or a rebuttal by Patrick only (solid line).

Patrick's rebuttal activity was fairly high (0.55 for Patrick and 0.64 for surrogates) right before the first post-LaGuer poll on October 8–10, which suggests that Patrick's rebuttals were not having much of an effect. After the October 8–10 poll, Patrick's rebuttal activity ramped up again. Patrick's campaign (himself plus surrogates) maintained a full week of rebuttal ratios of at least 0.6 from October 15 to October 22, culminating in the much-improved result from the October 20–23 poll.

TIMING

Patrick's first rebuttal appeared in the *Boston Globe* on October 1, two days after the LaGuer story broke on September 29. As we will see later, this two-day lag is swift when compared to the lag times of Harold Ford and Cory Booker, who did not offer rebuttals of their own until several days (or weeks, in Booker's case) after racial controversies emerged.

SURROGACY

The rise in Patrick's fortunes between the October 8–10 and October 20–23 polls coincides with the delegation of Patrick's message to surrogates (indicated by the split between the dashed and solid black lines on October 15 in figure 4.3). However, surrogacy is correlated with sustained volume, as October 15 marked the first of seven straight days of rebuttal ratios of 0.6 or higher. Although surrogates may have helped Patrick, we cannot definitively know whether it was the surrogates or the sustained high volume of rebuttals overall.

TYPE

To examine whether the content of Patrick's rebuttals coincided with improved performance, I compared Patrick's campaign rebuttals from September 29 through October 9 (pre–October 8–10 poll)[17] and October 10 through October 21 (post–October 8–10 poll). In table 4.2, I show the percentage of rebuttals by either Patrick or a surrogate that corresponds with rebuttal types outlined in chapter 3, plus one other type that was not discussed much in that chapter: *apologies*. They were not discussed as a strategy commonly used by candidates facing racial attacks because they are rare. Of the six Black candidates I examine in detail in this book, Patrick is the only one who offered an apology for the attacked action.

TABLE 4.2 Rebuttals offered by Deval Patrick or surrogates before and after first post-LaGuer (October 8–10) poll

	Before first post-LaGuer poll (Sept. 29–Oct. 9) (%)	After first post-LaGuer poll (Oct. 10–21) (%)
Negative	13	30
Justify	40	16
Distract	0	11
Counterimaging	7	14
Counterattack	20	25
Deny	0	5
Apology	20	2

Note: Columns may not add up to 100 percent because of rounding.

As shown in the center column of table 4.2, *justify* was the most commonly used strategy (40 percent). This did not appear to help Patrick, as his ratings among white voters fell in this period.

What changed in Patrick's rebuttal strategy after the concerning results of the October 8–10 poll? Patrick's use of *negative* increased from 13 percent to 30 percent, while his use of *justify* went down to 16 percent, and *apology* went down from 20 percent to 2 percent. These results should be read with caution, however, since none of the types are isolated enough to draw clear conclusions about their effects. Also, the rebuttal types are varying at the same time as changes in all of the other characteristics (volume, timing, and surrogacy).

What can we conclude, then, about the relationship between Patrick's rebuttals and his support among white voters? I have identified four features of rebuttals that are likely to matter: volume, timing, surrogacy, and type. Although I cannot tell with the available data which of these mattered for Patrick, at least one of them is likely to be associated with variation in approval. The other three case studies in chapters 4 and 5 will offer more suggestive evidence on volume, timing, and surrogacy, and the experiments in chapters 7 and 8 will offer a more conclusive test of type.

EFFECTS OF PATRICK REBUTTALS BY RACIAL RESENTMENT LEVEL

Turning to rebuttal effects among respondents at varying levels of racial resentment, I compare Patrick's lead over Healey/Mihos among white respondents in the October 8–10 poll (after crime became salient and Patrick's response was somewhat low) to white respondents in the October 20–23 poll (after Patrick's response was high) by levels of racial resentment—low, medium, and high. These levels were determined by dividing each sample into thirds by racial resentment. Rebuttals should have an effect on groups that are already receptive to the message—in this case, low-racial-resentment respondents. But if they also have an effect on the racially resentful, that would suggest that rebuttals can actually deactivate racial attitudes.

The results are shown in table 4.3. Though small sample sizes prevent any differences from reaching conventional levels of statistical significance, the magnitudes are nonetheless informative. Starting with high-racial-resentment respondents, it appears the rebuttals had little effect. Patrick's lead among this subgroup increased by only 2 percentage points. Among low-racial-resentment respondents, Patrick added 8 percentage points of support. Though only speculative, this suggests that Patrick's

TABLE 4.3 Support for Patrick over Healey/Mihos by racial resentment level, postattack vs. postrebuttal periods

Racial resentment level	Postattack (Oct. 8–10)	Postrebuttal (Oct. 20–23)	Difference
Low (<.52 for Oct. 8–10; <.50 for Oct. 20–23)	+22 (n = 392)	+30 (n = 368)	+8 (p = .22)
Med (> = .52 and <.62 for Oct. 8–10; > = .50 and <.62 for Oct. 20–23)	+6 (n = 286)	−2 (n = 330)	−8 (p = .40)
High (> = .62 for both surveys)	+2 (n = 446)	+4 (n = 426)	+2 (p = .88)

Note: Cell entries indicate the percentage point margin between Patrick and Healey/Mihos, with positive values indicating a Patrick lead and negative values indicating a Patrick deficit.

gains were made primarily by winning back low-resentment whites who were perhaps already inclined to support him. Finally, support among medium-resentment respondents declines by eight points, which is puzzling considering we might expect medium-resentment respondents to fall somewhere in between low- and high-resentment respondents. The clearest conclusion that can be drawn from this analysis is that Patrick's rebuttals may have worked not by deactivating the racially resentful but by winning back the racially sympathetic.

FORD CAMPAIGN

While Patrick was busy in Massachusetts fending off accusations that he was soft on crime, another viable Black candidate, Democrat Harold Ford Jr., had his hands full in Tennessee with a different line of attack that made national headlines in 2006. Ford's campaign for the U.S. Senate against Republican Bob Corker is perhaps best remembered for a Republican National Committee (RNC) ad now known as the "call me" ad that featured an actress playing a young blond woman who said she had met Ford at a *Playboy* party. At the end of the ad, the woman winks at the camera and says, "Harold, call me." The ad drew criticism from observers who argued that the strongly implied intimacy between Ford and a white woman was meant to stoke fear and anger over interracial sex in a part of the country where such fears have a long history.[18] Besides the theme of interracial sex, the "call me" ad contained a more general reference to Ford's sexual immorality when an actor portraying a fictitious Ford supporter said, "So he took money from porn movie producers. I mean, who hasn't?" Corker denounced the ad as "tacky" and called for the ad to be removed immediately after it started airing on October 20, but the ad remained on the airwaves through October 26.[19] Further evidence suggesting a link between the Corker campaign and the RNC comes from a Corker press release that cited the RNC's "call me" ad as one of the factors in Corker's improved poll numbers.[20]

In addition to the "call me" ad, another RNC ad called "Shaky," which began airing on October 23, again highlighted the theme of Ford's sexual deviance. The ad attacks Ford for taking contributions "from Hollywood's top X-rated porn moguls" and includes images of the letters "XXX" above the famous Hollywood sign with what appears to be the silhouettes of two strippers dancing on either side of the sign. Later in the ad, Ford is attacked for wanting "to give the abortion pill to our schoolchildren," accompanied by images of girls dressed in school uniforms in the foreground and background.

These two ads made the themes of interracial sex and sexual misbehavior salient during the last week and a half of October. In chapter 2, a content analysis of *Memphis Commercial Appeal* campaign stories found that 16 percent of all stories appearing in the last month of the campaign contained references to anti-Ford attacks on the theme of sex. That percentage goes up to 22 percent (17 of 77) when only considering stories that appeared in the *Commercial Appeal* from the first mention of the "call me" ad (October 21) until the end of the campaign (November 7). When only considering stories that ran between the first mention of the "call me" ad through the end of October, almost half—49 percent (17 of 35)—mentioned an anti-Ford attack on sex by Corker or a surrogate.[21]

RACIAL PRIMING DURING THE FORD CAMPAIGN

To test whether the anti-Ford sex attacks activated racial attitudes, I compare the relationship between racial resentment and vote choice before and after the "call me" ad began airing. Since estimating the relationship between racial resentment and vote choice requires regression analysis, I rely on surveys for which I have individual-level data. Fortunately, I have individual-level data for one pre-"call me" survey and one post-"call me" survey: the *USA Today*/Gallup poll conducted September 27–October 1 and the *Los Angeles Times*/Bloomberg poll conducted October 20–23.

Since neither survey included the racial resentment battery, I start by predicting racial resentment for each respondent using the same two-stage procedure as the one used for the 2006 Massachusetts gubernatorial surveys. First, I predicted racial resentment as a function of education, age, and sex using the 2010 CCES for white Tennessee respondents only.[22] These three variables did not account for much of the variance in racial resentment (adjusted R-squared = 0.047), so I included two additional predictors: income and community type (urban or rural).[23] This accounted for slightly more of the variance (adjusted R-squared = 0.054); plus the urban/rural variable was a significant predictor of racial resentment even after controlling for the other four variables (b = −0.05, se = 0.03, p < .05).[24] With the coefficients for the five variables from the CCES, I calculated racial resentment scores for respondents in each of the two surveys.

Next, I estimated the relationship between predicted racial resentment and vote choice in both surveys using logistic regression. Vote choice is coded 0 = Ford and 1 = Corker. As I did for the Massachusetts data, I included controls for party identification and ideology. The results are shown in table 4.4. While racial resentment was not correlated with vote choice before the "call me" ad aired, it was marginally so after. The difference between the pre- and post-"call me" racial resentment coefficients is quite large (3.55), though not statistically significant. Similar to the Massachusetts case, the unavoidable imprecision in the estimation of racial resentment is the likely explanation. However, the magnitude of the racial resentment difference is larger than the party identification and ideology differences. Both differences are not statistically significant,

TABLE 4.4 Was racial resentment associated with Republican (Corker) vote intention following sex attacks? (logistic regression)

	Pre-"Call Me" Sep. 27–Oct. 1 (USA Today / Gallup)	Post-"Call Me" Oct. 2–23 (LA Times / Bloomberg)	Difference
Predicted racial resentment (0–1 low-high)	3.56 (2.67)	7.11^ (3.79)	3.55 (4.64)
Party identification (0–1 Democrat-Republican)	4.50*** (0.39)	4.82*** (0.51)	0.32 (0.64)
Ideology (0–1 liberal-conservative)	1.99* (0.79)	3.14** (1.00)	1.15 (1.27)
Intercept	−6.36** (2.11)	−9.62** (3.10)	−3.26 (3.75)
N	411	351	

***p < .001; **p < .01; *p < .05; ^p < .1.
Note: Predicted racial resentment ranges from 0 for the least resentful attitudes to 1 for the most resentful attitudes. Party identification is coded 0 for Democrat, .5 for Independent, and 1 for Republican. Ideology is a five-category variable ranging from 0 (strong liberal) to 1 (strong conservative).

indicating that nonracial predispositions were not primed during this period.

The coefficients in table 4.4 are translated into predicted probabilities shown in figure 4.4, holding other variables in the model at their sample means. This display illustrates modest changes in racial resentment and ideology's predictive strength. The figure also makes clear that racial resentment may have faced a ceiling effect given that the association between racial resentment and vote choice was already sizable (though not statistically significant) in the pre-"call me" (September 27–October 1) poll. This may be attributable to the fact that there were several small-scale racial controversies earlier in the campaign, such as an anti-Ford radio ad that featured African drums playing the background; the anti-Ford radio ad mentioned in chapter 3 that criticized Ford's involvement with the Congressional Black Caucus, calling it "an all-black group of congressmen who represent the interests of black people above all others"; a pro-Corker campaign flyer circulated in rural eastern Tennessee counties that urged support for Corker in order to "preserve your way of life"; and accusations by the Ford campaign and the media that a Corker flyer had darkened Ford's skin.[25]

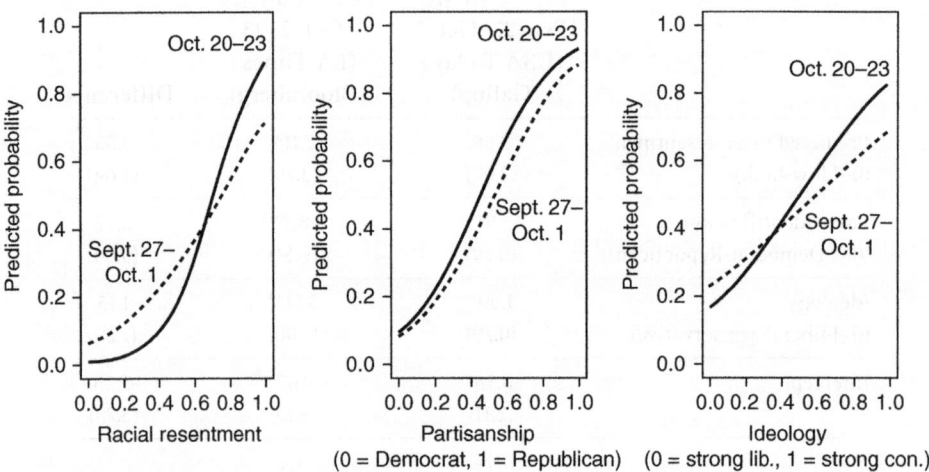

FIGURE 4.4 Predicted probability of Republican (Corker) vote intention as a function of predicted racial resentment, partisanship, and ideology, September 27–October 1 USA Today/Gallup versus October 20–23 LA Times/Bloomberg polls.

REBUTTALS AND WHITE OPINION DURING THE FORD CAMPAIGN

DATA

In order to see how Ford's support among white voters was influenced by his response to the "call me" ad, I first need to obtain as much polling data on white voters conducted across the course of the campaign as possible. To do this, I applied the same criteria used to obtain polls in the analysis of the Deval Patrick campaign: ones that published cross-tabulations of results for white voters only, ones for which the data set was publicly available, ones for which the organization responded to my request for the data set, and ones that were conducted over the course of the campaign.[26] Of the twenty-seven nonpartisan polls conducted after Labor Day according to the campaign Wikipedia page, I obtained data on white voters' preferences for six of them: the *USA Today*/Gallup poll from September 27–October 1 and the *Los Angeles Times*/Bloomberg poll from October 20–23 that were used in the racial priming analysis, which were publicly available; three surveys that were provided by SurveyUSA upon request, conducted on October 7–9, October 22–24, and November 3–5;[27] and a publicly available *USA Today*/Gallup poll conducted on November 3–5. Though not a complete set of polls, they cover a wide enough range of the campaign to see how Ford's white support changes over time.

VOLUME

Figure 4.5 shows how white support for Ford changed as the number of Corker attacks and Ford rebuttals rose and fell after the "call me" ad was first mentioned in the *Memphis Commercial-Appeal* on October 21 (marked by the vertical dashed line). Reported vote choice among white respondents in the six surveys is represented by the dots. The dashed trend line represents the number of anti-Ford sex attacks offered by Corker or his surrogates over the previous seven days, while the bold line represents the number of rebuttals to anti-Ford sex attacks offered by Ford's campaign over the previous seven days. Data on the frequency of attacks and

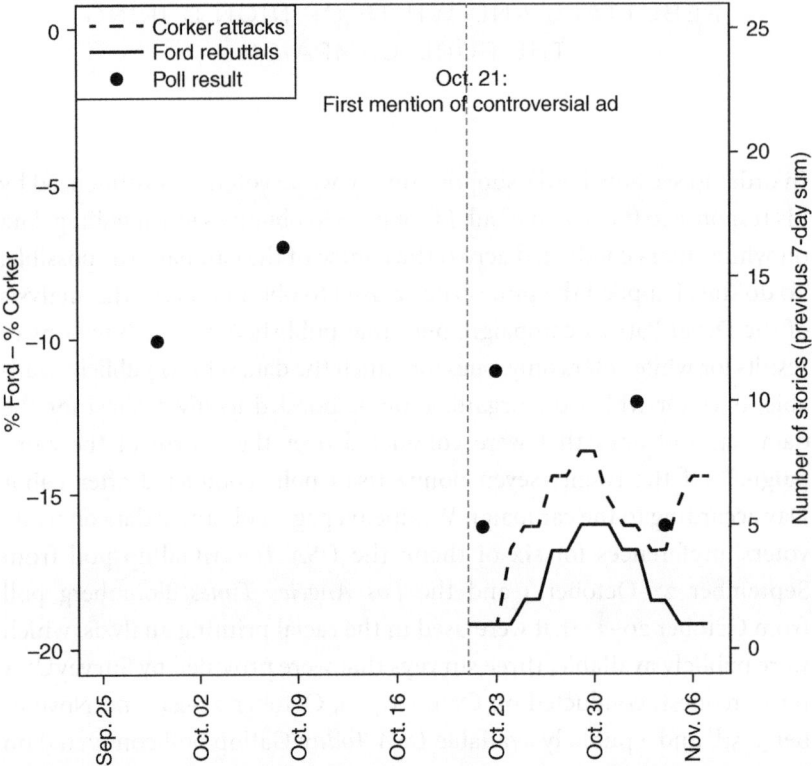

FIGURE 4.5 Polling in 2006 Tennessee U.S. Senate race (white voters only) versus campaign rhetoric on sex.

rebuttals come from an analysis of the *Memphis Commercial Appeal*. The main pattern is that Ford's white support declined from a 7–10 percentage point deficit in late September–early October before the "call me" ad aired to an 11–16 point deficit according to polls conducted October 20–23 right after the "call me" ad began airing. Despite a modest number of Ford rebuttals in the ten days after the "call me" ad first aired, Ford's deficit among whites stayed around 12–16 percentage points in polls conducted between November 1–5.

Though figure 4.5 comprehensively documents the campaign as it appeared in the pages of the *Commercial-Appeal*, the insight we can gather from it is limited by the fact that the *Commercial-Appeal*'s campaign coverage was sparse. In the last month of the campaign, only eighteen stories about the campaign mentioned a sexually themed attack (0.58 per day), compared to fifty-seven *Boston Globe* stories in the final month of the 2006 Massachusetts gubernatorial campaign that mentioned crime (1.84 per day).

Instead of looking at the absolute levels of attacks and rebuttals, which have limited variation, perhaps the proportion of stories mentioning a sex attack that also mentioned a rebuttal would be more informative. This measure, shown in figure 4.6, is the same measure ranging from 0 (no attacks rebutted) to 1 (every attack rebutted) that I introduced earlier when looking at the Massachusetts contest. The dashed line represents the proportion of attack stories containing a rebuttal from either Ford or a

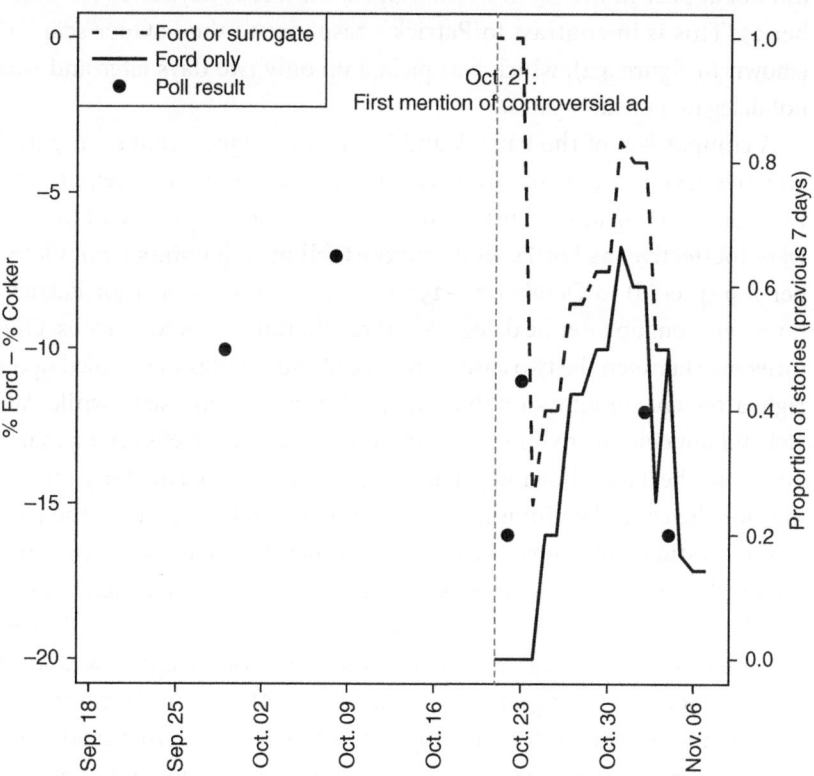

FIGURE 4.6 Polling in 2006 Tennessee U.S. Senate race (white voters only) versus proportion of rebuttal stories.

surrogate, while the bold line represents the proportion of attack stories containing a rebuttal by Ford only. This measure of rebuttal volume reveals the pattern shown earlier for the overall number of rebuttals: despite an increase in the proportion of attack stories that mentioned a rebuttal, Ford's ratings among white voters did not improve. This suggests that rebuttal volume did not help Ford.

TIMING/SURROGACY

The Ford campaign responded to the "call me" ad right away, with a rebuttal appearing in the same story that first mentioned the ad. However, the response was offered by a surrogate. A rebuttal offered by Ford himself did not appear in the *Commercial-Appeal* until four days later on October 25. This is in contrast to Patrick's response to the LaGuer scandal (shown in figure 4.2), which was picked up only two days later and was not delegated to surrogates.

A comparison of the Patrick and Ford cases suggest that surrogates' effectiveness may depend on when they are called upon to help. In the Ford case, surrogates' rebuttals immediately following the "call me" ad were ineffective, as Ford's white support fell by 4–9 points from October 7–9 (pre-ad) to October 20–23 (post-ad). White support for Patrick, however, went up after he delegated more rebuttals to his surrogates. One difference between the two cases is that Ford's surrogates were called upon right after a major attack (with no support from Ford himself), while Patrick did not delegate to his surrogates until about two weeks after a major attack. In the days following a major attack, it may be particularly important for the candidate himself to counter the attack. Silence on the part of the candidate may give the impression that the attack has merit, and the words of his surrogates may be discounted. In the next chapter, I examine the 2013 New Jersey U.S. Senate campaign in which Cory Booker relied entirely on surrogates to counter a month of racialized attacks. I find that Booker's surrogates were completely ineffective in stemming lost support among white voters, lending support to the notion that candidates should not rely on surrogates as a first line of defense following an attack.

Another difference between Ford's and Patrick's use of surrogates is that Ford's surrogates were the only pro-Ford voice in the four days after the attack, while Patrick's surrogates were always supported by Patrick, though he was somewhat in the background. This suggests that surrogates are likely to be more effective when they are amplifying the candidate's message rather than speaking in place of the candidate.

TYPE

Since Ford's rebuttals were ineffective, examining the types of rebuttals used may offer some insight into which types did not work. A surrogate called the "call me" ad "desperate" in the *Commercial Appeal*'s first story about the ad on October 21. Ford's next two rebuttals on October 25 and October 27 were to *justify* his attendance at a Super Bowl party sponsored by *Playboy* in 2005, saying, "I was there. I like football and I like girls. I don't have no apologies for that."[28] After confirming his attendance, he shifted to dismissing the attacks as *negative*, such as when he referred to the "call me" ad as "smut" and "slime" on October 29.[29] On two occasions, Ford surrogates directly used *racial* (the NAACP on October 27 and the civil rights leader Jesse Jackson on October 28).

A more systematic examination of the Ford campaign's post-"call me" sex rebuttals is shown in table 4.5, broken down by the percentage corresponding with the rebuttal types introduced in chapter 3. Since the

TABLE 4.5 Rebuttals offered by Harold Ford or surrogates to sex attacks after the first mention of the "Call Me" ad in the *Memphis Commercial-Appeal* on October 21

	Ford (%)	Ford or surrogates (%)
Racial	0	20
Negative	43	40
Justify	29	10
Distract	14	10
Counterimaging	14	10

Note: Columns may not add up to 100 percent because of rounding.

strategies used by surrogates (most notably their use of *racial*) differed in significant ways from the strategies used by Ford himself, I show the rebuttals offered by Ford separately. Ford relied mostly on *negative* and *justify*, with surrogates adding *racial*.

Since his evaluation among white voters did not improve, these responses did not appear to be effective. This should be read with caution, however, since all of the types occurred at the same time and covaried with other features of the rebuttals.

EFFECTS OF FORD REBUTTALS BY RACIAL RESENTMENT LEVEL

How did Ford fare among the three racial resentment subgroups after a modest period of rebuttals? Table 4.6 shows the results of this analysis for high- medium-, and low-racial-resentment subgroups, comparing the *LA Times*/Bloomberg poll right after the "call me" ad started airing (October 20–23) to the *USA Today*/Gallup poll from November 1–3 that reflected opinion after a week and half of Ford's rebuttals.[30] As with the

TABLE 4.6 Support for Ford over Corker by racial resentment level, postattack vs. postrebuttal periods

	Postattack Oct. 20–23 (LA Times / Bloomberg)	Postrebuttal Nov. 1–3 (USA Today / Gallup)	Difference
Low (< .69 in both surveys)	0 (n = 113)	–12 (n = 153)	–12 (p = .35)
Med (> = .69 and < .75 in both surveys)	–14 (n = 70)	–24 (n = 119)	–10 (p = .49)
High (> = .75 in both surveys)	–12 (n = 172)	–8 (n = 206)	+4 (p = .62)

Note: Cell entries indicate the percentage point margin between Ford and Corker, with positive values indicating a Ford lead and negative values indicating a Ford deficit.

Massachusetts analysis, differences do not reach standard levels of statistical significance given the small sample sizes, though again the magnitudes are still useful. Starting with the high-racial-resentment subgroup, Ford actually gained 4 percentage points of support following the rebuttal period. Somewhat unexpectedly, however, Ford lost 12 percentage points of support among low-racial-resentment whites.[31] Recall that Patrick regained support among this subgroup following his period of rebuttals. Immediately following the attacks, Ford was in a dead heat with Corker among low-racial-resentment white respondents—the only group of white voters who did not favor Corker. Following the rebuttal period, however, Ford faced deficits among all three subgroups. In sum, Ford's rebuttals were ineffective, particularly among low-resentment whites, the group that was most supportive of him before the attacks.

CONCLUSION

In this chapter, I examine two cases of high-level statewide Black candidates facing racialized attacks and what happens in the aftermath of those attacks. In both cases, white support is lost and racial considerations are activated in the period immediately following the attacks. Only Deval Patrick, however, managed to reverse the loss of white support that followed the attacks. By looking at subgroups of white voters by level of racial animus, I conclude that Patrick regained support among low-racial-resentment whites. Ford, on the other hand, actually lost support among this subgroup. Among high-racial-resentment whites, both candidates experienced modest levels of success winning back their support.

Though I suggest that messages and countermessages may be responsible for the opinion shifts, it is difficult to identify the causal link with the data I show here. One problem is that several weeks pass between polls, which leaves open the possibility that other events that are happening simultaneously to the messages I highlight are really causing the opinion shifts. It is impossible to rule that out entirely, though the various crime and sex attacks and the fallout from them were among the most salient events of the two campaigns. Also, the polls have small sample sizes, which increases the amount of error in the analyses. That is true, though I argue that attempts to show the effects of racial attacks and countermessages outside the laboratory setting are rare, and thus the analyses shown in this chapter are still valuable even though they are conducted with a fair amount of imprecision. Finally, a measurement of racial resentment would certainly be preferable to the predicted racial resentment measure constructed in this chapter. I attempt to improve on this in the next chapter when I turn my attention to Cory Booker's campaign to become New Jersey's first Black senator. As we will see shortly, the substantive conclusions of this chapter are supported when using more precise measurements of whites' racial attitudes.

5

THE 2013 CORY BOOKER AND 2014 ANTHONY BROWN CAMPAIGNS

In this chapter, I continue my examination of the effects of racial attacks and rebuttals in campaigns by turning to the 2013 New Jersey U.S. Senate election between Black Democrat Cory Booker and Republican Steve Lonegan and the 2014 Maryland gubernatorial election between Black Democrat Anthony Brown and Republican Larry Hogan. As shown in chapter 2, the New Jersey campaign featured a number of attacks by Lonegan on various racialized themes, while Hogan focused much of his rhetoric in the Maryland campaign on the issue of taxes. In the first part of the chapter, I focus on the Booker-Lonegan campaign in New Jersey, describing a variety of racialized attacks that Booker faced in that race. Second, I test whether these attacks activated whites' racial attitudes. This election is a good case for studying the effects of racial attacks because Booker did very little to respond to them until the last two weeks of the campaign, which allows for measuring the effects of unrebutted attacks. Third, I conduct a content analysis of stories that appeared in the *Star-Ledger*, New Jersey's most widely circulated daily newspaper, to examine how the frequency of attacks and rebuttals correspond with poll results among white voters. Fourth, I examine whether Booker's rebuttals were effective in reversing these trends. Finally, I conclude the chapter by examining what happened to Anthony Brown with respect to racialized attacks, responses, and white opinion in the 2014 Maryland gubernatorial election.

RACIALIZED ATTACKS IN BOOKER'S NEW JERSEY U.S. SENATE ELECTION

The question of what kind of campaign Booker would face was answered as soon as Lonegan emerged as his Republican opponent. Lonegan entered the contest with a reputation for being an outspoken conservative unafraid of generating controversy such as when he tried to ban Spanish-language billboards while he was mayor of Bogota, New Jersey, in 2006. An attack that happened early in the 2013 campaign provided an example of the types of racially charged controversies that he would spark throughout the campaign. During the final Democratic primary debate on August 8, a message was posted on Lonegan's campaign Twitter account that read: "just leaked—Cory Booker's foreign policy debate prep notes." Below it was a map of Newark with different neighborhoods labeled: "West Africa, Guyana, Portugal, Brazil" and "Middle East, Afghanistan, Pakistan, plus Bangladesh and Trinidad."[1]

During the fall, Lonegan attacked Booker on an array of racialized themes. On crime, Lonegan attacked Booker for campaigning while Newark, the city that Booker presided over as mayor, experienced a spike in homicides in early September. On September 5, Lonegan told the *Star-Ledger*, "This guy should not stepping foot out of Newark. He's got people getting shot every day. He's got a major crisis in Newark."[2] At the second debate on October 9, Lonegan responded to Booker's argument that environmental regulations are necessary to clean up Newark's Passaic River by saying, "You may not be able to swim in that river, but it's probably, I think, because of all the bodies floating around of shooting victims in your city."[3]

On sex, Lonegan suggested that Booker was gay. This type of attack is different than the ones Harold Ford Jr. faced in Tennessee, which suggested that he slept with white women and had ties to the porn industry. Nonetheless, rumors about Booker being gay might also bring to mind considerations of social difference that activate racial considerations.[4] In late August, after Booker denied being gay when interviewed by the *Washington Post*, Lonegan said in an interview that was broadcast on the conservative Newsmax TV:

> Maybe that helps to get him the gay vote by acting ambiguous. It's kind of weird. As a guy, I personally like being a guy. I don't know if

you saw the stories last year [referring to an interview in which Booker said he enjoys manicures and pedicures]. They've been out for quite a bit about how he likes to go out at 3 o'clock in the morning for a manicure and a pedicure. I don't like going out in the middle of the night, or any time of the day, for a manicure and a pedicure. It was described as his peculiar fetish. I have a more peculiar fetish. I like a good scotch and a cigar. That's my fetish, but we'll just compare the two.[5]

Five days before the election, Lonegan aide Bill Shaftan revisited the topic of Booker's sexuality in a lengthy, profanity-laced interview with the liberal political news site *Talking Points Memo*, in which he said Booker's G-rated Twitter correspondence with an Oregon stripper in late September was "what a gay guy would say to a stripper."[6]

On taxes, Lonegan decried the amount of money spent on Newark at the expense of suburban and rural parts of the state. During the second debate on October 9, Lonegan said, "The taxpayers in the suburbs and rural areas of this state have been ripped off now for 30 years. They gave us a sales tax. They said that was going to cut property taxes. Then they passed an income tax and that was going to cut property taxes. All that income tax and sales tax money gets poured into the big black hole of Newark."[7]

Aside from crime, sex, and taxes, other prominent lines of attack may have also strengthened the link between Booker and racial sentiments (see chapter 2). One was Lonegan painting Booker as the failed mayor of a dysfunctional Newark.[8] Following up on the "Twitter map" attack early in the campaign that highlighted Booker's connection to a city with a large Black and Latino population, Lonegan repeatedly argued that the quality of life in Newark declined as a result of Booker's leadership.[9] He also accused Booker of corruption for using the mayoral office for his own personal financial gain. Finally, Lonegan frequently associated Booker with President Obama. Lonegan often referred to Booker as a "rubber stamp" for President Obama's proposals. At one point during a debate, Lonegan's references to Obama prompted Booker to say he didn't know whether Lonegan is running "against me or Barack Obama." Lonegan replied, "Both, because you are one in [sic] the same."[10]

DID THE ATTACKS HAVE A RACIAL EFFECT?

The first question I address in this chapter is whether these attacks had a racial effect. As I did in the previous chapter, my test is a comparison of the relationship between racial resentment and vote choice before and after a period of heavy racial attacks. My "before" survey is Rutgers-Eagleton's first general election poll, conducted from September 3–7. Unlike all of the other surveys used thus far, however, I commissioned Rutgers-Eagleton to measure racial attitudes using three items from the racial resentment battery.[11] Respondents were asked to agree or disagree with these statements: (1) "Irish, Italian, Jewish, and many other minorities overcame prejudice and worked their way up. Blacks should do the same without any special favors." (2) "Generations of slavery and discrimination make it difficult for Blacks to work their way out of the lower class." (3) "It's really a matter of people not trying hard enough; if Blacks would only try harder they could be just as well off as whites." The five potential responses were 0 = disagree strongly, 0.25 = disagree somewhat, 0.5 = neither agree nor disagree, 0.75 = agree somewhat, and 1 = agree strongly. Item 2 was reverse coded so that a scale ranging from 0 being the most racially liberal response to 1 being the most racially conservative response could be constructed by taking the average score of the three items.

My "after" survey was a September 26–29 Monmouth poll that was conducted after what I show later in this chapter to be the end of a period of unrebutted Lonegan attacks. The September 26–29 Monmouth poll did not have a measure of racial attitudes, so I obtained predicted values using the same procedure I used for the 2006 Massachusetts and Tennessee polls described in the previous chapter. First, I regressed racial resentment on education, age, and sex using white New Jersey respondents in the 2014 CCES (n = 1,009).[12] Next, with the coefficients for education, age, and sex in hand, I predicted racial resentment using the data in the Monmouth poll.[13] Finally, I estimated the relationship between racial resentment and Republican vote intention, controlling for partisanship.[14] Since the Monmouth poll did not include a measure of ideology, I only control for partisanship. To preserve comparability with the Rutgers-Eagleton "before" poll, I only control for partisanship in that poll as well.

Table 5.1 displays the results. Racial resentment appears to have a much stronger relationship with the vote in the Monmouth poll compared to

TABLE 5.1 Was racial resentment associated with Republican (Lonegan) vote intention following weeks of unrebutted racialized attacks? (logistic regression)

	September 3–7 (Rutgers)	September 26–29 (Monmouth)	Difference
Racial resentment	2.04** (0.66)	5.60* (2.25)	3.56 (2.35)
Partisanship	4.58*** (0.47)	4.61*** (0.44)	0.02 (0.65)
Intercept	−4.08*** (0.49)	−5.87*** (1.47)	−1.79 (1.55)
Racial resentment measured or predicted?	Measured	Predicted	
N	384	397	

***p < .001, **p < .01, *p < .05.
Note: Racial resentment ranges from 0 for the least resentful attitudes to 1 for the most resentful attitudes. Party identification is a five-category variable ranging from 0 (strong Democrat) to 1 (strong Republican) in the Rutgers survey and a three-category variable ranging from 0 (Democrat) to 1 (Republican) in the Monmouth survey. Results do not substantively differ when a three-category measure of partisanship is used for the Rutgers survey.

the earlier Rutgers poll, though the result is not statistically significant because of the imprecision resulting from predicting racial resentment in the Monmouth poll. The magnitude of the difference, however, is considerable.

Figure 5.1 shows the predicted probability of voting for Lonegan obtained using the coefficients from table 5.1, holding the other predictor in the model at its mean level. The most racially resentful respondent in the late-September Monmouth poll (RR = .77) is 49 percentage points more likely to support Lonegan over Booker than the least racially resentful respondent (RR = .48). The difference in Lonegan support probability for early-September Rutgers respondents at those same levels of racial resentment (.48 and .77) is only 14 percentage points. Meanwhile, the relationship between partisanship and vote choice did not change over the course of September.

Though informative, comparing these two polls may not be the most definitive test of whether racial attitudes were primed for two reasons: one, because racial resentment was only measured in one of the polls, and two, because ideology was not accounted for when estimating the association between racial resentment and vote choice. To account for these

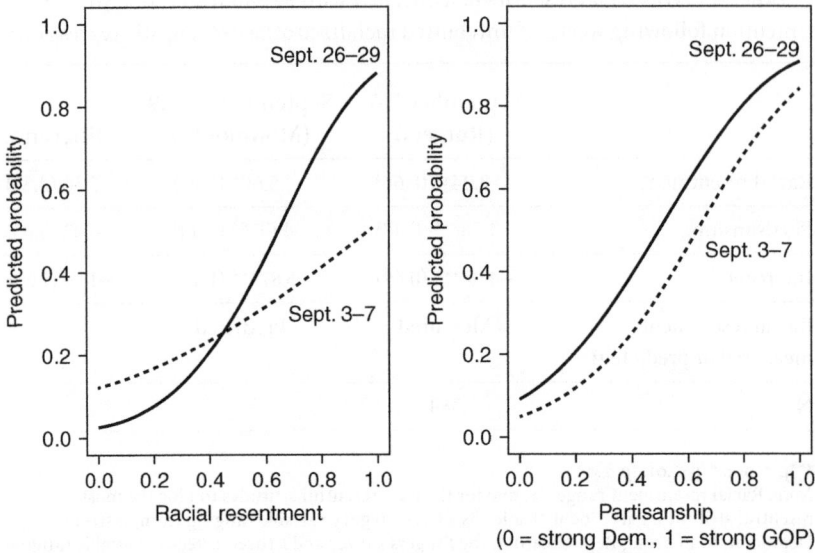

FIGURE 5.1 Predicted probability of Republican vote intention as a function of racial resentment and partisanship, September 3–7 Rutgers poll versus September 26–29 Monmouth poll.

shortcomings, I compare the September 3–7 Rutgers poll with another Rutgers poll conducted from October 7–13 (the final week of the campaign). As I did with the September 3–7 poll, I included the three racial resentment questions and an ideology question on the October 7–13 poll. This allows me to compare *measured* racial resentment's influence on vote choice controlling for partisanship, ideology, and a full set of demographic controls (age, sex, and education). The downside of the October Rutgers survey is that it was conducted after Booker started rebutting the attacks (see evidence on this later in the chapter), which may somewhat dilute the racial priming effect. However, racial attacks were still highly salient during this stage of the campaign, as I will show later in the chapter. Although the October survey was conducted a little later than would be ideal, it should still pick up the effects of Lonegan's attacks (albeit with the effects of Booker's rebuttals also included) in addition to having the advantages of measuring racial resentment and including a full set of control variables.

TABLE 5.2 Was racial resentment associated with Republican (Lonegan) vote intention following racialized attacks? (logistic regression; racial resentment measured in both Rutgers polls)

	Preattack Sept. 3–7 (Rutgers)	Postattack Oct. 7–13 (Rutgers)	Difference
Racial resentment	1.30^ (0.73)	3.10*** (0.81)	1.80^ (1.09)
Partisanship	4.11*** (0.52)	3.95*** (0.48)	−0.15 (0.71)
Ideology	1.68** (0.57)	2.39*** (0.54)	0.71 (0.79)
Education	−0.54 (0.62)	−0.38 (0.63)	0.15 (0.71)
Age	0.02 (0.01)	0.02 (0.01)	0.00 (0.02)
Male	0.61^ (0.32)	0.32 (0.34)	−0.29 (0.47)
(Intercept)	−5.22*** (1.01)	−6.38*** (1.18)	−1.17 (1.55)
N	384	401	

^p < 0.1; **p < 0.01; ***p < 0.001.
Note: The dependent variable is vote choice (1 = Lonegan; 0 = Booker). Partisanship is a five-category variable ranging from 0 (strong Democrat) to 1 (strong Republican). Ideology is a three-category variable ranging from 0 (liberal) to 1 (conservative). Age is the respondent's actual age in years. Male takes on a value of 0 for female and 1 for male. Education is a five-category variable ranging from 0 (less than a high school education) to 1 (post-college degree).

Table 5.2 displays the logistic regression coefficients for racial resentment, the two competing nonracial predispositions, and the demographic controls for the two Rutgers polls. The first row replicates the finding from earlier that racial resentment's association with the vote was stronger toward the end of the campaign. Racial resentment is marginally related to vote choice in the September model once ideology and the demographic controls are accounted for. However, by October, racial resentment's association with Lonegan preference is significant and stronger than its association in September after accounting for the same variables. The difference between the two racial resentment coefficients is marginally significant (p = 0.10, two-tailed). Meanwhile, partisanship's association with the vote remains unchanged, again replicating the result from the earlier analysis. Ideology becomes a slightly stronger

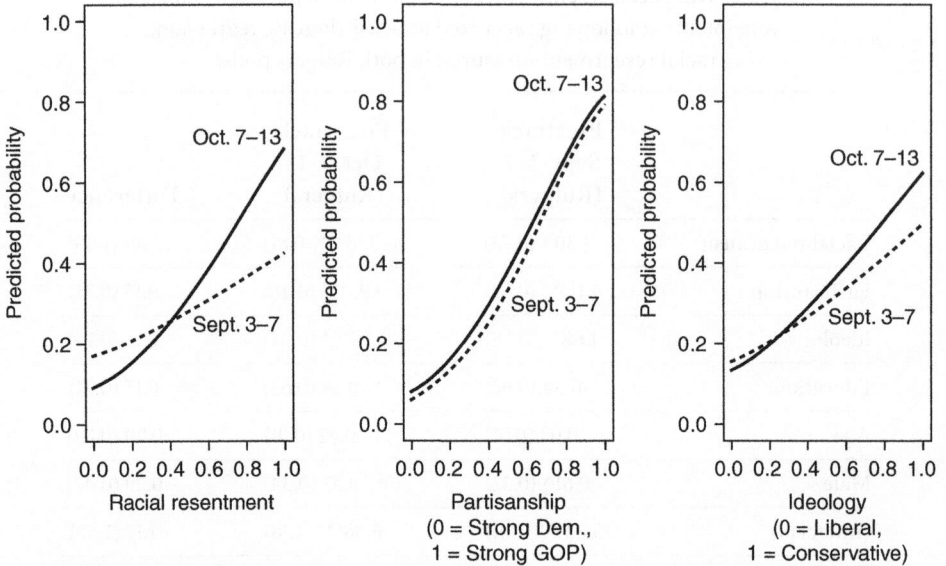

FIGURE 5.2 Predicted probability of Republican vote intention as a function of racial resentment, partisanship, and ideology, September 3–7 versus October 7–13 Rutgers polls (racial resentment measured in both polls; models include full set of demographic controls).

predictor of the vote between September and October, though the difference is statistically indistinguishable from zero (p = 0.37, two-tailed).[15]

Figure 5.2 shows the predicted probabilities of Lonegan support for each predisposition, holding the other variables in the model at their mean levels. The left panel shows that racial resentment was a stronger predictor of Lonegan preference in the October poll compared to September. In September, a white respondent one standard deviation above the mean for racial resentment (RR = .85) was 15 percentage points more likely to support Lonegan compared to a respondent who was one standard deviation below the mean (RR = .30). By October, the difference in likelihood of supporting Lonegan grew to 34 percentage points between a respondent who was one standard deviation above the mean (RR = .79) and a respondent who was one standard deviation below (RR = .28). In sum, these results support the claim that racial priming occurred during the 2013 New Jersey U.S. Senate election.

VALIDATION OF PREDICTED RACIAL RESENTMENT

Now that I have introduced the two Rutgers polls for which I have *measured* racial resentment, I conduct a very important validation of the *predicted* racial resentment variable that has been used in similar analyses presented thus far. I do this by showing that the priming effect obtained with the measured racial resentment variable also occurs when using the predicted racial resentment variable instead. First, I generated predicted racial resentment scores for each respondent in the September 3–7 and October 7–13 Rutgers surveys from their age, education, and sex just as I did for the September 26–29 Monmouth poll. Then, I show that this predicted racial resentment variable is a stronger predictor of the vote in the October 7–13 Rutgers poll compared to the September 7–13 Rutgers poll, consistent with the results when using the measured racial resentment variable. Results are shown in appendix table 5.3.

ALTERNATIVE EXPLANATIONS

Before moving on, I consider alternative explanations for the apparent racial priming effect. One possible explanation for the greater weight placed on racial resentment in October is that there are a large number of Republican undecided voters in early September (since Lonegan was lesser known) who learn that Lonegan is the Republican candidate as the campaign proceeds and "return home" to the Republican column by the end of the campaign. That scenario could explain the larger effect of racial resentment in October, with the cause being Republicans simply rediscovering their partisanship instead of racially resentful voters moving toward Lonegan, as I have assumed so far.

To assess this possibility, table 5.3 shows Booker's support among Republicans, Democrats, and independents in early September (left column), mid-October (center column), and the change between September and October (right column). Positive values in the early September and mid-October columns (left and center) indicate Booker's percentage point

TABLE 5.3 Change between September and October not caused by Republicans going home (vote choice by partisanship in September and October Rutgers-Eagleton surveys)

	Preattack (Sept. 3–7)	Postattack (Oct. 7–13)	Pro-Booker change following attacks
Republicans	−60 9% undecided (n=189)	−63 10% undecided (n=186)	−3
Democrats	+83 6% undecided (n=227)	+84 3% undecided (n=230)	+1
Independents	+17 18% undecided (n=85)	−14 9% undecided (n=78)	−31

lead over Lonegan, while negative values indicate Booker's percentage point deficit. Positive values in the change column (right) indicate that voters shifted toward Booker from September to October, while negative values indicate that voters shifted toward Lonegan.

If the alternative hypothesis that Republicans rediscovered their partisanship is true, we would expect to see a strong pro-Lonegan shift among Republicans between early September and mid-October. Instead, the right column of table 5.3 shows a small shift toward Lonegan among Republicans (3 percentage points) compared to a 31-point shift toward Lonegan among independents. The results suggest that Republican (and Democratic) partisans remained at roughly the same levels of support for their candidate from early September to mid-October, contrary to the alternative hypothesis of Republicans "going home."

Another test of the "returning home" hypothesis can be conducted by comparing the effects of the nonracial predispositions of partisanship and ideology from early in the campaign to late in the campaign. If respondents are returning home to their predispositions over the course of the campaign, we would expect to see a stronger relationship between those variables and vote choice at the end of the campaign. A glance at the partisanship and ideology effects plotted in figure 5.2, however, shows that only racial resentment's effect grew stronger by the end of the campaign. Thus, it appears that the "returning home" hypothesis is unlikely.

A second alternative explanation for the racial priming effect is that people merely learned that Booker was Black and thereafter moved their vote choice in line with their racial predispositions. This is unlikely because many white New Jersey likely voters were probably already aware of Booker's race in early September. The September Rutgers poll does not ask whether respondents knew Booker's race, but it does ask whether their opinion of Booker is favorable, unfavorable, or they have no opinion or don't know who Booker is. Only 23 percent of white likely voters in the September poll said they had no opinion or didn't know who Booker was. While this number is likely to be an underestimate given social desirability concerns, a majority—57 percent—felt comfortable admitting to a pollster that they had no opinion or didn't know who Lonegan was in the same September poll. Thus, the roughly three-quarters of white likely voters who had an opinion of Booker (and presumably knew his race) appears to be a reasonable estimate of how widespread knowledge of Booker's race was, and so it is unlikely that the racial activation effect was caused by new information about Booker's race.

Finally, another alternative hypothesis is that some other nonracial consideration besides partisanship and ideology was primed. One such nonracial consideration is the notion that Booker is a self-promoter. One of the central nonracial themes of Lonegan's attacks is that Booker is a celebrity more concerned with his own career ambitions than serving New Jersey. Thus, we want to know whether the racial priming effect is the spurious effect of the activation of the nonracial belief that Booker is a self-promoter.

Fortunately, this hypothesis can be tested using this question from the October Rutgers survey: "Some say Cory Booker has accomplished a lot as Newark's mayor and the city is better off than it was when he first took office. Others say Booker is mostly a self-promoter and that little has actually changed in the city. Do you think Booker has made a real difference in Newark or has it been mostly self-promotion and little has changed?"[16] Though it would be preferable to show that responses to this question were not a stronger predictor of vote choice in October versus September, the September Rutgers polls did not include this question. However, another way to test whether the racial priming effect is spurious is to account for

TABLE 5.4 "Booker is a self-promoter" does not decrease effect of racial resentment in October (logistic regressions; October Rutgers data; party identification, ideology, and demographic controls are included in the model, but not shown)

	Excluding self-promoter control (original model)	Including self-promoter control ("Don't know" coded NA)	Including self-promoter control ("Don't know" coded 0.5)
Racial resentment	3.10*** (0.81)	4.48*** (1.28)	3.28** (1.01)
Booker is a self-promoter		3.53*** (0.53)	3.44*** (0.49)
N	401	325	400

**p < 0.01; ***p < 0.001.

the self-promoter attitude and see if the strong association between racial resentment and vote choice in October goes away. Table 5.4 shows the results of logistic regressions including the belief that Booker is a self-promoter in the same model with racial resentment, partisanship, ideology, and the demographic controls for the October poll. The left column shows the results of the original model without the self-promoter attitude as a control. The middle column shows results coding "mostly self-promotion" as 1, "real difference" as 0, and throwing out "don't know" responses, while the right column shows results coding "don't know" responses as 0.5.

The results indicate that including the "Booker is a self-promoter" variable in the regression does not substantially alter the effect of racial resentment, regardless of how the self-promoter variable is coded. It appears that the rather large effect of racial resentment in October is robust to the inclusion of this alternative nonracial attitude.

In sum, it appears that racial attitudes were primed over the course of a campaign that featured numerous attacks on racialized themes. I also found that the effects of partisanship and ideology were not similarly primed during this same period. This supports the hypothesis that Lonegan's attacks primed racial and not nonracial considerations.

REBUTTALS AND WHITE OPINION DURING THE BOOKER CAMPAIGN

VOLUME

With the effects of racialized attacks now estimated, I now examine the relationship between rebuttals and white opinion by plotting them over the course of the campaign. As I did in the previous chapter on the Massachusetts and Tennessee campaigns, I start by gathering as many polls for which I can identify the results among white voters (whether the polling organization releases results by race, makes its data set publicly available, or provides the data set upon request) and that are conducted across the entire general election campaign (about six weeks in this case). Of the twelve nonpartisan surveys that were conducted during the general election campaign, I obtained estimates of white opinion for seven of the surveys: the September 3–9 Rutgers-Eagleton, September 26–29 Monmouth, and October 7–13 Rutgers-Eagleton polls mentioned in the previous section, plus four additional polls, three conducted by Quinnipiac from September 15–21, October 5–7, and October 10–14 and one by Monmouth from October 10–12.

With these surveys in hand, I plot the frequency of attacks by Lonegan on the six racialized themes outlined earlier (dashed line) and rebuttals by Booker (thin solid line) as recorded in the *Star-Ledger* along with polling among white voters (black dots, with the trend displayed as the thick solid line) in figure 5.3. One key feature to note about figure 5.3 is that the attacks are by Lonegan or a surrogate, while the rebuttals are only by Booker. Rebuttals offered by Booker surrogates will be discussed shortly. For now, the main pattern to draw attention to is Booker's precipitous decline among white voters during the month of September. A twenty-two-point lead on September 3–7 is erased by the end of the month. The dashed line shows that there was a steady stream of racial attacks by Lonegan during this period, while the flat thin solid line shows that Booker himself did not respond to any of these attacks until September 27, giving Lonegan three weeks of uncontested attacks. According to news reports, Booker was not even in the state of the New Jersey for an eight-day period from September 16–24, while he raised money in California.[17] From September 27 to October 7, both campaigns remained at roughly

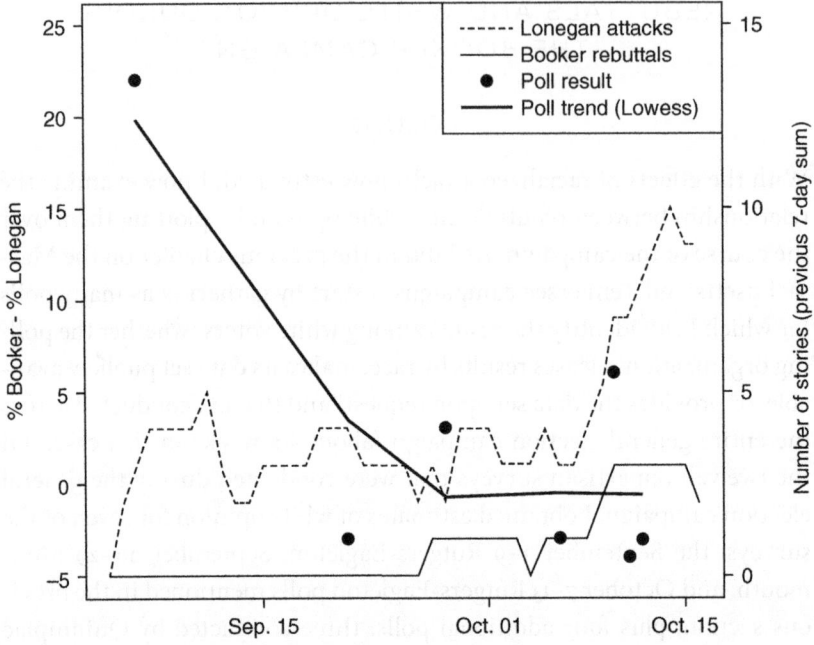

FIGURE 5.3 Polling in 2013 New Jersey U.S. Senate race (white voters only) versus campaign rhetoric on racialized topics.

the same level of attacks and rebuttals before a sharp increase in Lonegan attacks during the last week of the campaign was accompanied by an increase in Booker's level of contestation.

Booker's absence from the first several weeks of the campaign is corroborated by an analysis of spending on campaign ads shown in table 5.5. I tabulated the number of television ads bought and the amount of money spent on those ads by the two campaigns. The data comes from reports filed with the Federal Communications Commission (FCC) by ABC, CBS, and NBC affiliates in New York City, which is one of New Jersey's two media markets (Philadelphia is the other). Unfortunately, no advertising data was filed by either campaign for any Philadelphia affiliates or New York City's Fox affiliate. Also, the FCC does not collect data on local cable television ad purchases, though local cable television represented only a small fraction of the estimated political media share at that time according to estimates by the Kantar Media/CMAG research firm.[18] While not

TABLE 5.5 Number of ad showings bought and the amount spent by each campaign (ABC, NBC, and CBS affiliates in New York City)

	Number of ad showings bought by Lonegan	Amount spent by Lonegan	Number of ad showings bought by Booker	Amount spent by Booker
Aug. 28–Oct. 1	92	$78,350	0	$0
Oct. 2–Oct. 16	258	$240,650	136	$191,450

comprehensive, the ad data from New York City's ABC, CBS, and NBC affiliates still provide insight into the amount of airtime purchased by each campaign and the timing of those purchases.

Table 5.5 shows that Booker completely ceded the TV airwaves to Lonegan during the month of September, while both sides ramped up their spending during the last weeks of the campaign. The pattern is similar to the one shown for campaign rhetoric on racialized topics shown in figure 5.3. Lonegan enjoyed about a month of television presence that Booker did nothing to challenge.

SURROGACY/TIMING

In order to examine how surrogacy and timing influenced rebuttal effectiveness, rebuttals offered by surrogates need to be accounted for. Figure 5.4 shows the *proportion* of Lonegan attack stories that mentioned either a rebuttal by Booker himself or a surrogate (dashed line) or a rebuttal by Booker himself (thin solid line). This is the same measure that was introduced in the previous chapter. The figure shows distinct periods when Booker delegated rebuttals to his surrogates (September 5–27), when he handled them himself (September 27–October 9), and when he and surrogates responded to attacks together (October 9–16). Though Booker's surrogates responded to many of Lonegan's attacks during the September 5–27 period, they did nothing to stop Booker's slide among white voters. His white support stabilized right around the time when he stopped delegating rebuttals to his surrogates.

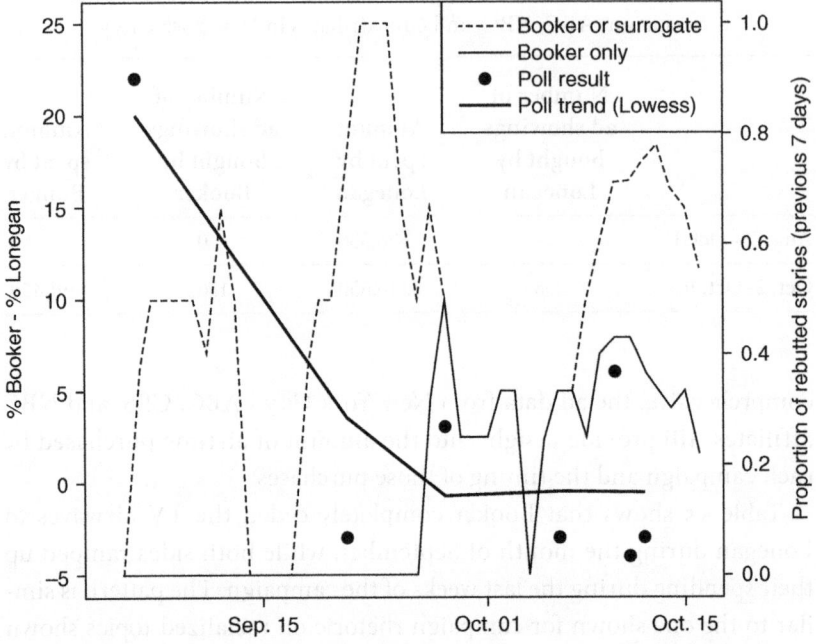

FIGURE 5.4 Polling in 2013 New Jersey U.S. Senate race (white voters only) versus proportion of rebuttal stories.

The patterns shown in figure 5.4 lend support to the hypothesis posed in the previous chapter that surrogates are only effective when they are amplifying the candidate's message rather than speaking in place of the candidate. During the "surrogates only" phase of September 5–27, there is no relationship between the poll trend and frequency of surrogate rebuttals. Recall from the previous chapter that Harold Ford had his own "surrogates only" phase (though it was much shorter than Booker's) right after the "call me" ad aired, during which his surrogates could not stop his support from dropping among white likely voters. While surrogates seemed to help Deval Patrick, the key differences in his case were that he did not delegate to surrogates until after he had already established himself as the main rebutter, and he did not delegate completely—he worked in tandem with his surrogates. In sum, with regard to the effectiveness of surrogates, the Patrick, Ford, and Booker campaigns suggest that surrogates can be effective, but only when they are not the first and only line of defense.

TYPE

The final rebuttal characteristic I consider is type. To examine whether Booker's improved performance toward the end of the campaign coincided with a shift in the types of rebuttals he used, I compared rebuttals offered by the Booker campaign during his "decline" phase (September 5–September 29) to rebuttals offered during his "stabilization" phase (September 30–October 16). The results are shown in table 5.6. After relying exclusively on *counterimaging*, *counterattack*, and *deny* during the decline phase, Booker shifted to a strategy of using *negative* and *distract* most frequently during the stabilization phase. This does not necessarily mean that these are effective strategies, however, given that Booker's stabilization also coincided with the point in the campaign at which he began rebutting attacks himself and more frequently compared to earlier in the campaign.

EFFECTS OF BOOKER REBUTTALS BY RACIAL RESENTMENT LEVEL

Was Booker able to deactivate the racial priming that occurred after he faced a wave of racialized attacks early in the campaign? To test this, I

TABLE 5.6 Rebuttals offered by Cory Booker or surrogates during "decline" vs. "stabilization" phase

	"Decline" phase (Sept. 5–29) (%)	"Stabilization" phase (Sept. 30–Oct. 16) (%)
Negative	0	25
Justify	0	8
Distract	0	25
Counterimaging	40	17
Counterattack	40	8
Deny	20	17

Note: Columns may not add up to 100 percent because of rounding.

compare Booker support among high-racial-resentment white likely voters at the height of the attacks using the September 26–29 Monmouth survey to Booker support among this subgroup at the end of the campaign by pooling the October 7–13 Rutgers survey and the October 10–12 Monmouth survey. I also show how opinion shifted among low-resentment subgroups for comparison.

The results are shown in table 5.7. As with the Massachusetts and Tennessee results presented in the previous chapter, the sample sizes are too small to draw conclusions that reach conventional levels of statistical significance, though the magnitudes are still worth examining. Among high-racial-resentment respondents, Booker appears unsuccessful. He lost 8 percentage points of support among this group, though we cannot be sure that this difference is distinguishable from zero. At the very least, however, it appears that Booker did not gain support among these respondents, thus supporting the claim that rebuttals were unsuccessful in terms of their ability to deactivate racial priming. In contrast, Booker

TABLE 5.7 Support for Booker over Lonegan by racial resentment level, postattack vs. postrebuttal periods

Racial resentment level	Postattack (Sept. 26–29 Monmouth)	Postrebuttal (Oct. 7–13 Rutgers and Monmouth combined)	Difference
Low (< .62 for Sept. 26–29; < .58 for Oct. 7–13)	+32 (n = 131)	+38 (n = 481)	+6 (p = .51)
Med (> = .62 and < = .65 for Sept. 26–29; > = .58 and < .67 for Oct. 7–13)	−8 (n = 140)	−6 (n = 394)	+2 (p = .96)
High (> .65 for Sept. 26–29; > = .67 for Oct. 7–13)	−18 (n = 138)	−26 (n = 571)	−8 (p = .50)

Note: Cell entries indicate the percentage point margin between Booker and Lonegan, with positive values indicating a Booker lead and negative values indicating a Booker deficit.

appears to have had some success winning back the low-racial-resentment subgroup.[19] He gained 6 percentage points more support in the October surveys over his mark in late September at the end of several weeks of Lonegan's uncontested racial attacks. Thinking back to the findings for Deval Patrick and Harold Ford in the previous chapter, Booker's results are similar to Patrick's in the sense that both were able to rally their bases of support among low-racial-resentment voters by challenging racial attacks. The fact that both Booker and Patrick won back low-racial-resentment support was not inevitable. Ford continued to lose support among low-racial-resentment voters even after challenging the sex attacks. On the other hand, neither Booker nor Patrick was able to deactivate high-racial-resentment whites.

In order to compensate for the small sample sizes for each individual campaign and to bolster confidence in conclusions about how rebuttals work among racial resentment subgroups, table 5.8 shows the change in support for the Black candidate between the postattack and postrebuttal periods, pooling across the Patrick, Booker, and Ford campaigns.[20] When pooling across comparable periods of each campaign, the results support earlier tentative conclusions about rebuttals having a positive effect among low-resentment whites. The candidates average an 8 percentage-point gain among this subgroup, a difference that just misses conventional levels of statistical significance (p = .12). Medium-resentment whites do not move a statistically appreciable amount in either direction. Finally, high-resentment whites move away from Black candidates by an average of

TABLE 5.8 Support for Black candidate over white candidate by racial resentment level, postattack vs. postrebuttal periods*

Racial resentment level	Postattack	Postrebuttal	Difference
Low	+20 (n = 636)	+28 (n = 1,002)	+8 (p = .12)
Med	0 (n = 496)	−6 (n = 843)	−6 (p = .27)
High	−4 (n = 756)	−12 (n = 1,203)	−8 (p = .12)

Note: Cell entries indicate the percentage point margin between the Black candidate and the white candidate, with positive values indicating the Black candidate leading and negative values indicating the Black candidate trailing. For definitions of low, medium, and high racial resentment levels in each campaign, see tables 4.3, 4.6, and 5.7.

8 percentage points following a rebuttal period, a difference that approaches conventional levels of statistical significance (p = .12). This is troubling, especially in light of the evidence presented in these chapters that the attacks mostly primed racial and not nonracial attitudes. If racial attacks activate racial thinking and if targeted candidates have a hard time neutralizing their effects, it suggests that Black candidates face an uphill battle in trying to get white voters to evaluate them based on the types of nonracial criteria that are used to evaluate white candidates.

DISCUSSION

It should come as no surprise that the 2013 New Jersey U.S. Senate election was a highly racialized campaign. Race has usually played a role whenever a Black American runs the first viable campaign for an important office.[21] It did in this contest because of Lonegan, who was eager to stir up controversy with racialized attacks. Booker also contributed to his own racialization by allowing Lonegan to control the message environment for a significant portion of the contest. It was exactly during this one-sided period that racial resentment became a strong predictor of vote choice and Lonegan made significant gains among white voters. However, Lonegan's gains among whites leveled off once the message environment became more competitive during the last two weeks of the campaign. In sum, it appears that contestation can benefit a Black candidate who is targeted by racialized attacks. Rebuttals may not reverse the slide, but the evidence presented in this chapter suggests that they can slow it considerably. With Booker able to keep Lonegan's edge among white voters to a small margin (see figures 5.3 and 5.4), Booker was able to win the election by about 11 percentage points, thanks to Booker's large edge among nonwhite voters. Had Lonegan been able to pile up larger margins among white voters, he might have been able to score an upset victory.

One of the contributions of this case study is that it extends the study of racial priming into statewide campaigns. Thus far, almost all of what we know about racial priming comes from lab experiments or two presidential campaigns—one featuring a high-profile racial attack (1988) and the other involving the first Black major-party candidate (2008). As Black Americans are now beginning to reach the offices of governor and senator, research on "campaigning while Black" needs to look at the role of racial attitudes in campaigns for these powerful and prestigious offices. This task has been difficult so far because statewide polls rarely include questions about racial attitudes and perceptions. By showing that racial attitudes remain central determinants of vote choice in statewide elections, this case study represents an important contribution to the study of Blacks running for statewide office.

The other main contribution of this case study is its treatment of rebuttals. Most of the voluminous literature on campaign effects, including the racial priming literature, examines the one-sided effects of campaign messages but ignores the effects of rebuttals. The literature on counterframing has emerged as a critique of these one-sided studies, producing interesting experimental work on whether framing effects hold up when opposing considerations are presented. This case study extends this literature, which has focused mostly on policy debates, to the study of campaigns.

The main limitation of this analysis is that it is difficult to detect the precise effect of attacks and rebuttals with survey data because the surveys are conducted a few weeks apart. Thus, it is possible that something occurring simultaneously with the attacks and rebuttals of the campaign are causing opinion to shift. For reassurance that attacks and rebuttals move opinion, I conducted several experiments that test attacks and rebuttals similar to the ones offered in this election. The results of these experiments are discussed in chapters 7 and 8. Nonetheless, the analysis presented in this chapter, while not without its limitations, is valuable because it shows how opinion shifts in response to different frequencies of attacks and rebuttals outside the lab.

In sum, the 2013 New Jersey U.S. Senate election provides another example of how campaign messages can activate negative racial thinking about a Black candidate. However, it appears that rebuttals can partially counteract this racialization. For one more case study on the racial dynamics of a campaign involving a viable Black candidate, I examine the 2014 Maryland gubernatorial candidacy of Anthony Brown.

ANTHONY BROWN AND THE 2014 MARYLAND GUBERNATORIAL CAMPAIGN

Larry Hogan, a Republican businessman who had never previously held office, won a stunning 51 percent to 48 percent victory over Brown, who was the lieutenant governor of Maryland under Governor Martin O'Malley. Hogan entered the race as a heavy underdog, given that Democrats outnumber Republicans in Maryland by a two-to-one margin, and Brown outspent Hogan five to one. Though virtually all preelection polls predicted a Brown victory, he lost by a significant margin in Maryland's nine suburban and twelve rural counties and was hurt by lower-than-expected turnout in the Democratic strongholds of the city of Baltimore and Montgomery and Prince George's Counties. Hogan's win made him only the second Republican governor of Maryland in the last forty-six years.

As reported in chapter 2, Hogan's rhetoric was *less* crime-focused than other white Republicans facing white Democratic challengers in recent Maryland gubernatorial elections. According to journalistic accounts of the 2014 Maryland campaign, however, Hogan focused his attacks on tax increases enacted by the O'Malley/Brown administration, frequently repeating phrases such as "40 consecutive tax increases" under the O'Malley/Brown administration resulting in a "mass exodus of businesses and families."[22] Brown did little to defend himself on taxes, instead choosing to attack Hogan on social issues, much to the puzzlement of the media, fellow Democrats, and O'Malley. "Brown left Hogan's narrative about the lagging economy only lightly challenged," according to one *Baltimore Sun* recap of the first debate.[23] "To counter Hogan's case that Maryland is overtaxed and its business climate is abysmal," according to a *Sun* postelection recap two days after the election, "Brown barely mounted a defense of the O'Malley administration's record. Critics said his program at times sounded like 'me too'—as when he pledged not to raise taxes and said it would be a top priority to make the state's business climate the best in the nation."[24] O'Malley, in his own election postmortem, agreed with this assessment, saying the Brown campaign "made a tactical decision not to defend the record or talk about it, and we saw the results that we saw."[25]

Were charges that Brown did not adequately defend himself true? If so, findings from previous research suggest that racial attitudes would play an important role in shaping voter attitudes in the election despite the fact that the issue of taxation does not contain any manifest racial content. Taxes and redistribution more generally have the image of funding social programs that cater to minorities and/or the poor, and so opinion on taxes is shaped by how citizens feel about the perceived beneficiaries of the state's tax revenue. In a thorough demonstration of the link between racial attitudes and opinion on taxation, the political scientists David Sears and Jack Citrin show that racial resentment was strongly correlated with antitax sentiment during California's "tax revolt" of the late 1970s and early 1980s even after controlling for a host of related attitudes such as ideology, partisanship, preferences for smaller and less intrusive government, trust in government, the belief that government is inefficient and wastes money, homeownership, personal financial situation, perceived high tax burden, and non-public-sector employment.[26] With many in the media calling the 2014 gubernatorial election "Maryland's tax revolt," perhaps unanswered attacks on taxes had a racializing effect similar to that of unanswered attacks on crime for Cory Booker. Unanswered attacks on taxes may be particularly damaging for a Black Democrat, who is already likely to be stereotyped as fiscally liberal.

RACIAL PRIMING DURING THE BROWN CAMPAIGN

I show in chapter 2 that Hogan focused heavily on the issue of taxes—over 36 percent of all stories appearing in the *Baltimore Sun* about the campaign mentioned either Hogan promoting his own position or attacking Brown on taxes. In chapter 3, I show that Brown rebuttals appeared in only 34 percent of all stories in which Hogan mentioned taxes, which was lower than Deval Patrick's crime rebuttal rate and in line with the rebuttal rates of Harold Ford Jr. (on sex) and Cory Booker (on various racialized themes). In the remainder of the chapter, I aim to show that Brown was racialized during the campaign and that his rebuttals did nothing to counter that racialization.

The first step is to show that Hogan's attacks had a racial effect. To do this, I compare two *Washington Post* polls: an October 2–5 poll (conducted right as tax mentions and rebuttals started to pick up, as I will later show) and a postelection poll conducted from February 5–8, 2015. Of course, there are many caveats to using a poll conducted that long after the end of the campaign, but I argue that the survey is still a reasonable approximation of opinion at the end of the campaign for two reasons: first, the February survey was much closer to the actual result than all of the preelection polls. Respondents to the February survey indicated that they voted for Hogan by a 49–44 margin when the actual result was 51–47 Hogan—only one percentage point off. All of the other preelection surveys conducted during the last five weeks of the campaign forecast Brown as the winner by margins as high as 17 percentage points. Second, there were no polls conducted after October 24, leaving eleven days of the campaign without any forecasts of the outcome. Given the accuracy of the February survey, I consider it a sensible measure of opinion at the end of the campaign. Since it was the only poll conducted after October 24, it is the closest existing measure of opinion during the campaign's final eleven days.

Since neither *Washington Post* poll included the racial resentment battery, I predict racial resentment using the same two-stage procedure used in the previous case studies. First, I regress racial resentment on age, education, and sex using white Maryland respondents in the 2014 CCES (n = 538).[27] Using the coefficients obtained from this regression, I predict racial resentment for the two *Washington Post* surveys. Finally, I estimate the relationship between predicted racial resentment and vote choice using logistic regression, including controls for partisanship and ideology.[28]

Table 5.9 shows the results. Racial resentment is not associated with Hogan preference in early October after accounting for partisanship and ideology, but it is in the postelection survey. In fact, the influence of racial resentment in the postelection survey is greater than that of partisanship or ideology.

To aid in interpreting the magnitude of these coefficients, figure 5.5 shows the predicted probabilities of Hogan support using the coefficients from table 5.9 while holding the other variables in the model at their mean value. Racial resentment is a much stronger predictor of Hogan preference in the February 2015 survey, as the respondent with the highest predicted racial resentment in that survey (RR = .87) is 44 percentage points

TABLE 5.9 Is racial resentment associated with Republican (Hogan) vote intention following tax attacks?

	Early campaign (*Wash. Post*, Oct. 2–5, 2014)	Late campaign (*Wash. Post*, Feb. 5–8, 2015)	Difference
Predicted racial resentment	1.36 (1.47)	4.03*** (1.15)	2.67 (1.87)
Partisanship	4.31*** (0.63)	3.00*** (0.47)	−1.31^ (0.79)
Ideology	2.39*** (0.65)	2.98*** (0.50)	0.58 (0.82)
Intercept	−3.48*** (0.98)	−4.29*** (0.79)	−0.81 (1.26)
N	278	407	

***p < .001, ^p <.1.

more likely to prefer Hogan over Brown than the respondent with the lowest predicted racial resentment (RR = .32), holding partisanship and ideology at their mean levels. In the early October 2014 survey, the most racially resentful respondent (RR = .87) is only 14 percentage points more likely to support Hogan over Brown than the least racially resentful respondent (RR = .38)—less than one-third of the comparable figure in the postelection poll. Partisanship's relationship with the vote was actually weaker in February 2015 compared to October 2014 (p < 0.1) because of greater Hogan support among Democrats in the February 2015 survey. The gap between Hogan's predicted support among Democrats (on the left side of the center panel of figure 5.5) in October 2014 compared to February 2015 makes very clear that Brown was hurt by a major white Democratic defection to Hogan.

Another way to demonstrate the racial effects of the unrebutted attacks is to test whether Democrats with higher levels of racial resentment defected at higher rates than less racially resentful Democrats. In essence, we are holding partisanship constant and seeing whether racial resentment is associated with Brown defection. To carry out this test, I divided white Democrats in the October 2014 and February 2015 polls into thirds by racial resentment score. The bottom third scored at or below .53 for the October 2014 poll and at or below .54 for the February 2015 poll. The middle third scored between .53 and .72 in October 2014 and between .54 and

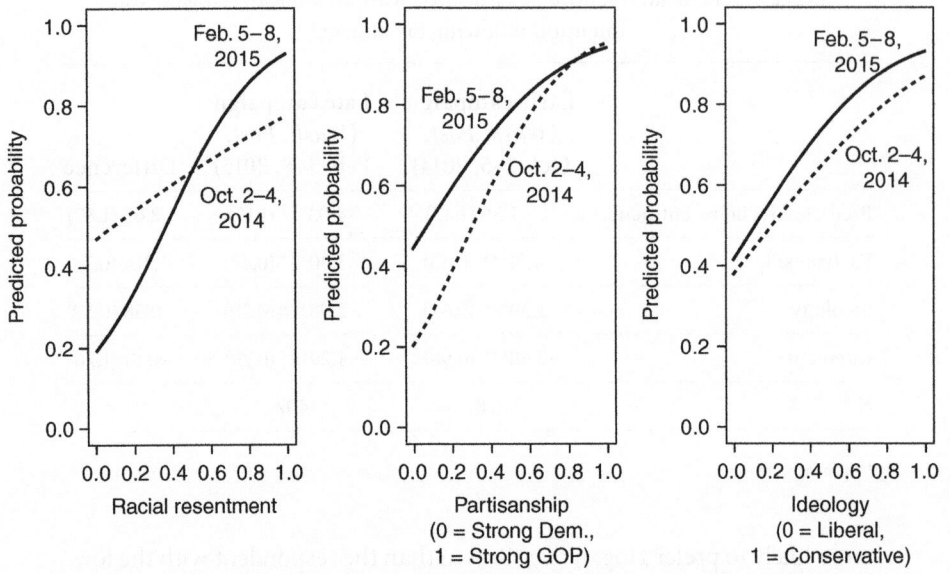

FIGURE 5.5 Predicted probability of Republican (Hogan) vote intention as a function of racial resentment, partisanship, and ideology, October 2–4, 2014, versus February 5–8, 2015, *Washington Post* polls.

.72 in February 2015. The top third scored at or above .72 in both polls. Then, I tabulated vote choice among Democrats who fell in each of the three categories for each poll. The results are shown in table 5.10. The middle two columns show the size (in percentage points) of Brown's lead over Hogan for each of the polls. The right column shows how much support Brown lost among each racial resentment subgroup. A glance at these numbers lends support to the hypothesis: though Brown lost substantial support among white Democrats at all racial resentment levels, he lost the most support among medium-, and especially, high-racial-resentment subgroups. The October 2–4, 2014, *Washington Post* poll found that Brown had a fifty-five-point lead (71 percent Brown versus 16 percent Hogan) among high-racial-resentment white Democrats. By February 5–8, 2015, respondents of that type reported equal levels of support for Brown and Hogan. This is further evidence that racial attitudes were primed during the contest.

Finally, ideology's role in shaping vote choice did not change much over the course of the campaign, as indicated by the near-parallel relationship

TABLE 5.10 Brown defection highest among high- and medium-racial-resentment white Democrats

Racial resentment level	Early campaign (Wash. Post, Oct. 2–4, 2014)	Late campaign (Wash. Post, Feb. 5–8, 2015)	Difference
Low (<=.53 for Oct. 2014 poll; <=.54 for Feb. 2015 poll)	96 (n=46)	78 (n=69)	−18
Medium (>.53 and <.72 for Oct. 2014 poll; >.54 and <.72 for Feb. 2015 poll)	52 (n=33)	9 (n=36)	−43
High (>=.72 for both polls)	55 (n=31)	0 (n=64)	−55

Note: Cell entries in the middle two columns represent Brown's percentage point lead over Hogan. Cell entries in the right column represent the difference between the middle two columns.

of the dashed and solid lines in the right panel of figure 5.5. In sum, the findings suggest that as the proportion of unrebutted Hogan tax statements went up, so did the association between racial resentment and Hogan preference. The unrebutted tax attacks did not coincide with a similar priming effect for partisanship or ideology, though a careful analysis of the effects of partisanship show that Brown lost a substantial amount of Democratic support that was concentrated among high- (and to a lesser, though still substantial extent) medium-racial-resentment white Democrats.

REBUTTALS AND WHITE OPINION DURING THE BROWN CAMPAIGN

The second objective is to demonstrate the inadequacy of Brown's response. To do so, I start by estimating how white opinion changed over the course of the campaign. My estimates of white opinion come from obtaining six of the seven nonpartisan polls conducted during the last five weeks of the campaign. The two *Washington Post* polls mentioned earlier in the racial priming analysis were conducted on October 2–5, 2014, and February 5–18, 2015. Since I consider the February 2015 poll to be a stand-in for opinion on Election Day, I assign it a date of Election Day, November 4. The other four polls were a CBS News/*New York Times*/YouGov poll conducted September 20–October 1, a *Baltimore Sun* poll conducted October 4–8, a CBS News/*New York Times*/YouGov poll conducted October 16–23, and a Gonzalez Research poll conducted October 20–24.[29]

Next, to see how white opinion changed as the frequency of Hogan attacks and Brown rebuttals changed, I plot those three trends in figure 5.6. All attacks and rebuttals were coded from the *Baltimore Sun*'s campaign coverage. With respect to white opinion, the most notable finding is that white voters moved away from Brown as the campaign progressed: a twelve-point Brown deficit among whites in late September turned into a twenty-eight-point deficit by late October and fell even further to a thirty-five-point deficit according to the postelection *Washington Post* poll. Turning to attacks and rebuttals, Hogan's tax rhetoric hit a peak between October 12 and October 18: the number of stories that

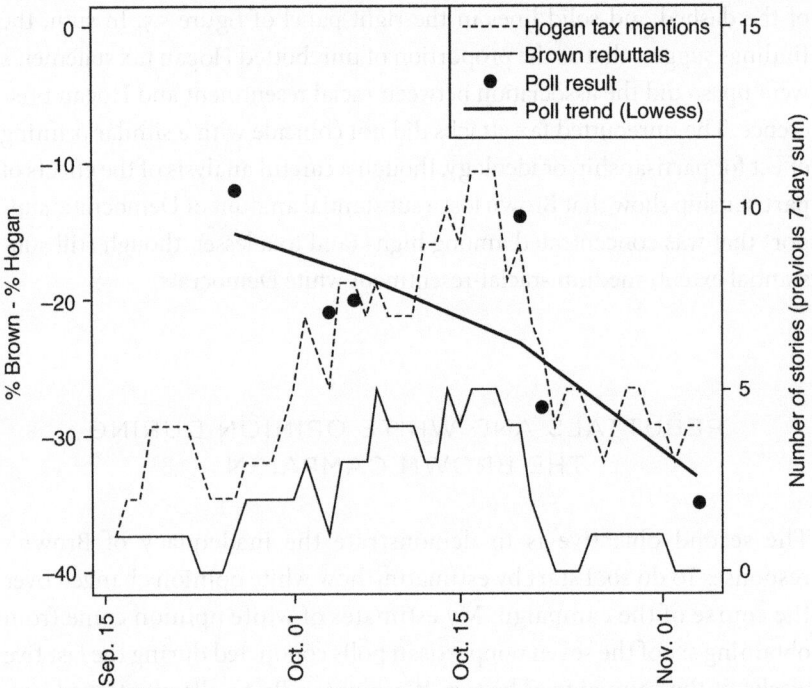

FIGURE 5.6 Polling in 2014 Maryland gubernatorial race (white voters only) versus campaign rhetoric on taxes.

appeared in the *Baltimore Sun* during the previous seven days never fell below nine during that period. Brown's response was sporadic—at no time from October 12–18 did the number of rebutted stories outnumber the number of unrebutted stories. Unlike Deval Patrick (who reversed his losses among white voters) and Harold Ford and Cory Booker (who at least did not lose any more ground once they started rebutting attacks), Brown's lack of a strong defense against racial attacks led to his white support falling sharply over the last two weeks of the campaign.

A clearer illustration of the relationship between Brown's level of contestation and his white support can be shown by comparing the proportion of tax stories that also mentioned a Brown rebuttal (the same measure used in previous chapters) to his level of white support over the course of the campaign. That relationship is shown in figure 5.7. The proportion rebutted by Brown himself is the solid black line. The proportion rebutted by Brown or a surrogate is the dashed black line, but surrogates only

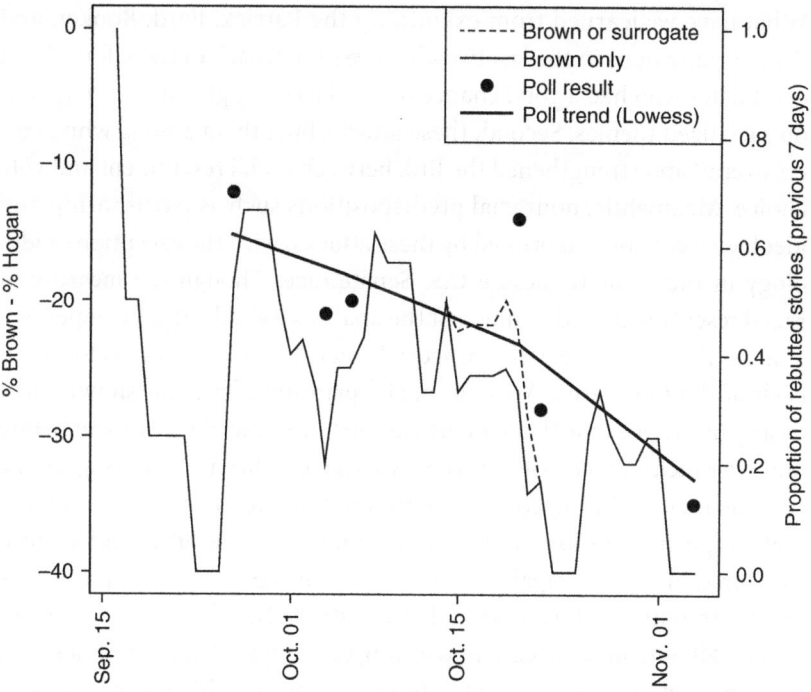

FIGURE 5.7 Polling in 2014 Maryland gubernatorial race (white voters only) versus proportion of rebuttal stories.

spoke on Brown's behalf for a short stretch of the campaign in mid-October. Most of the contestation of Hogan's tax charges was handled by Brown himself. Proportions range from 0 to 1, with 0 representing no stories over the previous seven days mentioning a Hogan tax statement also including a Brown rebuttal and 1 representing all stories mentioning a Hogan tax statement also including a rebuttal. The poll trend line (thick solid line) and the Brown rebuttal proportion line (thin solid line) track fairly well, suggesting that Brown's fortunes fell along with the amount of contestation he offered to Hogan's statements. Most of the stories that included tax mentions by Hogan did not also include a Brown rebuttal after October 15. In short, Brown's voice on taxes—and his support among white voters—became more and more faint as the campaign went on.

CONCLUSION

What have we learned from examining the Patrick, Ford, Booker, and Brown campaigns in the last two chapters? First, each of these four Black candidates who had a good chance to win faced a high volume of attacks on racialized themes. Second, these attacks hurt them among white voters overall and strengthened the link between racial resentment and vote choice. Meanwhile, nonracial predispositions such as partisanship and ideology were not also primed by these attacks, with the exception of ideology in the 2006 Tennessee U.S. Senate race. Though the measure of racial resentment used in much of the analysis was admittedly imperfect, a large (though imprecisely measured) racial priming effect is found in each of the four cases. Also, the racial priming effect was shown most clearly in the one case that had measurements of racial resentment before and after racial attacks—the 2013 New Jersey U.S. Senate race—suggesting that the racial priming effects reported in the other chapters are smaller and less precisely measured than they would be if racial attitudes had been measured in those campaigns. And finally, my comparison of postattack and postrebuttal polls shows that Deval Patrick, Harold Ford Jr., and Cory Booker all were unsuccessful in winning back support among whites with high levels of racial resentment—the same group of whites who were activated by the attacks. However, Patrick and Booker appeared to shore up support among low-racial-resentment respondents, while Ford's rebuttal efforts were particularly ineffective among this subgroup presumably inclined to be sympathetic to a Black candidate facing a racially tinged attack. Meanwhile, Anthony Brown was the outlier among the four candidates in terms of their rebuttal strategies. While Patrick, Ford, and Booker at least tried to counter racializing attacks, Brown grew more and more content to be defined by Hogan as a serial tax raiser—a reminder that candidates do not always pursue optimal strategies.

The disparate outcomes of these cases raise the question of whether the content of rebuttals matters. I have not yet focused much attention on the effects of specific types of rebuttals because it is difficult to pinpoint the precise effects of specific countermessages with the polling data I have used in these chapters. In real campaigns, multiple events happen, and multiple messages come from both sides every day, making it impossible to detect the effects of any one message with polls conducted weeks apart. Nonetheless, the chapters demonstrate that the general flow of attacks and rebuttals seems to influence how strongly racial thinking is activated among white voters in predictable ways. To show these patterns in the real world is necessary to justify experimental tests of specific messages in controlled settings. I turn to these tests in chapters 7 and 8 to better understand how specific attacks and rebuttals work. But before I test the effects of attacks and rebuttals, I consider one more case study. All of the case studies presented thus far have focused on Black men. What happens when Black women run for high-level offices? I address this question in the next chapter.

6

WHEN BLACK WOMEN RUN

The 2018 Stacey Abrams and 2020 Kamala Harris Campaigns

The central argument of the book so far is that race remains an obstacle for Black candidates, as their white opponents often emphasize issues that raise the salience of racial attitudes for white voters. With its focus on race, the book joins a number of other studies in examining the role of candidate race in shaping voting behavior.[1] Most of this research, however, focuses on the candidacies of Black men. When Black women run, race *and* gender are possible targets for their opponents. The question I address in this chapter is: When both factors are grounds for rejection by voters, which factor tends to be emphasized in the mind of the white public?

Since women have rarely run competitively for the high-level offices of governor or U.S. senator, the limited amount of evidence available on evaluations of Black female candidates focuses on elections at the mayoral and U.S. House levels.[2] In recent years, however, two Black women have broken through as viable candidates for high-level statewide office. In 2018, Stacey Abrams came very close to becoming the first Black female governor in U.S. history, losing the Georgia gubernatorial election to Republican Brian Kemp by just 1.4 percentage points.[3] In 2016, Kamala Harris became the second Black female U.S. senator in history and in 2020 became the first Black woman on a major party presidential ticket. The rise of these two prominent Black women provides an opportunity to assess the relative influences of racial and gender attitudes in campaigns for high-level offices when both are likely to be salient.

In this chapter, I focus on Abrams's 2018 senate contest in Georgia and Harris's 2020 run for the vice presidency. Of course, Harris won election to the Senate in 2016, but that contest is not examined because the unique circumstances of that campaign limit the conclusions we can draw from it. In particular, Harris ran against a fellow Democrat in the general election because of California's "top-two" primary system that advances the top two vote getters regardless of political party from a contest in which candidates from all parties are listed on the same primary ballot. Under this system, it is possible for two Democratic candidates to face off in the general election, which is exactly what happened in 2016: Harris faced fellow Democrat Loretta Sanchez. Running against a Latina Democrat is not representative of the type of opponent (and therefore, the types of attacks) a Black Democratic woman typically faces in a general election. The other reason why Harris's 2016 Senate race is not examined is the lack of available data—leading surveys like the Cooperative Congressional Election Study (CCES) and American National Election Study (ANES) lacked measures of modern sexism and vote choice in the Senate race that are essential to addressing the question of how much racial and gender attitudes influence vote choice.[4] However, as argued earlier, Harris's 2016 campaign may not be all that informative anyway because of the unusual circumstances.[5]

Harris's 2020 vice presidential campaign has the advantage of being a campaign where Harris faced a white Republican opponent, which is by far the most likely type of opponent a Black Democrat who is running for governor or senator is likely to face. Also, the 2020 ANES, my original survey from the 2020 campaign, and my 2021 survey experiment contain all of the measures necessary to evaluate the relative influence of racial and gender attitudes on vote choice. While a campaign for the vice presidency technically falls outside the scope of this book, the vice presidency is similar to the offices of governor and U.S. senator in that it is visible and prestigious but not quite at the level of the presidency. Thus, an examination of the racial and gender dynamics of a vice presidential run is likely to be relevant for gubernatorial and senatorial candidacies.

At the very least, this examination is new, as no Black American has ever run for the vice presidency before Harris.

APPROACH

The approach for evaluating the role of racial and gender attitudes for Black women candidates in this chapter adopts and builds on earlier studies in the racial and gender politics literatures. Previous studies evaluating the role of racial attitudes in evaluations of Black politicians have compared the effect of racial attitudes on evaluations of Black candidates (e.g., Barack Obama) to its effect on comparable white candidates such as Hillary Clinton, Bill Clinton, or John Edwards.[6] Research on the role of gender attitudes in evaluations of female politicians has used a similar strategy, comparing the effect of gender attitudes on evaluations of women (e.g., Hillary Clinton) to its effect on comparable men.[7]

I adopt the "comparison" strategy used in earlier studies in much of the analysis in this chapter. Unlike earlier studies, however, Black women require two comparison groups: Black men (in order to hold race constant when assessing the impact of gender attitudes) and white women (in order to hold gender constant when assessing the impact of racial attitudes). A number of analogues for Abrams and Harris will be introduced later in the chapter.

Though it has been frequently used in observational studies of racial and gender bias, the "comparison" strategy has an important limitation: since, say, Obama and John Edwards are not exactly the same in every respect except their race or Hillary Clinton and Joe Biden are not the same in every respect except their gender, it leaves open the possibility that any observed differences in voters' evaluations of the two candidates being compared is attributable to extraneous differences unrelated to race or gender. Experimental studies can more confidently isolate the causal effects of candidate race and gender but are limited by external validity concerns because of their reliance on fictional candidates.[8] The experiment discussed later in the chapter aims to address this concern by holding a real-world candidate—Harris—constant but varying the salience of her race or gender, building on other work that uses this novel identification strategy.⁹

EXPECTATIONS

Scholars of voter behavior have long been interested in how attitudes toward social groups—for instance, Blacks and women—influence how ordinary citizens think about politics. This line of research demonstrates that voters' decisions are "group-centric," meaning that people form their opinions on political candidates based on their attitudes toward the social groups the candidate appears to stand with or against.¹⁰ Although candidates signal their association with social groups in various ways, perhaps the most effective signal a candidate can send is to actually be a member of the group. By embodying the group, the candidate raises the salience of that group in voters' minds, which in turn leads voters to draw upon their attitudes toward that group when evaluating the candidate. The most extensive test of this "chronic accessibility" hypothesis is the presidential candidacy of Barack Obama in 2008. Researchers found that racial attitudes, measured a variety of ways, were a stronger predictor of evaluations of Obama than any of his white Democratic primary rivals and any of the previous white Democratic general election presidential candidates.¹¹ This large effect of racial animus, in spite of Obama's effort to neutralize its harmful effects, led researchers to conclude that racial attitudes were a chronically accessible consideration that were brought to bear on evaluations of Obama despite his attempts to reduce their salience.¹²

If the accessibility theory carries over to Harris and Abrams, we would expect racial attitudes to be a stronger influence on white voters' evaluations of them compared to white voters' evaluations of similar white candidates. Aside from the accessibility account, another reason to expect racial attitudes to matter a great deal for both candidates is that both campaigns featured no shortage of race-based attacks, which research suggests would strengthen the connection between racial attitudes and candidate evaluations.¹³ As discussed in chapters 2 and 3, crime was unusually salient during Abrams's campaign, as Abrams's opponent Brian Kemp sought to portray Abrams as soft on crime as well as possibly engaging in criminal behavior herself. Abrams also faced attacks for burning a Confederate flag as a college student and for her support for removing Confederate symbols. As for Harris, President Trump refused to state that Harris was eligible to serve as vice president when asked about a rumor that Harris was not actually an American citizen, a move that drew comparison to Trump's "birther" attacks against Obama.[14] Trump surrogates and conservative media figures frequently mispronounced her first name and questioned whether she was truly Black.[15] In an attack that resembled more conventional Republican attempts to stoke passions about crime, a Trump campaign ad accused Harris of wanting to "let terrorists and rapists vote from prison" and "give cop killers a pass."[16] These kinds of racial appeals are likely to keep race-based considerations at the forefront of voters' minds when evaluating Abrams and Harris.

On the other hand, the literature offers other reasons to believe that racial animus might not hurt Abrams or Harris very much. For one, the findings of strong racialization from research on Obama's campaigns may be unique to Obama, given that he was running for the presidency, the most visible and powerful office in American politics. Research suggests that the less important the office, the less racism influences voters.[17] The vice presidency is a peculiar office in that it is highly visible but usually not very powerful,[18] while the office of governor is clearly a notch below the presidency in terms of power and visibility. It is unclear whether a Black vice president or governor would evoke the same sense of upheaval that a Black president did. Another difference that sets Obama apart is simply that he was the first to make it to the highest position in American politics. It is possible that the influence of racial attitudes may be somewhat muted for Abrams or Harris compared to Obama, whose rise to the presidency was an achievement of such symbolic power and threat to many Americans that it may never be repeated for any major Black political figure who comes after him. Finally, political scientists have long known that racial attitudes are far from the only important influence on voting behavior. Two factors that have long been shown to affect candidate evaluations are partisanship and retrospective economic evaluations.[19] Combined with other nonracial factors—one example being concern about the coronavirus pandemic, which was a defining issue in the 2020 campaign—it is possible that racial attitudes might not play much of a role in shaping evaluations of Abrams or Harris after accounting for other factors.

In short, conflicting predictions about the impact of racism on evaluations of Abrams and Harris suggest a test of the *racial activation hypothesis*: racial predispositions will be a stronger predictor of Abrams and Harris support relative to comparable white candidates and when Harris's Black identity is highlighted in an experiment.

Just as Abrams and Harris make race salient by embodying it, they also do so with gender. Would we therefore expect gender attitudes to similarly influence evaluations of them? As one might expect, the most studied cases of how gender attitudes influence vote choice are the presidential candidacies of Hillary Clinton in 2008 and 2016. But unlike the literature on racial attitudes and evaluations of Obama, the findings from the Clinton literature are mixed. Studies from the 2008 campaign found that gender attitudes were not associated with voting against Clinton in the Democratic primary once racial attitudes were accounted for.[20] Several studies from the 2016 campaign, however, found that gender attitudes were a stronger predictor of vote choice than in previous male versus male presidential elections, even after accounting for the effect of racial attitudes.[21]

These findings raise the question of whether Abrams's circumstances in 2018 and Harris's in 2020 were more similar to Clinton's in 2016 or Clinton's in 2008. One similarity between the 2016 Clinton, Abrams, and Harris campaigns was the presence of Donald Trump in the political environment. Trump was Clinton's opponent in 2016 and Harris's in 2020, and Trump was a prominent endorser and key surrogate of Abrams's opponent Brian Kemp in 2018. Another similarity that Harris, especially, has in common with 2016 Clinton is the abundance of gender-based messages Harris faced from Trump and his surrogates. In the hours after Harris was announced as Biden's running mate, Trump frequently referred to her using some form of the word "nasty," an epithet Trump has used to describe other powerful women he has clashed with such as Clinton, Elizabeth Warren, and Nancy Pelosi.[22] Another example was the conservative radio host Rush Limbaugh and the Florida congressman Matt Gaetz (R-FL) pushing the claim that Harris was only able to move up in

California politics because of her relationship with former California state assembly speaker and former San Francisco mayor Willie Brown, a narrative that spread widely online.[23] Assuming such attacks raised the salience of Harris's gender, we would also expect them to raise the availability of gender considerations in the public mind. On the other hand, Harris and Abrams are different from Clinton in 2016 in that Harris and Abrams ran for lower offices, a distinction that is likely to matter given that scholars find that sexism matters more when women run for executive offices.[24]

Since studies offer reasons to think gender attitudes either are or are not a significant factor in shaping support for female candidates, this chapter offers a test of the *gender activation hypothesis* using Abrams and Harris as test cases: gender attitudes will be a stronger predictor of Abrams and Harris support relative to comparable male candidates and when Harris is framed as a woman.

RESEARCH DESIGN

I test these hypotheses using four sources of data: (1) CCES data from 2018; (2) ANES data from 2004, 2008, 2012, 2016, and 2020; (3) an original survey of 3,516 white American adults during the presidential campaign in October 2020 conducted by the survey firm Lucid; and (4) an original survey experiment conducted in February 2021. Study 1 uses the 2018 CCES to test whether racial and gender attitudes had larger effects on support for Abrams compared to other Democratic gubernatorial candidates during the 2018 cycle. Study 2 uses the ANES surveys to test whether racial and gender attitudes had larger effects on support for Harris compared to the white male Democratic vice presidential nominees in the 2004–2016 elections. Study 3 uses the October 2020 Lucid survey to compare the relationship between racial and gender attitudes and evaluations of Harris to their association with evaluations of other nationally prominent Democrats. Study 4 then turns to the February 2021 survey experiment to examine the causal impact of Harris's racial and gender identity on the relationship between racial and gender attitudes and opposition to Harris.

STUDY 1: THE 2018 STACEY ABRAMS GUBERNATORIAL CAMPAIGN

Study 1 examines the relationship between racial attitudes and gender attitudes and vote choice in the 2018 Georgia gubernatorial election between Abrams and Kemp. Since I am using the "comparison" strategy to evaluate the influence of these factors, I need to identify Black men and white women to serve as suitable comparison candidates. Fortunately, Abrams has a pretty good Black male analogue in 2018: Andrew Gillum, the Democratic candidate for Florida governor. Both were considered progressive, as they received endorsements from progressive U.S. Senator Bernie Sanders (I-VT) during their campaigns. They also share some key biographical details, as both are around the same age, held elected office before running for governor, and attended historically Black colleges. The political context in which they ran is also similar. They both ran in the midterm election year of 2018 as challengers for open seats for the same office (governor) of neighboring southern states. They both ran against white Republican men, Brian Kemp and Ron DeSantis, who embraced support from Donald Trump and adopted Trump's style of racially tinged campaigning (see chapters 2 and 3 for examples). Both barely lost: Gillum by less than 0.5 percent and Abrams by less than 1.5 percent. Thus, differences in the impact of gender attitudes on evaluations of Abrams and Gillum cannot be easily attributed to candidate-specific factors such as race, partisanship, previous officeholding, challenger status (i.e., not an incumbent), and age or campaign-specific factors such as office sought, running for an open seat, year, region, opponent characteristics, and competitiveness.

To find a suitable comparison group of white women for Abrams, I identified all of the white Democratic women running for the same office (governor) who matched Abrams on party (Democratic), challenger status (nonincumbents), and competitiveness (elections decided by less than 10 percentage points). There were four white women who met these criteria: Laura Kelly (D-KS), Janet Mills (D-ME), Gretchen Whitmer (D-MI), and Molly Kelly (D-NH). All four ran against white Republican men, so they also matched Abrams on opponent race, gender, and party.

The data used in this analysis is from the 2018 CCES. The dependent variable is vote choice (0 = Dem, 1 = GOP). The key independent variables are racial resentment and sexism. Racial resentment is measured using the four-item racial resentment battery.[25] It measures beliefs about racial inequality by asking respondents to agree or disagree with statements such as "Irish, Italian, Jewish, and many other minorities overcame prejudice and worked their way up. Blacks should do the same without any special favors" and "Generations of slavery and discrimination make it difficult for Blacks to work their way out of the lower class."[26] The battery was designed to measure how much white Americans agree with the belief that racial inequality is attributable primarily to deficiencies in Black culture such as the rejection of self-reliance and hard work instead of structural causes like discrimination. Sexism is measured using a two-item battery drawn from the psychologists Peter Glick and Susan Fiske's Ambivalent Sexism Inventory (ASI), which conceptualized sexism to be rooted in resistance to changing gender norms promoted by contemporary feminism, denial of discrimination, and resentment of unearned advantages in the workplace.[27] The two items were "When women lose to men in a fair competition, they typically complain about being discriminated against" and "Feminists are making entirely reasonable demands of men." In order to assess the independent effects of racial and gender attitudes on vote choice, controls for partisanship, ideology, age, gender, education, and income are included.[28]

Figure 6.1 shows two comparisons.[29] The left panel tests the racial activation hypothesis by comparing the probability of voting for the Republican Kemp in Abrams's contest versus the Republican candidate facing the four white Democratic female gubernatorial candidates as a function of racial resentment. Racial resentment was a marginally stronger predictor of voting for Kemp (over Abrams) compared to voting for the Republican opponents of the four white Democratic women ($p = 0.08$). The right panel tests the gender activation hypothesis by comparing the probability of voting for Kemp (over Abrams) versus DeSantis (over Gillum) as a function of sexism. Sexism was a marginally stronger predictor of voting for Kemp than DeSantis ($p = 0.09$). Though the results should be read with caution since they only reach marginal levels of statistical significance, the results provide modest support for both the racial and gender activation hypotheses.

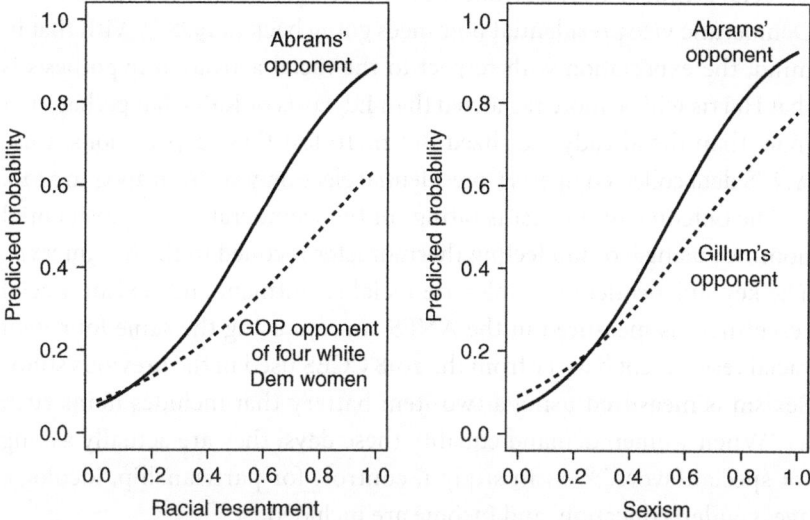

FIGURE 6.1 Predicted probability of GOP vote intention as a function of racial resentment (left panel, Abrams versus four white Democratic women) and sexism (right panel, Abrams versus Gillum).

Note: Probabilities are based on logistic regression coefficients from equations including controls for partisanship, ideology, age, gender, education, and income. For full results, see appendix table 6.1. Predicted probabilities were calculated by setting all other variables to their mean levels.

STUDY 2: KAMALA HARRIS VERSUS THE 2004–2016 DEMOCRATIC VICE PRESIDENTIAL NOMINEES

Study 2 examines the association between racial and gender attitudes and support for Harris compared to the Democratic vice presidential candidates in the previous four presidential election cycles. Since all were white men—John Edwards in 2004, Joe Biden in 2008, Biden again in 2012, and Tim Kaine in 2016—the racial and gender activation hypotheses suggest that racial attitudes and gender attitudes will be stronger predictors of support for Harris compared to any of the white Democratic men. One caveat, however, is that this assumes that all of those men are more or less equal to one another in terms of how strongly they evoke racialized and gendered thinking. The political scientist Michael Tesler demonstrates that Biden was racialized by his close association with President Obama, as racial attitudes were a stronger predictor of assessments of Biden than Democratic vice presidential nominees going back to 1988.[30] With that in mind, the expectation with respect to the racial activation hypothesis is that Harris will be more racialized than Edwards or Kaine but perhaps not more than the already racialized Biden. To test these expectations, I use ANES data collected in every presidential election year from 2004 to 2020.

The outcome of interest is ratings of the Democratic vice presidential nominee using a 0–100 feeling thermometer recoded to the 0–1 interval. The key independent variables are racial resentment and sexism. Racial resentment is measured in the ANES surveys using the same four-item racial resentment battery from the 2018 CCES used in the previous study. Sexism is measured using a two-item battery that includes items such as "When women demand equality these days, they are actually asking for special favors."[31] As in study 1, controls for partisanship, ideology, age, gender, education, and income are included.

The results shown in table 6.1 support the racial activation hypothesis but not the gender activation hypothesis. As expected, racial resentment was more strongly associated with evaluations of Harris than Edwards in 2004 ($p = .03$) and Kaine in 2016 ($p < .01$). Harris was not more racialized than Biden in 2008 or 2012, but that was not expected given that Biden was racialized by his association with Obama. Meanwhile, sexism was not significantly more strongly associated with evaluations of Harris than any of her male counterparts. Even when pooling all of the Democratic vice presidential candidates from 2004 to 2016 and comparing them to Harris, sexism's impact is not significantly stronger for Harris ($p = .17$).[32] Compared to previous vice presidential candidates, then, it appears that racial resentment had a uniquely large impact on support for Harris, while sexism did not.

STUDY 3: HARRIS VERSUS HILLARY CLINTON AND BARACK OBAMA

For another test of the racial and gender activation hypotheses, I adopt a strategy similar to that of study 1, but this time for Harris. This test will involve comparing Harris to two comparable political figures: a Black man

TABLE 6.1 (OLS) Racial resentment, sexism, and thermometer ratings of Democratic vice presidential candidates, 2004–2020, white respondents only

	2004 (Edwards)	2008 (Biden)	2012 (Biden)	2016 (Kaine)	2020 (Harris)
Racial resentment	−0.11** (0.04)	−0.16*** (0.04)	−0.19*** (0.02)	−0.09*** (0.02)	−0.20*** (0.02)
Sexism	−0.11** (0.04)	−0.05 (0.04)	−0.12*** (0.02)	−0.07* (0.03)	−0.11*** (0.02)
Partisanship (Republican)	−0.26*** (0.03)	−0.23*** (0.03)	−0.38*** (0.02)	−0.24*** (0.02)	−0.44*** (0.01)
Ideology (Conservative)	−0.21*** (0.05)	−0.17*** (0.04)	−0.30*** (0.02)	−0.21*** (0.03)	−0.26*** (0.02)
Age	0.00 (0.00)	0.00* (0.00)	0.00^ (0.00)	0.00*** (0.00)	0.00*** (0.00)
Male	−0.03 (0.02)	−0.03 (0.02)	−0.01^ (0.01)	−0.00 (0.01)	−0.01* (0.01)
Education	−0.07* (0.03)	0.03 (0.03)	−0.03^ (0.02)	0.01 (0.02)	0.01 (0.01)
Income	−0.04 (0.03)	−0.01 (0.03)	0.03^ (0.01)	−0.00 (0.02)	0.02 (0.01)
(intercept)	0.94*** (0.04)	0.80*** (0.04)	0.94*** (0.02)	0.68*** (0.02)	0.82*** (0.02)
Adjusted R²	0.41	0.35	0.55	0.37	0.68
N	561	683	2,851	1,701	4,224

Note: Entries are OLS coefficients with standard errors in parentheses. ***p < .001; **p < .01; *p < .05; ^p < .1, two-tailed tests.

Source: ANES 2004–2020.

(in order to hold race constant while assessing the influence of gender attitudes) and a white woman (in order to hold gender constant while assessing the influence of racial attitudes). Also, since this study uses measures of sexism and candidate evaluations from the same survey (the October 2020 Lucid survey), the influence of sexism on Harris is directly comparable to its influence on comparable politicians. Thus, this study addresses possible concerns that the results of study 2 are an artifact of using white men as the comparison group and that sexism is not measured consistently over time.

Since comparison figures should be of similar stature to Harris, I chose Barack Obama as her Black male comparison and Hillary Clinton as her white female comparison. In terms of name recognition, Harris is similar to Obama and Clinton. The Lucid survey found that 3.9 percent of respondents had never heard of Harris compared to 1.3 percent who had never heard of Obama and 1.6 percent who had never heard of Clinton. By comparison, 21.0 percent said they had never heard of Senator Cory Booker (D-NJ), and 9.0 percent said they had never heard of Senator Elizabeth Warren (D-MA), according to the same survey. Thus, it appears that Harris is closer in stature to Obama and Clinton than to her former colleagues in the U.S. Senate.

As mentioned earlier, the data for this investigation comes from the October 2020 Lucid survey. While the ANES uses a probability sample, Lucid does not. However, Lucid samples have been shown to be similar in quality to respected panels recruited using probability sampling such as Pew's American Trends Panel.[33] The dependent variable is ratings of Harris, Obama, and Clinton on the 0–100 feeling thermometer rescaled to the 0–1 interval. Racial resentment is measured using the same four-question battery used in studies 1 and 2. Sexism is a four-question battery consisting of the two sexism items from the 2018 CCES that were included in study 1 along with two sexism items from the 2004–2020 ANES that were used in study 2.[34] The controls from studies 1 and 2 of partisanship, ideology, age, gender, education, and income are included, as well as three variables intended to capture short-term political factors relevant to 2020: a four-category rating of Trump's performance as president, a five-category assessment of national economic conditions in the past year, and a four-category rating of fear of being infected with the coronavirus. Question wording and coding of all items can be found in the appendix.

TABLE 6.2 (OLS) Racial resentment, sexism, and thermometer ratings of Harris, Clinton, and Obama (white respondents only)

	Harris	Clinton	Obama	Difference
Racial resentment	−0.17*** (0.02)	−0.09*** (0.03)		−0.08* (0.03)
Sexism	−0.15*** (0.03)		−0.12*** (0.03)	−0.03 (0.04)
N	3,190	3,227	3,228	

Note: Entries are OLS coefficients with standard errors in parentheses.
***p < .001; *p < .05. Models include controls for partisanship, ideology, age, gender, education, income, Trump approval, economic evaluations, and coronavirus fear. See appendix table 6.2 in for full results.

Source: October 2020 Lucid survey.

Study 2 found support for the racial activation hypothesis but no support for the gender activation hypothesis for Harris in 2020. If those results hold in this study, we would expect racial attitudes to be a significantly stronger factor in evaluations of Harris compared to Clinton, while gender attitudes should not be a significantly stronger factor in evaluations of Harris compared to Obama. The results displayed in table 6.2 are consistent with that expectation.[35] Holding other factors in the model constant, moving from the least to most racially resentful respondent decreased support for Harris by about 17 percent of the scale's range. A similar shift decreased support for Clinton by only about 9 percent of the scale's range. The difference in racial resentment's impact on Harris and Clinton is statistically significant (p = .02). Turning to the impact of sexism on evaluations of Harris and Obama, it appears that sexism influences ratings of both, though slightly more for Harris. This difference, however, is not statistically significant (p = .50).

As a robustness test of these results, I leverage the fact that the Lucid survey also asked for feeling thermometer ratings of another prominent Black female political figure: former First Lady Michelle Obama.[36] When Mrs. Obama is substituted in place of Harris and compared to Clinton and President Obama, the results are similar (see appendix table 6.2 for full results). This lends reassurance that the results for Harris are not an anomaly and suggests that they apply more broadly to Black female political figures besides Harris.

STUDY 4: HARRIS EXPERIMENT

Studies 2 and 3 compare Harris to analogous white and male figures. Although this approach is widely used in previous observational studies evaluating the role of racial attitudes in evaluations Black candidates and gender attitudes in evaluations of women candidates, the two candidates being compared (e.g., Harris and Clinton or Harris and Barack Obama) are not exactly alike in every respect except their race or gender.[37] In order to improve upon the estimation of racial and gender effects, study 4 holds Harris constant and experimentally varies the salience of her race and gender.

Study 4 was a survey experiment conducted on 1,740 non-Hispanic white respondents from the Lucid panel from February 10–12, 2021. The experiment randomly assigns respondents to one of four conditions in which they read a short news article about Harris becoming vice president. Respondents in the first three conditions read a short news article that highlights an aspect of her identity by describing a political community expressing pride in her achievement: (1) Blacks, (2) women, and (3) South Asians. Respondents assigned to the fourth condition are in the control group and read a nonpolitical news article that is similar in length and formatting to the treatment conditions. Table 6.3 summarizes the key features of each condition. See the appendix for the full text of each article and the question wording for all items on the survey.

After reading the article, respondents were asked four questions about their views of Harris: a feeling thermometer rating of her, an evaluation of her likely effectiveness as vice president, the likelihood that the respondent would vote for Harris for president were she to be the Democratic nominee sometime in the near future, and an evaluation of her likely effectiveness as president. Responses to these questions are combined into a highly reliable (Cronbach's $\alpha = .95$) index running from 0 indicating the most negative evaluation of Harris to 1 indicating the most positive evaluation of Harris. Evaluations of Harris were followed by manipulation checks. To minimize the possibility of priming racial and gender attitudes before reading the news article, questions about racial attitudes and gender attitudes are asked at the end of the survey. Racial resentment was measured using the same four-question battery as the three previous studies. As an alternative measure of racial attitudes, a measure of belief in

TABLE 6.3 Summary of treatment conditions

	Blacks	Women	South Asians	Control
Headline	Harris Victory a Source of Pride for Many Blacks	Harris Victory a Source of Pride for Many Women	Harris Victory a Source of Pride for Many South Asians	Disney+ Surpasses 73 Million Subscribers Amid Streaming Boom
First paragraph	"Harris' rise was celebrated among Black political and community groups across the nation…"	"Harris' rise was celebrated among women's political and community groups across the nation…"	"Harris' rise was celebrated among South Asian political and community groups across the nation…"	Information about a nonpolitical news story
Second paragraph	Quote attributed to Congressman Hakeem Jeffries (D-NY), a member of the Congressional Black Caucus: "It sends a powerful message to Blacks everywhere that America is a land of opportunity."	Quote attributed to Congresswoman Madeleine Dean (D-PA), a member of the Congressional Women's Caucus: "It sends a powerful message to women everywhere that America is a land of opportunity."	Quote attributed to Congressman Raja Krishnamoorthi (D-IL), a member of the Congressional Asian Pacific American Caucus: "It sends a message to South Asians everywhere that America is a land of opportunity."	Information about a nonpolitical news story
Third paragraph	"As Vice President, Harris is clearly positioned to one day become president. She ran for president in 2020, but dropped out before any votes were cast in the Democratic primary. Some Democrats criticized her record as being too conservative, while Republicans criticized her during the campaign for being too liberal. Harris dismissed those charges, instead calling her approach to politics non-ideological and pragmatic."	Identical across conditions	Identical across conditions	Information about a nonpolitical news story

anti-Black stereotypes is included. Sexism is measured using the same four-question battery used in the October Lucid survey (study 3). All models include controls for partisanship, ideology, age, education, gender, and income.

Tests of the racial and gender activation hypotheses can be conducted by comparing the predictive strength of racial attitudes when Harris is framed as Black compared to when she is framed as something else (combining respondents in the Woman, South Asian, and control groups), and a similar comparison of the strength of gender attitudes can be conducted when Harris is framed as a woman compared to when she is framed as something else.[38] The results of these tests are shown in figure 6.2.[39]

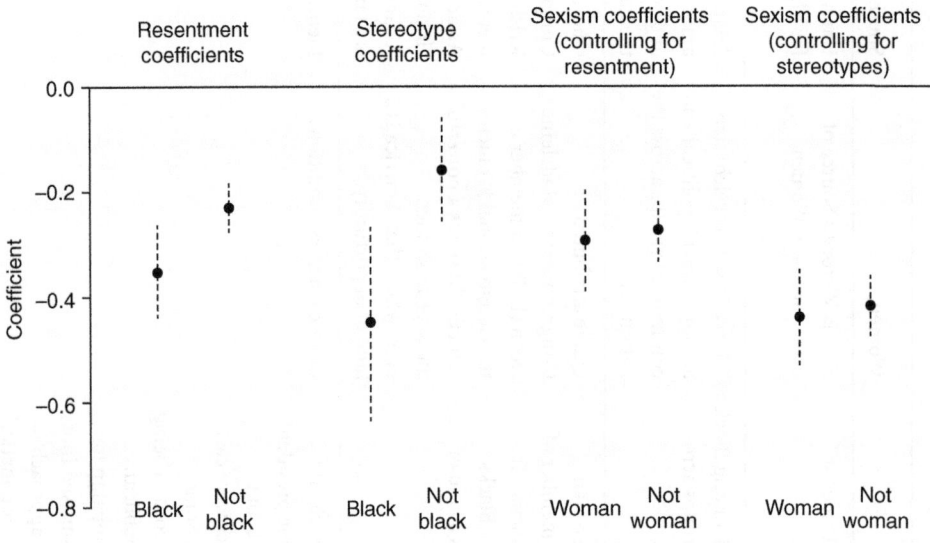

FIGURE 6.2 Association between racial and gender attitudes and evaluations of Harris by experimental condition.

Note: The points in this figure are based on OLS regression coefficients controlling for partisanship, ideology, age, education, gender, and income. Each point represents the change in Harris support (coded 0–1) associated with moving from the least to most racially conservative or gender conservative. Error bars represent 84% confidence intervals, which is consistent with a two-tailed test of overlap at $p = .05$. In other words, values are significantly different where error bars do not overlap.

Source: February 2021 Lucid survey experiment.

When examining all of the non-Black conditions as one group, racial resentment and anti-Black stereotypes are significantly weaker predictors of Harris evaluation compared to when Harris's Black identity is highlighted (p = .08 for resentment comparison and p = .05 for stereotype comparison). Meanwhile, sexism's influence on Harris evaluation does not vary much when Harris's gender is cued compared to when it is not. These findings are consistent with the earlier studies of Harris (studies 2 and 3): Harris's Black identity increases the salience of racial attitudes, but her identity as a woman does not do so for gender attitudes.

CONCLUSION

Returning to the chapter's opening question—when race and gender are available as targets for an opposing campaign, which one gets emphasized in the public mind?—we can now attempt to answer it in light of what we learned in this chapter's case studies. Of course, the chapter only examined two cases, so we cannot draw sweeping conclusions. But from those cases, we learned that race and gender mattered for Abrams, but only race mattered for Harris. Although I assumed similar reactions to Abrams and Harris based on their many similarities (shared race, gender, partisanship, and other social characteristics), there are clear differences between them that may account for the different results between them. For example: Abrams ran in a southern state, where support for traditional gender norms may be stronger than in other parts of the country;[40] Abrams is not married, while Harris is; and Abrams ran to be Georgia's chief executive while Harris ran to be Biden's second-in-command. It is possible that these differences mattered in their respective contests. In order to identify broader trends regarding how Black women are evaluated when running for high-level office, we need to observe what happens in future contests. Fortunately, the supply of candidates for the nation's highest offices seems likely to include more Black women, and so future research can shed light on how the intersectional nuances of race and gender influence campaign politics. This chapter's examination of Abrams and Harris—the first viable Black female candidates for high-level office in decades—represents a first step in that direction.

But as time goes on and we have a chance to observe more high-level Black women candidacies, I suspect that race will be the more consistent mobilizer, for two reasons. The first reason is that there are clearer electoral incentives to appealing to negative racial predispositions than negative gender predispositions. Think about it from the perspective of a gubernatorial candidate running against a Black woman in a majority-white state (which is all but four of the fifty states). The first thing to consider is simple math: about half of the electorate is women. Assuming that appealing to negative gender predispositions is unlikely to gain women's votes, the fact that half of the electorate is women disincentivizes this kind of strategy. The disincentive may be even stronger when you consider that a Black woman's opponent has race as an equally available line of attack. Consider the electoral math with respect to race. Blacks are less than half of the electorate in every state and much less than half in most states. According to the 2020 U.S. Census, Mississippi is the state with the largest Black population, at 36.6 percent. That is a large slice of the electorate but still far short of a majority. The median states with respect to their Black populations are Massachusetts (7.0 percent) and Oklahoma (7.3 percent). Another important consideration is that negative sentiments about Blacks are common among whites. Decades of survey evidence demonstrate that most whites consider inequality between whites and Blacks to be attributable mostly to the individual failings of Blacks, and a significant fraction of whites believe that Blacks are less hardworking, less intelligent, and more prone to violence than whites.[41] When the majority of the electorate is white and a large swath of that group believes that too many Blacks prefer crime, handouts, and unrestrained sex to honest living, the conditions are ripe for subtly (or perhaps not so subtly) suggesting that a Black woman running for governor represents a threat to the racial status quo.

The other reason to expect race to be mobilized more consistently is the salience of racial change versus gender change in America. The substantial racial change that has occurred in the last generation—from the country's population rapidly approaching majority-minority status, to the election of the first Black president, to the rise of the Black Lives Matter movement—has been noticed and felt by many whites in a way that has spawned a reaction against these changes. Research has demonstrated a growing sense of racial identity among whites (when the concept of racial identity had previously been thought to only be relevant among nonwhites) and that whites' racial attitudes are stronger predictors of their political views than at any point in recent decades.[42] Of course, gender norms and notions of gender identity are shifting during this time as well, but it is unlikely that these changes have been as broadly and powerfully felt as the threat to America's racial order. If this is true, then politicians facing an opponent who embodies racial and gender change will have a stronger incentive to appeal to the identity that resonates more strongly.

The argument here is not that sexism will not matter. It is just that it is likely to be more dependent on the context of a given election, such as who the target is. For instance, we know that sexism mattered more in the evaluation of Hillary Clinton in 2016 than any recent male Democratic presidential candidate.[43] It is not surprising that sexism mattered for Clinton given that she has been a lightning rod for criticism regarding her feminist persona dating back to at least the 1992 presidential campaign.[44] Her Republican critics know that casting Clinton as the symbol of everything that has gone wrong in America regarding feminism and gender norms is a sure way to fire up the Republican base. Of course, Harris also embodies gender and pursued an office that no woman had ever held before, so she may invite that criticism to a degree. However, she does not have the long history that Clinton does of symbolizing gender. The point here is that gender may be relevant in one campaign or another depending on whether the circumstances favor it. But race is likely to be a consistent factor in the campaigns of Black women given the structural reasons discussed earlier.

The case studies in the last three chapters demonstrate the power of racial appeals. One question that remains unaddressed is whether the content of rebuttals to racial appeals matters. I turn to these tests in the next two chapters to better understand how specific attacks and rebuttals work.

7

THE BOOKER EXPERIMENT

The main findings from chapters 4 and 5 on the Patrick, Ford, Booker, and Brown campaigns are that white support decreased and racial attitudes were activated after a period of unrebutted or lightly rebutted racial attacks, and white support either stabilized or even increased as rebuttals increased. However, for all of the reasons mentioned at the end of chapter 5, we cannot be sure that attacks and rebuttals caused these changes. In this chapter, I experimentally test a number of attacks against Booker in the 2013 New Jersey U.S. Senate election that likely led to racial activation. I also show how their effects change when followed by the actual rebuttal offered by the Booker campaign.

EXPERIMENTAL PROCEDURE AND DESIGN

I conducted a survey experiment from October 24 through November 4, 2014, to test the effects of frames used in the 2013 New Jersey U.S. Senate election. The study was conducted with 1,060 white adult respondents recruited by Survey Sampling International (SSI). The experiment was embedded in a survey of voters' preferences in the 2014 New Jersey U.S. Senate and Maryland gubernatorial elections, and so all respondents are residents of either New Jersey (n = 586) or Maryland (n = 474).[1]

At the beginning of the survey, respondents answered a battery of demographic and political attitudes questions. Following these questions, respondents read a short preamble to the experimental treatments that included a picture of both candidates to communicate that Booker is Black and Lonegan is white.[2] In the preamble, they were told that they were about to read about an event that happened in the New Jersey U.S. Senate election the previous year.[3]

After reading the preamble, respondents were randomly assigned to one of eight attacks or the control group that did not read about an attack. Then respondents rated Booker and Lonegan on feeling thermometers. After this first round of ratings, respondents then read a rebuttal to the attack. Next, respondents offered a second round of Booker and Lonegan feeling thermometer ratings. Finally, respondents answered the racial resentment battery and manipulation check questions regarding the content of their assigned treatment and Booker and Lonegan's race.

ATTACKS AND THEIR EFFECTS

For now, I focus on the attack treatments and their effects.[4] To identify a set of racializing frames, I turn to the themes identified by the existing racial communication literature outlined in chapter 2. From there, I identified attacks from Booker's 2013 contest that were similar to the themes identified in the literature as likely to racialize the target candidate.

1. *Associate the candidate with a racial constituency.* One example would be the "joke" that was posted to Lonegan's campaign Twitter account during the final Democratic primary debate on August 8. The tweet read, "Just leaked—Cory Booker's foreign policy debate prep notes," accompanied by a map of Newark with its different neighborhoods labeled as "West Africa, Guyana, Portugal, Brazil, Middle East, Afghanistan, Pakistan, plus Bangladesh and Trinidad."

2. *Attack the candidate on a racialized policy area such as crime or welfare.* Lonegan frequently criticized Booker for Newark's high crime rate during the campaign (see chapter 2 for more details).

3. *Attack the candidate for having stereotypically negative traits such as being prone to criminality or sexual deviance.* Booker was criticized for his Twitter correspondence with an Oregon stripper after facing earlier speculation about his sexuality.
4. *Link the candidate to President Obama.* One of Lonegan's main lines of attack was that Booker was a disciple of President Obama.

A fifth type of attack has been used against Booker and other Black candidates (like Obama and Abrams), which suggests that there may a racial dimension to it. However, since previous research has not tested whether this attack has a racializing effect, I have no strong prior expectation that it will be an effective racial prime:

5. *Call the candidate a celebrity, suggesting either that the candidate does not have any "substance" or that the candidate does not have the appropriately modest values of "everyday" people.* Lonegan claimed that Booker sees himself as having more in common with Hollywood celebrities and technology moguls than he does with ordinary New Jersey voters.

With these attacks in mind, I designed the treatments, which are listed in table 7.1. The first five attacks correspond with the four attack types described earlier (racial constituency, racialized policy, stereotypically negative traits, and link to Obama), with one attack combining the racial constituency and racialized policy types (see the third row of table 7.1, *black hole*). The expectation was that these attacks would racialize Booker. I did not have a strong expectation that the sixth attack—calling Booker a celebrity—would racialize him, though I thought it was possible given its earlier usage against Black candidates. In addition to the attack types described here, I also designed two placebo attacks that I did not expect to prime racial attitudes—one criticizing Booker's patriotism and another criticizing his performance in office. While these two attacks were designed as placebos, it is possible that they might activate racial thinking based on the notion that they suggest the candidate is an "outsider" (as in the patriotism attack) or is incompetent (as in the performance attack), both potentially anti-Black themes.[5] Thus, it is possible that the placebo messages will racialize somewhat. However, the expectation is that they will not racialize as strongly as the first five attacks.

Before I test the racializing effects of each attack, I start by showing the overall effects of each attack. In other words, how much of a hit did

TABLE 7.1 Attack treatments

Type	Label	Wording
Racial constituency	Twitter	Steve Lonegan, who ran against Newark Mayor Cory Booker, criticized Booker by **posting a map on Twitter that labeled Newark's neighborhoods as foreign countries, mostly African or Muslim.**
Racialized policy—crime	Crime	Steve Lonegan, who ran against Newark Mayor Cory Booker, criticized Booker by **saying that violent crime and murders have gone up in Newark for five years in a row.**
Combination of racial constituency and racialized policy—taxes	Black hole	Steve Lonegan, who ran against Newark Mayor Cory Booker, criticized Booker by **saying that money from suburban and rural taxpayers gets poured into the big black hole of Newark.**
Trait—sexual deviance	Stripper	Steve Lonegan, who ran against Newark Mayor Cory Booker, criticized Booker by **saying Booker had a brief online flirtation with a stripper.**
Link to Obama	Obama	Steve Lonegan, who ran against Newark Mayor Cory Booker, criticized Booker by **saying that Booker and President Obama are one in [sic] the same.**
Celebrity	Hollywood	Steve Lonegan, who ran against Newark Mayor Cory Booker, criticized Booker by **saying Booker spends too much time attending fundraisers in California with Hollywood celebrities.**
Placebo	Patriotism	Steve Lonegan, who ran against Newark Mayor Cory Booker, criticized Booker by **saying Booker had no confidence in America and didn't seem proud of his country.**
Placebo	Results	Steve Lonegan, who ran against Newark Mayor Cory Booker, criticized Booker by **saying Booker failed to deliver results while in office.**
Control	Control	[No attack]

Booker take from each of these attacks? To determine this, I calculated the Booker-minus-Lonegan feeling thermometer score (hereafter called the Booker score) for each attack minus the same score in the control group.[6] To see how this works, the mean Booker score in the control group was 0.11 on a −1 (most anti-Booker) to 1 (most pro-Booker) scale. This score is on the pro-Booker side of the scale, as one might expect given that the respondents are from the two Democratic states of New Jersey and Maryland. The mean Booker score among those who saw the crime attack was 0.04, a −0.07 difference compared to the mean Booker score in the control group. That score is plotted in figure 7.1, along with the same score for each attack. Negative values indicate that the attack hurt Booker, while positive values indicate that the attack actually improved perceptions of Booker (at least relative to Lonegan). Figure 7.1 shows some variation in the strength of attacks, as *Hollywood* (−0.08), *results* (−0.07), *crime* (−0.07), and *Obama* (−0.06) hurt Booker the most while *black hole* (0.02) and *Twitter* (0.00) appear to help Booker slightly. However, too much should not be made of these results, since they are not statistically significant.

Overall, the attacks do not appear to damage Booker much, but this may obscure important variation in the effectiveness of the attacks. If racially resentful respondents punish Booker after the attack and racially sympathetic respondents support Booker, that would suggest that the

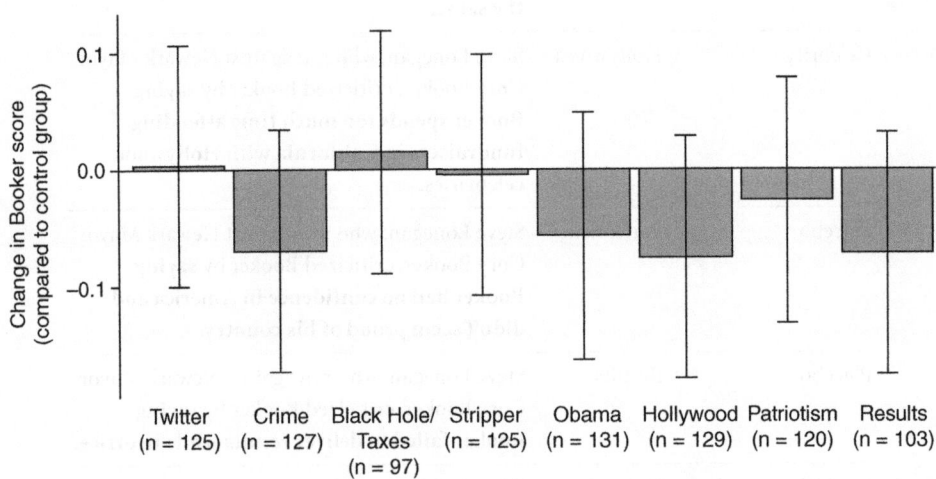

FIGURE 7.1 Main effects of each attack, white New Jersey and Maryland respondents.

attack had a racial priming effect even though the net effect of the attack is essentially zero. This is the main question of interest in this section: Did the attack make it more likely that respondents would bring their racial attitudes to bear on their evaluations of Booker?

To answer this question, I estimate the influence of racial resentment on the Booker score for each attack compared to racial resentment's influence in the control group. The first result to report is that attack effects differed substantially across the two states. For white New Jersey respondents, none of the attacks boosted racial resentment's impact compared to the control group.[7] This is because Booker was already racialized in the control group: racially resentful whites were much more likely to give Booker a lower rating than racially sympathetic whites.[8] In other words, no attack racialized Booker more than he already was to begin with. This makes sense: after two consecutive years on the ballot, Booker was a known public figure, and white New Jersey respondents' impressions of Booker had already been formed. For white Maryland respondents, however, Booker was an unknown commodity. As a result, racial resentment did not predict evaluations of Booker among respondents in the control group (b = −0.12, not statistically significant). So, would attacks significantly change how Maryland respondents evaluated Booker?

To answer this, figure 7.2 shows the predicted Booker score for white Maryland respondents at each point on the racial resentment scale compared to the predicted score at that same point for the control group. To account for the influence of competing nonracial predispositions, the scores were generated based on models that control for partisanship and ideology.[9] The scores were calculated by setting partisanship and ideology to their mean levels. Since I expect racial resentment to be primed for the first five attacks, I expect negative sloping lines indicating that as racial resentment goes up, evaluations of Booker go down. I have no expectation for the Hollywood attack, while I expect flat lines indicating no change in racial resentment's effect for the two placebo attacks.

The results are generally in line with these expectations. Of the five attacks that were expected to prime racial resentment (*Twitter*, *crime*, *black hole*, *stripper*, and *Obama*), all but *crime* do (p < .05 for the four attacks).[10] Pooling all five frames together, exposure to these cues magnifies the impact of racial resentment, as indicated by the negative-sloping solid line in the bottom right panel (p = .01). Meanwhile, *Hollywood* did not have a

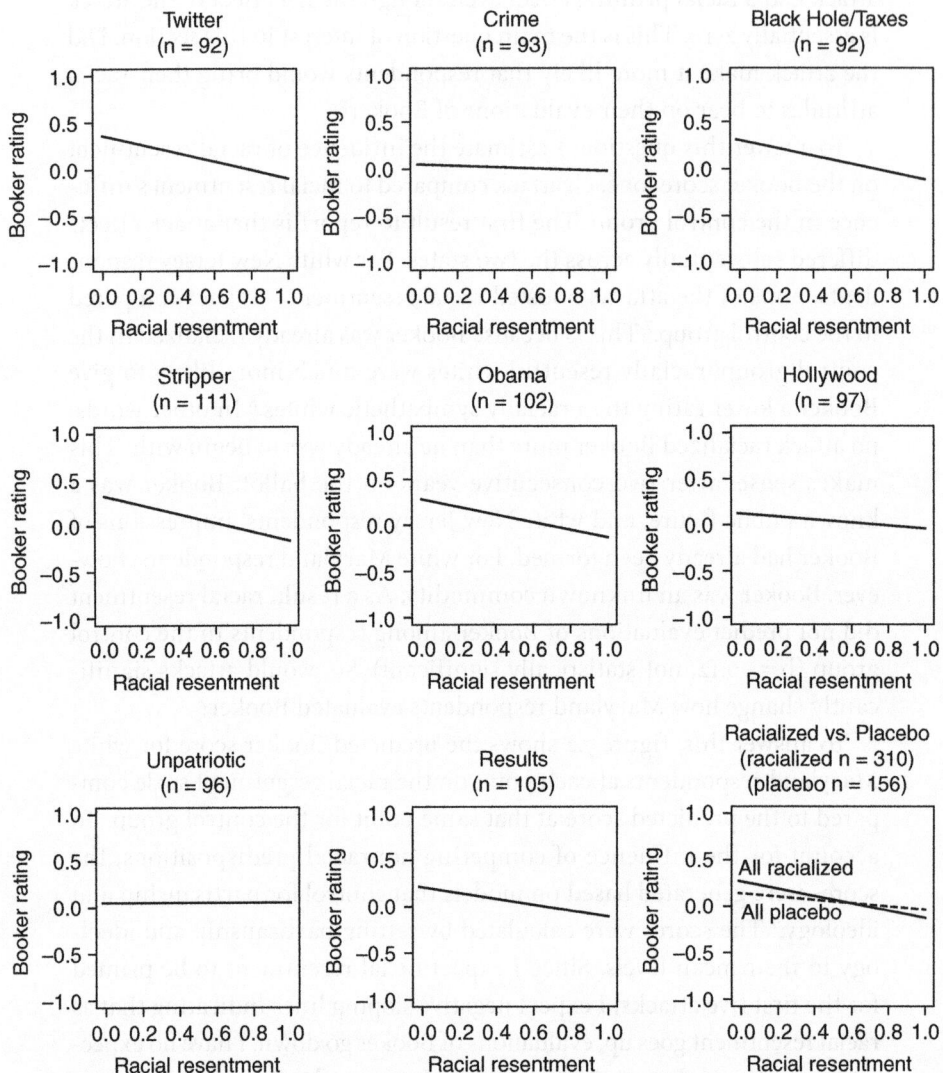

FIGURE 7.2 Impact of attacks on evaluations of Booker as a function of racial resentment, white Maryland respondents only.

significant priming effect. Of the two placebo attacks for which I did not expect to see a significant priming effect (*patriotism* and *results*), we see one for *results* (p = .03) but not for *patriotism*. This is in line with earlier speculation that either of these placebo messages might still racialize. However, pooling the two placebo frames together, we see a shallow-sloping dashed line in the bottom right panel that does not represent a statistically significant priming effect.

In sum, I conclude that attacks on racialized themes that frequently arose during the Booker campaign generally had negative racial effects even after accounting for the influence of competing nonracial predispositions. Furthermore, these negative racial effects were usually not replicated for attacks on less racialized themes. This lends support to earlier theorizing that racialized attacks are responsible for the racialization of Booker and other candidates who faced similar attacks that were documented in chapters 4 and 5.

REBUTTALS

Following exposure to an attack, each respondent read a rebuttal that corresponded to the rebuttal types detailed in chapter 3, based on existing studies of rebuttals[11] and a related literature on "political accounts."[12] Since my focus is on rebuttals to racial attacks, I only consider the rebuttals to the six attacks that were either hypothesized to have a negative racial effect or actually had one—*Twitter, crime, black hole, stripper, Obama,* and *results.*

I test five different rebuttal types that Booker used to counter these six attacks:

1. *Charge the attacker with being overly "negative."* For example, Booker's campaign manager responded to the "Twitter map" controversy (simulated in treatment 1 of the experiment) by calling the tweet "inappropriate, offensive, and fundamentally out of step."
2. *Call the opponent's attack "racist," suggest it had "racial overtones,"* etc. One Booker surrogate replied to the Twitter map controversy by saying that "such racially charged rhetoric has no place in our public discourse."
3. *Deny the attacker's charge.* A candidate usually does this by saying that they did not do what their opponent accuses them of doing or that they are not what their opponent accuses them of being. Booker countered accusations of being soft on crime by saying that crime statistics show that violent crime had actually gone down during this tenure as Newark's mayor.

4. *Counterattack: turn the attack back on the opponent.* This rebuttal involves the target attacking his opponent on the very same issue on which the target is being attacked. Booker responded to Lonegan's claim that tax dollars were unfairly allocated to Newark at the expense of suburban and rural parts of the state by attacking Lonegan for running up a large budget deficit while mayor of a suburban town and seeking financial assistance from New Jersey's governor.

5. *Justify: explain why your actions were reasonable or even necessary.* In response to criticism of his Twitter communication with a stripper, Booker surrogates argued that such communication was not unusual as Booker interacts with a wide range of people on Twitter.

I used these examples from the real campaign to design the rebuttal treatments. Table 7.2 shows the attacks in the left column and their corresponding rebuttals in the right column. Note that half of the respondents who were assigned to the Twitter attack were assigned to the *negative* rebuttal, while the other half were assigned to the *racial* rebuttal. All of the respondents who received the *crime* attack were assigned to the same *denial*, all respondents who received the *black hole* attack were assigned to the same *counterattack*, and so on.

EXPECTATIONS

The standing prediction in the racial priming literature is that calling attention to the racial nature of the appeal (or *racial*, as it is referred to in this experiment) is the most effective rebuttal strategy. Evidence in support of this claim comes from the political scientist Tali Mendelberg, who used survey data from the 1988 presidential campaign to show that racial attitudes had a significantly weaker effect on candidate evaluations during the last phase of the campaign, in which the Horton ads were explicitly called anti-Black message by leading Democrats, a charge that was widely disseminated by the media.[13] The reason for this weakening racial effect, according to this account, is that the rebuttal "uncovered" the racial content of the Horton ad, which led whites to reject the message, since it violated a widely held norm against openly racist derogation. The

TABLE 7.2 Rebuttals

Attack	Rebuttal
(Twitter) Steve Lonegan, who ran against Newark Mayor Cory Booker, criticized Booker by **posting a map on Twitter that labeled Newark's neighborhoods as foreign countries, mostly African or Muslim.**	(Negative) As the campaign went on, some said Lonegan's criticism was **inappropriate**. [half of the sample that received the Twitter map attack receives this rebuttal](Racial) As the campaign went on, some said Lonegan's criticism was **racist**. [the other half of the sample that received the Twitter map attack receives this rebuttal]
(Crime) Steve Lonegan, who ran against Newark Mayor Cory Booker, criticized Booker by **saying that violent crime and murders have gone up in Newark for five years in a row.**	(Denial) As the campaign went on, some said Lonegan's comment was **misleading because murders and assaults have actually gone down.**
(Black hole) Steve Lonegan, who ran against Newark Mayor Cory Booker, criticized Booker by **saying that money from suburban and rural taxpayers gets poured into the big black hole of Newark.**	(Counterattack) As the campaign went on, some said Lonegan's comment was misleading **because Lonegan recently sought financial assistance for his suburban town from New Jersey's governor.**
(Stripper) Steve Lonegan, who ran against Newark Mayor Cory Booker, criticized Booker by **saying Booker had a brief online flirtation with a stripper.**	(Justify) As the campaign went on, some said Lonegan's comment was **misleading because Booker talks to people from all walks of life on Twitter.**
(Obama) Steve Lonegan, who ran against Newark Mayor Cory Booker, criticized Booker by **saying that Booker and President Obama are one in [sic] the same.**	(Denial) As the campaign went on, some said Lonegan's comment was **misleading because Booker is not Obama; Booker has his own record.**
(Didn't deliver) Steve Lonegan, who ran against Newark Mayor Cory Booker, criticized Booker by **saying Booker failed to deliver results while in office.**	(Denial) As the campaign went on, some said Lonegan's comment was **misleading because businesses relocated to Newark under Booker's leadership.**
(Control) No attack	No rebuttal

rebuttal should work even among racially resentful whites, since supposedly they too have internalized this norm. Thus, a message that would have worked as long as it remained implicitly racial will no longer do so once it is uncovered as an explicitly negative reference to Blacks. From this perspective, racial rebuttals work precisely because they highlight the racial character of the implicit message.

On the other hand, there are reasons to believe that *racial* may be ineffective or even counterproductive. One reason for skepticism comes from scholars in the "deracialization" tradition, who argue that Black candidates who avoid explicit discussion of race stand the greatest chance of success.[14] A deracialized style is considered beneficial because it attempts to minimize the salience of racial considerations as much as possible. Thus, directly challenging an implicit appeal as racist makes little sense because it reinforces considerations that the candidate should be trying to suppress. From this perspective, racial rebuttals will not work because either whites may not find charges of racism to be credible or the norm of equality no longer acts as a constraint on their response, a hypothesis that is supported by recent research.[15]

Although *racial* has received the most attention in the racial priming literature, other rebuttal types suggest alternative mechanisms for explaining whether citizens revise their evaluations of public officials who are accused of wrongdoing. One possible strategy is to *justify*: accept ownership of the action but explain that there are credible reasons for it. For example, Deval Patrick defended his past legal defense of criminal suspects by arguing that the fairness of the American legal system requires that even unsavory defendants deserve legal defense.

Evidence consistent with the notion that *justify* can be persuasive is found in the political accounts literature developed by the political scientist Kathleen McGraw, who demonstrated the effective use of politicians' reason- and fact-based justifications for their controversial actions. According to McGraw, a justification does not deny responsibility for the action. Instead, "a justification focuses on the outcome and claims that contrary to accusations, the consequences are not so undesirable and therefore that less or no blame is warranted."[16] Thus, a successful justification should lead to a two-step inferential process. First, if the citizen is satisfied with the justification, it should lead to positive reevaluations of the outcome in light of the public official reframing its consequences in a more positive manner. Second, as a result of this reframing, the citizen may credit the public official for the outcome. This inferential process is quite different than the one implied by *racial*. While *racial* is theorized to work because it "unmasks" the racial intent of the attack, *justify* suggests that relevant and credible information can counteract an attack's harmful effects.

The other rebuttals tested in this experiment have been the subject of less theorizing and empirical testing than *racial* and *justify*. However, expectations can be derived from the literature on counterframing.[17] Earlier literature on framing found that exposure to a frame—say, that the Ku Klux Klan should be able to hold a rally because it is entitled to freedom of speech—elevates the importance citizens place on the framed consideration in political decision making.[18] However, the counterframing literature argues that framing effects weaken when pitted against a counterframe that emphasizes a different consideration. For racial attacks, it could be that rebuttals that emphasize compelling nonracial considerations (such as an opponent's negativity or hypocrisy) shift focus away from the racial considerations that were primed by the attack, thereby improving evaluations of the targeted candidate. Thus, the prediction here is that *negative* and *counterattack* will improve evaluations of the targeted candidate.

While *denial* seeks to refute the original charge rather than shift attention away from the original attack, the political scientists Stephen Craig, Paulina Rippere, and Marissa Grayson found that it improved evaluations of the target.[19] The authors tested this rebuttal in the context of a candidate (of undetermined race but likely assumed to be white) attacked for using the perks of elected office to enrich himself and his allies. They theorize that *denial* probably works better in situations in which the candidate is attacked for accusations of personal misconduct (like the one they tested) than for charges that are political in nature. In this chapter, Booker uses *denial* to rebut charges that violent crime has gone up in Newark, that he is a stand-in for President Obama, and that he failed to deliver results as mayor, charges that seem political in nature. Since existing research offers limited guidance for the scenario tested in this experiment, no prediction is offered regarding the effect of *denial*.

RESULTS

Turning now to the results, I pool New Jersey and Maryland respondents together (n = 1,060), since their rebuttal responses did not systematically differ.[20] I determine the effect of the rebuttal by calculating the change between postattack and postrebuttal Booker-minus-Lonegan feeling thermometer scores. It is measured by (1) calculating the Booker-Lonegan feeling thermometer difference after the attack, (2) calculating the same difference after the rebuttal, and (3) calculating the difference between the second quantity and the first quantity and dividing by 100 to map on the −2 to 2 scale. Positive values indicate that the rebuttal helped Booker, zero indicates that the rebuttal had no effect, and negative values indicate that the rebuttal backfired against Booker.[21]

Figure 7.3 shows the pro-Booker shift associated with each rebuttal. To aid in interpreting the magnitude of the rebuttal effects, the average attack resulted in a Booker-Lonegan difference that was 0.04 lower than the Booker-Lonegan difference in the control group. Therefore, rebuttal effects can be interpreted as the amount of the 0.04 hit that Booker gets back by using the rebuttal. Contrary to expectations, *racial* and *justify* do not improve evaluations of Booker. Instead, *negative*, *denial* (crime), and *denial* (didn't deliver) are the only rebuttals that leave Booker better off

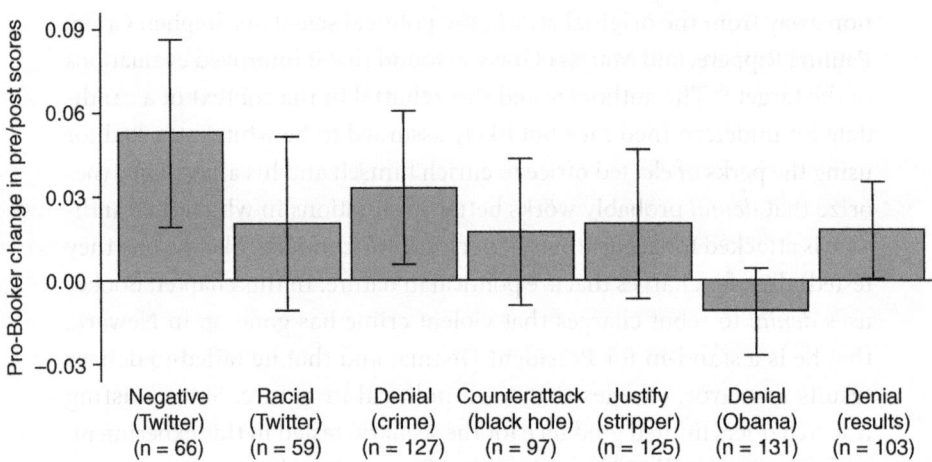

FIGURE 7.3 Rebuttal main effects, white New Jersey and Maryland respondents.

after the rebuttal than after the attack. Another notable finding is that none of the rebuttals leave Booker worse off. This suggests that Booker made a mistake by allowing a long stretch of his 2013 campaign go by without addressing racial attacks (see chapter 5). Some responses might not have helped him, but none would have hurt him.

Aside from the main effects of each rebuttal, the other important question to answer is their effects on racially resentful and sympathetic subgroups. Recall from chapter 5 that pooling across the Patrick, Ford, and Booker campaigns, rebuttals appear to have a positive effect among racially sympathetic whites while having no effect among racially moderate and racially resentful whites. Consistent with the analysis from earlier chapters, I divide the sample into thirds by racial resentment and compare Booker-minus-Lonegan feeling thermometer scores before the attack and after the rebuttal among low-, medium-, and high-racial-resentment respondents.[22] Since dividing the sample into thirds renders the sample sizes for each individual rebuttal too small for useful analysis, I pool all of the rebuttals together. This will allow for another test of which racial resentment subgroup is responsive to rebuttals in general. In the next chapter, I conduct another experiment with a large enough sample to test rebuttal effects by racial resentment subgroup for each rebuttal.

To assess the rebuttal effects, I compare Booker's standing before an attack to after a rebuttal among each of the three subgroups. Fortunately, the control group in the attack stage of the experiment did not receive an attack and therefore serves as the useful "before attack" baseline. Table 7.3 shows the Booker-minus-Lonegan feeling thermometer scores before an attack (for the control group) and after a rebuttal (pooling across the different types) for each racial resentment subgroup. Positive values in the first two columns represent Booker's feeling thermometer advantage over Lonegan, while negative values represent Booker's feeling thermometer deficit. The third column shows the difference between the Booker score before the attack and after the rebuttal. In other words, this column compares Booker's standing before he is hit with any negative information to after he's been put through an attack-rebuttal cycle. If rebuttals help Booker among the racially sympathetic and hurt him among the racially resentful, we would expect to see a positive difference among low-racial-resentment respondents and a negative difference among high-racial-resentment respondents in the fifth column.

TABLE 7.3 Booker-minus-Lonegan feeling thermometer scores before attack, after attack, and after rebuttal, by racial resentment level

	Before attack (control group)	After rebuttal	Difference: After rebuttal minus before attack
Low (0.50 <= RR)	0.24*** (0.05)	0.28*** (0.02)	0.04 (0.06)
Medium (0.50 > RR <= 0.69)	0.06 (0.06)	0.06* (0.03)	0.00 (0.07)
High (RR > 0.69)	−0.04 (0.07)	−0.09*** (0.03)	−0.05 (0.08)

***$p < .001$; *$p < .05$.

This is indeed what we observe. The third column shows that Booker emerges from an attack-rebuttal cycle 0.04 more favorably among low-racial-resentment respondents than he did before being hit with an attack, while he comes out 0.05 less favorably among high-racial-resentment respondents. Since this is a between-subjects comparison, standard errors are larger, and therefore the estimates are not statistically significant. But their direction is consistent with the findings from the pooled case studies: Booker is rewarded among the racially sympathetic and punished among the racially resentful.

CONCLUSION

What has this experiment taught us? The results point to the likelihood that the racial activation effects found in the case studies of Patrick, Ford, Booker, and Brown were indeed *caused by* the racial attacks. One of the limitations of the case studies was that they could not conclusively determine whether racial activation was caused by the racial attacks because the observational nature of the data did not allow for other possible causes to be ruled out. However, the fact that most attacks predicted to racialize Booker did, while the placebo attacks generally did not, suggests that the nonracial negative attacks that surely happened at the same time as the racial attacks did not cause Booker to be racialized. Instead, it was the frequent association of each candidate with a racialized theme that caused white voters to bring their racial attitudes to bear on their vote.

Another notable finding is the lack of racial priming effects in New Jersey and the abundance of them in Maryland. Such sharp differences between the two states were not expected, as the expectation before the experiment was that awareness of Booker would be more evenly distributed across the two states. It turns out that Booker was already racialized among New Jersey respondents: racial resentment predicted opposition to Booker (controlling for partisanship and ideology) even in the control group, and no additional information provided by the attacks increased racial resentment's negative effect on Booker support. It is unclear how much of the racialization found in 2014 was the residue of Booker's 2013 racialization. It is worth noting, however, that no high-profile racialized incident occurred during Booker's 2014 reelection battle with Republican Jeff Bell, which suggests that 2013 made a lasting mark on Booker's image. This conflicts with the political scientist Zoltan Hajnal's finding that incumbency reduces the weight that white citizens put on racial considerations when evaluating Black mayors.[23] Incumbency did not appear to have the same effect for Booker.

Meanwhile, Booker may as well have been a fictional candidate to the Maryland respondents. The finding that racial resentment did not predict negative Booker support in the control condition has interesting implications. One is that the racialization shown in the case study chapters likely did not occur simply because voters learned that one of the candidates running was Black. If knowledge of the candidate's race was all that was needed to activate racial resentment, we would expect Booker to have been racialized in the control group, since respondents in that group were still shown a picture of the two candidates. That did not occur. Second, this finding, plus the real-world finding from chapter 5 that Booker was not racialized in early September 2013, suggests that Black candidates have a honeymoon period in which they are known but not yet racialized. That means that campaign communications may still play an important role in Black campaigns. This is contrary to the "chronic accessibility" account of Barack Obama's 2008 presidential campaign offered by the political scientists Michael Tesler and David Sears. They argue that simply by being Black, Obama made racial considerations chronically accessible and that therefore the link between racial attitudes and the vote should be less dependent on situational cues like race-oriented campaign communications.[24] Of course, it is likely that Obama is a much more powerful racial symbol in the minds of white voters than Booker, and so perhaps chronic accessibility is more likely to operate at the presidential level. Nevertheless, the findings from this chapter suggest that a Black Senate candidate does not automatically evoke racial thinking and therefore may have more success in shaping how he is perceived by white voters.

In tests of various rebuttals, an important finding is the lack of an effect for the racial rebuttal. This is a longstanding hypothesis in the racial priming literature, but the results presented in this chapter do not support this claim. However, we do not know exactly why this is. Is it attributable to opposition from racially resentful whites? Or is there a lack of support for it across the racial resentment spectrum? I answer these questions with the help of a much larger sample in another experiment described in the next chapter.

The analysis presented in this chapter is not without its limitations. As mentioned earlier, the treatments are rather weak. They are very brief written snippets that may not register in the same way that real-life racial attacks, with the help of evocative imagery, often do. On one hand, presenting the attacks and rebuttals the way it was done in this experiment may actually be more realistic in the sense that people often learn about attacks in campaigns from reading a brief description in a news story or hearing a sound bite on television. However, would rebuttals work the same way in response to a more substantial attack—one that includes racially loaded imagery on a matter of substantial importance? Since attacks differ in terms of their presentation and effectiveness, it is possible that different rebuttals work for different types of attacks. Put another way, perhaps dismissing the frivolous Twitter map attack as overly negative may be more effective than using the same response for the weightier charge of being tied to a convicted rapist, as Deval Patrick was. Maybe in Patrick's case, a justification would fare better, as findings from earlier studies suggest.

Another limitation is that the rebuttals respond to different attacks, which was done to replicate the way they were used in the real campaign. However, this makes it hard to cleanly test their effects versus one another because they all start at different baselines (since they are paired with different attacks). A better test would compare their effects in response to the same attack. With these limitations in mind, I designed another set of experiments that would hopefully provide a better test of rebuttal strategies. I report the results of these experiments in the next chapter.

8

THE CRIMINAL PARDON EXPERIMENT

To build on the analysis from the previous chapter, I tested seven different rebuttals to the same attack in a set of four survey experiments from 2011–2014. One innovation of these experiments is that I manipulate the race of the target candidate to be either Black or white, which allows for a test of how much attacks hurt and rebuttals help Black candidates both in absolute terms and relative to an identical white candidate. These are informative tests that are not often found in the racial politics literature.

REBUTTAL STRATEGIES AND HYPOTHESES

In this chapter, I test seven rebuttal strategies. I start with the two that have received the most attention from previous research: *racial* and *justify*. As outlined in the previous chapter, both are expected to improve the target's standing, but for different reasons.[1] For *racial*, the key mechanism is norms. Whites will respond positively to rebuttals that "unmask" messages that violate widely held norms. For *justify*, the mechanism is information. Whites will change their minds when presented with relevant and credible information.

A third rebuttal type involves a more nuanced type of racial response—one that combines racial and compelling nonracial themes. In this experiment, this strategy is conceptualized as *justify + racial*, a hybrid response that combines a justification with a racial reference. One example of this response was Barack Obama's "A More Perfect Union" speech from March 2008, in which he addressed the controversial videos that emerged of his former pastor Jeremiah Wright denouncing the United States. In the speech, Obama tried to *justify* the origins of his relationship with Wright and how his former pastor, like many people, has strengths as well as shortcomings. Akin to *racial*, Obama acknowledged the existence of white racism in American society in a way that many observers considered unusual for a presidential candidate at the time.[2]

By disaggregating racial messages into subtypes based on their content, the experiment in this chapter builds on the work of the political scientist Christopher Stout, who distinguishes between negative racial appeals—ones that "are generally devoid of substantive policy proposals and usually take the form of an attack on a political opponent, the media, or a supposed ally"—and positive racial appeals—ones that "either advance black policy interests or highlight the candidate's connection to the black community without attacking outside political players or institutions."[3] In light of Stout's finding that white voters are amenable to racial messages that incorporate compelling nonracial themes, I expect *justify + racial* to improve evaluations of the target. The mechanism implied here is tone. Charges of racism may seem overly harsh to many whites, but relevant and credible information may soften the tone of *racial* and therefore make it more persuasive.[4]

In addition to providing a test of a more nuanced style of racial response, *justify + racial* also allows for a test of whether the effects of *racial* and *justify* are conditional on the other. In other words, it allows for an assessment of whether *racial*'s effect is conditional on it being packaged with a compelling nonracial consideration such as *justify*, in line with Stout's finding that racial messages that focus only on highlighting racism are less effective than other types of racial messages. It also allows for a test of whether *justify*'s effect is conditional on it being strictly nonracial.

The fourth and fifth rebuttal types tested in this experiment are *negative* and *counterattack*. Predictions derived from the counterframing literature[5] suggest that both would be effective, since both shift focus away from the racial considerations that were primed by the attack, but the test in chapter 7 found that while *negative* worked in response to the "Twitter map" attack, *counterattack* did not work in response to the "black hole" attack regarding Newark's relationship to the suburban and rural parts of New Jersey. Of course, the test in chapter 7 is not conclusive because the effect of a rebuttal is likely to be influenced by the nature of the attack it is responding to. This chapter provides a better test, since they are both responding to the same attack.

The sixth and seventh rebuttal types were defined in chapter 3 but not tested in chapter 7: *counterimaging* and *distract*. *Counterimaging* is when the target uses the attack as an opportunity to portray themselves as strong on the very issue they are being attacked on, such as how Deval Patrick responded to charges of being soft on crime by highlighting his experience as a federal prosecutor. The counterframing perspective suggests that this message shifts attention to nonracial considerations, but it does so in a specific way—by offering a counterstereotypical message. Previous studies find that counterstereotypical messages can positively affect white voters' evaluations of Black candidates.[6] Thus, the prediction here is that *counterimaging* will be effective. *Distract* involves pivoting away from the attack toward more favorable topics, such as how Barack Obama addressed racially tinged attacks by instead refocusing discussion on the economy. From the counterframing perspective, *distract* may be effective, as it focuses attention on nonracial considerations.

As in previous chapters, in addition to observing rebuttals' main effects I also examine how rebuttals work among high-, medium-, and low-racial-resentment subgroups. Studies in the racial priming literature emphasize that high-racial-resentment respondents are particularly receptive to racial attacks.[7] We know much less about whether rebuttals can undo the damage done by racial attacks among racially resentful respondents. Earlier chapters suggest that they do not, and this chapter offers another test of rebuttal effectiveness by racial resentment level.

EFFECTS OF CANDIDATE RACE ON REBUTTAL EFFICACY

Of course, the content of the rebuttal itself is only one variable that influences how effective it will be. By randomly assigning respondents to either a Black or white target issuing the same rebuttal, I test how the race of the messenger also influences how rebuttals are evaluated. This approach builds on rare studies on the effects of source cues.[8] Such studies have found instances in which messages offered by Black politicians are received less positively. For example, the political scientists Thomas Nelson, Kira Sanbonmatsu, and Harwood McClerking found that Black elites' charges of racism are perceived as less credible than the same charge made by white elites.[9] One implication of this finding is that since many observers may not view implicit appeals as being racial in nature, the effectiveness of the racial rebuttal hinges on whether the accusation of racial intent is perceived as credible. If Black claims of racism are perceived as less credible, then the racial rebuttal is also less likely to be effective when used by a Black candidate. This hypothesis will be tested in this chapter.

Other research suggests that the rhetorical penalty suffered by Black candidates extends beyond racial messages. Studies of negative advertising and ambiguous rhetoric find that white candidates enjoy greater payoffs from using these nonracial communication strategies.[10] The random assignment of respondents to a Black or white target allows us to see if Black candidates' rebuttals of all types will be less effective than white candidates' rebuttals.

In addition to observing how candidate race influences the main effects of the rebuttals, the behavior of high-, medium-, and low-racial-resentment respondents will also be examined. Of particular interest is whether rebuttals can work for Black candidates even among racially resentful whites. Previous research on white candidates finds that the extent to which they are evaluated through a racial lens depends on the nature of the campaign communications environment.[11] So presumably, if attacks can activate high-racial-resentment respondents, perhaps rebuttals can deactivate them. Research on Black candidates, however, suggests that by virtue of their race alone, racial considerations are "chronically accessible" to whites when evaluating Black candidates.[12] The political scientist Zoltan Hajnal, in a study of white attitudes toward Black mayoral candidates, finds that "black challengers can and usually do try to counter uncertainty surrounding their candidacies by running 'deracialized' or pro-white campaigns, but white voters tend to ignore these campaign statements, which they perceive as having little credibility."[13] This suggests that high-racial-resentment whites who respond negatively to racial attacks may not be very responsive to the rebuttals of Black candidates. Optimism regarding the potential to defuse the power of racial attacks among the racially resentful, then, is likely to apply more to white candidates than Black candidates. This is another hypothesis tested in this chapter.

SAMPLE

To test all of the hypotheses described in the previous section, I conducted four internet survey experiments from 2011 to 2014. The first two, conducted in December 2011 and March 2013, used a convenience sample of white respondents from Amazon.com's Mechanical Turk (MTurk).[14] The second two, conducted in February 2014 and December 2014, used samples provided by Survey Sampling International (SSI) that were drawn to match the U.S. white adult population.[15] Although the details of the design of each experiment differ in some respects, the core elements of the design are the same across all four experiments.[16] Results from the four experiments were substantively similar, so the four samples are combined in the following analyses.[17] Combining the samples yields a total of 3,482 white respondents.

METHOD

The experiments simulated an attack-rebuttal episode in a fictitious U.S. Senate campaign. Respondents were randomized into sixteen conditions: 1 (attack) × 8 (rebuttal types: *racial, justify, justify + racial, negative, counterattack, counterimaging, distract,* and a no rebuttal control group) × 2 (target race: Black or white).

Figure 8.1 shows the basic design of the experiments. They proceeded in two stages. In the first stage, respondents read a fictitious news story about an attack ad in a U.S. Senate race.[18] The story explains that the target of the ad was attacked by his opponent for pardoning a former U.S. Representative (the "criminal"), who was convicted of eight felonies, including assault of a police officer that left the officer hospitalized with a head injury.[19] After reading the news story, respondents provided

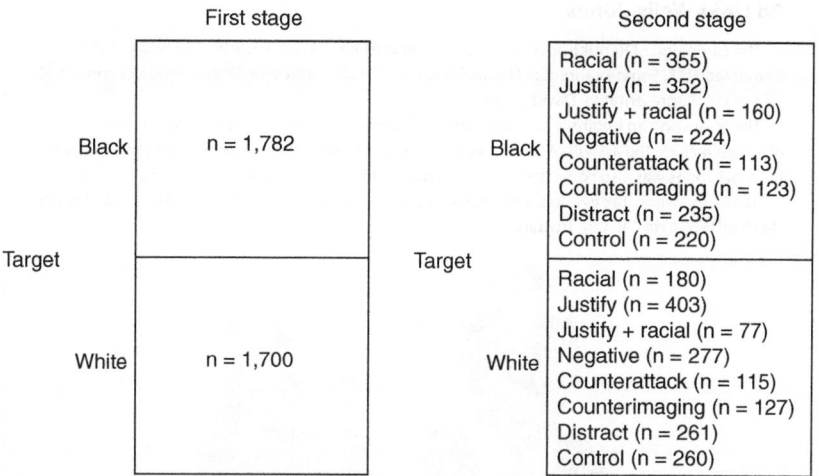

FIGURE 8.1 Experimental design.

feeling thermometer assessments (ranging from 0 = negative to 100 = positive) of the target and the attacker and answered a battery of demographic questions (but none about race, so that responses to remaining questions are not primed by race). In the second stage, respondents were randomly assigned to one of the eight rebuttal conditions and offered a second round of feeling thermometer evaluations for both candidates. To minimize the possibility of priming racial attitudes before reading the target's rebuttal, respondents answered the four-question racial resentment battery after the second round of candidate evaluations.[20]

The pardon of a convicted former politician was selected as the theme of the ad because linking candidates to Black criminality has been a theme in campaign ads such as the Willie Horton ad, the anti–Deval Patrick parking garage ad, and an ad from 2008 that tied Obama to Kwame Kilpatrick, the Black former mayor of Detroit who pleaded guilty to two counts of obstruction of justice and later resigned. The scenario examined in this chapter is intended to be similar to the Kilpatrick attack, as the former representative's crimes are loosely modeled on Kilpatrick's.[21] A side-by-side photo of the target and the criminal is embedded in the news article (see figure 8.2). The target is shown wearing a suit, while the criminal is shown in a mug shot. The race of the target was manipulated

Ad Links Wells, Jones

The campaign of Republican U.S. Senate candidate Peter Moore launched an ad against rival Democratic U.S. Senate candidate Michael Wells on Monday, criticizing Wells' pardon of convicted former U.S. Representative David Jones.

The 30-second ad begins with a description of Jones and the eight felonies he was convicted of, which include the assault of a police officer. The officer was hospitalized for injuries suffered to his head. Jones was also convicted of appointing 29 of his closest friends and relatives to public positions, extortion, tax evasion, and improper use of state funds. The ad ends with text that reads, "Michael Wells: He Can't Be Trusted."

Governor Michael Wells (left) and convicted former U.S. Representative David Jones (right) in a screenshot from an ad launched by U.S. Senate candidate Peter Moore.

Ad Links Wells, Jones

The campaign of Republican U.S. Senate candidate Peter Moore launched an ad against rival Democratic U.S. Senate candidate Michael Wells on Monday, criticizing Wells' pardon of convicted former U.S. Representative David Jones.

The 30-second ad begins with a description of Jones and the eight felonies he was convicted of, which include the assault of a police officer. The officer was hospitalized for injuries suffered to his head. Jones was also convicted of appointing 29 of his closest friends and relatives to public positions, extortion, tax evasion, and improper use of state funds. The ad ends with text that reads, "Michael Wells: He Can't Be Trusted."

Governor Michael Wells (left) and convicted former U.S. Representative David Jones (right) in a screenshot from an ad launched by U.S. Senate candidate Peter Moore.

FIGURE 8.2 Two versions of the attack news story used in experiment 4, Black target (top) and white target (bottom). The text of the attack news stories used in experiments 1–3 is shown in table 8.1 of the online appendix available at matthewtokeshi.com.

to be either Black or white in order to test whether race affects rebuttal effectiveness. Originally, the race of the criminal was also manipulated to be either Black or white. However, rebuttal effects do not substantively differ based on the criminal's race (see appendix table 8.3). Therefore, in order to simplify the presentation of results and increase statistical power, Black and white criminals are pooled together.

The white and Black versions of the target and criminal must be as close to identical as possible so that differences in ratings between them can be attributed to their skin color and not some other aspect of their appearance, such as their attractiveness. In order to do this, a morphing procedure developed in recent political science research was used.[22] This procedure yields a white face and a black face that are 60 percent identical, which controls for many extraneous (nonracial) sources of variation while still allowing realistic variation in skin tone and facial features.[23]

Turning to the second stage of the experiment, table 8.1 highlights the key features of the eight rebuttal conditions.[24] All conditions (except the control condition) contain the same first paragraph, explaining that a U.S. Senate candidate attacked his opponent for pardoning a convicted former U.S. Representative. The second and third paragraphs vary for each of the rebuttal conditions:

- In *racial*, the target says, "This ad is an attempt to stir up *racial fears* . . . Charges like this breed division in our country and our state. They divide us—*race against race*—so we blame each other instead of work together" (emphasis added). This statement is meant to resemble the one offered by then-governor Bill Clinton's speech announcing his run for the presidency in 1991 when he said, "For twelve years, Republicans have tried to divide us—race against race—so we get mad at each other and not at them."[25]
- The target in *justify* offers a justification for his action. He explains that the trial judge in the case recommended commuting the sentence and that the convicted representative received a 5–0 vote recommending parole from the state's bipartisan parole board. He concludes by saying that he does not condone the representative's actions, but he relied on the good judgment of the trial judge and parole board. This reasoning was similar to the real-life justification offered by former Arkansas governor Mike Huckabee in 2009 when he was criticized for pardoning an

TABLE 8.1 Description of rebuttal stories

Rebuttal	Racial	Justify	Justify + racial	Negative	Counterattack	Counterimaging	Distract	Control
Headline	Wells Claims Ad Had Racial Intent	Wells Claims Ad Is Unfair Attack	Wells Claims Ad Is Unfair, Racial Attack	Wells Claims Ad Is a Negative Attack	Wells Claims Ad Is Hypocritical Attack	Wells Claims Ad Misrepresents Pro-Victim Record	Wells Attacks Moore on Economy	YouTube Takes On Television
First paragraph	Wells fired back against ad...	Identical across conditions	Identical across conditions	Identical across conditions	Identical across conditions	Identical across conditions	Identical across conditions	Information about a nonpolitical news story
Second paragraph	"... ad is an attempt to stir up racial fears..."	"... ad is a distortion of the truth..."	"... ad is a distortion of the truth..."	"... ad is an attempt to stir up fears..."	"... ad is a hypocritical attack..."	"... ad is a misrepresentation of who I am..."	"My opponent's economic plan will spell disaster..."	Information about a nonpolitical news story
Third paragraph	"Charges like this... divide us—race against race..."	Wells explains reason for pardon: unanimous vote of bipartisan review board	Wells explains reason for pardon, plus: "Charges like this divide us—race against race..."	"Charges like this divide us..."	"My opponent is trying to look tough on crime when his record shows otherwise..."	"... I have aggressively fought for crime victims. In fact, I have sent people to jail..."	"I fought and delivered on behalf of all working families..."	Information about a nonpolitical news story
Photos	Candidate and criminal, race varying for each	Identical across conditions	Identical across conditions	Identical across conditions	Identical across conditions	Identical across conditions	Identical across conditions	Photos that go with a nonpolitical news story

Arkansas convict who murdered four Washington State police officers after Huckabee pardoned him. Huckabee justified the pardon by saying that he had received a recommendation to issue a pardon from the trial judge in the case and the unanimous vote of the parole board.[26]

- *Justify + racial* combines the credible justification of *justify* with *racial*'s claim that charges like this divide us "race against race."
- The target in *negative* issues the same rebuttal as the target in *racial*, except he leaves out *racial*'s two racial references—"racial fears" and "divide us—race against race"—and instead uses "fears" and "divide us."
- The target's *counterattack* charges the attacker with voting six times to limit employer access to criminal background checks on workers and that the attacker's proposed budget would cut funds for the state police. This is modeled after a rebuttal offered by Deval Patrick.
- In *counterimaging*, the target argues that he is the real tough-on-crime candidate because he sent people to jail when he was a federal prosecutor and that he has dedicated his life to working on criminal justice issues. This is also modeled after a Patrick rebuttal.
- In *distract*, the target avoids addressing the ad and instead criticizes the attacker's economic policy.
- Finally, respondents read a nonpolitical news article in the control condition that is similar in length and formatting to the other rebuttal conditions.

After reading the article, respondents evaluate the target and the attacker they read about in the first-stage news story. Thus, all respondents evaluate the fictional candidates twice. The control condition is needed in order to account for the possibility that the mere act of repeated measurement may influence treatment effects caused by anchoring, learning, fatigue, or some other time-related phenomenon. In other words, if a change in candidate evaluations is observed in one of the rebuttal conditions but no change is observed in the control condition, we can be confident that the change in the rebuttal condition is not an artifact of repeated measurement.

Racial and *justify* were each tested in all four experiments. *Negative, distract*, and control were tested in three out of four. *Justify + racial* was tested in two out of four, while *counterimaging* and *counterattack* were each tested once.[27]

RESULTS

Before examining the effects of the eight rebuttals, I verify that the attack ad news story worked as a racial attack against the Black target. To do this, I estimate the impact of racial resentment on target evaluation when the target is Black and compare this to racial resentment's impact when the target is white.[28] The dependent variable is the target-minus-attacker feeling thermometer difference measured after the attack (but before the rebuttal) rescaled to the −1 to 1 interval, with higher scores indicating greater support for the target. This score was regressed on racial resentment, a dummy variable indicating that the target is Black (with the white target as the comparison category), and the interaction between racial resentment and a Black target. The model also includes controls for partisanship, ideology, and the interactions between those variables and target race. If the news story worked as a racial attack against the Black target, we would expect a significant negative coefficient on the racial resentment × Black target interaction term, indicating that racial resentment's effect is stronger when the target is Black compared to when he is white. The coefficient displayed in the third row of table 8.2 supports this

TABLE 8.2 Did the attack work as a racial attack against the Black target? Predicting postattack target-minus-attacker difference score

	Support for the target
Racial resentment	−0.16*** (0.04)
Black target	0.09** (0.03)
Racial resentment × black target	−0.14** (0.05)
Intercept	0.03 (0.02)
Adjusted R-squared	0.07
N	3,234

Note: Entries are ordinary least-squares regression coefficients. Standard errors are in parentheses. The dependent variable is a −1 to 1 scale, ranging from strong opposition to strong support of the target. Controls for partisanship, ideology, and the interaction between those variables and exposure to a Black target are included but not shown. See appendix table 8.4 for full results. **$p < 0.05$; ***$p < 0.01$, two-tailed test.

expectation: racial resentment's association with target evaluation is more strongly negative when the target is Black. Thus, the news story appears to work as a racial attack against the Black target.[29]

Next, we turn to analysis of the rebuttal effects. The dependent variable used to test the main effect of the rebuttal is the change between the first round (postattack) and second round (postrebuttal) target-minus-attacker feeling thermometer ratings minus the same pre-post change in the appropriate control group (e.g., Black target's rebuttals are compared to the Black target control group, and white target's rebuttals are compared to the white target control group). The variable ranges from −2 to 2, with higher scores indicating better evaluations of the target relative to the appropriate control group.

Main effects are tested in three ways. First, is the effect positive and significantly different from the control group? Second, does the race of the target matter for the effect of a given rebuttal? After I conduct tests 1 and 2 for each rebuttal, I conduct test 3: which rebuttal is most effective for each target? These tests jointly cover all possible paired comparisons in an 8 × 2 design.

Tests 1–3 require a large number of pairwise comparisons, which increases the probability of incorrectly finding significant effects when the null hypothesis of no effect cannot be rejected (type I error). To guard against the possibility of finding significant effects simply as a result of conducting multiple comparisons, the False Discovery Rate (FDR) method is employed for these pairwise comparisons.[30] Applying the FDR correction requires adjusting the alpha level based on the number of tests conducted. Based on the sixty-three tests conducted in this study, the FDR-adjusted alpha level for pairwise comparisons is 0.014 instead of the usual 0.05.[31] All tests are two-tailed.

Figure 8.3 shows the effects of each rebuttal tested against a null hypothesis of no change relative to the appropriate control group (test 1) and all comparisons between pairs (tests 2 and 3). Each bar represents the rebuttal effect for each target-rebuttal pair with its 98.6 percent confidence interval to reflect the FDR-corrected alpha level of 0.014. To aid in interpreting the magnitude of the rebuttal effects, the attack resulted in a target rating that was 0.11 lower than the attacker's rating on average.[32] Therefore, rebuttal effects can be interpreted as the amount of the 0.11 hit that the target gets back by using the rebuttal.

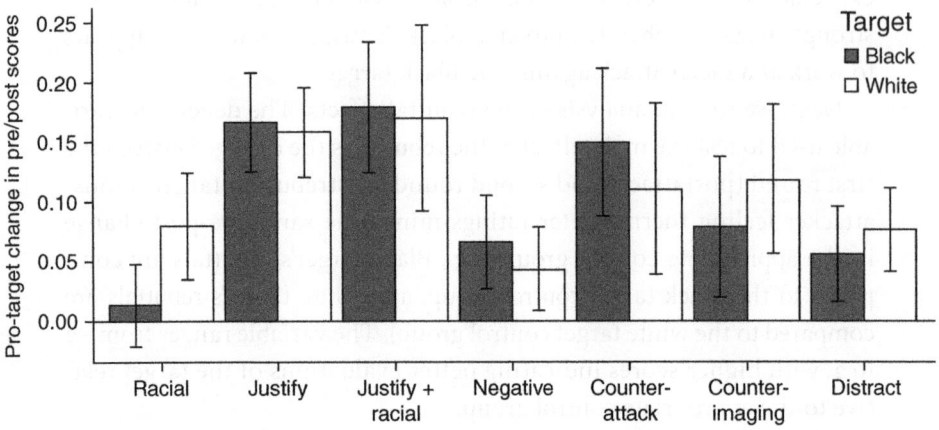

FIGURE 8.3 The impact of rebuttals on target-attacker evaluations. Positive values indicate that the rebuttal helped the target. Error bars represent 98.6% confidence intervals, which reflects the FDR-corrected alpha level of 0.014.

I start with *racial*. Looking at the average magnitudes compared to the control group (test 1), we see that it improves ratings of a white target by an average of 0.08 ($p < 0.01$) but the rebuttal's effect when used by a Black target by an average of only 0.01, which is statistically indistinguishable from zero ($p = 0.36$). A direct test of the racial disadvantage hypothesis (test 2) indicates that support for the white target is 0.06 higher on average than for a Black target using the same rebuttal ($p < 0.01$). Overall, the results provide mixed support for the racial priming literature's endorsement of *racial*. While it improves evaluations of a white target, a Black target does not enjoy the same benefit. This is consistent with previous research on the effects of racial rhetoric for Black versus white elites.[33]

Turning to *justify*, figure 8.3 shows that this rebuttal improves evaluations of Black and white targets alike (test 1). *Justify* improves evaluations by an estimated 0.17 for a Black target and 0.16 for a white target compared to each target's appropriate control group ($p < 0.01$ for both tests). The difference in *justify*'s effectiveness by target race is not statistically distinguishable from zero (test 2) ($p = 0.42$). In sum, *justify* is effective for a target of either race. This is also the case for *justify + racial*, as it boosts evaluations of a Black target by 0.18 and a white target by 0.17 compared to the relevant control group (test 1) ($p < 0.01$ for both tests). The difference between Black and white targets is also statistically indistinguishable from zero (test 2) (p = 0.66), which is notable given that *justify + racial*'s mention of race does not disadvantage Black targets in the same way that *racial* did.

The other four rebuttals—*negative, counterattack, counterimaging,* and *distract*—show the same pattern of (1) improvement for both Black and white targets relative to their respective control group (test 1) and (2) no differences between Black and white targets (test 2). The magnitudes of their effects, however, differ. On the high end of efficacy is *counterattack*, which improved evaluations of Black and white targets by amounts roughly on par with the effects of *justify* and *justify + racial*: 0.15 for Black targets and 0.11 for white targets. After that comes *counterimaging*, which added 0.08 more support for Black targets and 0.12 more support for white targets. Finally, *negative* and *distract* have the smallest effects, ranging from 0.05 to 0.08.

To summarize the findings so far, *justify, justify + racial,* and *counterattack* were highly and equally effective strategies for targets of either race. *Racial*, on the other hand, was mildly effective for a white target but ineffective for a Black target. In fact, *racial* used by a Black target was the only rebuttal tested that did not improve evaluations of the target compared to the control group. All other rebuttals showed at least modest effects for targets of either race with no racial differences.

Next, we turn to test 3: which rebuttal works best for each target? Starting with the Black target, we learned from test 2 that all rebuttals except *racial* were successful relative to the control group. Among the successful rebuttals from test 2, a clear hierarchy emerges. *Justify, justify + racial,* and *counterattack* make up the top tier of rebuttals. All are more effective than the closest competitor, *counterimaging* ($p < 0.01$ for *justify* versus *counterimaging* and *justify + racial* versus *counterimaging*; $p = .03$ for *counterattack* versus *counterimaging*). The next tier consists of *negative, counterimaging,* and *distract*, which are all more effective than *racial* ($p < 0.01$ for *negative* and *counterimaging* and $p = 0.01$ for *distract*). That leaves *racial* at the bottom, though it is worth noting that at least *racial* does not cause a backlash effect compared to the control group. The rebuttal simply leaves a Black target no better or worse off than offering no response.

For the white target, test 2 revealed that all rebuttals were successful relative to the control group. Turning to test 3, the set of four strategies that cannot be dominated by any other are *justify, justify + racial, counterattack,* and *counterimaging.* Compared to the next best strategy, *racial,* however, only *justify* and *justify + racial* are clearly better than *racial* ($p < 0.014$, the FDR-corrected alpha level, for both comparisons). Thus, the top tier of rebuttals is *justify* and *justify + racial,* while the next tier is *counterimaging, counterattack, racial,* and *distract.* The bottom tier consists of *negative,* which is marginally less effective than the closest competitor, *distract* ($p = 0.05$).

To better understand the main effects of each rebuttal, I examine how rebuttal effects differ among low-, medium-, and high-racial-resentment respondents. Replicating analyses in earlier chapters, I divide the sample into thirds by racial resentment.[34] As argued earlier, it is particularly important to know whether rebuttal effects persist for respondents with high levels of racial resentment. The analysis also allows for a closer examination of why each rebuttal succeeds or fails. It could be that positive effects are concentrated primarily among the racially sympathetic or that effects are consistent across the racial resentment spectrum.

To distinguish between these possibilities, figure 8.4 shows each rebuttal's effect among respondents with low, medium, and high levels of racial resentment. Effects for Black targets are shown on top, while effects for white targets are shown on the bottom. Starting with *racial* on the top panel far left, the Black target's success declines as racial resentment increases. *Racial* has a marginally positive effect on low-racial-resentment respondents ($p = .02$) but essentially no effect for medium- or high-racial-resentment respondents. Meanwhile, white targets (bottom panel far left) enjoy positive effects among low- and medium-racial-resentment respondents ($p < .01$ for both tests). But in an important departure from the overall sample, they do not enjoy a statistically significant improvement among high-racial-resentment respondents.

While the Black target's success with *racial* is shaped by the racial resentment level of the audience, their success with *justify* (top panel second from the left) is stable across the racial resentment spectrum. White targets (bottom panel second from the left) also enjoy improved ratings at all three levels of racial resentment. The same holds true for *justify + racial* (third from the left). Black and white targets benefit from statistically significant positive effects at each level of racial resentment. One difference is that racial resentment appears to shape the rebuttal's

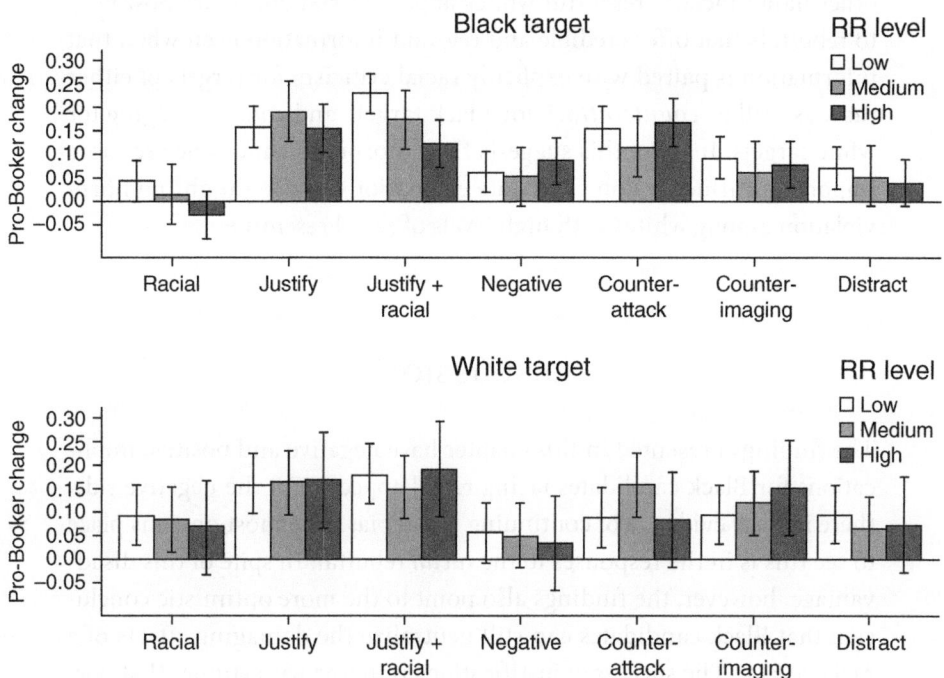

FIGURE 8.4 Rebuttal effects by racial resentment level. Positive values indicate that the rebuttal helped the target. Error bars represent 98.6% confidence intervals, which reflects the FDR-corrected alpha level of 0.014.

effect more strongly for a Black target, as effects weaken as racial resentment increases. But notably, Black targets still enjoy success using *justify + racial* among the racially resentful. This is particularly striking given that the rebuttal contains the same phrase in *racial*—"Charges like this . . . divide us—race against race"—that had a negative (though statistically indistinguishable from zero) effect among the racially resentful.

Overall, one important takeaway from figure 8.4 is that the results among the racially resentful are surprisingly similar to the results for the overall sample. The key difference is that *racial* no longer appears to benefit a white target. This suggests that a rebuttal that criticizes a racialized attack in explicitly racial terms does not necessarily lead racially resentful whites to reevaluate the racialized attack, contrary to the political scientist Tali Mendelberg's theory of internalized racial norms.[35] On the other hand, racially resentful whites appear to respond more positively to rebuttals that offer credible and relevant information even when that information is paired with explicitly racial criticism for targets of either race, as well as *counterattack* for Black targets and *counterimaging* for white targets. In sum, this suggests that information and tone are more important influences on candidate evaluation than highlighting norm violation among whites with high levels of racial resentment.

DISCUSSION

The findings presented in this chapter have negative and positive implications for Black candidates facing racial appeals. On the negative side, there is clear evidence of continuing racial bias. The most obvious place to see this is in the responses to the *racial* rebuttal. In spite of this disadvantage, however, the findings also point to the more optimistic conclusion that Black candidates can still neutralize the damaging effects of a racial attack. The success of justifications is in line with studies that portray white voters, even racially resentful ones, as receptive to reasonable information.[36] The success of the hybrid *justify + racial* also suggests that adopting a strictly deracialized style in the face of racial attacks may be unnecessary. To be sure, Black targets who only highlight the racial nature of the attack fare poorly. But Black targets can succeed with nuanced rebuttals that highlight compelling racial and nonracial themes.

The results also speak to an important theoretical question in the study of American racial politics. A key debate that has emerged during the Obama and Trump presidencies is whether the norm against explicit racial derogation still acts as a constraint on white Americans. Mendelberg argued that even whites with high levels of racial resentment reject explicitly racialized rhetoric, an argument that has been challenged by recent research suggesting that many whites no longer consider explicitly hostile racial rhetoric to be inappropriate.[37] The findings in this chapter support the view of the newer research. While *racial* improved evaluations of the white target among the overall sample, the analysis by racial resentment level shows that only the racially sympathetic and racially moderate respond positively. Racially resentful whites were not moved by a rebuttal that made visible a message that likely would have violated norms in earlier decades.

The results of the last two chapters suggest that no one or two rebuttal types dominate all others. Instead, a variety of strategies are effective in helping Black candidates fend off racial attacks. In chapter 7, *negative* and *denial* helped Cory Booker gain back approval lost to the original attack. In this chapter, the top tier of responses for a Black candidate were *justify*, *justify + racial*, and *counterattack*. The challenge appears to be finding the rebuttal that most appropriately responds to the situation at hand. For charges that can be credibly denied, such as Steve Lonegan criticizing Booker for Newark's rising crime rate, perhaps it is best to deny those charges by pointing out that the crime rate is actually declining (assuming that is true, of course). Charges like Lonegan's "Twitter map" attack, which are not clearly connected to anything relevant to either Booker's character or issue positions, can be brushed aside by using *negative*. But the same response is unlikely to work against the weightier charge of pardoning a convicted criminal. In this situation, there is no way to sever the link between the actions of the candidate and the controversy created by that action. Other acts of political misconduct, such as a controversial policy vote or a demonstrated link to a figure like Jeremiah Wright, have this same character. In situations like this where there is no way to deny responsibility for the act, perhaps it is best to either offer a good reason for *why* one took such action or land an effective counterpunch rather than to criticize the incivility of the opposition.

Another important finding from this chapter is that several rebuttals help the attacked candidate even among racially resentful white respondents. In contrast, the results from the case studies in chapters 4 and 5 indicate that rebuttals were unsuccessful among the racially resentful. Perhaps rebuttals can influence racially resentful whites under the circumstances simulated by the experiment in this chapter—an attack regarding a controversial act that gains attention for a previously low-profile candidate. Nonetheless, optimism regarding rebuttals' ability to influence the racially resentful still warrants support from studies of real campaigns.

Finally, a few limitations of the results are considered. First, the data was collected before Donald Trump became president, so it is worth considering how these findings hold up in the post-Trump era. Given recent findings that suggest white liberals have grown more racially sympathetic since the 2016 election, it is possible that Black candidates charging racism may have a more receptive audience than the one found in this study.[38] Second, only one attack-rebuttal sequence is tested, and thus the question of how multiple iterations of attack-rebuttal sequences influence candidate evaluation cannot be addressed. Third, this chapter does not consider rebuttals offered by a candidate's surrogates, though the political scientists Antoine Banks and Heather Hicks find that the racial rebuttal offered by a surrogate is effective among racially sympathetic whites but not racially resentful whites.[39] This is line with the findings from this chapter.

In spite of these limitations, the chapter's key contribution is its focus on how Black candidates combat racial appeals, a departure from typical research that focuses on the effects of racial appeals on white candidates.[40] This line of research often portrays the American public as being easily manipulated by racial cues. The current chapter builds on this research by showing that implicit racial attacks do not necessarily determine the role of race in campaigns. Instead, Black (and white) candidates can counter the negative effects of these attacks depending on how they respond.

CONCLUSION

In this final chapter, I take a step back to consider what the findings from earlier chapters have to say about the current state of race and American politics and consider avenues for future research. The book's central lessons, I argue, are that candidate race still matters to white voters; Black candidates with a good chance to win high-level statewide office are likely to face racial attacks that are effective, and this is likely to continue in the foreseeable future; and Black (and white) candidates can counteract these attacks, but with some important qualifications regarding which subgroups of white voters respond favorably and to what types of messages. After summarizing the main findings and discussing their practical implications, I consider a few important normative questions that they raise. Finally, I identify areas for future research and close with concluding thoughts.

CANDIDATE RACE MATTERS

One clear conclusion that can be drawn from the findings is that candidate race matters in high-level statewide campaigns. In chapter 1, I show that Black candidates are about half as likely to win and receive about 8 percent less support among white voters compared to white candidates from the same party running in the same state for the same office around the same time. In chapter 2, I find that Black candidates who have a decent chance of winning face a higher rate of attacks on topics that evoke stereotypically anti-Black themes when compared to white candidates with similar characteristics. In chapters 4 and 5, I show that all four viable Black candidates from 2006 to 2014—Deval Patrick, Harold Ford Jr., Cory Booker, and Anthony Brown—suffered losses in white support following racial attacks. In chapter 6, I show that racial resentment was a stronger predictor of opposition to Stacey Abrams and Kamala Harris than comparable white Democrats. And finally, in chapter 8, I show that Black candidates' use of the racial rebuttal is much less effective than its use by an identical white candidate.

These findings may underestimate the penalty faced by Black candidates because most of my analysis only examines the very last stage in the process of becoming a governor or U.S. senator—the general election. While my brief examination of the 2020 primary election candidate pool in chapter 1 finds that Black candidates ran in numbers proportional to their share of the electorate, I also found evidence that Black candidates were underrepresented in the candidate pool in 2010. Political scientists have documented reasons for why that happens. In one study, the political scientists Gbemende Johnson, Bruce Oppenheimer, and Jennifer Selin examine the decision of all U.S. House members to run for the U.S. Senate from 1992–2008 and find that Black members are about half as likely to run as white members.[1] They attribute this to a number of factors linked to race, such as state size (most of the Black population lives in larger states, so Black U.S. House members who represent Black constituencies represent less of the state's population and therefore have lower name recognition and more competition), ideological extremity (Black U.S. House members often represent liberal Black constituencies, making it harder to recalibrate for a statewide campaign), and fundraising ability (Black U.S. House members represent poorer districts on average, which imposes a fundraising handicap). Another study found that local party chairs of both political parties view white candidates as significantly more likely to perform better among their party's primary voters than Black candidates.[2] Since recruitment of prospective candidates is among the most common tasks of local party chairs, this is likely to lead to less integration into established, predominantly white state- and national-level party organizations. Also, the lack of support among party officials may contribute to prospective candidates having less confidence in their ability to win. Future work should examine all of these factors in order to understand whether bias is still occurring at earlier stages of the process. A better understanding of how racial disparities shape the earlier stages of the process will not only provide a more complete picture of the factors hindering Blacks from reaching high-level statewide positions but may also point the way to overcoming those hurdles.

RACIAL ATTACKS ARE STILL COMMON AND POTENT

I also find that racial attacks are still common and politically consequential for Black candidates. Chapter 2 demonstrates that whenever a Black candidate has a good chance to win, they can expect to face more racially tinged attacks than they would face if they were white. In the case studies of chapters 4 and 5, I examine the association between whites' racial attitudes and vote choice in Black versus white statewide contests and find that following a highly salient racially charged event (in the cases of Patrick and Ford) or a series of racial attacks that go lightly rebutted (in Brown's case) or not rebutted at all (in the first half of the Booker campaign), racial resentment is a stronger predictor of opposition to Black candidates even after accounting for the effects of nonracial predispositions such as partisanship and ideology. The experiment in chapter 7 suggests that the attacks *caused* this racialization, as racial resentment was negatively associated with support for Booker mostly in the conditions in which he was targeted on a racial theme.

The findings also suggest that a Black candidate's race is not the only necessary ingredient for their racialization—racial attacks matter, too. As noted in the conclusion of chapter 7, the political scientists Michael Tesler and David Sears put forth a "chronic accessibility" hypothesis to explain the way racial attitudes shaped evaluations of Barack Obama in 2008.[3] According to this account, the mere fact of Obama being Black made racial considerations salient, and so the usual work of racializing a candidate through attacks was unnecessary. My findings do not support the chronic accessibility hypothesis, at least for Cory Booker. Booker's race alone did not activate racial attitudes. In the Booker experiment in chapter 7, I found that for Maryland respondents in the control condition in which Booker's picture was shown (signaling his race) but no other information was provided, racial resentment was not associated with vote choice. Also, in the Booker case study in chapter 5, racial resentment was not associated with vote choice in the early stages of his 2013 U.S. Senate campaign. Both experimental and observational data show that racial attacks are what racialized Booker. Thus, racial attacks still play a critical role in campaigns involving Black candidates.

With respect to the current significance of racial attacks, it is likely that they will remain a significant part of campaigns in the near future. Perhaps the best indication of the continuing relevance of these attacks is the way Donald Trump has shown that politicians suffer no penalty from making them the centerpiece of their political strategy. In 2008, John McCain was reluctant to campaign on racial fear against Obama in part because he thought that such tactics would hurt him politically.[4] But Trump believed that McCain's reluctance meant that Obama had not been effectively attacked.[5] In March 2011, when he was a reality television star with no political experience, Trump first began publicly airing his accusation that President Obama was born outside the United States and was therefore ineligible for the presidency. For the next six weeks, Trump promoted this "birther" theory, which was once relegated to the fringes of political discourse, into the mainstream, as he appeared on ABC's *The View*, Fox News's *On the Record*, and NBC's *Today Show*. "The more Mr. Trump questioned the legitimacy of Mr. Obama's presidency," according to a *New York Times* piece about the birther episode, "the better he performed in early polls of the 2012 Republican field, springing from fifth place to a virtual tie for first."[6] The Obama White House did not want to respond to the rumors at first, thinking that to respond would only give them credibility. But after the issue kept coming up at town-hall events and following a major address on the budget, Obama finally responded at a press conference in which he released his long-form birth certificate. By that time, six weeks had passed, and a connection between Trump and a segment of the Republican base was already forged. Though Trump did not end up running in 2012, the birther attacks demonstrated that a significant part of the Republican electorate was open to candidates who abandoned McCain's self-imposed restraint on race.[7]

As president, Trump called Haiti and African countries "shitholes"; told Black congressman and civil rights icon John Lewis to fix his "crime-infested" district; called Black congressman Elijah Cummings's district a "disgusting, rat and rodent infested mess"; vowed to protect the "suburban housewife" from "low income" people moving in under a federal program run by Cory Booker; and refused to state that 2020 Democratic vice presidential nominee Kamala Harris was eligible to serve as vice president when asked about a rumor that Harris was not actually an American citizen due to her parents being immigrants.[8] But even after Trump has left office, his style of racial provocation appears to have found a home in the Republican Party. An estimated 42 percent of the Republicans in the U.S. House at the beginning of the Trump presidency either retired or lost reelection and were replaced by Trump acolytes, according to an August 2020 *Politico* analysis.[9] As the seeds of Trumpism bloom within the Republican Party over the next few decades, the chances of a Black Democrat facing a Trump-style racial provocateur in the general election increase. In fact, this is already happening, as the two viable high-level statewide Black candidates in 2018—Stacey Abrams for Georgia governor and Andrew Gillum for Florida governor—each faced Trump-style Republicans in Brian Kemp (Georgia) and Ron DeSantis (Florida). Kemp touted his pickup truck large enough to "round up criminal illegals," while DeSantis warned Florida voters not to "monkey this up" by electing Gillum, whom he attacked as being corrupt and soft on crime.[10] Trump, acting as a DeSantis surrogate, called Gillum "a stone-cold thief."[11]

Of course, Black Democrats might face racialized attacks without running against a Kemp or DeSantis. The case studies in this book demonstrate that three of the six Republicans running against viable Black candidates—Kerry Healey, Bob Corker, and Larry Hogan—were seen as moderate at the time, and Corker and Hogan have since become among the most high-profile anti-Trump voices in the Republican Party. Yet all three embraced racialized strategies when running against viable Black opponents. As long as white candidates sense that racial animus can be tapped for political gain, it is likely that they will see a strategic incentive in highlighting racial fear of their Black opponents. Trump showed that it can launch a political career, and the wave of Trump imitators that are entering office today suggests that fewer and fewer Republican politicians share John McCain's belief that the politics of racial fear can backfire.

REBUTTALS HELP, BUT WITH SOME QUALIFICATIONS

The main conclusion to draw from the various tests of rebuttals is that some form of contestation is preferable to silence. Consider the precipitous loss of white support during the first half of the Booker campaign and across the entire Brown campaign. Whether inspired by overconfidence or strategic miscalculation, silence is a failed strategy. This conclusion is supported by comparing the no-rebuttal control group to every rebuttal in chapter 8's criminal pardon experiment. Even rebuttals that were found to be ineffective, such as the racial rebuttal when used by a Black candidate, leave the candidate no worse off than remaining silent.

This finding is important because the temptation to remain silent in the face of racial attacks is strong. As mentioned in the introduction, most studies of Black and white candidates facing racial attacks find that they usually either ignore them or try to change the subject.[12] Recall from the previous section that Obama took six weeks to respond to the birther attacks. The analysis of the Booker and Brown campaigns in chapter 5 and the criminal pardon experiment in chapter 8 suggest that not responding for long stretches of a campaign following racial attacks is likely to result in a substantial loss of white support.

In addition to the general conclusion that silence does not work, we also learned that rebuttals generally do not do much to win back high-racial-resentment voters. None of the three candidates for whom I analyzed the effect of rebuttals (Patrick, Ford, or Booker) made statistically significant gains among this subgroup. Although I found evidence of rebuttals positively influencing evaluations of a Black candidate among high-racial-resentment whites in the criminal pardon experiment reported in chapter 8, most of the positive effects of rebuttals reported in this book occurred among racially sympathetic whites. This has implications for how Black candidates should think about their response options when facing racial attacks. My findings suggest that Black candidates should look at rebuttals as a way to reassure likely supporters who may be wavering and pitch their responses to them, not to racially resentful voters who are unlikely to change their mind after exposure to a racial attack. The case of Harold Ford is instructive here. Ford was the only candidate who actually lost ground among the racially sympathetic following his rebuttals. His response to the "Call Me" attack may have alienated racially sympathetic whites.

With regard to specific rebuttal types, we learned in chapter 3 that Black candidates rarely use the racial rebuttal themselves, though in some instances, they delegate it to surrogates. As we learned in chapters 7 and 8, they do so with good reason: it is ineffective. White candidates, however, do not face a similar constraint when using the racial rebuttal. This finding helps explain why President Obama was reluctant to mention race in his public speeches,[13] while at the same time, 2016 Democratic presidential nominee Hillary Clinton and 2020 nominee Joe Biden did not shy away from explicit discussion of racial justice issues. For instance, both Clinton and Biden distanced themselves from the 1994 crime bill that Bill Clinton signed and Biden supported as a U.S. senator for disproportionately hurting Black families.[14] In the aftermath of the police killings of Black Americans Alton Sterling and Philando Castile in 2016 and George Floyd and Breonna Taylor in 2020, Clinton and Biden vowed to fight "systemic racism," with Biden saying that the killings were "a wake-up call for our nation" where "too often, just the color of your skin puts your life at risk."[15] By virtue of their race, whites may find Clinton and Biden to be more credible messengers of the idea that white racism and discrimination against Black Americans still plague American society. When endorsing Biden at the 2020 Democratic National Convention, former Democratic presidential candidate Andrew Yang observed, "The magic of Joe Biden is, everything he does becomes the new reasonable."[16] Although Yang meant this as a compliment, he, perhaps unwittingly, made a trenchant observation about the built-in advantage of being white, particularly a white man with a moderate reputation. The criminal pardon experiment in chapter 8 shows that white candidates indeed enjoy a "magic" touch when it comes to calling attention to racism that can be attributed simply to being white.

Regarding the other rebuttal types, the results from chapter 7's Booker experiment and chapter 8's criminal pardon experiment suggest that a range of strategies can be used to combat racial attacks. The differences between what worked in chapter 7 and chapter 8 suggest that rebuttals need to be tailored to the attack that they are responding to. For instance, *negative* left Booker better off than he was before the "Twitter map" attack, but the same rebuttal won back only a little more than half of what the

Black target lost from the criminal pardon attack. Meanwhile, *justify* was among the most effective responses to the criminal pardon attack, but its positive effect was much smaller for the "stripper" attack. For a fairly trivial attack like the "Twitter map" attack, in which the candidate is not tied to a specific controversial action, perhaps it is sufficient to dismiss such attacks as negative and silly. But for a more serious attack, such as a pardon of a convicted former politician, a credible justification for *why* one took such action appears to be a better strategy. Denial of having issued the pardon is not credible, and brushing off the attack as negative, silly, or racist will not suffice. More work needs to be done to develop a better theoretical account of which rebuttals are best suited to different types of attacks, but the link between the candidate and a specific controversial action is likely to be important.

NORMATIVE IMPLICATIONS

From a normative perspective, some readers may be troubled by the idea that avoiding race is necessary for Black politicians. If you think of campaigns as "our primary occasions for political education" and among "the most important and influential means of discourse about race," then a case could be made that the best strategy for dealing with racialized attacks is to use them as an opportunity to educate the public about the racially harmful nature of such communication.[17] In the long run, shaping public consciousness around the boundaries of acceptable racial discourse could have a greater impact on bringing about racial equality than the election of more Black candidates. From this perspective, the finding from the criminal pardon experiment in chapter 8 that Black targets who call out the attack as racial do not fare well is disappointing.

However, recall another finding from chapter 8: that *justify + racial*, a modified version of the racial rebuttal that includes a racial component packaged with a credible justification, can be quite effective, even among high-racial-resentment respondents. This suggests that strict deracialization may be unnecessary. While it is true that Black targets who only highlight the racial nature of the attack do not fare well, they can succeed by packaging the racial critique with a credible justification. In short, the packaging of racial defense matters.

This calls to mind perhaps the best real-world example of white voters evaluating a Black candidate responding to a racially charged situation: Barack Obama's "A More Perfect Union" speech from March 2008, in which he addressed the controversial videos that emerged of his former pastor Jeremiah Wright denouncing the United States. To be sure, there are differences between the situation Obama faced and the one faced by the fictitious candidate in chapter 8, most notably that the racial aspect of the Wright controversy was explicit. Still, the themes Obama laid out in that speech mirror the strategies tested in the rebuttals from the criminal pardon experiment in chapter 8. Akin to *racial*, he acknowledged the existence of white racism in American society to a much greater degree than most presidential candidates. But the whole speech was more than just a recounting of the nation's ugly racial past. It included a *justification* of sorts when Obama tried to explain the nature of his relationship with Wright. It also included appeals to unity (similar to how I operationalized *negative* in the chapter 8 experiment) and a call to move the national conversation back to more important topics such as the economy, health care, and foreign policy (similar to *distract*). Although it is impossible to know without better data what elements of the speech were effective and among which subgroups of the public, there is suggestive evidence that the speech had an overall positive effect for Obama.[18] This suggests that a Black candidate can defuse a racially charged situation with *justify* + *racial* or some other combination of racial and nonracial rhetoric. However, it is also possible that the circumstances that allowed Obama to survive this crisis were unusual and that Black candidates are still generally punished for discussing racial matters no matter what other messages they package with it. Remember that Obama's other forays into racial issues, such as his July 2009 comments following the arrest of Black Harvard professor Henry Louis Gates Jr. and his July 2013 comments about the death of Black Florida teenager Trayvon Martin, were not as well received by many whites. Obama's mixed success in handling racial controversies suggests that researchers and practitioners will continue to debate best practices for self-presentation when Black candidates are embroiled in racial controversies.

Some readers, though, may find such "bias hacking" efforts to be inadequately cosmetic. They may wonder what the point of such efforts is when it is unclear that increasing the number of Black elected officials actually advances the larger project of racial equality. We now have "Black faces in high places," yet basic indicators of racial inequality remain largely unchanged in recent decades.[19] Research on the effects of representation on the material well-being of Black Americans is mixed.[20] But research also points to representation having positive effects on outcomes such as political interest, political participation, and trust in the political process.[21] In an era of growing cynicism, minorities view the presence of their own in office as an indicator of the legitimacy of the political system.[22] Representation also appears to positively affect white racial attitudes.[23] There may also be positive long-run benefits of Black office-holding on racial prejudice. Political scientists have demonstrated the effects of the events and contexts of adolescence on attitudes in later adulthood.[24] Findings from the political socialization literature suggest that children growing up today when Black representation in politics and other societal domains is becoming more normalized are learning lessons about who deserves to hold positions of power that are likely to shape their racial attitudes decades later.

In sum, the benefits of representation, admittedly, appear to be indirect. Representation is not the panacea that many had hoped for. But it would also be a mistake to dismiss it as irrelevant. In the long sweep of American history, the path to greater racial equality has never been linear.[25] To expect representation to cure all of America's racial problems was never realistic. But if Black candidates can better navigate challenging campaign dynamics and ultimately reach the highest offices in the United States, that would be a step on the road to greater racial equality that could continue to pay even larger dividends in the future.

FUTURE RESEARCH

BLACK WOMEN CANDIDATES

While this book sheds light on a number of important questions about racial communication and its effects on Black candidates, it also raises several questions that should be addressed by future research. For one, the chapter on Stacey Abrams and Kamala Harris represents a first step in understanding how race and gender influence the evaluations of Black women candidates for high-level offices. We learned that while race and gender mattered for Abrams, only race mattered for Harris. In that chapter's conclusion, I listed a number of reasons why we should expect race to be a more consistent mobilizer of opposition to Black women candidacies than gender. Fortunately, the emergence of more Black women candidates for high-level offices in the future seems likely, and so future researchers will have an opportunity to test this hypothesis.

BLACK VOTERS

Another important topic that deserves more attention is how Black voters respond to Black candidacies. Since Blacks make up no more than 15 percent of the population in any state outside the South, white voters play a pivotal role in deciding the electoral fortunes of most Black statewide candidates. But maintaining the loyalty and enthusiasm of Black voters is a key strategic consideration for Black candidates, especially in the South, as well as for Black candidates in municipal and congressional elections, where the behavior of white voters is less relevant because they may not be part of the base of support that would vote for a Black candidate anyway. Existing research suggests that explicitly racial campaign communications activate in-group identification among Black voters.[26] However, I found in chapter 3 that Black candidates are reluctant to engage in such communications. Thus, Black candidates may have difficulty mobilizing their Black base. That problem may have contributed to the defeat of Anthony Brown, who, as mentioned in chapter 5, suffered from lower-than-average turnout in the heavily Black city of Baltimore and Prince George's County. Perhaps a more robust defense against Larry Hogan's attacks would have energized Black voters. This is a question that has not been answered yet but is worthy of further research.

A separate question with respect to Black voters is how they respond to racial attacks. One possibility is that they mobilize Black voters in defense of the attacked Black candidate, which may neutralize their overall effectiveness. Given the literature's focus on how white voters respond to racial attacks, we do not yet know whether Black voters provide enough of a countervailing force to cancel out the effects among white voters. However, if the large volume of Republican attacks against Black candidates on crime in the 2022 midterm elections for high-level statewide offices are any indication—see Republican attacks against Mandela Barnes in Wisconsin and Cheri Beasley in North Carolina—it appears that many Republicans still believe that they have more to gain among whites than they have to lose among Blacks by attacking Black Democrats in this way. Future research on how Black voters respond to racial attacks can illuminate the conditions under which they are politically advantageous for white candidates.

BLACK REPUBLICAN CANDIDATES

The experience of Black Republican statewide candidates is another topic that future researchers should examine. The reason for their omission in this book is that there have been no relevant cases—that is, viable Black Republicans running against a white opponent—until 2020.[27] That year, John James lost by 2 percentage points in his bid to become Michigan's first Black U.S. senator. If the definition of viability is expanded to include candidates who came within 10 percentage points of winning, the list expands to include James's 2018 bid for a Michigan U.S. Senate seat (which he lost by 7 percentage points) and Darryl Glenn, who lost a U.S. Senate election in Colorado by 6 percentage points in 2016. If the trend of Black Republicans running competitively for high-level statewide offices continues, researchers will have an opportunity to examine how race and racial attacks influence their campaigns. One reason why Black Republicans are unlikely to face the same volume of racial attacks as Black Democrats is the difference in the racial constituencies courted by the two parties. White Republican candidates may see something to gain by stoking anti-Black sentiment because they typically appeal to a predominantly white base. But given that white Democrats in many states must put together a coalition of whites and nonwhites, it is unlikely that they will see the same value in subtly appealing to anti-Black sentiment. This may not hold true in states with very few nonwhite voters, however. If Black Republicans run competitively in these states, future researchers will have an opportunity to examine whether Black Republicans face as many racialized attacks and suffer the same damage from them as their Black Democratic counterparts.[28]

While Black Republicans may receive a comparable volume of racialized attacks under some circumstances, they may actually be *more* likely to appeal to anti-Black animus than comparable white Republican candidates. If Black candidates who defend conservative racial stances are particularly attractive to Republican voters because support for Black candidates can be used to deflect against charges of racism, then Black Republican candidates would have an incentive to cater to this demand in the political marketplace. Recent Black Republican presidential candidates Herman Cain and Ben Carson built their political brands on sharp criticism of Blacks for not working hard enough and being too willing to depend on government programs that they do not deserve.[29] Of course, without the ability to observe a larger number of cases, we cannot know whether Cain and Carson are outliers. However, the fact that Cain and Carson quickly rose from political unknown status to nationally known presidential candidates by embracing what the political scientist LaFleur Stephens-Dougan calls "racial distancing" suggests that other Black Republicans may see the value in taking a similar approach.[30]

AMERICA'S MAJORITY-MINORITY FUTURE

Another broad area for further research is how the growing diversity of the United States will affect the future of campaigns. The time period in which the Black candidates in this book ran for office (2000–2020) most likely represents the end of the era in which all of them had to appeal to a white median voter. According to the 2020 Census, whites are a majority of the electorate in forty-six of the fifty states and at least two-thirds of the electorate in thirty-three states.[31] As demographers expect racial and ethnic minorities to surpass non-Hispanic whites as a majority of the U.S. population sometime in the 2040s, more states are expected to have majority-minority electorates.

How will changing demographics fueled by immigration affect the nature of campaigns and the diversity of America's highest political offices? One optimistic possibility is that this "diversity explosion" will result in a more pluralistic political leadership.[32] Evidence in favor of this scenario can be found in the progress in Black representation made at the congressional, state legislative, and mayoral levels. Today, Blacks make up 12.9 percent of the U.S. House in the 117th Congress (2021–2023) and about 10 percent of state legislatures, according to a 2020 study by the National Conference of State Legislatures, approximating their 11 percent share of the 2020 presidential electorate.[33] Gains have also occurred at the mayoral level, as half of the nation's fifty largest cities have elected a Black mayor, including the four largest cities of New York, Los Angeles, Chicago, and Houston. If many American states come to resemble the diverse cities and legislative districts that have elected Black mayors, representatives, and state legislators, it could follow that leadership at the level of governor and senator will similarly diversify.

On the other hand, there are reasons to question whether this "diversity explosion" scenario will happen. For one, whites are unlikely to fade into irrelevance as they reach minority status. The political scientist Ashley Jardina documents the emergence of a sense of group attachment, pride, and solidarity among many white Americans that results from the belief that they are losing social, economic, and political power to racial minorities.[34] This feeling of white identity is a strong predictor of opposition to Barack Obama in 2012 and support for Donald Trump in 2016 even after controlling for other considerations such as partisanship, ideology, and attitudes toward Blacks.[35] If whites increasingly feel a sense of threat and consolidate their support behind candidates who they believe will preserve their group's status, that is likely to lower the chances of America's political leadership diversifying significantly in the coming decades. Another reason to question predictions about more pluralistic leadership is that they ignore the reality of conflict among minority groups. Research on Latinos and Asian Americans, for example, finds considerable heterogeneity in these groups' attitudes toward Blacks.[36] If wide swaths of the Latino, Asian American, and other nonwhite populations are receptive to anti-Black messaging, politicians will continue to benefit from stoking resentment of Blacks. Future research should examine how effective those efforts are.

The growing diversity of the United States is also likely to increase the pool of Latino and Asian American candidates for high-level statewide offices. As I mentioned in the introduction, I do not examine how race affects Latino and Asian candidacies in this book, but they deserve attention of their own. Race is likely to matter for these candidates for the same reasons it does for African Americans: negative stereotyping and group competition. Latinos are stereotyped by whites as lazy, criminal, and unintelligent,[37] while Asians are often seen by whites as foreign and inscrutable.[38] The political scientist Zoltan Hajnal points to several examples of whites feeling threatened by large or rapidly growing Latino or Asian populations; he also notes that candidates of both groups frequently offer reassurances that they will not favor their coethnics over whites.[39] But there are other reasons to believe that the racial penalty observed by Black candidates will be larger than the ones we might observe for Latino or Asian candidates. One is simply that anti-Black animus has a unique and unrivaled position in the history of American racism, as it remains strong even as prejudice against newer immigrant groups weakens over successive generations.[40] Another is that Latinos' and Asians' policy views are not as distinct from white views as are the views of Blacks, and so the prospect of Latino or Asian leadership is likely to be perceived as less threatening to white voters.

DEMONSTRATION OF EXPERIMENTAL EFFECTS IN REAL CAMPAIGNS

Finally, the case study chapters and the criminal pardon experiment reach different conclusions about the effects of rebuttals on racially resentful whites. While the experimental results point to an optimistic appraisal of the capacity of racially resentful whites to respond to reasonable communication, ultimately, we need corroborating evidence from real campaigns in order for optimism to be justified. Of course, this will not be an easy endeavor because it is hard to cleanly measure the effects of messages in the real world. But clarifying the effect of rebuttals on the racially resentful could matter a great deal to the electoral prospects of future Black candidates.

CONCLUDING THOUGHTS

To conclude, I consider how the findings shed light on whether racial considerations will be less consequential in future high-profile level Black candidacies. One possibility is that it depends on whether Black candidates are running as challengers or incumbents. Black challengers, as I have shown, have been racialized every time they have come close to breaking the color barrier. Trump's influence on the Republican Party suggests that Black challengers are likely to face more attacks that are pitched at racially resentful whites. Black incumbents, however, may be less racialized when running for reelection. Hajnal's research on Black mayors finds that once Black mayors win public office, they provide white citizens with information about what life is like under Black leadership.[41] That is to say, for most whites, life looks quite similar under Black leadership as it does under white leadership. This information, he argues, causes whites to deemphasize stereotypes and instead base their evaluations of Black candidates on the same criteria they use to evaluate white candidates: candidate quality, the economy, and endorsements collected by the candidate. If Black governors and senators follow a similar path, then racial considerations will be less consequential once a candidate breaks the color barrier.

However, one piece of evidence I have from a Black candidate's reelection campaign does not line up with this theory. In chapter 7, I showed results of an experiment conducted during Cory Booker's 2014 reelection bid. In that experiment, racial resentment was associated with Booker evaluation among New Jersey respondents who were assigned to the control group in which no information other than his picture was presented (see appendix table 8.1). This suggests that Booker was still racialized in 2014 even though he faced no major racial attacks in that year's reelection campaign. Based on Hajnal's findings, we might expect that racial resentment would fade as a predictor of Booker support, but that did not happen. The ongoing racialization of Booker in 2014 is in line with the political scientist Michael Tesler's work on the racialization of President Obama.[42] Incumbency did not reduce the weight that whites put on racial attitudes when evaluating Obama. In fact, Obama's presidency had the opposite effect: it made racial attitudes a stronger determinant of Obama evaluation and many other political evaluations that previously had no association with racial attitudes. If the white electorate remains hyperracialized after the memory of the Obama and Trump presidencies fade, racial considerations are likely to remain central to the evaluation of future Black statewide candidates.

Regardless of the role that racial attitudes play in future campaigns, it is apparent that Black candidates are likely to encounter racialized attacks when attempting to reach the highest offices in the United States. But it is also true that they respond to these attacks in a number of ways that influence the evaluations of white voters. In sum, the central argument of the book is that while race remains a major obstacle for Black candidates, it is not an insurmountable one. The United States is just beginning to witness a shift in the supply of candidates for high-level offices to include people like the candidates discussed in this book. The ability of future candidates to navigate challenging racial campaign dynamics will shape what the highest corridors of political power in the United States look like in the coming decades. The question of whether our leaders reflect our diversifying citizenry is likely to tell us a lot about the health of America's experiment in multiracial democracy.

APPENDIXES

APPENDIX FOR CHAPTER 1

APPENDIX TABLE 1.1 Black challengers facing white opponents from 2000–2020 (left); white comparison candidates, 3–4 white per one Black (right)

Black candidates					White candidates				
Name	State	Office	Year	Party	Name	State	Office	Year	Party
Jack Robinson	MA	U.S. Senate	2000	R	Mitt Romney	MA	U.S. Senate	1994	R
					William Weld	MA	U.S. Senate	1996	R
					Kenneth Chase	MA	U.S. Senate	2006	R
Troy Brown	MS	U.S. Senate	2000	D	Ken Harper	MS	U.S. Senate	1994	D
					Bootie Hunt	MS	U.S. Senate	1996	D
					Ronnie Musgrove	MS	U.S. Senate	2008	D
Ron Kirk	TX	U.S. Senate	2002	D	Victor Morales	TX	U.S. Senate	1996	D
					Gene Kelly	TX	U.S. Senate	2000	D
					Barbara Ann Radnofsky	TX	U.S. Senate	2006	D
					Rick Noriega	TX	U.S. Senate	2008	D

(continued)

APPENDIX TABLE 1.1 Black challengers facing white opponents from 2000–2020 (left); white comparison candidates, 3–4 white per one Black (right) (*continued*)

Black candidates					White candidates				
Name	State	Office	Year	Party	Name	State	Office	Year	Party
Joe Neal	NV	Governor	2002	D	Jan Laverty Jones	NV	Governor	1998	D
					Dina Titus	NV	Governor	2006	D
					Rory Reid	NV	Governor	2010	D
H. Carl McCall	NY	Governor	2002	D	Peter Vallone	NY	Governor	1998	D
					Eliot Spitzer	NY	Governor	2006	D
					Andrew Cuomo	NY	Governor	2010	D
Denise Majette	GA	U.S. Senate	2004	D	Max Cleland	GA	U.S. Senate	1996	D
					Michael Coles	GA	U.S. Senate	1998	D
					Jim Martin	GA	U.S. Senate	2008	D
Marvin Scott	IN	U.S. Senate	2004	R	Paul Helmke	IN	U.S. Senate	1998	R
					Dan Coats	IN	U.S. Senate	2010	R
					Richard Mourdock	IN	U.S. Senate	2012	R
Wayne Sowell	AL	U.S. Senate	2004	D	Clayton Suddith	AL	U.S. Senate	1998	D
					Susan Parker	AL	U.S. Senate	2002	D
					William Barnes	AL	U.S. Senate	2010	D
Deval Patrick	MA	Governor	2006	D	Scott Harshbarger	MA	Governor	1998	D
					Shannon O'Brien	MA	Governor	2002	D
					Martha Coakley	MA	Governor	2014	D
Harold Ford Jr.	TN	U.S. Senate	2006	D	Jeff Clark	TN	U.S. Senate	2000	D
					Bob Clement	TN	U.S. Senate	2002	D
					Bob Tuke	TN	U.S. Senate	2008	D
					Mark Clayton	TN	U.S. Senate	2012	D

Black candidates					White candidates				
Name	State	Office	Year	Party	Name	State	Office	Year	Party
Erik Fleming	MS	U.S. Senate	2006	D	Ronnie Musgrove	MS	U.S. Senate	2008	D
					Albert Gore	MS	U.S. Senate	2012	D
					Travis Childers	MS	U.S. Senate	2014	D
Ken Blackwell	OH	Governor	2006	R	Bob Taft	OH	Governor	1998	R
					John Kasich	OH	Governor	2010	R
					Mike DeWine	OH	Governor	2018	R
Michael Steele	MD	U.S. Senate	2006	R	Paul Rapaport	MD	U.S. Senate	2000	R
					E. J. Pipkin	MD	U.S. Senate	2004	R
					Eric Wargotz	MD	U.S. Senate	2010	R
					Dan Bonigno	MD	U.S. Senate	2012	R
Lynn Swann	PA	Governor	2006	R	Tom Ridge	PA	Governor	1994	R
					Mike Fisher	PA	Governor	2002	R
					Tom Corbett	PA	Governor	2010	R
					Scott Wagner	PA	Governor	2018	R
Vivian Davis Figures	AL	U.S. Senate	2008	D	Susan Parker	AL	U.S. Senate	2002	D
					William Barnes	AL	U.S. Senate	2010	D
					Ron Crumpton	AL	U.S. Senate	2016	D
Erik Fleming	MS	U.S. Senate	2008	D	Ronnie Musgrove	MS	U.S. Senate	2008	D
					Albert Gore	MS	U.S. Senate	2012	D
					Travis Childers	MS	U.S. Senate	2014	D
Kendrick Meek	FL	U.S. Senate	2010	D	Bill Nelson	FL	U.S. Senate	2000	D
					Betty Castor	FL	U.S. Senate	2004	D
					Patrick Murphy	FL	U.S. Senate	2016	D
Mike Thurmond	GA	U.S. Senate	2010	D	Jim Martin	GA	U.S. Senate	2008	D
					Michelle Nunn	GA	U.S. Senate	2014	D
					Jim Barksdale	GA	U.S. Senate	2016	D

(continued)

APPENDIX TABLE 1.1 Black challengers facing white opponents from 2000–2020 (left); white comparison candidates, 3–4 white per one Black (right) *(continued)*

Black candidates					White candidates				
Name	State	Office	Year	Party	Name	State	Office	Year	Party
Alvin Greene	SC	U.S. Senate	2010	D	Inez Tenenbaum	SC	U.S. Senate	2004	D
					Bob Conley	SC	U.S. Senate	2008	D
					Brad Hutto	SC	U.S. Senate	2014	D
Johnny Dupree	MS	Governor	2011	D	John Eaves	MS	Governor	2007	D
					Robert Gray	MS	Governor	2015	D
					Jim Hood	MS	Governor	2019	D
Randy Brock	VT	Governor	2012	R	Brian Dubie	VT	Governor	2010	R
					Scott Milne	VT	Governor	2014	R
					Phil Scott	VT	Governor	2016	R
Cory Booker	NJ	U.S. Senate	2013	D	Jon Corzine	NJ	U.S. Senate	2000	D
					Frank Lautenberg	NJ	U.S. Senate	2002	D
					Bob Menendez	NJ	U.S. Senate	2006	D
Anthony Brown	MD	Governor	2014	D	Parris Glendening	MD	Governor	1994	D
					Kathleen Kennedy Townsend	MD	Governor	2002	D
					Martin O'Malley	MD	Governor	2006	D
Constance Johnson	OK	U.S. Senate	2014	D	Jim Rogers	OK	U.S. Senate	2010	D
					Matt Silverstein	OK	U.S. Senate	2014	D
					Mike Workman	OK	U.S. Senate	2016	D
Darryl Glenn	CO	U.S. Senate	2016	R	Bob Schaffer	CO	U.S. Senate	2008	R
					Ken Buck	CO	U.S. Senate	2010	R
					Cory Gardner	CO	U.S. Senate	2014	R

	Black candidates				White candidates				
Name	State	Office	Year	Party	Name	State	Office	Year	Party
Ben Jealous	MD	Governor	2018	D	Parris Glendening	MD	Governor	1994	D
					Kathleen Kennedy Townsend	MD	Governor	2002	D
					Martin O'Malley	MD	Governor	2006	D
Andrew Gillum	FL	Governor	2018	D	Jim Davis	FL	Governor	2006	D
					Alex Sink	FL	Governor	2010	D
					Charlie Crist	FL	Governor	2014	D
Stacey Abrams	GA	Governor	2018	D	Mark Taylor	GA	Governor	2006	D
					Roy Barnes	GA	Governor	2010	D
					Jason Carter	GA	Governor	2014	D
John James	MI	U.S. Senate	2018	R	Jack Hoogendyk	MI	U.S. Senate	2008	R
					Pete Hoekstra	MI	U.S. Senate	2012	R
					Terri Lynn Land	MI	U.S. Senate	2014	R
Mike Espy	MS	U.S. Senate	2018	D	Albert Gore	MS	U.S. Senate	2012	D
					Travis Childers	MS	U.S. Senate	2014	D
					David Baria	MS	U.S. Senate	2018	D
Tony Campbell	MD	U.S. Senate	2018	R	Eric Wargotz	MD	U.S. Senate	2010	R
					Dan Bonigno	MD	U.S. Senate	2012	R
					Kathy Szeliga	MD	U.S. Senate	2016	R
Woody Myers	IN	Governor	2020	D	Jill Thompson	IN	Governor	2008	D
					John Gregg	IN	Governor	2012	D
					John Gregg	IN	Governor	2016	D
Mike Espy	MS	U.S. Senate	2020	D	Albert Gore	MS	U.S. Senate	2012	D
					Travis Childers	MS	U.S. Senate	2014	D
					David Baria	MS	U.S. Senate	2018	D

(continued)

APPENDIX TABLE 1.1 Black challengers facing white opponents from 2000–2020 (left); white comparison candidates, 3–4 white per one Black (right) *(continued)*

Black candidates					White candidates				
Name	State	Office	Year	Party	Name	State	Office	Year	Party
Raphael Warnock	GA	U.S. Senate	2020	D	Michelle Nunn	GA	U.S. Senate	2014	D
					Jim Barksdale	GA	U.S. Senate	2016	D
					Jon Ossoff	GA	U.S. Senate	2020	D
Jaime Harrison	SC	U.S. Senate	2020	D	Inez Tenenbaum	SC	U.S. Senate	2004	D
					Bob Conley	SC	U.S. Senate	2008	D
					Brad Hutto	SC	U.S. Senate	2014	D
Marquita Bradshaw	TN	U.S. Senate	2020	D	Bob Tuke	TN	U.S. Senate	2008	D
					Gordon Ball	TN	U.S. Senate	2014	D
					Phil Bredesen	TN	U.S. Senate	2018	D
John James	MI	U.S. Senate	2020	R	Jack Hoogendyk	MI	U.S. Senate	2008	R
					Pete Hoekstra	MI	U.S. Senate	2012	R
					Terri Lynn Land	MI	U.S. Senate	2014	R

APPENDIX TABLE 1.2 (OLS) Impact of candidate race on three key outcome measures

	% chance of victory (OLS)	Margin of victory among white voters (OLS)	Margin of victory among all voters (OLS)
Black (0 = white, 1 = Black)	**−12.99** (6.66)	**−10.73*** (3.09)	**−6.87*** (2.37)
Quality—previous experience (0 = least, 3 = most)	2.23 (3.32)	2.18* (1.54)	1.13 (1.19)
Quality—fundraising total (in millions)	0.20 (0.41)	0.46*** (0.19)	0.39*** (0.14)
Open seat (0 = no, 1 = yes)	7.84 (7.03)	6.72** (3.26)	10.70*** (2.51)
Ideological extremity (absolute value of CF score)	−15.63 (14.97)	2.71 (6.95)	−1.03 (5.34)
State economic performance	−0.57 (0.79)	−0.21 (0.37)	−0.02 (0.28)
Party advantage (%; neg = favors opp party, pos = favors own party)	0.27 (0.35)	0.06 (0.16)	0.38*** (0.13)
Black population in state (%)	0.34 (3.18)	−1.91* (1.48)	0.33 (1.14)
Male (0 = female, 1 = male)	27.33*** (8.08)	5.08* (3.75)	4.40* (2.88)
Running for U.S. Senate (0 = running for governor, 1 = running for U.S. Senate)	32.36*** (12.53)	12.03** (5.82)	5.59 (4.47)
(intercept)	10.39 (80.63)	−26.07 (37.42)	−37.82* (28.77)
State fixed effects	Yes	Yes	Yes
Party-Year fixed effects	Yes	Yes	Yes
N	129	129	129
Adjusted R-squared	0.56	0.84	0.68

*p < .1; **p < .05; ***p < .01, one-tailed test.

APPENDIX FOR CHAPTER 2

TABLE 2.1 Examples and nonexamples of crime, sex, and tax mentions

	Example	Nonexample	Reason for exclusion
Crime	"I will not be looking out to release dangerous offenders into society prematurely" "There is no benefit to hiding someone's criminal history" "Republican candidate Kerry Healey says that his [Patrick's] assistance [of the rapist] was a mistake." "[Abrams's] Republican opponent, Secretary of State Brian Kemp, has blasted Abrams for lending her campaign $50,000 while owing taxes, saying: 'If that's not criminal, it should be.'"	"You can have all the gun control you want. Criminals are always going to find a way to get guns on the street." "Lonegan later said he thought it was up to states to decide whether recreational use of marijuana should be permitted. 'It's really a state's rights issue,' he said."	Though Lonegan states his position on gun control, I considered gun control to be a separate issue from crime. The debate over whether an activity should be legal (in this case, marijuana use) is different from how to reduce activities that are clearly illegal (like murder or rape) or what to do with people who are found guilty of such activities.
Sex	"Ads for Corker portray Ford as part of a political machine with a Washington mentality and backing from the porno industry. In one ad, a blonde woman says she met 'Harold' at a Playboy party and asks, seductively, for him to call her."	"An unapologetic and slightly amused Cory Booker took questions yesterday regarding his brief online flirtation with Portland stripper Lynsie Lee, saying he will continue 'to just be me' on Twitter."	The narrator references Booker's flirtation with a stripper, which I considered a sexually themed topic. But since the mention was not made by Lonegan or a surrogate, it was not counted.

	Example	Nonexample	Reason for exclusion
		"Lonegan said, 'marriage is the greatest institution made by man' because 'it's about the children.' Asked whether he believed gay couples should have children, he quipped, 'That would be a biological phenomenon.'"	Issue positions (in this case, same-sex marriage) were not considered the same as attacks on personal sexual conduct.
Taxes	"Some of Hogan's oft-used phrases about Maryland's financial health include '40 consecutive tax increases,' 'mass exodus of businesses and families,' and '8,000 businesses killed.'"	"Hogan claimed repeatedly that 10 of Maryland's Fortune 500 companies left the state during the first seven years of the O'Malley-Brown administration."	At other times during the campaign, Hogan specifically linked the decision of businesses to relocate to high taxes. But unless the statement explicitly mentions taxes, it was not counted as a tax mention.

APPENDIX FOR CHAPTER 3

APPENDIX TABLE 3.1 Examples of rebuttal types

Rebuttal type	Brief description	Example
Racial	Call attention to the racial nature of the attack	A Republican political consultant severed his ties with Wal-Mart Friday night in the fallout over an ad in Tennessee's Senate race that critics deem racist.... The commercial does not mention that Ford is black, but [Jesse] Jackson and union-funded wakeupwal-mart.com had jointly called on Wal-Mart to fire [the consultant] to show it does not tolerate racism.
Negative	Denounce the attack, but using general, nonracial terms (e.g., "negative" or "inappropriate")	"I was a little surprised to see the smut and the slime coming into my living room during family time," Ford said of the two ads sponsored by the Republican National Committee.
Justify	Offer a justification for the attacked action	"This is a huge issue," [Healey running mate Reed] Hillman said. "It's Tim Murray [Patrick's running mate] who's been a defense attorney. It's Deval Patrick that's been a defense attorney. It's Kerry Healey that's always and consistently been on the side of victims." Murray responded by saying that he and Patrick had an obligation to defend criminals. "People in this country have a right to an equal protection under the law and due process," Murray said. "And yes, sometimes that does mean criminal defendants, as unsavory as they might be.
Distract	Pivot to a more favorable topic	Yesterday, Patrick poked fun at Healey, who has attacked him for his legal work on behalf of a convicted rapist and murderer ... and excoriated her record on the Big Dig, the economy, and other issues.

Rebuttal type	Brief description	Example
Counterimaging	Reframe the attack in a way that allows them to talk about their strengths on the very topic on which they are being attacked	In the past few weeks, as Healey has charged increasingly that Patrick is soft on crime, Patrick has referred to himself more and more as a former prosecutor who has had the personal "experience of sending people to jail. No, I'm not a criminologist," he said at a recent Boston Common rally, "but I have been in the crucible, breaking a sweat."
Counterattack	Turn the attack back on the opponent by attacking him on the same issue	And then [Patrick running mate Tim] Murray accused Healey of hypocrisy by portraying Patrick as soft on crime because of his advocacy for convicted rapist Benjamin LaGuer. "We just learned today Kerry Healey hired an attorney that represented LaGuer," he said.
Deny	Deny doing what candidate's opponent accuses them of doing, or stating they are not what their opponent accuses them of being	Hogan, meanwhile, attacked Brown relentlessly over what he called "40 consecutive tax increases" under the administration of Gov. Martin O'Malley. Brown declared unequivocally that he would not raise taxes. "I don't see the need, as governor, to raise taxes. There will be no new taxes in the Brown-Ulman administration," he declared.

APPENDIX FOR CHAPTER 5

APPENDIX TABLE 5.1 Was racial resentment associated with Republican (Lonegan) vote intention following racialized attacks? (no controls; logistic regression; racial resentment measured in both Rutgers polls)

	Before attacks (Rutgers September 3–7)	After attacks (Rutgers October 7–13)	Difference
Racial resentment	4.03*** (0.51)	5.23*** (0.56)	1.19 (0.76)
Intercept	−2.85*** (0.34)	−3.18*** (0.34)	−0.33 (0.48)
N	385	398	

***$p < .001$.

APPENDIX TABLE 5.2 Was racial resentment associated with Republican (Lonegan) vote intention following racialized attacks? (controlling for partisanship, no other controls; logistic regression; racial resentment measured in both Rutgers polls)

	Before attacks (Rutgers September 3–7)	After attacks (Rutgers October 7–13)	Difference
Racial resentment	2.04** (0.66)	3.95*** (0.74)	1.92^ (0.99)
Partisanship	4.58*** (0.47)	4.53*** (0.46)	−0.06 (0.66)
Intercept	−4.08*** (0.49)	−4.71 (0.53)	−0.63 (0.72)
N	384	399	

***$p < .001$; **$p < .01$; ^$p < .1$.

APPENDIX TABLE 5.3 Validation of predicted racial resentment. Racial priming occurs using predicted and measured racial resentment variables (compare with table 5.2)

	Before attacks (Rutgers September 3–7)	After attacks (Rutgers October 7–13)	Difference
Predicted racial resentment	1.67 (2.15)	4.37^ (2.27)	2.70 (3.12)
Partisanship	4.30*** (0.47)	4.32*** (0.45)	0.02 (0.65)
Ideology	1.99*** (0.53)	2.83*** (0.51)	0.85 (0.73)
Intercept	−4.79*** (1.41)	−6.80*** (1.55)	−2.01 (2.10)
N	437	443	

***p < .001; ^p < .1.

APPENDIX FOR CHAPTER 6

APPENDIX TABLE 6.1 (logistic regression) Racial resentment, sexism, and voting for GOP in 2018 gubernatorial contests (white respondents only, full results)

	Vote for Kemp (vs. Abrams)	Vote for GOP (vs. four white Dem women: L. Kelly, Mills, Whitmer, and M. Kelly)	Vote for DeSantis (vs. Gillum)
Racial Resentment	4.78*** (0.88)	3.04*** (0.47)	3.60*** (0.46)
Sexism	5.35*** (0.96)	2.20*** (0.52)	3.55*** (0.46)
Partisanship	6.89*** (0.75)	6.04*** (0.45)	6.12*** (0.36)
Ideology	2.15* (0.86)	3.15*** (0.57)	3.18*** (0.51)
Age	0.01 (0.01)	−0.00 (0.01)	−0.01 (0.01)
Male	−1.13** (0.40)	0.13 (0.22)	−0.08 (0.19)
Education	0.91 (0.63)	−0.39 (0.39)	−0.19 (0.36)
Income	−0.39 (0.93)	0.76 (0.59)	1.65** (0.51)
(Intercept)	−10.19*** (1.08)	−7.82*** (0.56)	−8.84*** (0.59)
N	934	1,805	2,390

***p < .001; **p < .01; *p < .05.

SEXISM MEASURE IN STUDY 2

Sexism is measured slightly differently across surveys. The 2004 and 2008 ANES measured it identically, using the following three items:

1. When women demand equality these days, they are actually seeking special favors. [agree strongly, agree somewhat, neither agree nor disagree, disagree somewhat, or disagree strongly]
2. Women often miss out on good jobs because of discrimination. [agree strongly, agree somewhat, neither agree nor disagree, disagree somewhat, or disagree strongly]

3. Women who complain about harassment cause more problems than they solve. [agree strongly, agree somewhat, neither agree nor disagree, disagree somewhat, or disagree strongly]

In 2012, the first question was repeated, but with a different response format.

1. When women demand equality these days, how often are they actually seeking special favors? [always, most of the time, about half the time, some of the time, or never]
2. When women complain about discrimination, how often do they cause more problems than they solve? [always, most of the time, about half the time, some of the time, or never]

The second item is very similar to item 3 on the 2004 and 2008 ANES, but with the different response format.

Four new items were added:

3. How serious a problem is discrimination against women in the United States? [not a problem at all, a minor problem, a moderately serious problem, a very serious problem, or an extremely serious problem]
4. Should the news media pay more attention to discrimination against women, less attention, or the same amount of attention they have been paying lately? [a great deal more attention, somewhat more attention, a little more attention, the same amount of attention, a little less attention, somewhat less attention, or a great deal less attention]
5. When employers make decisions about hiring and promotion, how often do they discriminate against women? [never, some of the time, about half the time, most of the time, or always]
6. In the U.S. today, do men have more opportunities for achievement than women have, do women have more opportunities than men, or do they have equal opportunities? [men have many more, men have moderately more, men have slightly more, equal, women have slightly more, women have moderately more, women have many more]

In 2016, the three-item scale returned:

1. When women demand equality these days . . . (identical to 2012 item 1)
2. When women complain about discrimination . . . (identical to 2012 item 2)
3. Should the news media . . . (identical to 2012 item 4)

In 2020, the ANES pared the scale down to two items:

1. When women demand equality these days . . . (identical to 2012 item 1 and 2016 item 1)
2. When women complain about discrimination . . . (identical to 2012 item 2 and 2016 item 2)

In selecting the two items that were most similar across years, the first one was easy: item 1 ("when women demand equality these days . . .") was the same across years despite minor differences in response format.

For the second item, the downplaying of discrimination was a theme that was consistent across all five surveys. The 2020 ANES had only one other item (item 2), and it was discrimination themed ("When women complain about discrimination"). So I decided to try to select items from other years that were as similar to that item as possible. This was easy for 2012 and 2016, as item 2 from those surveys ("When women complain about discrimination") is identical to 2020 ANES item 2. As for the 2004 and 2008 ANES, item 3 ("When women complain about harassment . . .") was similar in construction to 2020 ANES item 2, but I considered discrimination and harassment to be two different topics. So I selected the discrimination-themed item 2 from 2004 and 2008 ("Women often miss out of good jobs because of discrimination.")

QUESTION WORDING FROM OCTOBER 2020 LUCID SURVEY (STUDY 3)

Items provided by Lucid before the survey

Income

How much total combined income do all members of your household earn before taxes? [less than $5,000; $5,000 to $9,999; $10,000 to $14,999; $15,000 to $19,999; $20,000 to $24,999; $25,000 to $29,999; $30,000 to

$34,999; $35,000 to $39,999; $40,000 to $44,999; $45,000 to $49,999; $50,000 to $54,999; $55,000 to $59,999; $60,000 to $64,999; $65,000 to $69,999; $70,000 to $79,999; $80,000 to $84,999; $85,000 to $89,999; $90,000 to $94,999; $95,000 to $99,999; $100,000 to $124,999; $125,000 to $149,999; $150,000 to $174,999; $175,000 to $199,999; $200,000 to $249,999; $250,000 or over; prefer not to say]

Education

What is the highest level of education you have completed? [3rd grade or less; middle school—grades 4–8; completed some high school; high school graduate; other post–high school vocational training; completed some college, but not degree; associate degree; college degree (such as BA, BS); completed some graduate, but no degree; masters degree; doctorate degree; none of the above]

Party identification

The scale was constructed using branched questions: "Generally speaking, do you think of yourself as a . . . ?" [Democrat, Republican, Independent, Other] [If R considers self a Democrat/Republican] "Would you call yourself a strong Democrat or not so strong Democrat/ Would you call yourself a strong Republican or not so strong Republican?" [strong, not very strong] [If R is Independent or Other] "Do you think of yourself as closer to the Republican or Democratic Party?" [Closer to the Republican Party, closer to the Democratic Party, Neither] Coded as a seven-category variable from the branching questions ranging from 0 (strong Democrat) to 1 (strong Republican).

Age

What is your age? [fill in the blank]

Items asked on the survey (in order)

Feeling thermometer ratings

We would like to get your feeling toward some of our political leaders and other people who are in the news these days. If we come to a person whose name you don't recognize, you don't need to rate that person. Just click the "Never heard of person" box and we'll move on to the next one.

How would you rate [randomized order]: Democratic vice presidential candidate Kamala Harris; former President Barack Obama; former First Lady Michelle Obama; former Democratic presidential candidate Hillary Clinton [rating on 0–100 scale or never heard of person]

Trump approval

Do you approve or disapprove of the way President Trump is doing his job? [strongly approve, somewhat approve, somewhat disapprove, strongly disapprove, or not sure]

Economic assessment

Would you say that OVER THE PAST YEAR the nation's economy has [gotten much better, gotten better, stayed about the same, gotten worse, gotten much worse, or not sure]

COVID fear

How worried are you about you or someone in your family being infected with Coronavirus? [very worried, somewhat worried, not very worried, or not at all worried]

Ideology

In general, how would you describe your own political viewpoint? [very liberal, liberal, somewhat liberal, moderate/middle of the road, somewhat conservative, conservative, very conservative, or not sure]

Income [if respondent did not provide income to Lucid before the survey]

Thinking back over the last year, what was your total combined household income before taxes? This question is completely confidential and just used to help classify the responses, but it is very important to the research [Less than $40,000; $40,000 to $79,999; Over $80,000; Prefer not to say]

Education [if respondent did not provide education to Lucid before the survey]

What's the highest level of education you have completed? [some high school or less; high school diploma or equivalent certificate; some college or 2-year degree; college degree; post-college degree]

Racial resentment battery

The scale was constructed from responses to the following items: (1) "Irish, Italians, Jewish, and many other minorities overcame prejudice and worked their way up. Blacks should do the same without any special favors." [strongly agree, somewhat agree, neither agree nor disagree, somewhat disagree, or strongly disagree] (2) "Generations of slavery and discrimination have created conditions that make it difficult for blacks to work their way out of the lower class." [strongly agree, somewhat agree, neither agree nor disagree, somewhat disagree, or strongly disagree] (3) "Over the past few years, blacks have gotten less than they deserve." [strongly agree, somewhat agree, neither agree nor disagree, somewhat disagree, or strongly disagree] (4) "It's really a matter of not trying hard enough; if blacks would only try harder they could be just as well off as whites" [strongly agree, somewhat agree, neither agree nor disagree, somewhat disagree, or strongly disagree] Coded from 0 (least resentful) to 1 (most resentful).

Sexism battery

The scale was constructed from responses to the following items: (1) "When women lose to men in a fair competition, they typically complain about being discriminated against." [strongly agree, somewhat agree, neither agree nor disagree, somewhat disagree, or strongly disagree] (2) "Feminists are making entirely reasonable demands of men." [strongly agree, somewhat agree, neither agree nor disagree, somewhat disagree, or strongly disagree] (3) "When women demand equality these days, they are actually seeking special favors." [strongly agree, somewhat agree, neither agree nor disagree, somewhat disagree, or strongly disagree] (4) "Women often miss out on good jobs because of discrimination."

[strongly agree, somewhat agree, neither agree nor disagree, somewhat disagree, or strongly disagree] Coded from 0 (least sexist) to 1 (most sexist).

Race

In order to get a representative sample of everyone, please indicate your race or ethnicity. [White, not-Hispanic; Black or African American; Hispanic or Latino; Asian American; American Indian/Native American; Middle Eastern or Arab American; other]

Gender

Please indicate your current gender. [Man, Woman, Other]

APPENDIX TABLE 6.2 (OLS) Racism, sexism, and feeling thermometer ratings of Harris, Clinton, Barack Obama, and Michelle Obama (white respondents only)

	Harris	Clinton	B. Obama	M. Obama
Racial resentment	−0.17*** (0.02)	−0.09*** (0.03)	−0.20*** (0.02)	−0.23*** (0.02)
Sexism	−0.15*** (0.03)	−0.13*** (0.03)	−0.12*** (0.03)	−0.18*** (0.03)
Partisanship (Republican)	−0.22*** (0.02)	−0.30*** (0.02)	−0.18*** (0.02)	−0.14*** (0.02)
Ideology (conservative)	−0.20*** (0.02)	−0.21*** (0.02)	−0.22*** (0.02)	−0.20*** (0.02)
Age	−0.00*** (0.00)	−0.00*** (0.00)	−0.00*** (0.00)	−0.00*** (0.00)
Male	0.06*** (0.01)	0.06*** (0.01)	0.04*** (0.01)	0.03*** (0.01)
Education	0.12*** (0.02)	0.11*** (0.02)	0.07*** (0.02)	0.06** (0.02)
Income	0.10*** (0.02)	0.12*** (0.02)	0.12*** (0.02)	0.11*** (0.02)
Trump approval	−0.25*** (0.02)	−0.12*** (0.02)	−0.26*** (0.02)	−0.25*** (0.02)
Economic evaluations	0.09*** (0.02)	0.11*** (0.02)	0.06*** (0.02)	0.05** (0.02)
Coronavirus fear	0.21*** (0.02)	0.21*** (0.02)	0.20*** (0.02)	0.19*** (0.02)
(intercept)	0.74*** (0.03)	0.63*** (0.03)	0.94*** (0.03)	0.98*** (0.03)
Adjusted R^2	0.59	0.50	0.60	0.58
N	3,190	3,227	3,228	3,233

Note: Entries are OLS coefficients with standard errors in parentheses. Michelle Obama's racial resentment coefficient (−0.23) is significantly larger than Clinton's (−0.09; p < .001), while Michelle Obama's sexism coefficient (−0.18) is not significantly larger than Barack Obama's (−0.12; p = 0.18).

Source: 2020 Lucid survey.

***p < .001; **p < .01, two-tailed tests.

QUESTION WORDING FROM FEBRUARY 2021 LUCID SURVEY EXPERIMENT (STUDY 4)

Items provided by Lucid before the survey

Age

What is your age? [fill in the blank]

Education

What is the highest level of education you have completed? [3rd grade or less; middle school—grades 4–8; completed some high school; high school graduate; other post–high school vocational training; completed some college, but not degree; associate degree; college degree (such as BA, BS); completed some graduate, but no degree; masters degree; doctorate degree; none of the above]

Party identification

The scale was constructed using branched questions: "Generally speaking, do you think of yourself as a . . .?" [Democrat, Republican, Independent, Other] [If R considers self a Democrat/Republican] "Would you call yourself a strong Democrat or not so strong Democrat/Would you call yourself a strong Republican or not so strong Republican?" [strong, not very strong] [If R is Independent or Other] "Do you think of yourself as closer to the Republican or Democratic Party?" [Closer to the Republican Party, closer to the Democratic Party, Neither] Coded as a seven-category variable from the branching questions ranging from 0 (strong Democrat) to 1 (strong Republican).

Income

How much total combined income do all members of your household earn before taxes? [less than $5,000; $5,000 to $9,999; $10,000 to $14,999; $15,000 to $19,999; $20,000 to $24,999; $25,000 to $29,999; $30,000 to $34,999; $35,000 to $39,999; $40,000 to $44,999; $45,000 to $49,999; $50,000 to $54,999; $55,000 to $59,999; $60,000 to $64,999; $65,000 to $69,999; $70,000 to $79,999; $80,000 to $84,999; $85,000 to $89,999;

$90,000 to $94,999; $95,000 to $99,999; $100,000 to $124,999; $125,000 to $149,999; $150,000 to $174,999; $175,000 to $199,999; $200,000 to $249,999; $250,000 or over; prefer not to say]

Pretreatment questions

Ideology

In general, how would you describe your own political viewpoint? [very liberal, liberal, somewhat liberal, moderate/middle of the road, somewhat conservative, conservative, very conservative, or not sure]

Income [if respondent did not provide income to Lucid]

Thinking back over the last year, what was your total combined household income before taxes? This question is completely confidential and just used to help classify the responses, but it is very important to the research [Less than $40,000; $40,000 to $79,999; Over $80,000; Prefer not to say]

Education [if respondent did not provide education to Lucid]

What's the highest level of education you have completed? [some high school or less; high school diploma or equivalent certificate; some college or 2-year degree; college degree; post-college degree]

Post-treatment questions

Harris feeling thermometer

Please rate Kamala Harris using something called the feeling thermometer. Ratings between 50 degrees and 100 degrees mean that you feel favorable and warm toward her. Ratings between 0 degrees and 50 degrees mean that you don't feel favorable toward Harris and that you don't care too much for her. Rate her at the 50 degree mark if you don't feel particularly warm or cold toward her. [*control group only:* If you don't know who Harris is, you don't need to provide a rating. Just click the "Never heard of this person" box and we'll move on.] [rating on 0–100 scale or never heard of this person]

Harris job as VP

How good of a job do you think Kamala Harris will do as vice president? [a very poor job, a poor job, a below-average job, an average job, an above-average job, a good job, or a very good job; *control group only*: I have never heard of Kamala Harris]

Harris presidential vote

How likely would you be to vote for Kamala Harris if she were the Democratic nominee for president in the near future? [extremely unlikely, not very likely, neither likely nor unlikely, very likely, or extremely likely; *control group only*: I have never heard of Kamala Harris]

Harris job as president

How good of a job do you think Kamala Harris would do as president? [a very poor job, a poor job, a below-average job, an average job, an above-average job, a good job, or a very good job; *control group only*: I have never heard of Kamala Harris]

Manipulation check—Harris's race

How would you describe Kamala Harris's ethnic or racial background? (please write in the space below); *control group only*: If you have never heard of Kamala Harris, write "I don't know who Harris is" in the space below.

Manipulation check—article topic

What was the central topic of the story you read about earlier? [the 2020 election, cell phones, the Olympics, bears, Disney+]

Racial resentment battery

The scale was constructed from responses to the following items: (1) "Irish, Italians, Jewish, and many other minorities overcame prejudice and worked their way up. Blacks should do the same without any special favors." [strongly agree, somewhat agree, neither agree nor disagree, somewhat disagree, or strongly disagree] (2) "Generations of slavery and discrimination have created conditions that make it difficult for blacks to work their way out of the lower class." [strongly agree, somewhat agree, neither agree nor disagree, somewhat disagree, or strongly disagree] (3) "Over the past few years, blacks have gotten less than they deserve." [strongly agree, somewhat agree, neither agree nor disagree, somewhat disagree, or strongly disagree] (4) "It's really a matter of not trying hard enough; if blacks would only try harder they could be just as well off as whites" [strongly agree, somewhat agree, neither agree nor disagree, somewhat disagree, or strongly disagree] Coded from 0 (least resentful) to 1 (most resentful).

Anti-Black stereotypes battery

The scale was constructed from responses to the following items: (1) "Where would you rate whites in general on this scale? [1 (hard-working), 2, 3, 4, 5, 6, 7 (lazy)]; (2) "Where would you rate blacks in general on this scale? [1 (hard-working), 2, 3, 4, 5, 6, 7 (lazy)]; (3) "Where would you rates white in general on this scale? [1 (peaceful), 2, 3, 4, 5, 6, 7 (violent)] (4) "Where would you rate blacks in general on this scale? [1 (peaceful), 2, 3, 4, 5, 6, 7 (violent)]. Responses are coded to the 0–1 interval. Belief in the stereotype that Blacks are lazy is calculated by subtracting the white score from the Black score on items 1 and 2. Belief in the stereotype that Blacks are violent is calculated by subtracting the white score from the Black score on items 3 and 4. The overall stereotypes score is calculated by averaging the belief in the two stereotypes and coding it 0 (least stereotypical) to 1 (most stereotypical).

Sexism battery

The scale was constructed from responses to the following items: (1) "When women lose to men in a fair competition, they typically complain about being discriminated against." [strongly agree, somewhat agree, neither agree nor disagree, somewhat disagree, or strongly disagree] (2) "Feminists are making entirely reasonable demands of men."

[strongly agree, somewhat agree, neither agree nor disagree, somewhat disagree, or strongly disagree] (3) "When women demand equality these days, they are actually seeking special favors." [strongly agree, somewhat agree, neither agree nor disagree, somewhat disagree, or strongly disagree] (4) "Women often miss out on good jobs because of discrimination." [strongly agree, somewhat agree, neither agree nor disagree, somewhat disagree, or strongly disagree] Coded from 0 (least sexist) to 1 (most sexist).

Race

In order to get a representative sample of everyone, please indicate your race or ethnicity. [White, not Hispanic; Black or African American; Hispanic or Latino; Asian American; American Indian/Native American; Middle Eastern/Arab American; Other]

Gender

Please indicate your current gender. [Man, Woman, Other]

NEWS ARTICLE AND TREATMENTS IN FEBRUARY 2021 LUCID SURVEY EXPERIMENT

A version of the following news article appeared on a major national news website in November 2020. Please read the article carefully before answering questions about it.

Treatments 1–3

Kamala Harris a Source of Pride for Many [Blacks/Women/South Asians]

After taking the oath of office on Wednesday, Kamala Harris became the nation's 49th vice president. Harris' rise is celebrated among [*Black political and community groups across the nation/women's political and community groups across the nation/South Asian political and community groups across the nation/*], who expressed joy at the prospect of seeing one of their own in the nation's second highest office.

"The election of Kamala Harris as vice president is an occasion worth celebrating," said [*Congressman Hakeem Jeffries (D-NY), a member of the Congressional Black Caucus / Congresswoman Madeleine Dean (D-PA), a member of the Congressional Women's Caucus / Congressman Raja Krishnamoorthi (D-IL), a member of the Congressional Asian Pacific American Caucus*]. "It sends a powerful message to [Blacks/women/South Asians] everywhere that America is a land of opportunity."

As vice president, Harris is clearly positioned to one day become president. She ran for president in 2020, but dropped out before any votes were cast in the Democratic primary. Some Democrats criticized her record as being too conservative, while Republicans criticized her during the campaign for being too liberal. Harris dismissed those charges, instead calling her approach to politics non-ideological and pragmatic.

Control

Disney+ Surpasses 73 Million Subscribers Amid Streaming Boom

The Disney streaming service Disney+ announced that it had 73.7 million subscribers as of October 3, surpassing its five-year projections in only 11 months. The announcement was hailed as a major success by industry analysts, who were surprised that Disney gained a foothold in the competitive streaming environment so quickly.

"In order to continue their strong early performance, they need to invest heavily in original programming," said David Jones, a media business analyst. "Netflix and Amazon are the industry leaders in producing new content, and Disney must keep up if they hope to add new subscribers."

Despite the good news regarding its streaming business, streaming is still not profitable for Disney due to startup costs. Disney is hoping that streaming becomes profitable soon in order to offset losses suffered by its theme park division.

APPENDIX TABLE 6.3 (OLS) Association between racial and gender attitudes and evaluations of Harris by experimental condition

	Black	Woman	p	Black	South Asian	p	Black	Control	p
Racial resentment	-0.35*** (0.06) (N = 403)	-0.23** (0.06) (N = 418)	0.15	-0.35*** (0.06) (N = 403)	-0.22*** (0.05) (N = 460)	0.09	-0.35*** (0.06) (N = 403)	-0.24*** (0.06) (N = 382)	0.19
Anti-Black stereotypes	-0.45*** (0.13) (N = 339)	-0.10 (0.12) (N = 365)	0.05	-0.45*** (0.13) (N = 339)	-0.15 (0.11) (N = 397)	0.08	-0.45*** (0.13) (N = 339)	-0.26^ (0.14) (N = 333)	0.33
	Woman	Black	p	Woman	South Asian	p	Woman	Control	p
Sexism (controlling for racial resentment)	-0.29*** (0.07) (N = 418)	-0.25*** (0.08) (N = 403)	0.66	-0.29*** (0.07) (N = 418)	-0.35*** (0.06) (N = 460)	0.56	-0.29*** (0.07) (N = 418)	-0.19* (0.08) (N = 382)	0.35
Sexism (controlling for anti-Black stereotypes)	-0.44*** (0.06) (N = 365)	-0.38*** (0.08) (N = 339)	0.58	-0.44*** (0.06) (N = 365)	-0.46*** (0.06) (N = 397)	0.78	-0.44*** (0.06) (N = 365)	-0.37*** (0.08) (N = 333)	0.49

Note: Estimates for correlations between racial attitudes, gender attitudes, and evaluations of Harris includes controls for partisanship, ideology, age, education, gender, and income.

APPENDIX TABLE 6.4 (OLS) Association between racial and gender attitudes and evaluations of Harris by experimental condition (Black vs. Not Black and Woman vs. Not woman), full results

	Black	Not Black	Black	Not Black	Woman	Not woman	Woman	Not woman
Racial resentment	−0.35*** (0.06)	−0.23*** (0.03)			−0.23*** (0.06)	−0.27*** (0.03)		
Anti-Black stereotypes			−0.45*** (0.13)	−0.16* (0.07)			−0.10 (0.12)	−0.26*** (0.07)
Sexism	−0.25** (0.08)	−0.29*** (0.04)	−0.38*** (0.08)	−0.44*** (0.04)	−0.29*** (0.07)	−0.27*** (0.04)	−0.44*** (0.06)	−0.42*** (0.04)
Partisanship	−0.37*** (0.03)	−0.50*** (0.02)	−0.38*** (0.04)	−0.53*** (0.02)	−0.44*** (0.03)	−0.47*** (0.02)	−0.51*** (0.04)	−0.49*** (0.02)
Ideology	−0.11* (0.05)	−0.05* (0.02)	−0.17** (0.06)	−0.09*** (0.03)	−0.07 (0.04)	−0.07* (0.03)	−0.07 (0.05)	−0.13*** (0.03)
Age	−0.00 (0.00)	−0.00* (0.00)	−0.00 (0.00)	−0.00*** (0.00)	−0.00* (0.00)	−0.00^ (0.00)	−0.00* (0.00)	−0.00* (0.00)
Male	0.04^ (0.02)	0.04** (0.01)	0.02 (0.03)	0.05*** (0.01)	0.04^ (0.02)	0.04*** (0.01)	0.04^ (0.02)	0.04** (0.01)
Income	0.05 (0.04)	0.08** (0.02)	−0.02 (0.05)	0.06* (0.03)	0.09* (0.04)	0.06* (0.03)	0.04 (0.04)	0.03 (0.03)
Education	0.04 (0.06)	0.02 (0.03)	0.08 (0.06)	0.01 (0.03)	0.05 (0.05)	0.03 (0.03)	0.01 (0.05)	0.03 (0.03)
(Intercept)	1.10*** (0.05)	1.06*** (0.03)	1.25*** (0.07)	1.14*** (0.04)	1.07*** (0.05)	1.07*** (0.03)	1.12*** (0.07)	1.18*** (0.04)
Adjusted R^2	0.57	0.64	0.55	0.64	0.61	0.62	0.64	0.61
N	403	1,260	339	1,096	418	1,245	365	1,070

APPENDIX FOR CHAPTER 7

APPENDIX TABLE 7.1 Impact of racial resentment on Booker-minus-Lonegan rating by attack, white NJ respondents only

	Twitter	Crime	Black hole	Stripper	Obama	Holly-wood	Patriotism	Results	All racialized	All placebo
Racial resentment	−0.75** (0.24)	−0.75*** (0.22)	−0.75** (0.23)	−0.75** (0.24)	−0.75*** (0.21)	−0.75** (0.23)	−0.75*** (0.23)	−0.75** (0.22)	−0.75** (0.23)	−0.75** (0.23)
Partisanship	−0.62** (0.19)	−0.62** (0.18)	−0.62** (0.19)	−0.62** (0.19)	−0.62*** (0.17)	−0.62*** (0.18)	−0.62** (0.19)	−0.62*** (0.18)	−0.62*** (0.19)	−0.62** (0.19)
Ideology	0.26 (0.28)	0.26 (0.26)	0.26 (0.27)	0.26 (0.28)	0.26 (0.25)	0.26 (0.27)	0.26 (0.27)	0.26 (0.26)	0.26 (0.27)	0.26 (0.27)
Attack	0.15 (0.18)	0.19 (0.17)	0.00 (0.19)	0.27 (0.20)	0.19 (0.17)	0.30 (0.18)	0.01 (0.18)	0.33 (0.22)	0.17 (0.15)	0.14 (0.17)
Attack* racial resentment	0.19 (0.31)	0.40 (0.29)	0.12 (0.32)	0.24 (0.33)	0.17 (0.28)	0.22 (0.29)	0.25 (0.31)	0.22 (0.34)	0.23 (0.25)	0.28 (0.28)
Attack* partisanship	0.41^ (0.24)	0.17 (0.22)	0.25 (0.28)	0.11 (0.26)	−0.05 (0.21)	0.26 (0.23)	−0.13 (0.25)	0.25 (0.24)	0.19 (0.20)	0.08 (0.22)
Attack* ideology	−0.85* (0.34)	−0.99** (0.31)	−0.30 (0.38)	−0.91* (0.37)	−0.54^ (0.31)	−1.15*** (0.33)	−0.14 (0.36)	−1.22*** (0.34)	−0.76** (0.29)	−0.64* (0.32)
(intercept)	0.72*** (0.14)	0.72*** (0.13)	0.72*** (0.14)	0.72*** (0.14)	0.72*** (0.13)	0.72*** (0.14)	0.72*** (0.14)	0.72*** (0.13)	0.72*** (0.14)	0.72*** (0.14)
Adjusted R²	0.41	0.54	0.39	0.46	0.56	0.54	0.43	0.53	0.50	0.46
N	131	132	104	112	127	130	122	96	393	165

Note: Dependent variable is the Booker-minus-Lonegan feeling thermometer score recoded from −1 (most anti-Booker) to 1 (most pro-Booker). Each regression equation includes measures of partisanship, ideology, attack exposure and the interaction between the two attitudinal variables and attack exposure. ***p < .001; **p < .01; *p < .05, two-tailed tests.

APPENDIX TABLE 7.2 Impact of racial resentment on Booker-minus-Lonegan rating by attack, white MD respondents only

	Twitter	Crime	Black hole	Stripper	Obama	Hollywood	Patriotism	Results	All racialized	All placebo
Racial resentment	0.23 (0.24)	0.23 (0.22)	0.23 (0.21)	0.23 (0.22)	0.23 (0.24)	0.23 (0.22)	0.23 (0.25)	0.23 (0.19)	0.23 (0.23)	0.23 (0.23)
Partisanship	−0.50** (0.16)	−0.50** (0.15)	−0.50** (0.15)	−0.50** (0.15)	−0.50** (0.17)	−0.50** (0.15)	−0.50** (0.17)	−0.50*** (0.13)	−0.50** (0.16)	−0.50** (0.16)
Ideology	−0.21 (0.21)	−0.21 (0.19)	−0.21 (0.19)	−0.21 (0.19)	−0.21 (0.21)	−0.21 (0.19)	−0.21 (0.22)	−0.21 (0.17)	−0.21 (0.20)	−0.21 (0.20)
Attack	0.33^ (0.19)	0.05 (0.16)	0.24 (0.16)	0.36* (0.15)	0.32^ (0.17)	0.07 (0.16)	0.07 (0.18)	0.21 (0.13)	0.27* (0.14)	0.14 90.15)
Attack* racial resentment	−0.68* (0.32)	−0.29 (0.29)	−0.64* (0.28)	−0.70** (0.26)	−0.65* (0.31)	−0.38 (0.30)	−0.24 (0.34)	−0.53* (0.24)	−0.61* (0.24)	−0.41 (0.27)
Attack* partisanship	0.17 (0.24)	−0.00 (0.22)	0.09 (0.20)	0.38^ (0.20)	0.16 (0.24)	0.27 (0.20)	−0.24 (0.23)	0.46** (0.17)	0.19 (0.17)	0.10 (0.19)
Attack* ideology	0.04 (0.31)	0.15 (0.29)	0.22 (0.26)	−0.28 (0.25)	−0.08 (0.32)	0.00 (0.29)	0.32 (0.34)	−0.29 (0.24)	−0.01 (0.22)	0.06 (0.25)
(intercept)	0.26^ (0.13)	0.26* (0.12)	0.26* (0.12)	0.26* (0.12)	0.26^ (0.14)	0.26* (0.12)	0.26^ (0.14)	0.26* (0.11)	0.26* (0.13)	0.26* (0.13)
Adjusted R^2	0.31	0.36	0.36	0.38	0.41	0.28	0.32	0.42	0.39	0.31
N	92	93	92	111	102	97	96	105	310	156

Note: Dependent variable is the Booker-minus-Lonegan feeling thermometer score recoded from −1 (most anti-Booker) to 1 (most pro-Booker). Each regression equation includes measures of partisanship, ideology, attack exposure and the interaction between the two attitudinal variables and attack exposure. ***p < .001; **p < .01; *p < .05, two-tailed tests.

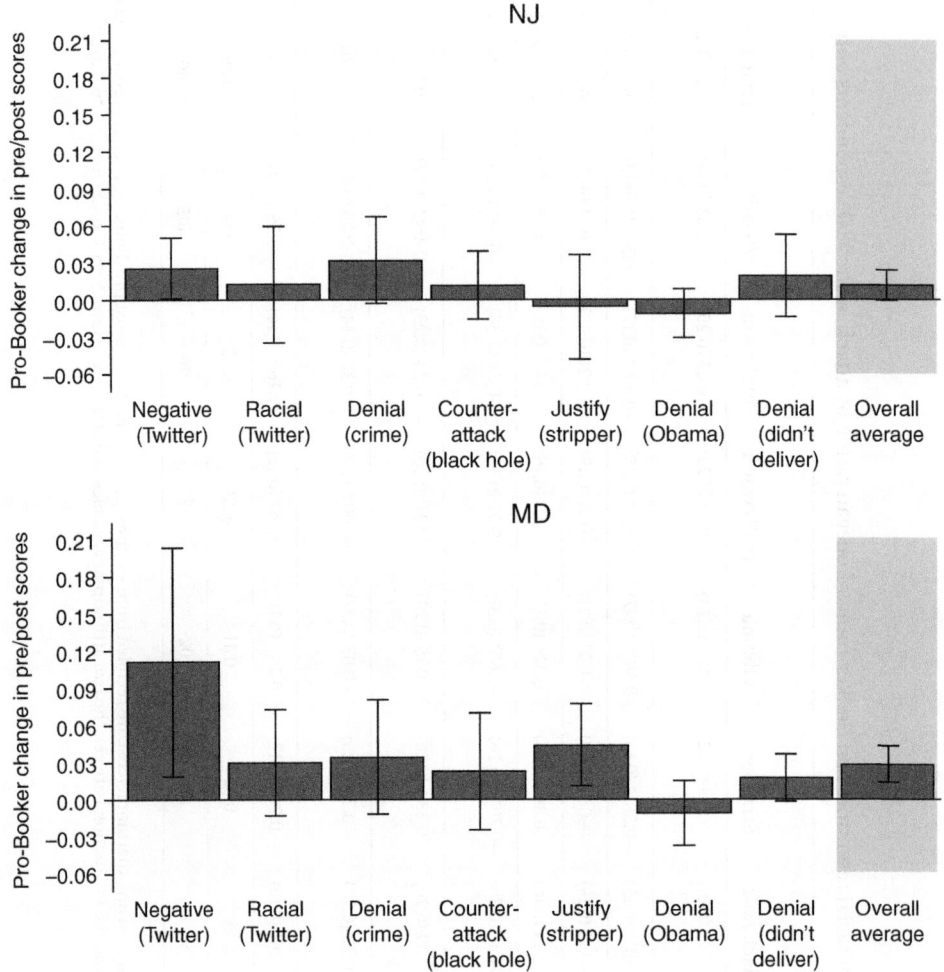

APPENDIX FIGURE 7.1. Rebuttal effects, white New Jersey respondents (top panel) and white Maryland respondents (bottom panel).

APPENDIX FOR CHAPTER 8

APPENDIX TABLE 8.1 Overview of key design features of each experiment

Experiment	Date	Subject pool	n	Attack details	Election type	Candidate party labels	Rebuttals tested	Realistic images?
1	Dec. 2011 and Feb. 2012	MTurk	670	Extortion, tax evasion, appointment of friends and relatives to public positions, and assault of a police officer	General	No party labels given	1. Racial (n = 114) 2. Justify (n = 152) 3. Negative (n = 140) 4. Distract (n = 149) 5. Control (n = 115)	No
2	March 2013 and July 2013	MTurk (97%) and Mercer County (NJ) Panel (3%)	766	Emphasize assault on police officer; list other crimes (extortion, tax evasion, etc.)	Primary	Both candidates' party matched to respondent's	1. Racial (n = 101) 2. Justify (n = 144) 3. Justify + racial (n = 96) 4. Negative (n = 144) 5. Distract (n = 138) 6. Control (n = 143)	Yes

(*continued*)

APPENDIX TABLE 8.1 Overview of key design features of each experiment (*continued*)

Experiment	Date	Subject pool	n	Attack details	Election type	Candidate party labels	Rebuttals tested	Realistic images?
3	February 2014	SSI	1,149	Emphasize assault on police officer; list others (extortion, tax evasion, appointment of friends and relatives)	Primary	Both candidates' party matched to respondent's	1. Racial (n = 140) 2. Justify (n = 220) 3. Justify + racial (n = 141) 4. Negative (n = 217) 5. Distract (n = 209) 6. Control (n = 222)	Yes
4	December 2014	SSI	897	Emphasize assault on police officer; list others (extortion, tax evasion, appointment of friends and relatives)	General	Targeted candidate is a Democrat and attacking candidate is a Republican	1. Racial (n = 180) 2. Justify (n = 239) 3. Counterimaging (n = 250) 4. Counterattack (n = 228)	Yes

APPENDIX TABLE 8.2 Rebuttal effects in each experiment
(standard errors are displayed in parentheses)

	Black target				White target			
	Exp. 1	*Exp. 2*	*Exp. 3*	*Exp. 4*	*Exp. 1*	*Exp. 2*	*Exp. 3*	*Exp. 4*
Racial	0.01 (0.02) n = 75	0.00 (0.02) n = 71	−0.05 (0.02) n = 90	0.03 (0.02) n = 119	0.01 (0.04) n = 39	0.04 (0.04) n = 30	0.08 (0.03) n = 50	0.08 (0.03) n = 61
Justify	0.16 (0.03) n = 80	0.17 (0.04) n = 63	0.13 (0.02) n = 93	0.15 (0.03) n = 116	0.15 (0.03) n = 72	0.15 (0.02) n = 81	0.09 (0.02) n = 127	0.16 (0.03) n = 123
Justify + racial	N/A	0.23 (0.03) n = 65	0.11 (0.02) n = 95	N/A	N/A	0.19 (0.04) n = 31	0.11 (0.04) n = 46	N/A
Negative	0.05 (0.02) n = 69	0.03 (0.02) n = 58	0.06 (0.02) n = 97	N/A	0.04 (0.02) n = 71	−0.01 (0.02) n = 86	0.03 (0.02) n = 120	N/A
Counterattack	N/A	N/A	N/A	0.13 (0.02) n = 113	N/A	N/A	N/A	0.09 (0.03) n = 115
Counterimaging	N/A	N/A	N/A	0.06 (0.02) n = 123	N/A	N/A	N/A	0.10 (0.02) n = 127
Distract	0.06 (0.03) n = 77	0.05 (0.03) n = 61	0.02 (0.02) n = 97	N/A	0.09 (0.03) n = 72	0.06 (0.02) n = 77	0.03 (0.02) n = 112	N/A
Control	−0.01 (0.01) n = 56	−0.02 (0.01) n = 66	−0.02 (0.02) n = 98	N/A	−0.02 (0.01) n = 59	−0.02 (0..01) n = 77	−0.02 (0..01) n = 124	N/A

APPENDIX TABLE 8.3 Rebuttal effects in each experiment, Black criminal and white criminal conditions disaggregated (standard errors are displayed in parentheses)

	Black target/black criminal				Black target/white criminal				White target/black criminal				White target/white criminal			
	Exp. 1	Exp. 2	Exp. 3	Exp. 4	Exp. 1	Exp. 2	Exp. 3	Exp. 4	Exp. 1	Exp. 2	Exp. 3	Exp. 4	Exp. 1	Exp. 2	Exp. 3	Exp. 4
Racial	0.00 (0.03) n=40	0.01 (0.03) n=36	−0.05 (0.04) n=41	0.01 (0.03) n=59	0.01 (0.03) n=35	−0.00 (0.03) n=35	−0.06 (0.03) n=49	0.04 (0.03) n=60	0.01 (0.04) n=39	0.04 (0.04) n=30	0.08 (0.03) n=50	0.08 (0.03) n=61	N/A	N/A	N/A	N/A
Justify	0.13 (0.03) n=40	0.12 (0.05) n=28	0.11 (0.03) n=47	0.16 (0.05) n=54	0.20 (0.04) n=40	0.21 (0.06) n=35	0.15 (0.03) n=46	0.14 (0.03) n=62	0.12 (0.03) n=37	0.19 (0.04) n=36	0.06 (0.04) n=52	0.17 (0.04) n=63	0.18 (0.04) n=35	0.13 (0.03) n=45	0.11 (0.03) n=75	0.15 (0.04) n=60
Justify + racial	N/A	0.24 (0.04) n=33	0.10 (0.04) n=45	N/A	N/A	0.23 (0.05) n=32	0.12 (0.03) n=50	N/A	N/A	0.19 (0.04) n=31	0.11 (0.04) n=46	N/A	N/A	N/A	N/A	N/A
Negative	0.05 (0.04) n=34	0.03 (0.03) n=27	0.04 (0.03) n=46	N/A	0.05 (0.03) n=35	0.02 (0.03) n=31	0.09 (0.03) n=51	N/A	0.06 (0.03) n=32	0.01 (0.03) n=29	0.03 (0.04) n=51	N/A	0.03 (0.03) n=39	−0.01 (0.03) n=57	0.02 (0.02) n=69	N/A
Counterattack	N/A	N/A	N/A	0.11 (0.03) n=59	N/A	N/A	N/A	0.16 (0.03) n=54	N/A	N/A	N/A	0.07 (0.05) n=57	N/A	N/A	N/A	0.10 (0.03) n=58
Counterimaging	N/A	N/A	N/A	0.08 (0.03) n=61	N/A	N/A	N/A	0.05 (0.04) n=62	N/A	N/A	N/A	0.07 (0.03) n=64	N/A	N/A	N/A	0.12 (0.04) n=63
Distract	0.09 (0.03) n=41	0.02 (0.03) n=27	0.01 (0.03) n=48	N/A	0.02 (0.05) n=36	0.08 (0.04) n=34	0.03 (0.03) n=49	N/A	0.05 (0.03) n=37	0.11 (0.03) n=27	0.06 (0.03) n=41	N/A	0.12 (0.04) n=35	0.04 (0.02) n=50	0.01 (0.02) n=71	N/A
Control	0.01 (0.02) n=30	−0.02 (0.02) n=38	−0.01 (0.03) n=48	N/A	−0.03 (0.02) n=26	−0.01 (0.02) n=28	−0.03 (0.01) n=50	N/A	0.00 (0.01) n=32	−0.01 (0.02) n=33	−0.00 (0.01) n=51	N/A	−0.04 (0.03) n=27	−0.03 (0.02) n=44	−0.04 (0.02) n=77	N/A

Note: Racial and *justify + racial* were considered to be unrealistic rebuttals for a white target paired with a white criminal, so they were not tested for that pair.

APPENDIX TABLE 8.4 Did the attack work as a racial attack against the Black target? Predicting postattack target-minus-attacker difference score (full model)

	Support for the target
Racial resentment	−0.16*** (0.04)
Partisanship	−0.05 (0.03)
Ideology	−0.05 (0.04)
Black target	0.09** (0.03)
Racial resentment × black target	−0.14** (0.05)
Partisanship × black target	0.09* (0.05)
Ideology × black target	−0.10^ (0.05)
Experiment 2	−0.06*** (0.02)
Experiment 3	−0.01 (0.01)
Experiment 4	0.04* (0.02)
Intercept	0.03 (0.02)
Adjusted R-squared	0.07
N	3,234

Note: Entries are ordinary least-squares regression coefficients. Standard errors are in parentheses. The dependent variable was measured on a −1 to 1 scale ranging from strong opposition to strong support of the target. Partisanship was measured on a 7-point scale collapsed to the 0–1 interval ranging from 0 (strong Democrat) to 1 (strong Republican). Ideology was measured on a 7-point scale collapsed to the 0–1 interval ranging from 0 (very liberal) to 1 (very conservative). ^p < 0.1; *p < 0.05; **p < 0.01; ***p < 0.001, two-tailed test.

NOTES

INTRODUCTION

1. Aaron Navarro and Sarah Ewell-Wice, "GOP Uses Crime in Closing Message Against Democrats in Wisconsin, Pennsylvania Senate Races," *CBS News*, October 31, 2022, https://www.cbsnews.com/news/republicans-crime-democrats-wisconsin-pennsylvania-senate-races/.
2. Antoine J. Banks, "The Public's Anger: White Racial Attitudes and Opinions Toward Health Care Reform," *Political Behavior* 36, no. 3 (2013): 493–514; Antoine J. Banks and Melissa A. Bell, "Racialized Campaign Ads: The Emotional Content in Implicit Racial Appeals Primes White Racial Attitudes," *Public Opinion Quarterly* 77, no. 2 (2013): 549–60; Adam J. Berinsky, Vincent L. Hutchings, Tali Mendelberg, Lee Shaker, and Nicholas A. Valentino, "Sex and Race: Are Black Candidates More Likely to Be Disadvantaged by Scandals?," *Political Behavior* 33, no. 2 (2011): 179–202; Christopher DeSante, "Working Twice as Hard to Get Half as Far: Race, Work Ethic, and America's Deserving Poor," *American Journal of Political Science* 57, no. 2 (2013): 342–56; Jon Hurwitz and Mark Peffley, "Playing the Race Card in the Post–Willie Horton Era: The Impact of Racialized Code Words on Support for Punitive Crime Policy," *Public Opinion Quarterly* 69, no. 1 (2005): 99–112; Donald R. Kinder and Allison Dale-Riddle, *The End of Race? Obama, 2008, and Racial Politics in America* (New Haven, CT: Yale University Press, 2012); Donald R. Kinder and Lynn Sanders, *Divided by Color: Racial Politics and Democratic Ideals* (Chicago: University of Chicago Press, 1996); Tali Mendelberg, *The Race Card: Campaign Strategy, Implicit Appeals, and the Norm of Equality* (Princeton, NJ: Princeton University Press, 2001); Michael Tesler, "The Spillover of Racialization Into Health Care: How President Obama Polarized Public Opinion by Racial Attitudes and Race," *American Journal of Political Science* 56, no. 3 (2012): 690–704; Michael Tesler and David O. Sears, *Obama's Race: The 2008 Election and the*

Dream of a Post-Racial America (Chicago: University of Chicago Press, 2010); Nicholas A. Valentino, Vincent L. Hutchings, and Ismail K. White, "Cues That Matter: How Political Ads Prime Racial Attitudes During Campaigns," *American Political Science Review* 96, no. 1 (2002): 75–90; Ismail K. White, "When Race Matters and When It Doesn't: Racial Group Differences in Response to Racial Cues," *American Political Science Review* 101, no. 2 (2007): 339–54.

3. Mandela Barnes, "Truth," YouTube, August 30, 2022, https://www.youtube.com/watch?v=kjXzioemqgY.
4. Adam Edelman, "Ron Johnson and Mandela Barnes Duel Over Crime and Abortion in Wisconsin Senate Debate," *NBC News*, October 7, 2022, https://www.nbcnews.com/politics/2022-election/ron-johnson-mandela-barnes-duel-crime-abortion-wisconsin-senate-debate-rcna51313.
5. Susan Milligan, "How Race Entered the Midterms in the Guise of 'Crime,'" *US News and World Report*, October 14, 2022.
6. Julia Jacobs, "DeSantis Warns Florida Not to 'Monkey This Up,' and Many Hear a Racist Dog Whistle," *New York Times*, August 28, 2018.
7. Of those ten winners, only seven defeated white opponents in the general election. Barack Obama (D-IL), Tim Scott (R-SC), and Kamala Harris (D-CA) defeated nonwhite opponents to win their Senate elections.
8. John Sides, Michael Tesler, and Lynn Vavreck, *Identity Crisis: The 2016 Presidential Campaign and the Battle for the Meaning of America* (Princeton, NJ: Princeton University Press, 2018).
9. Donald R. Kinder and Allison Dale-Riddle, *The End of Race? Obama, 2008, and Racial Politics in America* (New Haven, CT: Yale University Press, 2012); Spencer Piston, "How Explicit Prejudice Hurt Obama in the 2008 Election," *Political Behavior* 32, no. 4 (2010): 431–51; Seth Stephens-Davidowitz, "The Cost of Racial Animus on a Black Candidate: Evidence Using Google Search Data," *Journal of Public Economics* 118 (2014): 26–40; Michael Tesler, *Post-Racial or Most-Racial? Race and Politics in the Obama Era* (Chicago: University of Chicago Press, 2016); Michael Tesler and David O. Sears, *Obama's Race: The 2008 Election and the Dream of a Post-Racial America* (Chicago: University of Chicago Press, 2010).
10. Paul M. Sniderman and Edward H. Stiglitz, "Race and the Moral Character of the Modern American Experience," *The Forum* 6, no. 4 (2008): 1–15; Abigail Thernstrom and Stephan Thernstrom, "Taking Race out of the Race," *Los Angeles Times*, March 2, 2008.
11. Kinder and Dale-Riddle, *The End of Race?*; Michael Lewis-Beck, Charles Tien, and Richard Nadeau, "Obama's Missed Landslide: A Racial Cost?," *PS: Political Science and Politics* 43, no. 1 (2010): 69–76; Piston, "How Explicit Prejudice Hurt Obama in the 2008 Election"; Stephens-Davidowitz, "The Cost of Racial Animus on a Black Candidate"; Tesler, *Post-Racial or Most-Racial?*; Tesler and Sears, *Obama's Race*.
12. Tesler and Sears, *Obama's Race*.
13. Nayda Terkildsen, "When White Voters Evaluate Black Candidates: The Processing Implications of Candidate Skin Color, Prejudice, and Self-Monitoring," *American Journal of Political Science* 37, no. 4 (1993): 1032–53; Vesla Weaver, "The Electoral

Consequences of Skin Color: The 'Hidden' Side of Race in Politics," *Political Behavior* 34, no. 1 (2012): 159–92.

14. Rufus P. Browning, Dale Rogers Marshall, and David H. Tabb, *Racial Politics in American Cities VII* (New York: Longman, 1997); Charles S. Bullock, "Partisan Changes in Southern Congressional Delegation and the Consequences," in *Continuity and Change in House Elections*, ed. David W. Brady, John F. Cogan, and Morris Fiorina (Stanford, CA: Stanford University Press, 2000), 39–64; Charles S. Bullock and Richard E. Dunn, "The Demise of Racial Districting and the Future of Black Representation," *Emory Law Journal* 48, no. 4 (1999): 1209–53; Zoltan Hajnal, *Changing White Attitudes Toward Black Political Leadership* (New York: Cambridge University Press, 2007); Donald R. Kinder and David O. Sears, "Prejudice and Politics: Symbolic Racism Versus Racial Threats to the Good Life," *Journal of Personality and Social Psychology* 40, no. 3 (1981): 414–31; Stephen D. Voss and David Lublin, "Black Incumbents, White Districts: An Appraisal of the 1996 Congressional Elections," *American Politics Research* 29, no. 2 (2001): 141–82.

15. Jack Citrin, Donald Philip Green, and David O. Sears, "White Reactions to Black Candidates: When Does Race Matter?" *Public Opinion Quarterly* 54 (1990): 74–96; Benjamin Highton, "White Voters and African American Candidates for Congress," *Political Behavior* 26, no. 1 (2004): 1–25.

16. Highton, "White Voters and African American Candidates for Congress," 17.

17. Linda F. Williams, "White/Black Perceptions of the Electability of Black Political Candidates," *National Political Science Review* 2 (1990): 145–64.

18. Charles Cameron, David Epstein, and Sharyn O'Halloran, "Do Majority-Minority Districts Maximize Substantive Black Representation in Congress?," *American Political Science Review* 90, no. 4 (1996): 794–812; David Lublin and Stephen D. Voss, "Racial Redistricting and Realignment in Southern State Legislatures," *American Journal of Political Science* 44 (2000): 792–810; Raphael J. Sonenshein, "Can Black Candidates Win Statewide Elections?," *Political Science Quarterly* 105, no. 2 (1990): 219–41.

19. Christopher H. Achen and Larry M. Bartels, *Democracy for Realists: Why Elections Do Not Produce Responsive Government* (Princeton, NJ: Princeton University Press, 2016), 313.

20. For an examination of how race influences state legislative elections, see Christopher J. Clark, *Gaining Voice: The Causes and Consequences of Black Representation in the American States* (New York: Oxford University Press, 2019).

21. Charles V. Hamilton, "Deracialization: Examination of a Political Strategy," *First World* 1 (1977): 3–5; Huey L. Perry, "Deracialization as an Analytical Construct in American Politics," *Urban Affairs Quarterly* 27, no. 2 (1991): 181–91.

22. Sekou Franklin, "Situational Deracialization, Harold Ford, and the 2006 Senate Race in Tennessee," in *Whose Black Politics? Cases in Post-Racial Black Leadership*, ed. Andra Gillespie (New York: Routledge, 2010), 214–40; Angela K. Lewis, "Making History, Again, So Soon? The Massachusetts Gubernatorial Election," in *Beyond the Boundaries: A New Structure of Ambition in African American Politics*, ed. Georgia A. Persons (New Brunswick, NJ: Transaction, 2009); Charlton D. McIlwain and Stephen M.

Caliendo, *Race Appeal: How Candidates Invoke Race in U.S. Political Campaigns* (Philadelphia: Temple University Press, 2011); Byron D'Andra Orey, "Racial Threat, Republicanism, and the Rebel Flag: Trent Lott and the 2006 Mississippi Senate Race," *National Political Science Review* 12 (2009): 83–96.

23. Mendelberg, *The Race Card*.
24. Sekou M. Franklin and Ray Block Jr., *Losing Power: African Americans and Racial Polarization in Tennessee Politics* (Athens: University of Georgia Press, 2020).
25. Kinder and Sanders, *Divided by Color*; Valentino, Hutchings, and White, "Cues That Matter."
26. Mendelberg, *The Race Card*.
27. Thomas B. Edsall and Mary D. Edsall, *Chain Reaction: The Impact of Race, Rights, and Taxes on American Politics* (New York: Norton, 1991); Hamilton, "Deracialization"; Perry, "Deracialization as an Analytical Construct in American Politics."
28. I will have more to say about viability in chapter 2, but for now, I define viability as either winning the election by any margin or losing the election by less than five percentage points.
29. Since 2016, the *New York Times* has published stories on the lack of diversity at the top levels of law, finance, media, entertainment, academia, medicine, science, technology, arts, professional sports, the military, journalism, and politics.
30. Haeyoun Park, Josh Keller, and Josh Williams, "The Faces of American Power, Nearly as White as the Oscar Nominees," *New York Times*, February 26, 2016, http://www.nytimes.com/interactive/2016/02/26/us/race-of-american-power.html.
31. Of those forty-four minority leaders, seventeen were Black (3.3% of the total), fifteen were Hispanic (3.0%), and twelve were Asian/Asian American (2.4%).
32. Denise Lu, Jon Huang, Ashwin Seshagiri, Haeyoun Park, and Troy Griggs, "Faces of Power: 80% Are White, Even as U.S. Becomes More Diverse," *New York Times*, September 9, 2020, https://www.nytimes.com/interactive/2020/09/09/us/powerful-people-race-us.html.
33. Jennifer L. Lawless and Richard L. Fox, *It Takes a Candidate: Why Women Don't Run for Office* (New York: Cambridge University Press, 2005); Michele L. Swers, *The Difference Women Make: The Policy Impact of Women in Congress* (Chicago: University of Chicago Press, 2002); Nicholas Carnes, *The Cash Ceiling: Why Only the Rich Run for Office—and What We Can Do About It* (Princeton, NJ: Princeton University Press, 2018).
34. I focus on Black candidates because they are the most likely among minority candidates to arouse anxiety among white voters about representation. Although the last few decades have seen an influx of people who do not fit the traditional Black/white paradigm of U.S. race relations, the central racial divide in American politics today is still between whites and Blacks. The racial divide in voting, policy views, and life circumstances is much sharper between whites and Blacks than it is between whites and Latinos or Asian Americans. See Paul R. Abramson, John H. Aldrich, and David W. Rohde, *Change and Continuity in the 2004 and 2006 Elections* (Washington, DC: CQ

Press, 2007); Kinder and Sanders, *Divided by Color*; Douglas S. Massey and Nancy A. Denton, *American Apartheid* (Cambridge, MA: Harvard University Press, 1993); and David O. Sears and Victoria Savalei, "The Political Color Line in America: Many Peoples of Color or Black Exceptionalism?," *Political Psychology* 27 (2006): 895–924. This divide in experience and political views gives rise to whites' negative stereotypes and other forms of anti-Black attitudes that in turn arouse fear about Black representation. This is not to say, however, that race is irrelevant to Latino and Asian American candidacies. It likely is, and such candidacies are worthy of their own examination.

35. Dennis Chong and James N. Druckman, "Framing Public Opinion in Competitive Democracies," *American Political Science Review* 101, no. 4 (2007): 637–55; Paul M. Sniderman and Sean M. Theriault, "The Structure of Political Argument and the Logic of Issue Framing," in *Studies in Public Opinion: Attitudes, Nonattitudes, Measurement Error, and Changes*, ed. Willem E. Saris and Paul M. Sniderman (Princeton, NJ: Princeton University Press, 2004).

36. Sides, Tesler, and Vavreck, *Identity Crisis*.

1. WHY ARE BLACK GOVERNORS AND U.S. SENATORS SO RARE? RACIAL BIAS AGAINST BLACK CHALLENGERS, 2000-2020

1. Nicholas Carnes, *The Cash Ceiling: Why Only the Rich Run for Office—and What We Can Do About It* (Princeton, NJ: Princeton University Press, 2018); Jennifer L. Lawless and Richard L. Fox, *It Takes a Candidate: Why Women Don't Run for Office* (New York: Cambridge University Press, 2005); Pippa Norris and Joni Lovenduski, *Political Recruitment: Gender, Race, and Class in the British Parliament* (Cambridge: Cambridge University Press, 1995).
2. Although southern states have larger Black populations, they have also historically shown the strongest opposition to Black political advances.
3. Christopher H. Achen and Larry M. Bartels, *Democracy for Realists: Why Elections Do Not Produce Responsive Government* (Princeton, NJ: Princeton University Press, 2016); Charles Cameron, David Epstein, and Sharyn O'Halloran, "Do Majority-Minority Districts Maximize Substantive Black Representation in Congress?," *American Political Science Review* 90, no. 4 (1996): 794–812; David Lublin and Stephen D. Voss, "Racial Redistricting and Realignment in Southern State Legislatures," *American Journal of Political Science* 44 (2000): 792–810; Raphael J. Sonenshein, "Can Black Candidates Win Statewide Elections?," *Political Science Quarterly* 105, no. 2 (1990): 219–41.
4. Looking exclusively at challengers narrows the set of Black candidacies by six, since Edward Brooke (R-MA) (twice), Carol Moseley-Braun (D-IL), Deval Patrick (D-MA), Cory Booker (D-NJ), and Tim Scott (R-SC) ran as incumbents.
5. Challenger candidacies include open-seat races. In other words, a challenger can be running against an incumbent or running for an open seat.

6. Hiram Revels (R) and Blanche Kelso (R) represented Mississippi in the U.S. Senate during Reconstruction, but neither was popularly elected: U.S. senators were elected by state legislatures before 1913.
7. Bradley's narrow defeat in 1982 despite leading his opponent George Deukmejian (R) in the pre-election polls gave rise to the term "Bradley effect," which refers to the underperformance of Black candidates compared to pre-election forecasts. This results from survey respondents telling pollsters that they support the Black candidate but not actually doing so at the ballot box. For evidence of the Bradley effect until 1996, see Daniel J. Hopkins, "No More Wilder Effect, Never a Whitman Effect: When and Why Polls Mislead About Black and Female Candidates," *Journal of Politics* 71, no. 3 (2009): 769–81.
8. P. B. S. Pinchback (R) became the first Black governor in U.S. history in 1872 when he became governor of Louisiana. Pinchback was not elected, however. He succeeded the previous governor, who was removed during Reconstruction.
9. Michael Tesler, *Post-Racial or Most-Racial? Race and Politics in the Obama Era* (Chicago: University of Chicago Press, 2016).
10. Jack Citrin, Donald Philip Green, and David O. Sears, "White Reactions to Black Candidates: When Does Race Matter?," *Public Opinion Quarterly* 54 (1990): 74–96.
11. Benjamin Highton, "White Voters and African American Candidates for Congress," *Political Behavior* 26, no. 1 (2004): 1–25.
12. Paul M. Sniderman and Thomas Piazza, *The Scar of Race* (Cambridge, MA: Harvard University Press, 1993); Stephan Thernstrom and Abigail Thernstrom, *America in Black and White: One Nation, Indivisible* (New York: Simon and Schuster, 1997).
13. Zoltan Hajnal, *Changing White Attitudes Toward Black Political Leadership* (New York: Cambridge University Press, 2007).
14. Seth K. Goldman and Diana C. Mutz, *The Obama Effect: How the 2008 Campaign Changed White Attitudes* (New York: Russell Sage Foundation, 2014).
15. Adam J. Berinsky, Vincent L. Hutchings, Tali Mendelberg, Lee Shaker, and Nicholas A. Valentino, "Sex and Race: Are Black Candidates More Likely to Be Disadvantaged by Scandals?," *Political Behavior* 33, no. 2 (2011): 179–202; Monika L. McDermott, "Race and Gender Cues in Low-Information Elections," *Political Research Quarterly* 51, no. 4 (1998): 895–918; Carol K. Sigelman, Lee Sigelman, Barbara J. Walkosz, and Michael Nitz, "Black Candidates, White Voters: Understanding Racial Bias in Political Perceptions," *American Journal of Political Science* 39, no. 1 (1995): 243–65; Nayda Terkildsen, "When White Voters Evaluate Black Candidates: The Processing Implications of Candidate Skin Color, Prejudice, and Self-Monitoring," *American Journal of Political Science* 37, no. 4 (1993): 1032–53; Matthew Tokeshi and Tali Mendelberg, "Countering Implicit Racial Appeals: Which Strategies Work?," *Political Communication* 32, no. 4 (2015): 648–72.
16. Donald R. Kinder and Allison Dale-Riddle, *The End of Race? Obama, 2008, and Racial Politics in America* (New Haven, CT: Yale University Press, 2012); Spencer Piston, "How Explicit Prejudice Hurt Obama in the 2008 Election," *Political Behavior* 32, no. 4 (2010):

431–51; Tesler, *Post-Racial or Most-Racial?*; Michael Tesler and David O. Sears, *Obama's Race: The 2008 Election and the Dream of a Post-Racial America* (Chicago: University of Chicago Press, 2010).

17. Kinder and Dale-Riddle, *The End of Race?*; Michael Lewis-Beck, Charles Tien, and Richard Nadeau, "Obama's Missed Landslide: A Racial Cost?," *PS: Political Science and Politics* 43, no. 1 (2010): 69–76; Seth Stephens-Davidowitz, "The Cost of Racial Animus on a Black Candidate: Evidence Using Google Search Data," *Journal of Public Economics* 118 (2014): 26–40; but see Alexandre Mas and Enrico Moretti, "Racial Bias in the 2008 Presidential Election," *American Economic Review: Papers and Proceedings* 99, no. 2 (2009): 323–29.
18. Hajnal, *Changing White Attitudes Toward Black Political Leadership*; Highton, "White Voters and African American Candidates for Congress."
19. Citrin, Green, and Sears, "White Reactions to Black Candidates."
20. Terkildsen, "When White Voters Evaluate Black Candidates"; Vesla Weaver, "The Electoral Consequences of Skin Color: The 'Hidden' Side of Race in Politics," *Political Behavior* 34, no. 1 (2012): 159–92.
21. Tesler and Sears, *Obama's Race*.
22. Evidence consistent with the notion that some forms of racial animus have declined since the 1960s comes from many sources, including national surveys showing an increasing number of whites who say they would support a qualified Black presidential candidate and social arrangements such as interracial marriage, integrated schools, and integrated neighborhoods. See Howard Schuman, Charlotte Steeh, Lawrence Bobo, and Maria Krysan, *Racial Attitudes in America: Trends and Interpretations* (Cambridge, MA: Harvard University Press, 1997).
23. Looking exclusively at challengers narrows the set of Black candidacies by only three, since Deval Patrick (D-MA), Cory Booker (D-NJ), and Tim Scott (R-SC) ran as incumbents between 2000 and 2020.
24. The omitted cases are Barack Obama's 2004 U.S. Senate campaign (against Black Republican Alan Keyes) and Tim Scott's 2014 U.S. Senate campaign (against Black Democrat Joyce Dickerson).
25. In cases where there was a tie for the third most recent white candidate, both candidates were included, resulting in some Black candidates having four (instead of three) white comparison observations. This explains why the number of white comparison candidates is 115 (instead of 111). The median number of years separating a white comparison election from the Black candidate election is six, with 67 percent of white comparison elections taking place within six years and 85 percent of white comparison elections taking place within ten years of the Black candidate election.
26. Research assistants Kaitlin Braband, Jose Manuel Corichi Gomez, Sam Mermin, and Yannick Davidson assisted in the collection of the data.
27. The surveys had an average error of 4.8 percentage points when compared to the actual result of the election. For comparison, a FiveThirtyEight analysis of more than 8,500 polls from 1998 to 2018 conducted within the final three weeks of a campaign found an

average error of 5.9 percentage points. See Nate Silver, "The Polls Are All Right," *FiveThirtyEight*, May 30, 2018, https://fivethirtyeight.com/features/the-polls-are-all-right/.

28. Gary King, *A Solution to the Ecological Inference Problem* (Princeton, NJ: Princeton University Press, 1997).

29. EI is commonly used to measure the voting behavior of groups when survey data is unavailable or unreliable. Perhaps the most prominent example of EI's use is in voting rights court cases, which often turn on whether plaintiffs can demonstrate patterns of racially polarized voting. Other recent applications of EI to estimate vote choice for subgroups of the population include Gary King, Ori Rosen, Martin Tanner, and Alexander F. Wagner, "Ordinary Economic Voting Behavior in the Extraordinary Election of Adolf Hitler," *Journal of Economic History* 68, no. 4 (2008): 951–96; Matt A. Barreto, "¡Si Se Puede! Latino Candidates and the Mobilization of Latino Voters," *American Political Science Review* 101, no. 3 (2007): 425–41; and Matt A. Barreto, Tyler Reny, and Bryan Wilcox-Archuleta, "Survey Methodology and the Latina/o Vote: Why a Bilingual, Bicultural, Latino-Centered Approach Matters," *Atzlán: A Journal of Chicano Studies* 42, no. 2 (2017): 209–25. For a critique of EI's reliability, see David A. Freedman, "Ecological Inference and the Ecological Inference and the Ecological Fallacy," in *International Encyclopedia of the Social and Behavioral Sciences*, ed. Neil J. Smelser and Paul B. Baltes (New York: Elsevier, 1999), 4027–30.

30. To address concerns that differences in turnout between Black versus white and white versus white contests render margin of victory comparisons inconclusive, no significant differences in turnout were found between the two types of contests. Black versus white contests had an average turnout of 50.83 percent of eligible voters, while turnout for white versus white contests averaged 48.59 percent ($p = 0.34$, two-tailed test).

31. Gary C. Jacobson and Samuel Kernell, *Strategy and Choice in Congressional Elections* (New Haven, CT: Yale University Press, 1981).

32. Jonathan S. Krasno and Donald Philip Green, "Preempting Quality Challengers in House Elections," *Journal of Politics* 50 (1988): 920–36.

33. Gary C. Jacobson, *The Politics of Congressional Elections*, 8th ed. (Boston: Pearson, 2012).

34. Alan Gerber, "African Americans' Congressional Careers and the Democratic House Delegation," *Journal of Politics* 58, no. 3 (1996): 831–45.

35. Adam Bonica, *Database on Ideology, Money in Politics, and Elections: Public Version 2.0* (Stanford: Stanford University Libraries, 2016), http://data.stanford.edu/dime.

36. Keith T. Poole and Howard Rosenthal, *Congress: A Political-Economic History of Roll-Call Voting* (New York: Oxford University Press, 1997); Boris Shor and Nolan McCarty, "The Ideological Mapping of American Legislatures," *American Political Science Review* 105, no. 3 (2011): 530–51.

37. James Adams and Lawrence Kenny, "The Retention of State Governors," *Public Choice* 62 (1989): 1–13; Randall W. Bennett and Clark Wiseman, "Economic Performance and U.S. Senate Elections, 1958–1986," *Public Choice* 69, no. 1 (1991): 93–100; John Chubb,

"Institutions, the Economy, and the Dynamics of State Elections," *American Political Science Review* 82 (1988): 133–54; John R. Hibbing and John R. Alford, "Economic Conditions and the Forgotten Side of Congress: A Foray into U.S. Senate Elections," *British Journal of Political Science* 12, no. 4 (1982): 505–13; William Levernier, "The Effect of Relative Economic Performance on the Outcome of Gubernatorial Elections," *Public Choice* 74 (1992): 181–90; Richard Niemi, Harold Stanley, and Ronald Vogel, "State Economies and State Taxes: Do Voters Hold Governors Accountable?," *American Journal of Political Science* 39 (1995): 936–57; Sam Peltzman, "Economic Conditions and Gubernatorial Elections," *American Economic Review* 7 (1987): 293–97.

38. Clara Kulich, Michelle K. Ryan, and S. Alexander Haslam, "The Political Glass Cliff: Understanding How Seat Selection Contributes to Minority Candidates," *Political Research Quarterly* 67, no. 1 (2014): 84–95.
39. Jacobson, *The Politics of Congressional Elections*.
40. Hopkins, "No More Wilder Effect, Never a Whitman Effect."
41. For example, the estimate of the Black population for Mississippi in 1995 is the linear interpolation of the Black population estimates provided by the 1990 and 2000 U.S. Census.
42. "Party advantage" is the state partisanship variable recoded so that Democratic partisanship is coded positive for Democratic candidates and Republican partisanship is coded positive for Republican candidates. In other words, the negative values in the table for both Black and white candidates indicate that on average, they run in states whose partisanship favors the opposing party (Democrats running in Republican-dominated states and vice versa).
43. For full regression results, see appendix table 1.2.
44. William H. Frey, "The Nation Is Diversifying Even Faster Than Predicted, According to New Census Data," *Brookings*, July 1, 2020, https://www.brookings.edu/research/new-census-data-shows-the-nation-is-diversifying-even-faster-than-predicted/.
45. LaFleur Stephens-Dougan, *Race to the Bottom: How Racial Appeals Work in American Politics* (Chicago: University of Chicago Press, 2020); Nicholas A. Valentino, Fabian G. Neuner, and L. Matthew Vandenbroek, "The Changing Norms of Political Rhetoric and the End of Racial Priming," *Journal of Politics* 80, no. 3 (2018): 757–71.
46. Kinder and Dale-Riddle, *The End of Race?*; Lewis-Beck, Tien, and Nadeau, "Obama's Missed Landslide"; Piston, "How Explicit Prejudice Hurt Obama in the 2008 Election"; Stephens-Davidowitz, "The Cost of Racial Animus on a Black Candidate"; Tesler and Sears, *Obama's Race*.

2. THE RACIALIZATION OF BLACK CANDIDATES

1. Antoine J. Banks, "The Public's Anger: White Racial Attitudes and Opinions Toward Health Care Reform," *Political Behavior* 36, no. 3 (2013): 493–514; Antoine J. Banks and Melissa A. Bell, "Racialized Campaign Ads: The Emotional Content in Implicit Racial Appeals Primes White Racial Attitudes," *Public Opinion Quarterly* 77, no. 2 (2013):

549–60; Adam J. Berinsky, Vincent L. Hutchings, Tali Mendelberg, Lee Shaker, and Nicholas A. Valentino, "Sex and Race: Are Black Candidates More Likely to Be Disadvantaged by Scandals?," *Political Behavior* 33, no. 2 (2011): 179–202; Christopher DeSante, "Working Twice as Hard to Get Half as Far: Race, Work Ethic, and America's Deserving Poor," *American Journal of Political Science* 57, no. 2 (2013): 342–56; Jon Hurwitz and Mark Peffley, "Playing the Race Card in the Post–Willie Horton Era: The Impact of Racialized Code Words on Support for Punitive Crime Policy," *Public Opinion Quarterly* 69, no. 1 (2005): 99–112; Donald R. Kinder and Allison Dale-Riddle, *The End of Race? Obama, 2008, and Racial Politics in America* (New Haven, CT: Yale University Press, 2012); Donald R. Kinder and Lynn Sanders, *Divided by Color: Racial Politics and Democratic Ideals* (Chicago: University of Chicago Press, 1996); Tali Mendelberg, *The Race Card: Campaign Strategy, Implicit Appeals, and the Norm of Equality* (Princeton, NJ: Princeton University Press, 2001); Michael Tesler, "The Spillover of Racialization Into Health Care: How President Obama Polarized Public Opinion by Racial Attitudes and Race," *American Journal of Political Science* 56, no. 3 (2012): 690–704; Michael Tesler and David O. Sears, *Obama's Race: The 2008 Election and the Dream of a Post-Racial America* (Chicago: University of Chicago Press, 2010); Nicholas A. Valentino, Vincent L. Hutchings, and Ismail K. White, "Cues That Matter: How Political Ads Prime Racial Attitudes During Campaigns," *American Political Science Review* 96, no. 1 (2002): 75–90; Ismail K. White, "When Race Matters and When It Doesn't: Racial Group Differences in Response to Racial Cues," *American Political Science Review* 101, no. 2 (2007): 339–54.

2. Mendelberg, *The Race Card*, 175; Berinsky et al., "Sex and Race."
3. Mendelberg, *The Race Card*, 28–66.
4. Mendelberg, *The Race Card*, 35.
5. Taeku Lee, *Mobilizing Public Opinion: Black Insurgency and Racial Attitudes in the Civil Rights Era* (Chicago: University of Chicago Press, 2002); Mendelberg, *The Race Card*, 67–108; John R. Zaller, *The Nature and Origins of Mass Opinion* (Cambridge: Cambridge University Press, 1992).
6. Kinder and Sanders, *Divided By Color*.
7. Donald R. Kinder, "Prejudice and Politics," in *The Oxford Handbook of Political Psychology*, 2nd ed., ed. Leonie Huddy, David O. Sears, and Jack S. Levy (New York: Oxford University Press, 2013), 820.
8. Mendelberg, *The Race Card*.
9. Michael Tesler, *Post-Racial or Most-Racial? Race and Politics in the Obama Era* (Chicago: University of Chicago Press, 2016), 78–80.
10. "Full Transcript of the Mitt Romney Secret Video," *Mother Jones*, September 19, 2012, http://www.motherjones.com/politics/2012/09/full-transcript-mitt-romney-secret-video.
11. Ashley Parker, "Romney Blames Loss on Obama's 'Gifts' to Minorities and Young Voters," *New York Times*, November 14, 2012, http://thecaucus.blogs.nytimes.com/2012/11/14/romney-blames-loss-on-obamas-gifts-to-minorities-and-young-voters/.

12. "Bill O'Reilly: 'The White Establishment Is Now the Minority,'" *Fox News*, November 7, 2012, http://nation.foxnews.com/bill-oreilly/2012/11/07/bill-o-reilly-white-establishment-now-minority.
13. David O. Sears and Jack Citrin, *Tax Revolt: Something for Nothing in California* (Cambridge, MA: Harvard University Press, 1985).
14. Kinder and Sanders, *Divided by Color*.
15. Thomas B. Edsall and Mary D. Edsall, *Chain Reaction: The Impact of Race, Rights, and Taxes on American Politics* (New York: Norton, 1991); Robert M. Entman and Andrew Rojecki, *The Black Image in the White Mind: Media and Race in America* (Chicago: University of Chicago Press, 2000); Martin Gilens, *Why Americans Hate Welfare: Race, Media, and the Politics of Anti-Poverty Policy* (Chicago: University of Chicago Press, 1999); Franklin D. Gilliam Jr. and Shanto Iyengar, "Prime Suspects: The Influence of Local Television News on the Viewing Public," *American Journal of Political Science* 44, no. 3 (2000): 560–73.
16. Andra Gillespie, *The New Black Politician: Cory Booker, Newark, and Post-Racial America* (New York: New York University Press, 2012).
17. Paul Frymer, *Uneasy Alliances: Race and Party Competition in America* (Princeton, NJ: Princeton University Press, 1999); LaFleur Stephens-Dougan, "Priming Racial Resentment Without Stereotypic Cues," *Journal of Politics* 78, no. 3 (2016): 687–704.
18. Eric Foner, *Forever Free: The Story of Emancipation and Reconstruction* (New York: Vintage, 2006).
19. Zoltan Hajnal, *Changing White Attitudes Toward Black Political Leadership* (New York: Cambridge University Press, 2007); Charlton D. McIlwain and Stephen M. Caliendo, *Race Appeal: How Candidates Invoke Race in U.S. Political Campaigns* (Philadelphia: Temple University Press, 2011).
20. Tesler, "The Spillover of Racialization into Health Care."
21. Angela K. Lewis, "Making History, Again, So Soon? The Massachusetts Gubernatorial Election," in *Beyond the Boundaries: A New Structure of Ambition in African American Politics*, ed. Georgia A. Persons (New Brunswick, NJ: Transaction, 2009); Richard T. Middleton IV and Sekou M. Franklin, "Southern Racial Etiquette and the 2006 Tennessee Senate Race: The Racialization of Harold Ford's Deracialized Campaign," in *Beyond the Boundaries: A New Structure of Ambition in African American Politics*, ed. Georgia A. Persons (New Brunswick, NJ: Transaction, 2009); Byron D'Andra Orey, "Racial Threat, Republicanism, and the Rebel Flag: Trent Lott and the 2006 Mississippi Senate Race," *National Political Science Review* 12 (2009): 83–96.
22. McIlwain and Caliendo, *Race Appeal*.
23. The NewsBank database was used to find articles in the *Star-Ledger*; the ProQuest database was used to find articles in all other newspapers.
24. For specific examples and nonexamples of what I coded as crime, sex, and tax mentions, see appendix table 2.1. To address concerns about coding validity, two coders were used. The alpha between the two coders is 0.95. The data set has 2,106 articles that were coded for crime, sex, and tax references for a total of 6,318 codable units. Research

assistants Grace Kim, Ondine Jevremov, Stephanie Teng, Sonya Chen, and Chaya Crowder assisted with the collection and coding of the articles.

25. Vesla M. Weaver, "Frontlash: Race and the Development of Punitive Crime Policy," *Studies in American Political Development* 21 (Fall 2007): 230–65.
26. Ralph Martin II, "Righting a Wrong Isn't Being 'Soft' on Crime," *Boston Globe*, October 8, 2006.
27. David Metz and Katherine Tate, "The Color of Urban Campaigns," in *Classifying by Race*, ed. Paul Peterson (Princeton, NJ: Princeton University Press, 1995).
28. Bernard L. Fraga and Eitan D. Hersh, "Voting Costs and Voter Turnout in Competitive Elections," *Quarterly Journal of Political Science* 5, no. 4 (2011): 339–56.
29. Eight of the thirty-seven candidates in the data set are viable according to the five-percent threshold, while eleven are viable according to the ten-percent threshold.
30. Polls accessed from Roper iPoll database, http://ropercenter.cornell.edu/ipoll.
31. The viability threshold for white comparison candidates is set at ten percentage points in order to preserve at least one comparison candidate for Ford and Abrams. Clement lost the 2002 Tennessee U.S. Senate election by 9.9 percentage points, and Clayton, Tuke, and Clark all lost by at least 30 percentage points. Carter lost the 2014 Georgia gubernatorial election by 8.8 percentage points, Barnes lost by just over 10, and Taylor lost by almost 20.
32. Previous studies find that Latino U.S. Senate and House candidates face crime attacks at a similar rate as African American candidates for those offices. See McIlwain and Caliendo, *Race Appeal*. As it turns out, crime was a major theme of Menendez's opponent Thomas Kean's campaign, as Kean claimed throughout the campaign that Menendez was under federal criminal investigation. See Ray Rivera, "A Show of Hostility for Menendez and Kean," *New York Times*, October 8, 2006.
33. Booker's white comparison candidates are Frank Lautenberg (2002) and Jon Corzine (2000). Patrick's are Martha Coakley (2014), Shannon O'Brien (2002), and Scott Harshbarger (1998). Brown's are Martin O'Malley (2006), Kathleen Kennedy Townsend (2002), and Parris Glendening (1994). Gillum's are Charlie Crist (2014), Alex Sink (2010), and Jim Davis (2006).

3. THE RESPONSE OF BLACK CANDIDATES

1. Donald R. Kinder and Lynn Sanders, *Divided by Color: Racial Politics and Democratic Ideals* (Chicago: University of Chicago Press, 1996); Tali Mendelberg, *The Race Card: Campaign Strategy, Implicit Appeals, and the Norm of Equality* (Princeton, NJ: Princeton University Press, 2001); Nicholas A. Valentino, Vincent L. Hutchings, and Ismail K. White, "Cues That Matter: How Political Ads Prime Racial Attitudes During Campaigns," *American Political Science Review* 96, no. 1 (2002): 75–90.
2. Jack Citrin, Donald Philip Green, and David O. Sears, "White Reactions to Black Candidates: When Does Race Matter?," *Public Opinion Quarterly* 54 (1990): 74–96; Kristopher A. Fredrick and Judson L. Jeffries, "A Study in African American Candidates for

High-Profile Statewide Office," *Journal of Black Studies* 39 (2009): 689–718; Judson L. Jeffries and Charles E. Jones, "Blacks Who Run for Governor and the U.S. Senate: An Examination of Their Candidacies," *Negro Educational Review* 57, nos. 3–4 (2006): 243–65; Huey L. Perry, "Deracialization as an Analytical Construct in American Politics," *Urban Affairs Quarterly* 27, no. 2 (1991): 181–91; Raphael J. Sonenshein, "Can Black Candidates Win Statewide Elections?," *Political Science Quarterly* 105, no. 2 (1990): 219–41.

3. Thomas B. Edsall and Mary D. Edsall, *Chain Reaction: The Impact of Race, Rights, and Taxes on American Politics* (New York: Norton, 1991); Paul Frymer, *Uneasy Alliances: Race and Party Competition in America* (Princeton, NJ: Princeton University Press, 1999); James M. Glaser, *Race, Campaign Politics, and Realignment in the South* (New Haven, CT: Yale University Press, 1996).

4. Andrea Estes and Kay Lazar, "Letter Slams Patrick Over LaGuer Case," *Boston Globe*, October 8, 2006.

5. Stephen C. Craig, Paulina S. Rippere, and Marissa Silber Grayson, "Attack and Response in Political Campaigns: An Experimental Study in Two Parts," *Political Communication* 31, no. 4 (2014): 647–74; Kathleen M. McGraw, "Managing Blame: An Experimental Test of the Effects of Political Accounts," *American Political Science Review* 85, no. 4 (1991): 1133–57; Tali Mendelberg, "Deliberation, Incivility, and Race in Electoral Campaigns," in *Democratization in America: A Comparative-Historical Analysis*, ed. Desmond King, Robert C. Lieberman, Gretchen Ritter, and Laurence Whitehead (Baltimore, MD: Johns Hopkins University Press, 2009); Matthew Tokeshi and Tali Mendelberg, "Countering Implicit Racial Appeals: Which Strategies Work?," *Political Communication* 32, no. 4 (2015): 648–72.

6. Two coders were used to assess reliability. The percent agreement and Krippendorff's alpha were 96 percent and 0.76, respectively. Research assistants Grace Kim, Ondine Jevremov, Stephanie Teng, Sonya Chen, and Chaya Crowder helped with the collection and coding of the articles.

7. Mark Mooney, "Obama Aide Concedes 'Dollar Bill' Remark Referred to His Race," *ABC News*, August 1, 2008, http://abcnews.go.com/GMA/Politics/story?id=5495348.

8. Michael D. Shear, "Obama Releases Long-Form Birth Certificate," *New York Times*, April 27, 2011. Emphasis added.

9. Jason Zengerle, "Deval Patrick, Machine Slayer. Mass Appeal," *New Republic*, November 6, 2006.

10. One type of response that was observed in the Deval Patrick campaign that did not fit into the first seven rebuttal categories was *apology*. Patrick apologized for misrepresenting his involvement in convicted rapist Benjamin LaGuer's legal defense. Patrick's apologies were found in the *Boston Globe*'s campaign coverage four times from October 6–11, 2006. For more on the role of apologies in Patrick's rebuttal strategy, see the next chapter.

11. Estes and Lazar, "Letter Slams Patrick Over LaGuer Case."

12. Frank Phillips and Andrea Estes, "Healey, Patrick Get Testy; Republican Calls Rival Big Spender; Democrat Rips Incumbents," *Boston Globe*, October 26, 2006.

13. Frank Phillips and Matt Viser, "Race Remark Draws Campaign Barbs," *Boston Globe*, September 22, 2006.
14. Richard Locker, "Caution Prevails in Last TV Debate—Ford, Corker Sidestep Controversy, Criticize Attack Ads," *Memphis Commercial Appeal*, October 29, 2006.
15. Tom Humphrey, "Corker, Ford Agree: Ad Goes Too Far—Racial Issues Broached by Tennesseeans for Truth," *Memphis Commercial Appeal*, October 14, 2006.
16. Ryan Hutchins, "Booker-Lonegan Campaign Insults Get Local," *Star-Ledger*, October 9, 2013.
17. Mendelberg, *The Race Card*; Carol K. Sigelman, Lee Sigelman, Barbara J. Walkosz, and Michael Nitz, "Black Candidates, White Voters: Understanding Racial Bias in Political Perceptions," *American Journal of Political Science* 39, no. 1 (1995): 243–65.
18. Elizabeth Titus, "Booker Wins New Jersey Senate Seat," *Politico*, October 16, 2013, http://www.politico.com/story/2013/10/cory-booker-new-jersey-senate-election-098436.
19. Dan Rodricks, "Brown's Negative Ads May Be a Hogan Plus: Democratic Gubernatorial Candidate Needs to Draw His Base to the Polls with a Positive Message," *Baltimore Sun*, October 12, 2014.
20. Steve Contorno and Emily L. Mahoney, "Debate Is All Attack, Evade: Andrew Gillum and Ron DeSantis Snipe at Each Other, Sidestep the Tough Questions," *Tampa Bay Times*, October 22, 2018. Emphasis added.
21. Jeremy Redmon, "Democratic: Meet Stacey Abrams," *Atlanta Journal-Constitution*, October 14, 2018.
22. Greg Bluestein, "Abrams' Flag-Burning Protest Becomes Issue: 'Permitted' and 'Peaceful' Event Took Place in 1992," *Atlanta Journal-Constitution*, October 24, 2018.
23. James Salzer, "State Spending Hot Issue for Candidates: Budget Priorities Define Differences Between Abrams and Kemp," *Atlanta Journal-Constitution*, October 7, 2018.
24. David Metz and Katherine Tate, "The Color of Urban Campaigns," in *Classifying by Race*, ed. Paul Peterson (Princeton, NJ: Princeton University Press, 1995).
25. Dennis Chong and James N. Druckman, "Framing Public Opinion in Competitive Democracies," *American Political Science Review* 101, no. 4 (2007): 637–55; Paul M. Sniderman and Sean M. Theriault, "The Structure of Political Argument and the Logic of Issue Framing," in *Studies in Public Opinion: Attitudes, Nonattitudes, Measurement Error, and Changes*, ed. Willem E. Saris and Paul M. Sniderman (Princeton, NJ: Princeton University Press, 2004). Also see Kinder and Sanders, *Divided by Color*; Thomas E. Nelson, Rosalee A. Clawson, and Zoe M. Oxley, "Media Framing of a Civil Liberties Conflict and Its Effect on Tolerance," *American Political Science Review* 91, no. 3 (1997): 567–83; Thomas Nelson and Donald R. Kinder, "Issue Frames and Group-Centrism in American Public Opinion," *Journal of Politics* 58 (1996): 1055–78.
26. I assume that campaigns respond to one another within the same news cycle, a reasonable assumption given the rise of the twenty-four-hour news cycle during the 1990s.
27. Of the three instances of the racial rebuttal's use by Ford surrogates, two were by African American sources (Jesse Jackson and the NAACP), and one was from a racially unidentified senior advisor to the Ford campaign.

28. Mendelberg, *The Race Card*; Mendelberg, "Deliberation, Incivility, and Race in Electoral Campaigns."

4. THE DEVAL PATRICK AND HAROLD FORD JR. CAMPAIGNS OF 2006

1. The evidence presented in the next two chapters tying the outcome to rebuttals is descriptive observational analysis—not causal—but experimental tests conducted in chapters 7 and 8 will complement the analyses in the next two chapters.
2. Donald R. Kinder and Lynn Sanders, *Divided by Color: Racial Politics and Democratic Ideals* (Chicago: University of Chicago Press, 1996); Tali Mendelberg, *The Race Card: Campaign Strategy, Implicit Appeals, and the Norm of Equality* (Princeton, NJ: Princeton University Press, 2001); Nicholas A. Valentino, Vincent L. Hutchings, and Ismail K. White, "Cues That Matter: How Political Ads Prime Racial Attitudes During Campaigns," *American Political Science Review* 96, no. 1 (2002): 75–90.
3. James N. Druckman, Jordan Fein, and Thomas J. Leeper, "A Source of Bias in Public Opinion Stability," *American Political Science Review* 106, no. 2 (2012): 430–54.
4. Michael Dukakis, "Enough," *Boston Globe*, October 29, 2006; Jason Sokol, "Past Imperfect," *American Prospect*, October 25, 2006.
5. Frank Phillips, "Healey Keeps Up Attack; Patrick Toughens His Ad," *Boston Globe*, October 11, 2006.
6. Deval Patrick, "Statement from Deval Patrick," *Boston Globe*, October 13, 2006.
7. The quotations in this paragraph are from Jason Zengerle, "Deval Patrick, Machine Slayer. Mass Appeal," *New Republic*, November 6, 2006.
8. Ideally, I would like to measure the effect of each of the different types of responses. However, no one type of response dominated during any period of the campaign, making it impossible to untangle the effect of any one type. I will address the question of the effects of different types of responses in chapters 7 and 8.
9. All Massachusetts interviews for the 2006 CCES took place over the last eighteen days of the campaign. Of the 412 white respondents interviewed, 366 (or 89 percent) were interviewed during the last ten days of the campaign.
10. Kinder and Sanders, *Divided by Color*; Paul M. Sniderman and Thomas Piazza, *The Scar of Race* (Cambridge, MA: Harvard University Press, 1993).
11. Charles H. Franklin, "Estimation Across Data Sets: Two-Stage Auxiliary Instrumental Variables Estimation (2SAIV)," *Political Analysis* 1, no. 1 (1989): 1–23.
12. See appendix table 5.3.
13. Mendelberg, *The Race Card*; Michael Tesler and David O. Sears, *Obama's Race: The 2008 Election and the Dream of a Post-Racial America* (Chicago: University of Chicago Press, 2010).
14. Education was a four-category variable ranging from 0=high school or less, .33=some college, .66=college, and 1=postgraduate education. Age was a three-category variable ranging from 0=18–34, .5=35–44, and 1=45 or older. Sex was a dummy variable, 0=female

and 1=male. The education and age categories were chosen by looking at racial resentment values across a more fine-grained breakdown of each variable (such as looking at 18–24, 25–34, 35–44, etc. for age) and grouping the fine-grained categories that had similar racial resentment values. The standard errors for the education, age, and sex coefficients were 0.04 (p<.001), 0.03 (p=.07), and 0.02 (p<.001), respectively. The adjusted R-squared for the regression was 0.09.

15. The dependent variable was coded 0=Patrick vote intention and 1=Healey or Christy Mihos vote intention, with all others excluded. Mihos was a Republican who left his party to run as an independent and ended up receiving 7 percent of the vote. Since Mihos was a credible (white) Republican alternative to Patrick, Mihos supporters are included in the analysis.

16. https://en.wikipedia.org/wiki/2006_Massachusetts_gubernatorial_election.

17. I chose October 9 as the cutoff because it is the midpoint of the October 8–10 polling period.

18. Robin Toner, "Ad Seen as Playing to Racial Fears," *New York Times*, October 26, 2006; Eugene Robinson, "Does the Code Still Work?," *Washington Post*, October 27, 2006.

19. "Republicans Still Run Dirty Ad," *Chattanooga Times Free Press* (Editorial), October 28, 2006.

20. "Tacky? No, Disgraceful," *Memphis Commercial Appeal* (Editorial), October 27, 2006.

21. While data on how many times the "Call Me" ad ran would be ideal, that data does not exist. Although the Wisconsin Advertising Project began collecting data on television advertisements aired on broadcast and cable stations for all U.S. Senate elections in presidential election years from 1996 through 2008, there is no data for the midterm year of 2006. Instead, I rely on newspaper accounts describing the ad, which likely underestimates the ad's true audience. However, the findings reported in this paragraph regarding the frequency of anti-Ford attacks on sexual themes—almost 50 percent of all *Commercial Appeal* articles from the first mention of the "Call Me" ad on October 21 through October 31—suggest that the newspaper data did not fail to capture the ad's salience during this phase of the campaign.

22. Education was a dummy variable coded 0=less than college and 1=college graduate or more. Age was a three-category variable coded 0=18–24, .5=25–34, and 1=35 or older. Sex was a dummy variable coded 0=female, 1=male. Consistent with how I coded variables for the Massachusetts sample, these cutpoints were chosen based on the fact that meaningful differences in racial resentment appeared for each variable at those cutpoints.

23. Income was a three-category variable coded 0=<$40k/year, .5=$40k/year–$80k/year, 1=>$80k/year. Urban was a dummy variable coded 0=nonurban, 1=urban. A respondent was considered to live in an urban area if she lived in one of the three Tennessee counties (out of ninety-five) for which at least 90 percent of the county's population was considered "urban" by the U.S. Census Bureau in 2010: Davidson, Hamilton, or Shelby. These counties are home to three of Tennessee's four largest cities: Memphis (Shelby), Nashville (Davidson), and Chattanooga (Hamilton).

5. THE BOOKER AND BROWN CAMPAIGNS 259

24. The coefficients for education, age, sex, and income were b= −0.11 (se=0.03, p< .001), b= 0.10 (se=0.04, p<.05), b= 0.03 (se=0.02, not significant), and b= 0.04 (se=0.03, not significant), respectively. Sample size was 648.
25. Richard T. Middleton IV and Sekou M. Franklin, "Southern Racial Etiquette and the 2006 Tennessee Senate Race: The Racialization of Harold Ford's Deracialized Campaign," in *Beyond the Boundaries: A New Structure of Ambition in African American Politics*, ed. Georgia A. Persons (New Brunswick, NJ: Transaction, 2009).
26. Like in Massachusetts, the majority (86 percent) of interviews with white Tennesseeans in the 2006 CCES were conducted in the last ten days of the campaign, which renders it unhelpful for my purposes.
27. The SurveyUSA polls were not used for the earlier racial priming analysis because the October 7–9 poll did not include a measure of educational attainment for each respondent, which is necessary to calculate a predicted racial resentment score. Also, the universe of SurveyUSA respondents is all Tennessee adults, while the universe of respondents in the *USA Today*/Gallup and *Los Angeles Times*/Bloomberg polls used in the racial priming analysis is all Tennessee likely voters. Since likely voters are more similar to the target population of actual voters than adults generally, the SurveyUSA polls were omitted.
28. Richard Locker, "Neck and Neck—Ford Fights Off Allegations in Latest Attack Ad, While Corker Appeals to GOP Stronghold in Jr.'s Backyard—Democratic Nominee Claims He's a Catalyst for Change," *Memphis Commercial-Appeal*, October 25, 2006.
29. Richard Locker, "Caution Prevails in Last TV debate—Ford, Corker Sidestep Controversy, Criticize Attack Ads," *Memphis Commercial Appeal*, October 29, 2006.
30. In order to preserve the comparison between white likely voters in these polls, the November 3–5 SurveyUSA poll was not included in this analysis.
31. Though these are "low-racial-resentment whites" given their scoring in the bottom third of the sample on racial resentment, they are not low compared to national samples. The national mean for racial resentment among whites fluctuated between .58 and .62 (on a 0–1 scale) in every American National Election Survey between 1988 and 2008. See Tesler and Sears, *Obama's Race*.

5. THE 2013 CORY BOOKER AND 2014 ANTHONY BROWN CAMPAIGNS

1. David Giambusso and Brent Johnson, "Racially Charged Lonegan Tweet Draws Fire from Booker Campaign, Newark Leaders," *Star-Ledger*, August 9, 2013.
2. James Queally and David Giambusso, "Newark's Carnage Lacks Common Thread," *Star-Ledger*, September 5, 2013.
3. Matt Friedman and Brent Johnson, "Senate Debate at Rowan Anything but Collegial," *Star-Ledger*, October 10, 2013.
4. Donald R. Kinder and Cindy D. Kam, *Us Against Them: Ethnocentric Foundations of American Opinion* (Chicago: University of Chicago Press, 2009); Donald R. Kinder and

Lynn Sanders, *Divided by Color: Racial Politics and Democratic Ideals* (Chicago: University of Chicago Press, 1996).
5. David Giambusso, "Booker, Lonegan Spar as Fallout Continues from Sexuality Issue," *Star-Ledger*, August 29, 2013.
6. David Giambusso, "Lonegan Fires Aide Over Profane Rant About Booker, Stripper," *Star-Ledger*, October 12, 2013.
7. Elizabeth Titus, "Steve Lonegan Blasts Cory Booker's City: 'Big Black Hole,'" *Politico*, October 9, 2013, http://www.politico.com/story/2013/10/steve-lonegan-blasts-cory-booker-new-jersey-special-senate-election-2013-98116.html
8. Andra Gillespie, *The New Black Politician: Cory Booker, Newark, and Post-Racial America* (New York: New York University Press, 2012).
9. To be sure, attacks linking Booker to Newark are inevitable given that Booker was Newark's mayor. Some may therefore question whether every attack linking Booker to Newark is racialized. I acknowledge that it is hard to argue that every linking of Booker to Newark is done with the intent of racializing the campaign. However, as I argue in chapter 2, intent is not necessary for an attack to be racialized. Attacks that highlight a Black candidate's association with Black places have been shown to diminish support among racially resentful whites. See LaFleur Stephens-Dougan, "Priming Racial Resentment Without Stereotypic Cues," *Journal of Politics* 78, no. 3 (2016): 687–704. It is likely that at least some white candidates recognize this and try to use this to their advantage. Part of the challenge of "campaigning while Black" is that Black candidates are more likely than white candidates to emerge as leaders of places with large Black populations, such as Newark—consider that Newark has elected an unbroken string of Black mayors since 1970. Therefore, association with Black places is another kind of attack that they are more likely to face than white candidates.
10. Brent Johnson, "Booker, Lonegan Amp Up Attacks in Second U.S. Senate Debate," *Star-Ledger*, October 9, 2013.
11. Kinder and Sanders, *Divided by Color*.
12. Education was a three-category variable taking on values of 0=high school or less, .5=some college or college grad, and 1=postgraduate education. Age was a three-category variable with values of 0=18–24, .5=25–34, and 1=35 or older. Sex was a dummy variable coded 0=female and 1=male.
13. The coefficients for education, age, and sex were b= −0.21 (se=0.03, p<.001), b=0.07 (se=0.03, p<.05), and b= 0.02 (se=0.02, not significant), respectively. The adjusted R-squared of the regression was 0.06.
14. Vote choice is coded 0=Booker and 1=Lonegan.
15. The regression coefficients for racial resentment only (without controls) and racial resentment controlling for partisanship (with no other controls) are shown in appendix tables 5.1 and 5.2, respectively. The results are similar: racial resentment is a stronger predictor in the later poll with no other controls (though the difference is not quite statistically significant, p=0.12, two-tailed) and controlling for partisanship (p=.05, two-tailed).
16. The answer choices were "real difference," "mostly self-promotion," and "don't know."

17. Ryan Hutchins, "Lonegan Dines with Everyday 'Stars' From N.J.," *Star Ledger*, September 24, 2013.
18. According to Kantar Media/CMAG, local broadcast television receives by far the largest share of political advertising dollars, making up 57 percent of the estimated political media share in 2014. Local cable television and mail are tied for second at 15 percent apiece, followed by digital (7 percent), radio (4 percent), and print (2 percent). See http://us.kantar.com/public-affairs/politics/2014-political-media-projections/.
19. Low-racial-resentment whites in the New Jersey polls examined here are not low on racial resentment compared to national samples of whites, as is true of Tennessee whites examined in the previous chapter (who are more racially resentful than the New Jersey whites examined here). Low-racial-resentment whites in this chapter's New Jersey analysis (<.62 for the postattack Monmouth poll and <.58 for the postrebuttal Rutgers and Monmouth polls) include respondents who are right around the national average for whites as measured by the American National Election Studies (ANES). The national average has fluctuated between .58 and .62 in every ANES between 1988 and 2008. See Michael Tesler and David O. Sears, *Obama's Race: The 2008 Election and the Dream of a Post-Racial America* (Chicago: University of Chicago Press, 2010).
20. Since Anthony Brown did not experience a high-profile racialized attack like Patrick and Ford or begin defending himself after a long-dormant period like Booker, the effects of rebuttals are harder to measure, and therefore Brown is excluded from this analysis. For more on the racialization of Brown, continue reading this chapter.
21. Zoltan Hajnal, *Changing White Attitudes Toward Black Political Leadership* (New York: Cambridge University Press, 2007).
22. Michael Dresser and Erin Cox, "A Tale of Two Very Different Marylands: Fundamental Disagreement Among Candidates Over the Course in Past Eight Years," *Baltimore Sun*, October 5, 2014.
23. Michael Dresser and Erin Cox, "What to Look for in Monday's Televised Debate: Brown and Hogan Are Scheduled to Face Off for 2nd Time in Race for Governor," *Baltimore Sun*, October 12, 2014.
24. Michael Dresser, "No-Show Democrats Helped Hogan Win," *Baltimore Sun*, November 6, 2014.
25. Robert McCartney. "Martin O'Malley Blames Anthony Brown's Campaign for Md. Democrats' Loss," *Washington Post*, January 10, 2015.
26. David O. Sears and Jack Citrin, *Tax Revolt: Something for Nothing in California* (Cambridge, MA: Harvard University Press, 1985).
27. Education is a four-category variable taking on values of 0=high school graduate or less, .33=some college; .66=college graduate, and 1=postcollege education. Age is a three-category variable taking on values of 0=18–24, .5=25–44, and 1=45 or older. Sex is a dummy variable ranging from 0=female to 1=male. The coefficients for education, age, and sex are b= −0.34 (se=0.03, p<.001), b=0.22 (se=0.04, p<.001), and b=0.04 (se=0.02, not significant), respectively. The intercept coefficient is b=0.62 (se=0.04, p<.001).
28. Vote choice is coded 0=Brown and 1=Hogan.

29. White opinion was determined by looking at vote choice–by-race cross-tabulations published by each organization. The CBS News/*New York Times*/YouGov and Gonzales Research polls were left out of the racial priming analysis because those organizations did not make their data sets available, while the *Baltimore Sun* poll did not include a question about respondent ideology that was necessary for the racial priming analysis.

6. WHEN BLACK WOMEN RUN: THE 2018 STACEY ABRAMS AND 2020 KAMALA HARRIS CAMPAIGNS

1. Zoltan Hajnal, *Changing White Attitudes Toward Black Political Leadership* (New York: Cambridge University Press, 2007); Benjamin Highton, "White Voters and African American Candidates for Congress," *Political Behavior* 26, no. 1 (2004): 1–25; Keith Reeves, *Voting Hopes or Fears? Black Candidates, White Voters, and Racial Politics in America* (New York: Oxford University Press, 1997); Stephen Thernstrom and Abigail Thernstrom, *America in Black and White: One Nation, Indivisible* (New York: Simon and Schuster, 1997); Nayda Terkildsen, "When White Voters Evaluate Black Candidates: The Processing Implications of Candidate Skin Color, Prejudice, and Self-Monitoring," *American Journal of Political Science* 37, no. 4 (1993): 1032–53.
2. Dewey M. Clayton and Angela M. Stallings, "Black Women in Congress: Striking the Balance," *Journal of Black Studies* 30, no. 4 (2000): 574–603; Tasha S. Philpot and Hanes Walton Jr., "One of Our Own: Black Female Candidates and the Voters Who Support Them," *American Journal of Political Science* 51, no. 1 (2007): 49–62; Katherine Tate, *Black Faces in the Mirror* (Princeton, NJ: Princeton University Press, 2003).
3. Abrams ran for governor again in 2022 against the incumbent Kemp. Abrams lost the rematch by 7.5 percentage points.
4. The 2016 CCES does not contain a measure of sexism (it did not start measuring sexism until 2018), while the 2016 ANES codes Sanchez voters as part of a residual category that includes people who said they did not intend to vote or did not have a preference. Thus, there is no way to separate people who preferred Sanchez from those who did not intend to vote or had no preference.
5. Harris's successful campaign for attorney general of California in 2010 is another possible campaign to examine. It has the advantage of Harris winning a close race against a white Republican opponent. However, the 2010 CCES does not contain a measure of sexism. Also, the office of state attorney general is much less visible and prestigious than the offices of governor or U.S. senator, and so the racial and gender dynamics of a state attorney general campaign may not carry over to campaigns for higher-level offices.
6. Adam J. Berinsky, Vincent L. Hutchings, Tali Mendelberg, Lee Shaker, and Nicholas A. Valentino, "Sex and Race: Are Black Candidates More Likely to Be Disadvantaged by Scandals?," *Political Behavior* 33, no. 2 (2011): 179–202; Jack Citrin, Donald Philip Green, and David O. Sears, "White Reactions to Black Candidates: When Does Race Matter?,"

Public Opinion Quarterly 54 (1990): 74–96; Donald R. Kinder and Allison Dale-Riddle, *The End of Race? Obama, 2008, and Racial Politics in America* (New Haven, CT: Yale University Press, 2012); Donald R. Kinder and Corrinne McConnaughy, "Military Triumph, Racial Transcendence, and Colin Powell," *Public Opinion Quarterly* 70, no. 2 (2006): 139–65; Michael Tesler, *Post-Racial or Most-Racial? Race and Politics in the Obama Era* (Chicago: University of Chicago Press, 2016); Michael Tesler and David O. Sears, *Obama's Race: The 2008 Election and the Dream of a Post-Racial America* (Chicago: University of Chicago Press, 2010).

7. Mary McThomas and Michael Tesler, "The Growing Influence of Gender Attitudes on Public Support for Hillary Clinton, 2008–2012," *Politics & Gender* 12, no. 1 (2016): 28–49; John Sides, Michael Tesler, and Lynn Vavreck, *Identity Crisis: The 2016 Presidential Campaign and the Battle for the Meaning of America* (Princeton, NJ: Princeton University Press, 2018).

8. Adam Berinsky and Tali Mendelberg, "The Indirect Effects of Discredited Stereotypes in Judgments of Jewish Leaders," *American Journal of Political Science* 49, no. 4 (2005): 845–64.

9. Claire L. Adida, Lauren D. Davenport, and Gwyneth McClendon, "Ethnic Cueing Across Minorities: A Survey Experiment on Candidate Evaluation in the United States," *Public Opinion Quarterly* 80, no. 4 (2016): 815–36.

10. Philip E. Converse, "The Nature of Belief Systems in Mass Publics," in *Ideology and Discontent*, ed. David E. Apter (New York: Free Press, 1964); Thomas E. Nelson and Donald R. Kinder, "Issue Frames and Group-Centrism in American Public Opinion," *Journal of Politics* 58, no. 4 (1996): 1055–78.

11. Kinder and Dale-Riddle, *The End of Race?*; Spencer Piston, "How Explicit Prejudice Hurt Obama in the 2008 Election," *Political Behavior* 32, no. 4 (2010): 431–51; Seth Stephens-Davidowitz, "The Cost of Racial Animus on a Black Candidate: Evidence Using Google Search Data," *Journal of Public Economics* 118 (2014): 26–40; Michael Tesler, "The Return of Old-Fashioned Racism to White Americans' Partisan Preferences in the Early Obama Era," *Journal of Politics* 75, no. 1 (2013): 110–23; Tesler and Sears, *Obama's Race*.

12. Marc Ambinder, "Race Over?" *The Atlantic*, January/February 2009; Kinder and Dale-Riddle, *The End of Race?*; Tesler and Sears, *Obama's Race*.

13. Donald R. Kinder and Lynn Sanders, *Divided by Color: Racial Politics and Democratic Ideals* (Chicago: University of Chicago Press, 1996); Tali Mendelberg, *The Race Card: Campaign Strategy, Implicit Appeals, and the Norm of Equality* (Princeton, NJ: Princeton University Press, 2001); Nicholas A. Valentino, Vincent L. Hutchings, and Ismail K. White, "Cues That Matter: How Political Ads Prime Racial Attitudes During Campaigns," *American Political Science Review* 96, no. 1 (2002): 75–90.

14. Katie Rogers, "Trump Encourages Racist Conspiracy Theory About Kamala Harris," *New York Times*, August 13, 2020.

15. Annie Karni and Jeremy W. Peters, "Her Voice? Her Name? G.O.P.'s Raw Personal Attacks on Kamala Harris," *New York Times*, August 25, 2020.

16. Trump War Room, "Meet Phony Kamala Harris, Joe Biden's New Liberal Handler," YouTube, August 12, 2020, https://www.youtube.com/watch?v=ZjSpFECJhJ8. For more on the effects of crime attacks on Black candidates, see Mendelberg, *The Race Card*.
17. Linda F. Williams, "White/Black Perceptions of the Electability of Black Political Candidates," *National Political Science Review* 2 (1990): 145–64.
18. Joel K. Goldstein, *The White House Vice Presidency: The Path to Significance, Mondale to Biden* (Lawrence: University of Kansas Press, 2016).
19. Larry M. Bartels, "Partisanship and Voting Behavior, 1952–1996," *American Journal of Political Science* 44, no. 1 (2000): 35–50; Angus Campbell, Philip E. Converse, Warren E. Miller, and Donald E. Stokes, *The American Voter* (Chicago: University of Chicago Press, 1960); Morris P. Fiorina, *Retrospective Voting in American National Elections* (New Haven, CT: Yale University Press, 1981).
20. Kinder and Dale-Riddle, *The End of Race?*; Tesler and Sears, *Obama's Race*. To be sure, this does not mean that sexism did not hurt Clinton in 2008. Tesler and Sears suggest that sexism could have hurt Clinton in two ways that would be hard to detect in their individual-level statistical models. First, some evidence suggests that Obama received more positive media coverage than Clinton. See Katherine Q. Seelye and Julie Bosman, "Media Charged with Sexism in Clinton Coverage," *New York Times*, June 13, 2008. Second, the anticipated effect of sexism may have caused Clinton to emphasize her ability to provide tough leadership at the cost of being perceived as unlikeable—what experts call the "double bind" of women's leadership. See Kathleen Hall Jamieson, *Beyond the Double Bind: Women and Leadership* (Oxford: Oxford University Press, 1995).
21. Brian F. Schaffner, Matthew MacWilliams, and Tatishe Nteta, "Understanding White Polarization in the 2016 Vote for President: The Sobering Role of Racism and Sexism," *Political Science Quarterly* 133, no. 1 (2018): 9–34; Sides, Tesler, and Vavreck, *Identity Crisis*; Nicholas A. Valentino, Carly Wayne, and Marzia Oceno, "Mobilizing Sexism: The Interaction of Emotion and Gender Attitudes in the 2016 US Presidential Election," *Public Opinion Quarterly* 82, no. S1 (2018): 799–821.
22. Katie Rogers, "Kamala Harris Crystallizes Trump's View of Women: They're 'Nasty' or Housewives," *New York Times*, August 19, 2020.
23. Karen Tumulty, Kate Woodsome, and Sergio Peçanha, "How Sexist, Racist Attacks on Kamala Harris Have Spread Online—a Case Study," *Washington Post*, October 7, 2020.
24. Kathleen Dolan, "Gender Differences in Support for Women Candidates," *Women & Politics* 17, no. 2 (1997): 27–41; Leonie Huddy and Nayda Terkildsen, "The Consequences of Gender Stereotypes for Women Candidates at Different Levels and Types of Offices," *Political Research Quarterly* 46, no. 3 (1993): 503–25.
25. Kinder and Sanders, *Divided by Color*.
26. The other two statements in the racial resentment battery are "Over the past few years, Blacks have gotten less than they deserve" and "It's really a matter of not trying hard enough; if Blacks would only try harder they could be just as well off as whites." The five potential responses to each statement are strongly agree, somewhat agree, neither agree nor disagree, somewhat disagree, and strongly disagree.

27. Peter Glick and Susan T. Fiske, "The Ambivalent Sexism Inventory: Differentiating Hostile and Benevolent Sexism," *Journal of Personal and Social Psychology* 70, no. 3 (1996): 491–512.
28. All variables except age range from 0–1. Age is coded as number of years old.
29. See appendix table 6.1 for full regression results.
30. Tesler, *Post-Racial or Most-Racial?*
31. Since sexism is measured slightly differently in each survey, the two items are not identical from year to year. However, I chose the two items that were most consistent across surveys. The first item ("when women demand equality these days . . .") is asked in all five surveys, although the response options were slightly different in 2012 and 2016. For the second item, I used "Women often miss out on good jobs because of discrimination" (2004 and 2008) or "When women complain about discrimination, how often do they cause more problems than they solve?" (2012, 2016, and 2020). Of course, I prefer to have identical question wordings across years. However, studies 3 and 4 use a single measure of sexism, and the results are consistent with results found in this study. That lends reassurance that the findings from this study are not attributable to measurement idiosyncrasy. See the appendix for measurement details.
32. Racial resentment's impact, however, is stronger ($p<.01$).
33. Chris Tausanovitch, Lynn Vavreck, Tyler Reny, Alex Rossell Hayes, and Aaron Rudkin, "Democracy Fund + UCLA Nationscape Methodology and Responsiveness Assessment," 2019, https://www.voterstudygroup.org/uploads/reports/Data/NS-Methodology-Representativeness-Assessment.pdf.
34. The two sexism items from study 1 that were included in the Lucid survey were: (1) "When women lose to men in a fair competition, they typically complain about being discriminated against" and (2) "Feminists are making entirely reasonable demands of men." The two sexism items from study 2 were: (1) "When women demand equality these days, they are actually seeking special favors" and (2) "Women often miss out on good jobs because of discrimination."
35. See appendix table 6.2 for full results.
36. About 1.3 percent of Lucid respondents indicated that they had never heard of Michelle Obama, suggesting that Harris and Mrs. Obama are comparable in name recognition.
37. Adam Berinsky et al., "Sex and Race"; Citrin, Green, and Sears, "White Reactions to Black Candidates"; Kinder and Dale-Riddle, *The End of Race?*; Kinder and McConnaughy, "Military Triumph, Racial Transcendence, and Colin Powell"; Tesler and Sears, *Obama's Race*; McThomas and Tesler, "The Growing Influence of Gender Attitudes on Public Support for Hillary Clinton, 2008–2012"; Sides, Tesler, and Vavreck, *Identity Crisis*.
38. The predictive strength of racial and gender attitudes for each experimental condition are shown in appendix table 6.3. The coefficients for racial resentment and anti-Black stereotypes in the Black condition are larger than the same coefficients in other conditions, though not always at conventional levels of statistical significance. In contrast, gender attitudes are not always a stronger predictor of Harris evaluations when she is

framed as a woman, and never do the differences in sexism's predictive power approach statistical significance.
39. See appendix table 6.4 of the for full regression results.
40. Rebecca S. Powers, J. Jill Suitor, Susan Guerra, Monisa Shackelford, Dorothy Mecom, and Kim Gusman, "Regional Differences in Gender-Role Attitudes: Variations by Gender and Race," *Gender Issues* 21 (2003): 40–54.
41. LaFleur Stephens-Dougan, *Race to the Bottom: How Racial Appeals Work in American Politics* (Chicago: University of Chicago Press 2020); Tesler and Sears, *Obama's Race*.
42. Adam M. Enders and Jamil S. Scott, "The Increasing Racialization of American Electoral Politics, 1988–2016," *American Politics Research* 47, no. 2 (2019): 275–303; Ashley Jardina, *White Identity Politics* (New York: Cambridge University Press, 2019); Tesler, *Post-Racial or Most Racial?*
43. Schaffner, MacWilliams, and Nteta, "Understanding White Polarization in the 2016 Vote for President"; Sides, Tesler, and Vavreck, *Identity Crisis*; Valentino, Wayne, and Oceno, "Mobilizing Sexism."
44. Jamieson, *Beyond the Double Bind*.

7. THE BOOKER EXPERIMENT

1. Booker was on the ballot again in 2014 running as an incumbent against Republican Jeff Bell.
2. Manipulation checks revealed that 86 percent of respondents identified Booker as Black and 91 percent identified Lonegan as white.
3. The alternate version of the preamble, which was presented to people in the control group (who thus did not receive information about an attack), was: "As you may or may not know, New Jersey had a U.S. Senate election last year. The candidates were Democrat Cory Booker and Republican Steve Lonegan. Booker was the mayor of Newark, the largest city in New Jersey. Lonegan was the mayor of a small suburb in a different part of the state." The same photo of Booker and Lonegan that appeared in the main preamble is shown below the text.
4. I will describe the rebuttals and their effects in the next section.
5. Eduardo Bonilla-Silva, *Racism Without Racists*, 5th ed. (Lanham, MD: Rowman & Littlefield, 2018); Michael Tesler and David O. Sears, *Obama's Race: The 2008 Election and the Dream of a Post-Racial America* (Chicago: University of Chicago Press, 2010).
6. The Booker-minus-Lonegan score is used instead of simply looking at Booker's score to account for the possibility that Lonegan's ratings may be damaged by the attacks. See Richard R. Lau and Ivy Brown Rovner, "Negative Campaigning," *Annual Review of Political Science* 12 (2009): 285–306.
7. The functional form of the model is Booker score = racial resentment + partisanship + attack + attack*racial resentment + attack*partisanship + attack*ideology. The key coefficient for testing my hypothesis is the attack*racial resentment interaction term. See

appendix table 7.1 for full results for New Jersey respondents. Full results for Maryland respondents are shown in appendix table 7.2.

8. The difference in the Booker rating between the most and least racially resentful respondent is about half of the scale's range: about one full point on a −1 to 1 scale (p<.001).

9. Partisanship is measured on a seven-category scale ranging from 0 (strong Democrat) to 1 (strong Republican). Ideology is measured on a seven-category scale ranging from 0 (extremely liberal) to 1 (extremely conservative). For full regression results, see appendix table 7.2.

10. The null result for *crime* is puzzling considering that so much previous research finds that crime attacks have a priming effect on their targets. See Franklin D. Gilliam Jr. and Shanto Iyengar, "Prime Suspects: The Influence of Local Television News on the Viewing Public," *American Journal of Political Science* 44, no. 3 (2000): 560–73; Mark Peffley and Jon Hurwitz, "Persuasion and Resistance: Race and the Death Penalty in America," *American Journal of Political Science* 51, no. 4 (2007): 996–1012; and Tali Mendelberg, "Executing Hortons: Racial Crime in the 1988 Presidential Campaign," *Public Opinion Quarterly* 61, no. 1 (1997): 134–57. However, it is worth noting that the attacks in this experiment are weak in the sense that they are only a few sentences long and contain none of the evocative racial imagery that is featured in many real-life attacks on crime—for instance, the mug shot featured in the Willie Horton campaign ads in 1988 (see Tali Mendelberg, *The Race Card: Campaign Strategy, Implicit Appeals, and the Norm of Equality* [Princeton, NJ: Princeton University Press, 2001]) or the "parking lot rape" ad in the 2006 Massachusetts gubernatorial campaign (see introduction of this book). In the next chapter, I test another crime attack accompanied by a vivid image of a criminal suspect's mug shot and find the familiar racializing effect.

11. Stephen C. Craig, Paulina S. Rippere, and Marissa Silber Grayson, "Attack and Response in Political Campaigns: An Experimental Study in Two Parts," *Political Communication* 31, no. 4 (2014): 647–74.

12. Kathleen M. McGraw, "Managing Blame: An Experimental Test of the Effects of Political Accounts," *American Political Science Review* 85, no. 4 (1991): 1133–57. The other rebuttal types outlined in chapter 3—*distract* and *counterimaging*—are tested in the next chapter.

13. Mendelberg, *The Race Card*.

14. Jack Citrin, Donald Philip Green, and David O. Sears, "White Reactions to Black Candidates: When Does Race Matter?," *Public Opinion Quarterly* 54 (1990): 74–96; Kristopher A. Fredrick and Judson L. Jeffries, "A Study in African American Candidates for High-Profile Statewide Office," *Journal of Black Studies* 39 (2009): 689–718; Charles V. Hamilton, "Deracialization: Examination of a Political Strategy," *First World* 1 (1977): 3–5; Judson L. Jeffries and Charles E. Jones, "Blacks Who Run for Governor and the U.S. Senate: An Examination of Their Candidacies," *Negro Educational Review* 57, nos. 3–4 (2006): 243–65; Huey L. Perry, "Deracialization as an Analytical Construct in American Politics," *Urban Affairs Quarterly* 27, no. 2 (1991): 181–91; Raphael J.

Sonenshein, "Can Black Candidates Win Statewide Elections?," *Political Science Quarterly* 105, no. 2 (1990): 219–41.

15. Nicholas A. Valentino, Fabian G. Neuner, and L. Matthew Vandenbroek, "The Changing Norms of Political Rhetoric and the End of Racial Priming," *Journal of Politics* 80, no. 3 (2018): 757–71.
16. McGraw, "Managing Blame," 1136.
17. Dennis Chong and James N. Druckman, "Framing Public Opinion in Competitive Democracies," *American Political Science Review* 101, no. 4 (2007): 637–55.
18. Thomas E. Nelson, Rosalee A. Clawson, and Zoe M. Oxley, "Media Framing of a Civil Liberties Conflict and Its Effect on Tolerance," *American Political Science Review* 91, no. 3 (1997): 567–83.
19. Craig, Rippere, and Grayson, "Attack and Response to Political Campaigns."
20. Results for New Jersey and Maryland respondents shown separately are in appendix figure 7.1. Rebuttal effects are somewhat larger for Maryland respondents, though not dramatically so. Larger effects for Maryland respondents are expected given that Booker and Lonegan are lesser known in Maryland, and therefore information provided in the experiment is more likely to sway candidate evaluations.
21. For example, imagine a respondent who gave a postattack rating of 30 to Booker and 50 to Lonegan and postrebuttal ratings of 40 to Booker and 35 to Lonegan. The change in the candidate thermometer ratings would be (40−35, the postrebuttal difference) − (30−50, the postattack difference) = 25, which divided by 100 equals 0.25, a strong endorsement of Booker's rebuttal. Although the theoretical range of this variable is −2 to 2, the actual range for the sample was −1.03 to 0.90, with most of the data clustering between −0.01 and 0.05 (the interquartile range).
22. Low-racial-resentment respondents scored at or below 0.50, medium-racial-resentment respondents scored above 0.50 but at or below 0.69, and high-racial-resentment respondents scored above 0.69.
23. Zoltan Hajnal, *Changing White Attitudes Toward Black Political Leadership* (New York: Cambridge University Press, 2007).
24. Tesler and Sears, *Obama's Race*.

8. THE CRIMINAL PARDON EXPERIMENT

1. Kathleen M. McGraw, "Managing Blame: An Experimental Test of the Effects of Political Accounts," *American Political Science Review* 85, no. 4 (1991): 1133–57; Tali Mendelberg, *The Race Card: Campaign Strategy, Implicit Appeals, and the Norm of Equality* (Princeton, NJ: Princeton University Press, 2001).
2. Donald R. Kinder and Allison Dale-Riddle, *The End of Race? Obama, 2008, and Racial Politics in America* (New Haven, CT: Yale University Press, 2012), 45.
3. Christopher Stout, *Bringing Race Back In: Black Politicians, Deracialization, and Voting Behavior in the Age of Obama* (Charlottesville: University of Virginia Press, 2015), 8, 11–12.

4. While racial priming studies focus primarily on how messages influence the association between racial resentment and candidate evaluation, Stout (2015) examines how messages influence candidate evaluations. This is in line with the counterframing and political accounts literatures discussed in earlier chapters. The analysis presented later examines how messages influence candidate evaluations (the main effects) and racial resentment's role in shaping those evaluations.
5. Dennis Chong and James N. Druckman, "Framing Public Opinion in Competitive Democracies," *American Political Science Review* 101, no. 4 (2007): 637–55.
6. Seth K. Goldman and Diana C. Mutz, *The Obama Effect: How the 2008 Campaign Changed White Attitudes* (New York: Russell Sage Foundation, 2014).
7. Donald R. Kinder and Lynn Sanders, *Divided by Color: Racial Politics and Democratic Ideals* (Chicago: University of Chicago Press, 1996); Mendelberg, *The Race Card*; Nicholas A. Valentino, Vincent L. Hutchings, and Ismail K. White, "Cues That Matter: How Political Ads Prime Racial Attitudes During Campaigns," *American Political Science Review* 96, no. 1 (2002): 75–90.
8. James H. Kuklinski and Normal L. Hurley, "On Hearing and Interpreting Political Messages: A Cautionary Tale of Citizen Cue-Taking," *Journal of Politics* 56, no. 3 (1994): 729–51.
9. Thomas E. Nelson, Kira Sanbonmatsu, and Harwood K. McClerking, "Playing a Different Race Card: Elite Influence on Perceptions of Racism," *Journal of Politics* 69, no. 2 (2007): 416–29.
10. Yanna Krupnikov and Spencer Piston, "Accentuating the Negative: Candidate Race and Campaign Strategy," *Political Communication* 32, no. 1 (2015): 152–73; Spencer Piston, Yanna Krupnikov, Kerri Milita, and John Barry Ryan, "Clear as Black and White: The Effects of Ambiguous Rhetoric Depend on Candidate Race," *Journal of Politics* 80, no. 2 (2018): 662–74.
11. Kinder and Sanders, *Divided by Color*; Mendelberg, *The Race Card*; Valentino, Hutchings, and White, "Cues That Matter."
12. Michael Tesler and David O. Sears, *Obama's Race: The 2008 Election and the Dream of a Post-Racial America* (Chicago: University of Chicago Press, 2010).
13. Zoltan Hajnal, *Changing White Attitudes Toward Black Political Leadership* (New York: Cambridge University Press, 2007), 16.
14. In the March 2013 study, 28 out of 766 respondents (3.7 percent) were recruited from the Princeton Survey Research Center's Mercer County (New Jersey) panel, while the remaining 96.3 percent were recruited from MTurk.
15. In the February 2014 study, the sample was drawn to match the national white adult population on age, sex, and region. In the December 2014 study, the sample was drawn to match on age, sex, region, and educational attainment.
16. For an overview of the key design differences across the four experiments, see appendix table 8.1.
17. The rebuttal effects in each experiment shown separately are in appendix table 8.2.
18. The election type (general or primary) and the partisanship of the target and the attacker vary across experiments (see appendix table 8.1).

19. The target is the sitting governor of the state, which explains how he issued a pardon. In the first experiment, the assault of a police officer was listed among the former representative's crimes instead of being emphasized as it was in the other three experiments. For details on the wording of the attack news stories across experiments, see figure 8.2 and table 8.1 in the online appendix available at matthewtokeshi.com.

20. Racial resentment is an average score (ranging from 0=low to 1=high) on a four-item battery designed to measure "symbolic racism," a concept developed to measure anti-Black affect by asking respondents to agree or disagree with statements such as "Over the past few years, Blacks have gotten less than they deserve" or "It's really a matter of not trying hard enough; if Blacks would only try harder they could be just as well off as whites." For more on the measurement of racial resentment, see Kinder and Sanders, *Divided by Color*. To address concerns that measuring racial resentment after the second round of candidate evaluations opens the possibility of post-treatment bias, the average racial resentment score of respondents assigned to a Black target was not significantly higher than that of respondents assigned to a white target (Black target RR mean=0.58, white target RR mean=0.58, p=0.43, two-tailed test).

21. Although Kilpatrick was arrested for assaulting a police officer, the detail about the officer requiring hospitalization was added. The aim was to make the assault seem severe enough to capture respondents' attention in an internet interview mode where attention is scarce.

22. This procedure was used to generate the faces used in experiments 2–4. For other examples of morphing used to generate faces in political science experiments, see Jeremy N. Bailenson, Shanto Iyengar, Nick Yee, and Nathan A. Collins, "Facial Similarity Between Voters and Candidates Causes Influence," *Public Opinion Quarterly* 72, no. 5 (2008): 935–61; and Vesla Weaver, "The Electoral Consequences of Skin Color: The 'Hidden' Side of Race in Politics," *Political Behavior* 34, no. 1 (2012): 159–92. In experiment 1, the faces were created using FaceGen Modeller 3.2, a 3-D face-generating software program that creates "identical" Black and white faces. These faces, however, lack the realism of the faces created using the morphing procedure. The FaceGen faces used in experiment 1 are shown in figure 8.2 of the online appendix available at matthewtokeshi.com.

23. For more details on how the faces were created, see Matthew Tokeshi and Tali Mendelberg, "Countering Implicit Racial Appeals: Which Strategies Work?," *Political Communication* 32, no. 4 (2015): 648–72. To verify that the white and Black versions of the target and criminal used in experiments 2–4 were perceived by human subjects as equivalent, pilot studies were conducted in 2012 on MTurk to assess how people rate the faces along six trait dimensions identified by psychologists as critical for social judgment: likeable, threatening, dominance, competence, trustworthiness, and attractiveness. See Nikolaas N. Oosterhof and Alexander Todorov, "The Functional Basis of Face Evaluation," *Proceedings of the National Academy of Sciences of the United States of America* 105, no. 32 (2008): 11087–92. There were no differences at the 0.05 level in mean rating along any of these dimensions. See table 8.2 in the online appendix (available at matthewtokeshi.com) for ratings of Black and white versions of the target and criminal.

24. See figures 8.3–8.10 of the online appendix (available at matthewtokeshi.com) for the full text of each rebuttal.
25. Mendelberg, *The Race Card*, 104.
26. Amanda Sterling, "Huckabee Calls Criticism Over Clemency 'Disgusting,'" *CBS News*, December 1, 2009, http://www.cbsnews.com/news/huckabee-calls-criticisms-over-clemency-disgusting/.
27. Some rebuttals were tested more often than others because rebuttals were added and dropped for each experiment. Specifically, the original set of five rebuttals tested in experiment 1 was *racial, negative, justify, distract, and ignore*. A sixth rebuttal, *justify + racial*, was added to experiments 2 and 3. Experiment 4 kept *racial* and *justify*, dropped all other rebuttals, and replaced them with *counterimaging* and *counterattack*. Racial and *justify* were kept because they were consistently effective (at least for the white target) in experiments 1–3, and therefore replication of their effects in a fourth experiment justified their inclusion.
28. Since this analysis pools data across the four experiments, heterogeneity across experiments is captured using a fixed effect term for each experiment.
29. Notably, the coefficient on racial resentment in the first row is also negative and statistically significant, indicating that racial resentment is also associated with lower ratings of a white target. For results of the full model, see appendix table 8.4.
30. Yoav Benjamini and Daniel Yekutieli, "The Control of False Discovery Rate in Multiple Testing Under Dependency," *Annals of Statistics* 29, no. 4 (2001): 1165–88.
31. The alpha level accounts for sixty-three tests conducted (14 test 1s, 7 test 2s, and 42 test 3s). For calculation details, see Jenifer Larson-Hall, *A Guide to Doing Statistics in Second Language Research Using R* (London: Routledge, 2009), appendix B.
32. The attack results in an average target rating that is 0.11 lower than the attacker's rating for both Black and white targets. This difference is statistically indistinguishable from zero (p=0.98).
33. Nelson, Sanbonmatsu, and McClerking, "Playing a Different Race Card."
34. The bottom third of the sample (the "low" group) are respondents who scored at or below 0.5 on the 0–1 racial resentment scale (n=1,507). The middle third ("middle") are respondents who are above 0.5 but below 0.69 (n=968). The top third ("high") are respondents who scored above 0.69 (n=1,013).
35. Mendelberg, *The Race Card*.
36. Goldman and Mutz, *The Obama Effect*; Hajnal, *Changing White Attitudes Toward Black Political Leadership*.
37. Vincent L. Hutchings, Hanes Walton Jr., and Andrea Benjamin, "The Impact of Explicit Racial Cues on Gender Differences in Support for Confederate Symbols and Partisanship," *Journal of Politics* 72, no. 4 (2010): 1175–88; Mendelberg, *The Race Card*; Nicholas A. Valentino, Fabian G. Neuner, and L. Matthew Vandenbroek, "The Changing Norms of Political Rhetoric and the End of Racial Priming," *Journal of Politics* 80, no. 3 (2018): 757–71.
38. Andrew M. Englehardt, "Trumped by Race: Explanations for Race's Influence on Whites' Votes in 2016," *Quarterly Journal of Political Science* 14, no. 3 (2019): 313–28;

Ashley Jardina, *White Identity Politics* (New York: Cambridge University Press, 2019); "The Partisan Divide on Political Values Grows Even Wider," Pew Research Center, October 5, 2017, https://www.pewresearch.org/politics/2017/10/05/the-partisan-divide-on-political-values-grows-even-wider/.

39. Antoine J. Banks and Heather M. Hicks, "The Effectiveness of a Racialized Counterstrategy," *American Journal of Political Science* 63, no. 2 (2019): 305–22.
40. Mendelberg, *The Race Card*.

CONCLUSION

1. Gbemende Johnson, Bruce I. Oppenheimer, and Jennifer L. Selin, "The House as a Stepping Stone to the Senate: Why Do So Few African American House Members Run?," *American Journal of Political Science* 56, no. 2 (2012): 387–99.
2. David Doherty, Conor M. Dowling, and Michael G. Miller, "Do Local Party Chairs Think Women and Minority Candidates Can Win? Evidence from a Conjoint Experiment," *Journal of Politics* 81, no. 4 (2019): 1282–97.
3. Michael Tesler and David O. Sears, *Obama's Race: The 2008 Election and the Dream of a Post-Racial America* (Chicago: University of Chicago Press, 2010).
4. Tesler and Sears, *Obama's Race*, 54–55. To be sure, McCain's restraint did not mean that Obama did not face race-based attacks. In particular, McCain's vice presidential running mate, Sarah Palin, often raised questions about Obama's background as a way of portraying him as fundamentally un-American. See Tesler and Sears, *Obama's Race*, 127–42.
5. Maggie Haberman and Katie Rogers, "Trump's Tactic: Sowing Distrust in Whatever Gets in His Way," *New York Times*, September 3, 2020.
6. Ashley Parker and Steve Eder, "Inside the Six Weeks Donald Trump Was a Nonstop 'Birther,'" *New York Times*, July 2, 2016.
7. Obama's 2012 Republican rivals Rick Santorum, Newt Gingrich, and Mitt Romney seemed to pick up on this, as all three made stereotypical appeals about Black dependency. Gingrich won the South Carolina primary a few days after receiving a standing ovation at a debate for dismissing criticism by a Black Fox News commentator that calling Obama "the food-stamp president" was offensive to Black Americans. See Michael Tesler, *Post-Racial or Most Racial? Race and Politics in the Obama Era* (Chicago, University of Chicago Press, 2016), 60–61.
8. Aubree Eliza Weaver. "Trump's 'Shithole' Comment Denounced Across the Globe," *Politico*, January 12, 2018; Donald Trump, "mention crime infested) rather than falsely complaining about election results," Twitter, January 14, 2017, https://twitter.com/realDonaldTrump/status/820255947956383744; Donald Trump, "... as proven last week during a Congressional tour, the border is clean, efficient & well run," Twitter, July 27, 2019, https://twitter.com/realDonaldTrump/status/1155073965880172544; Donald Trump, "The 'suburban housewife' will be voting for me," Twitter, August 12, 2020, https://twitter.com/realdonaldtrump/status/1293517514798960640; Katie Rogers, "Trump

Encourages Racist Conspiracy Theory Against Kamala Harris," *New York Times*, August 13, 2020.

9. Ally Mutnick, "Win or Lose, Trump's New GOP Is Here to Stay," *Politico*, August 19, 2020. One Trump acolyte elected to the U.S. House in 2020 was the QAnon conspiracy theorist Marjorie Taylor Greene.

10. Richard Fausset, "Stacey Abrams and Brian Kemp Renew Attacks in Georgia Debate," *New York Times*, October 23, 2018; Julia Jacobs, "DeSantis Warns Florida Not to 'Monkey This Up,' and Many Hear a Racist Dog Whistle," *New York Times*, August 28, 2018.

11. Mark Skoneki, "President Trump Calls Andrew Gillum a 'Stone Cold Thief' on Fox News," *Orlando Sentinel*, October 30, 2018.

12. Thomas B. Edsall and Mary D. Edsall, *Chain Reaction: The Impact of Race, Rights, and Taxes on American Politics* (New York: Norton, 1991); James M. Glaser, *Race, Campaign Politics, and Realignment in the South* (New Haven, CT: Yale University Press, 1996); Charles V. Hamilton, "Deracialization: Examination of a Political Strategy," *First World* 1 (1977): 3–5; Huey L. Perry, "Deracialization as an Analytical Construct in American Politics," *Urban Affairs Quarterly* 27, no. 2 (1991): 181–91.

13. Daniel Q. Gillion, *Governing with Words: The Political Dialogue on Race, Public Policy, and Inequality in America* (New York: Cambridge University Press, 2016).

14. Matthew Nussbaum, "Clinton Calls Parts of 1994 Crime Bill 'A Mistake,'" *Politico*, March 6, 2016, http://www.politico.com/blogs/2016-dem-primary-live-updates-and-results/2016/03/hillary-clinton-1994-crime-bill-220344; Arlette Saenz, "Biden: 'I Haven't Always Been Right' on Criminal Justice," CNN, January 21, 2019, https://www.cnn.com/2019/01/21/politics/joe-biden-criminal-justice/index.html.

15. "Joe Biden's Remarks on Civil Unrest and Nationwide Protests," CNN, June 2, 2020, https://www.cnn.com/2020/06/02/politics/biden-philadelphia-transcript/index.html.

16. Nick Corasanti, "What We Learned from Biden's Big Night at the D.N.C.," *New York Times*, August 20, 2020, https://www.nytimes.com/2020/08/20/us/politics/biden-dnc-highlights.html.

17. Larry M. Bartels, "Campaign Quality: Standards for Evaluation, Benchmarks for Reform," in *Campaign Reform: Insights and Evidence*, ed. Larry M. Bartels and Lynn Vavreck (Ann Arbor: University of Michigan Press, 2000), 1; Tali Mendelberg, "Deliberation, Incivility, and Race in Electoral Campaigns," in *Democratization in America: A Comparative-Historical Analysis*, ed. Desmond King, Robert C. Lieberman, Gretchen Ritter, and Laurence Whitehead (Baltimore, MD: Johns Hopkins University Press, 2009), 163.

18. Kinder and Dale-Riddle report results from a series of national surveys of Democrats conducted by Gallup in March 2008 that found Obama leading Democratic rival Hillary Clinton by 3 percentage points following the speech, overturning the five-point lead Clinton held in the period after the Wright story broke but before Obama's speech. See Donald R. Kinder and Allison Dale-Riddle, *The End of Race? Obama, 2008, and Racial Politics in America* (New Haven, CT: Yale University Press, 2012), 44.

19. Keeanga-Yamahtta Taylor, *From #BlackLivesMatter to Black Liberation* (Chicago: Haymarket, 2016), 75–106.

20. John D. Griffin, "When and Why Minority Legislators Matter," *Annual Review of Political Science* 17 (2014): 327–36; John D. Griffin and Brian Newman, "The Unequal Representation of Latinos and Whites," *Journal of Politics* 69, no. 4 (2007): 1032–46; Grace Hall Saltzstein, "Black Mayors and Police Policies," *Journal of Politics* 51, no. 3 (1989): 525–54; but see Rodney E. Hero and Caroline J. Tolbert, "Latinos and Substantive Representation in the U.S. House of Representatives: Direct, Indirect, or Nonexistent?," *American Journal of Political Science* 39, no. 3 (1995): 640–52; Carol M. Swain, *Black Faces, Black Interests: The Representation of African Americans in Congress* (Cambridge, MA: Harvard University Press, 1995).
21. Lawrence Bobo and Franklin Gilliam Jr., "Race, Sociopolitical Participation, and Black Empowerment," *American Political Science Review* 84, no. 2 (1990): 377–93.
22. Christian Grose, *Congress in Black and White: Race and Representation in Washington and at Home* (New York: Cambridge University Press, 2011); Jane Mansbridge, "Should Blacks Represent Blacks and Women Represent Women? A Contingent 'Yes,'" *Journal of Politics* 61, no. 3 (1999): 628–57.
23. Seth K. Goldman and Diana C. Mutz, *The Obama Effect: How the 2008 Campaign Changed White Attitudes* (New York: Russell Sage Foundation, 2014); Zoltan Hajnal, *Changing White Attitudes Toward Black Political Leadership* (New York: Cambridge University Press, 2007); but see Tesler, *Post-Racial or Most Racial?*
24. Seth K. Goldman and Daniel J. Hopkins, "Past Place, Present Prejudice: The Impact of Adolescent Racial Context on White Racial Attitudes," *Journal of Politics* 82, no. 2 (2020): 529–42; Andrew Healy and Neil Malhotra, "Childhood Socialization and Political Attitudes: Evidence from a Natural Experiment," *Journal of Politics* 75, no. 4 (2013): 1023–37; Tali Mendelberg, Katherine T. McCabe, and Adam Thal, "College Socialization and the Economic Views of Affluent Americans," *American Journal of Political Science* 61, no. 3 (2017): 606–23; David O. Sears and Nicholas A. Valentino, "Politics Matters: Political Events as Catalysts for Preadult Socialization," *American Political Science Review* 91, no. 1 (1997): 45–65; Laura Stoker and M. Kent Jennings, "Of Time and the Development of Partisan Polarization," *American Journal of Political Science* 52, no. 3 (2008): 619–35.
25. Philip A. Klinkner and Rogers M. Smith, *The Unsteady March: The Rise and Decline of Racial Equality in America* (Chicago: University of Chicago Press, 1999).
26. Ismail K. White, "When Race Matters and When It Doesn't: Racial Group Differences in Response to Racial Cues," *American Political Science Review* 101, no. 2 (2007): 339–54.
27. Tim Scott (R-SC) was elected to the U.S. Senate in 2014, but his opponent in the general election was an African American Democrat.
28. Of course, Black Republicans might not run competitively in these states precisely because they are more likely to face racialized attacks. However, eight out of the ten Black Republicans who ran for governor or U.S. senator between 2000 and 2020 ran in states that had a larger white population than the national average. Whether or not they can run competitively in predominantly white states is an open question, but as of now, they are at least willing to run in these states.

29. LaFleur Stephens-Dougan, *Race to the Bottom: How Racial Appeals Work in American Politics* (Chicago: University of Chicago Press, 2020).
30. Stephens-Dougan, *Race to the Bottom*.
31. U.S. Census Bureau, "Voting and Registration in the Election of November 2020," table 4b, https://www.census.gov/data/tables/time-series/demo/voting-and-registration/p20-585.html.
32. William H. Frey, *Diversity Explosion: How New Racial Demographics Are Remaking America* (Washington, DC: Brookings Institution Press, 2015).
33. Amanda Zoch, "The 'Average' State Legislator Is Changing, Slowly," *State Legislatures Magazine*, October 29, 2020, https://www.ncsl.org/research/about-state-legislatures/who-s-the-average-state-legislator-depends-on-your-state-magazine2020.aspx.
34. Ashley Jardina, *White Identity Politics* (New York: Cambridge University Press, 2019).
35. Jardina, *White Identity Politics*; John Sides, Michael Tesler, and Lynn Vavreck, *Identity Crisis: The 2016 Presidential Campaign and the Battle for the Meaning of America* (Princeton, NJ: Princeton University Press, 2018).
36. Michael Jones-Correa, "Commonalities, Competition, and Linked Fate," in *Just Neighbors? Research on African American and Latino Relations in the United States*, ed. Edward Telles, Mark Q. Sawyer, and Gaspar Rivera-Salgado (New York: Russell Sage Foundation, 2011), 63–95; Paula D. McClain, Niambi M. Carter, Victoria M. DeFrancesco Soto, Monique L. Lyle, Jeffrey D. Grynaviski, Shayla C. Nunnally, Thomas J. Scotto, J. Alan Kendrick, Gerald F. Lackey, and Kendra Davenport Cotton, "Racial Distancing in a Southern City: Latino Immigrants' Views of Black Americans," *Journal of Politics* 68, no. 3 (2006): 571–84; J. Eric Oliver and Janelle Wong, "Intergroup Prejudice in Multiethnic Settings," *American Journal of Political Science* 47, no. 4 (2003): 567–82; Bettina Cutaia Wilkinson, *Partners or Rivals? Power and Latino, Black, and White Relations in the Twenty-First Century* (Charlottesville: University of Virginia Press, 2015).
37. Lawrence D. Bobo and Devon Johnson, "Racial Attitudes in a Prismatic Metropolis: Mapping Identity, Competition, and Views on Affirmative Action," in *Prismatic Metropolis: Inequality in Los Angeles*, ed. Lawrence D. Bobo, Melvin L. Oliver, James H. Johnson Jr., and Abel Valenzuela Jr. (New York: Russell Sage Foundation, 2000).
38. Claire Jean Kim, "The Racial Triangulation of Asian Americans," *Politics & Society* 27, no. 1 (1999): 105–38; Taeku Lee, "Racial Attitudes and the Color Line(s) at the Close of the Twentieth Century," in *Transforming Race Relations: A Public Policy Report*, ed. Paul M. Ong (Los Angeles: LEAP Asian Pacific American Public Policy Institute and UCLA Asian American Studies Center, 2000).
39. Hajnal, *Changing White Attitudes Toward Black Political Leadership*, 151–52.
40. David O. Sears and Victoria Savalei, "The Political Color Line in America: Many Peoples of Color or Black Exceptionalism?," *Political Psychology* 27 (2006): 895–924.
41. Hajnal, *Changing White Attitudes Toward Black Political Leadership*.
42. Tesler, *Post-Racial or Most Racial?*

INDEX

Abrams, Stacey, 11, 13–14, 130–46, 148–49, 197; Harris contrasted with, 147; *justify* rebuttals used by, 63–64; Kemp criticizing, 212; rebuttals by, 63–65, *64*; white candidates compared with, *209*
ACS. *See* American Community Survey
advertisements (ads), for campaigns: attacks, 1, 172, *174*, 178; Black criminality emphasized in, 173; "cop-killer," 6, 34; crime attacks emphasized in, 1; against Ford, 34, 36; on local broadcast television, 261n18; "parking-lot rape," 6; against Patrick, 34, 36; racial resentment affected by, 178; in Senate elections, 172; spending on, 112–13, *113*; Willie Horton, 2, 6, 37, 74, 173. *See also* "call me" ad
age (variable), Lucid survey questions on, 221, 226, 257n14
Amazon.com's Mechanical Turk, 172
Ambivalent Sexism Inventory (ASI), 138
American Academy of Motion Picture Arts and Sciences, 9
American Community Survey (ACS), 28
American National Election Study (ANES), 14, 131, 136, 261n19, 262n4; Lucid survey

compared with, 142; sexism measured in, 218–20
anti-Black stereotypes, 40, 229
apology rebuttals, 84, 255n10
ASI. *See* Ambivalent Sexism Inventory
Asian American candidates, 200–201, 246n34
Atlanta Journal-Constitution (newspaper), 42
attacks, 260n9; *counterimaging* rebuttals reframing, 55–56; effects of, 151–57; Maryland respondents influenced by, *154*; New Jersey respondents influenced by, *154*; nonracial, 40; racial effects of, 102–6; racialization caused by, 189; racial resentment influenced by, *234*, *235*; rebuttals contrasted with, 113, 158, *159*, 166–68, 193–94; vote choice affected by, 77–78. *See also counterattack* rebuttals; crime attacks; *Hollywood* attacks; *Obama* attacks, against Booker; *patriotism* attacks; racial attacks; *results* attacks; *sex* attacks; *stripper* attacks; taxes attacks; *Twitter* attacks
attitudes, gender. *See* gender attitudes

attitudes, racial. *See* racial attitudes
attorney general, Harris campaigning for, 262n5

Ball, Gordon, *210*
Baltimore Sun (newspaper), 42, 44, 61–62, 120, 121
Banks, Antoine, 186
Baria, David, *209*
Barksdale, Jim, *207*, *210*
Barnes, Mandela, 1, 2, 198, 254n31
Barnes, Roy, 47, *209*
Barnes, William, *206*, *207*
Beasley, Cheri, 2, 198
bias, racial. *See* racial bias
Biden, Joe, 139–40, *141*, 193
"birther" theory, about B. Obama, disproving, 190
Black Americans, 17–18, 21; police killing, 193; in political leadership, 200; in Senate elections, 19–20
Black candidates, Democratic, 3–4, 250n30; Black voters responding to, 197–98; "Bradley effect" on, 248n7; crime attacks faced by, *48*, *51*; data on, 23–25; *denial* rebuttals helping, 161; general elections screening out, 10, 17, 19, 188–89; in gubernatorial elections, *18*, *20*; for high-level statewide offices, 1–2, 7, 71; as incumbents, 247n4; *justify* + *racial* rebuttals benefiting, 184; *justify* rebuttals helping, 180–81; margins of defeat among white and all voters, *31*; margins of victory among white and all voters, 25–26, *211*; nonracial attacks against, 40; B. Obama linked with, 152, *153*; primary elections underrepresenting, 188–89; race affecting, 21–23, 28–31, *31*; racial appeals combated by, 186; racial attacks faced by, 11–12, *46*, 53, 65–66, 128, 188, 203, *241*; racial bias against, 16–17; racial constituency associated with, 151, *153*; racialization of, 46–51, *48*, *49*, *50*, *51*, 67;

racial rebuttals avoided by, 68–69; racism affecting, 5; rebuttals by, *180*, 180–82; Republican, 198–99; in Senate elections, *18*, *20*; sex attacks faced by, *49*, *51*; taxes attacks faced by, *50*, *51*; viability of, 35, 44–45; volume of rebuttals helping, 70; white candidates compared with, 29, *30*, *31*, 32–33, *33*, 41, *48*, *49*, *50*, *51*, 168, 171, *174*, 174–75, 178, *183*, 205–10, *239*, *240*, 249n25; white voters penalizing, 11, 15–17, 21–23, 31, 34, 130. *See also* Abrams, Stacey; Black women candidates; Booker, Cory; Brown, Anthony; Ford, Harold, Jr.; Gillum, Andrew; Harris, Kamala; high-level statewide candidates; Patrick, Deval; surrogates
Black Caucus, Congressional, 59–60, 90
black hole attacks, against Booker: *counterattack* rebuttals against, *159*, *162*, 170, *235*; effects of, *154*; racial resentment influenced by, 156, *234*, *235*; wording of, 153
Black Lives Matter (movement), 32, 148
Black population: electorate contrasted with, 148; of Mississippi, 148, 251n41; in southern states, 247n2
Black Republicans, 198–99, 274n28
Black voters, evaluations of Black candidates by, 197–98
Blackwell, Ken, *207*
Black women candidates, Democratic: future research on, 196–97; gender attitudes and support for, 130–32; racial attitudes and support for, 13–132, 148. *See also* Abrams, Stacey; Harris, Kamala
Bonica, Adam, 27
Bonigno, Dan, *207*, *209*
Booker, Cory, 11, 34, 98, 142, 193–94, 266n7; celebrities and, 152, *153*; crime attacks against, *153*, *154*, 156, *159*, *234*, *235*; decline phase vs. stabilization phase of 2013 campaign by, *115*; *denial* rebuttals helping, 162–63, 185; feeling thermometer ratings of, *154*, *162*, *164*, 267n21; against Lonegan,

12–14, 39, 43, 99–101, *112*, 151, *153*, *234*, *235*, 266n3, 266n6; Lynsie Lee and, *212*; *negative* rebuttals used by, 157, 162–63; Newark linked to, 60–61, 101, 151, 260n9; Patrick compared with, 117; racial attacks affecting, 100–101, *108*; racialization of, 165; racial priming deactivated by, 115–16; racial resentment toward, 155, *156*; rebuttals by, 60–61, *61*, 111–13, *112*, *113*, *114*, *115*, 163; self-promotion and, 109–10, *110*; volume of, 111–13, *112*, *113*; white candidates compared with, *208*, 254n33; white opinion of, 111–13, *112*, *113*. *See also* Hollywood attacks; *Obama* attacks; *patriotism* attacks; *results* attacks; *stripper* attacks; *Twitter* attacks
Booker experiment, 152–57; expectations of, 158–61; procedure and design of, 150–51; results of, 162–64
Boston Globe (newspaper), 41–42, 54, 57, 75, 81
Bradley, Tom, 20, 22, 248n7
"Bradley effect," on underperformance of Black candidates, 248n7
Bradshaw, Marquita, *210*
Brannen, James, 20
Bredesen, Phil, *210*
Brock, Randy, *208*
Brooke, Edward, 19–20
Brooks, Darrell, 1
Brown, Anthony, 11, 44, 48, 197, 261n20; campaign for, 121–28, *126*, *127*; high-racial-resentment whites leaving, 123–24, *125*; Hogan attacking, 13, 99, *215*; Patrick compared with, 127; racial attacks not challenged by, 127; racial priming against, 121–25, *123*, *124*, *125*; rebuttals by, 61–62, *62*, 125–28, *126*, *127*; taxes attacks not challenged by, 120; white candidates compared with, *208*; white Democrats leaving, 123–24, *125*; white opinion of, 125–28, *126*, *127*; white voters lost by, 8
Brown, Troy, *205*

Brown, Willie, 136
Buck, Ken, *208*
Budd, Ted, 2
Bush, George, 2, 37

Cain, Herman, 199
California, 262n5; primary system in, 24–25; Senate elections in, 131; "tax revolt" in, 38, 121
"call me" ad, 88, 90, *95*, *212*; data lacked on, 258n21; by RNC, 6, 87; surrogates responding to, 94–95
campaign finance (CF) scores, 27
campaigns. *See* specific topics
Campbell, Tony, *209*
Carson, Ben, 199
Carter, Jason, *209*, 254n31
Castor, Betty, *207*
CCES. *See* Cooperative Congressional Election Study
celebrities, Booker and, 152, *153*
CF scores. *See* campaign finance
Chase, Kenneth, *205*
Childers, Travis, *207*, *209*
Chong, Dennis, 65–66
"chronic accessibility," B. Obama and, 133, 165, 189–90
Citrin, Jack, 22, 38, 121
Clark, Jeff, 47, *206*, 254n31
Clayton, Mark, 47, *206*, 254n31
Cleland, Max, *206*
Clement, Bob, *206*, 254n31
Clinton, Bill, 39, 54
Clinton, Hillary, 135, 193, 225; Harris versus, 140–43, *143*; B. Obama compared with, 273n18; sexism and, 149, 264n20
Coakley, Martha, 24, *206*
Coats, Dan, *206*
Coles, Michael, *206*
"comparison" strategy, limitations of, 132–33
Congressional Black Caucus, 59–60, 90
congressional elections. *See* gubernatorial elections; Senate elections

Conley, Bob, *208*, *210*
Cooperative Congressional Election Study (CCES), 14, 80, 102, 142; interviews by, 257n9; racial resentment predicted using, 77–78; sexism not measured in, 262nn4–5; in Tennessee, 259n26
"cop-killer" ad, 6, 34
Corbett, Tom, *207*
Corker, Bob: Republican vote intention for, 89, *90*; RNC linked with, 87; sexual misbehavior emphasized by, 48
Corzine, Jon, *208*
counterattack rebuttals, 158, 169, 177; against *black hole* attacks, *159*, *162*, *170*, 235; description of, *176*; effects of, *236*, *239*, *240*; example of, *215*; Patrick using, 56–58
counterframing, 65–66, 72, 119, 161, 170, 269n4
counterimaging rebuttals, 57, 60, 177; attacks reframed with, 55–56; description of, *176*; effects of, *236*, *239*, *240*; example of, *215*; Patrick using, 170
COVID fear, Lucid survey questions on, 222
Craig, Stephen, 161
crime attacks, 35, 151; advertisements emphasizing, 1; Black candidates facing, 48, *51*; against Booker, *153*, *154*, *156*, *159*, 234, 235; *denial* rebuttals against, *159*, *162*, 235; evocative racial imagery and, 267n10; examples and nonexamples of, 212–13, 253n24; against Gillum, 47; gubernatorial elections affected by, 81; Healey emphasizing, 47, 74; by Kemp, 134; Latino candidates facing, 254n32; by Lonegan, 100–101; Patrick challenging, 54, 57, 75–76; racial resentment influenced by, 78–79, *79*, 155–56, *156*; rebuttals in proportion to, 82–83; rhetoric included in, 42; white voters influenced by, 81; wording of, *153*
criminal pardon experiment, 270n19, 270n22; discussion of, 184–86; method for, 172–77; recruitment of respondents for, 269n14; results of, 178–84; samples for, 172, 269n15

Crist, Charlie, *209*
Crumpton, Ron, *207*
Cummings, Elijah, 191
Cuomo, Andrew, *206*

Dale-Riddle, Allison, 273n18
Davis, Jim, *209*
Demings, Val, 2
Democratic vice presidential candidates, 141
Democrats, 107–8, *108*. *See also* Black candidates, Democratic; Black women candidates, Democratic
denial rebuttals, 56, 60, 157; Black candidates helped by, 161; Booker helped by, 162–63, 185; against crime attacks, *159*, *162*, 235; effects of, *236*, *239*, *240*; example of, *215*; against *Obama* attacks, *159*, *162*, 235; against *results* attacks, *159*, *162*, 235
deracialization, *racial* rebuttals contrasted with, 160
DeSantis, Ron, 3, 62, 137, 191, *218*
Deukmejian, George, 248n7
DeWine, Mike, *207*
Disney+ (streaming service), 145, 231
distract rebuttals, 55, *176*, 177; effects of, *239*, *240*; example of, *214*; by B. Obama, 170; taxes attacks responded to by, 64–65
diversity, and majority-minority electorates, 199–201
Druckman, James N., 65–66, 73
Dubie, Brian, *208*
Dukakis, Michael, 2, 37, 69, 74
Dupree, Johnny, *208*

Eaves, John, *208*
ecological inference (EI) procedure, 5, 250n29
economic assessment, Lucid survey questions on, 222
economic dependency (racialized theme), 35–38
economies, national and state, 27

education, Lucid survey questions on, 221–23, 226–27, 257n14, 258n22, 260n12, 261n27
Edwards, John, 139, *141*
Ehrlich, Robert, 49
EI. *See* ecological inference
elections. *See* general elections; gubernatorial elections; primary elections; Senate elections
electorate, Black population contrasted with, 148
Espy, Mike, 209
experiments: design of, 150–51, *173*, *237–38*; on Harris, 144–47, *145*, *146*; Senate campaigns simulated in, 172, *237–38*. *See also* Booker experiment; criminal pardon experiment

FaceGen Modeller 3.2 (software program), 270n22
"Faces of American Power, Nearly as White as the Oscar Nominees, The" (graphic), 9
False Discovery Rate (FDR) method, for pairwise comparisons, 179
FCC. *See* Federal Communications Commission
FDR. *See* False Discovery Rate
fear of COVID, Lucid survey questions on, 222
FEC. *See* Federal Election Commission
Federal Communications Commission (FCC), 112–13
Federal Election Commission (FEC), 26
feeling thermometer ratings, 140, 142–43, 151, 225; of Booker, 154, 162, *164*, 267n21; of Harris, 144, 227; of Lonegan, 267n21; Lucid survey questions on, 221–22, 227
Fein, Jordan, 73
Figures, Vivian Davis, *207*
Fisher, Mike, *207*
Fiske, Susan, 138
FiveThirtyEight (website), 249n27
Fleming, Erik, *207*

Florida, 75, 191
Ford, Harold, Jr., 6, 11, 43, 114, 129, *214*; advertisements against, 34, 36; campaign for, 87–96; *negative* rebuttals by, 95; Patrick compared with, 12, 71, 94–95; racially sympathetic whites lost by, 192–93; racial priming against, 88–90, *89*, *90*; against racial resentment, 96, 96–97; rebuttals by, 58–59, *59*, 91–94, *92*, *93*; sex attacks against, 87–88, 91–92; surrogates and, *95*; volume of, 91–94, *92*, *93*; white candidates compared with, *206*; white opinion of, 91–94, *92*, *93*
Fraga, Bernard, 45

Gaetz, Matt, 135–36
Gardner, Cory, *208*
Gates, Henry Louis, Jr., 195
gender: Black women candidates affecting, 130–31; Lucid survey questions on, 224, 229–30; race contrasted with, 147, 197
gender activation hypothesis, 136, 139, 143, 146–47
gender attitudes: Black women candidates affecting, 132; toward Harris, *146*, *232*, *233*, 265n38; vote choice and, 135, 137
general elections, 3–4; Black candidates screened out in, 10, 17, 19, 188–89; Harris in, 244n7; B. Obama in, 244n7; white voters dominating, 5
Georgia, 130, 131, 147
Gillum, Andrew, 11, 137; crime attacks against, 47; *racial* rebuttals used by, 62–63; Trump criticizing, 3; white candidates compared with, *209*
Gingrich, Newt, 272n7
Glendening, Parris, 49, *208*, *209*
Glenn, Darryl, 198, *209*
Glick, Peter, 138
GOP. *See* Republican Party
Gore, Albert, *207*, *209*
governor campaigns, racialized issues mentioned in, *46*

governors, Black, 3, 16, 17–18, 21, 248n8
Gray, Robert, 208
Grayson, Marissa, 161
Green, Donald, 22, 26
Greene, Alvin, 208
Greene, Marjorie Taylor, 273n9
Gregg, John, 209
gubernatorial candidates, white Democratic women, 138
gubernatorial elections, 137–39; Black candidates in, *18, 20*; crime attacks affecting, *81*; economies shaping, 27; in Georgia, 130, 147; in Maryland, 99, 120–25, *126, 127*; in Massachusetts, 34, 47, 74, *81*, 83, 257n9; Republican vote intention in, *218. See also* Abrams, Stacey; Brown, Anthony; Gillum, Andrew

Hajnal, Zoltan, 165, 171, 201, 202
Harper, Ken, 205
Harris, Kamala, 13–14, 24, 130–49, *141*, 191, 197, 225; Abrams contrasted with, 147; approach to evaluating, 132–33; attorney general campaigned for by, 262n5; Blacks' pride in, 144, *145*, 230–31, *232*; H. Clinton versus, 140–43, *143*; expectations for, 133–36; experiment on, 144–47, *145, 146*; feeling thermometer ratings of, 144, 227; gender attitudes toward, 146, *232, 233*, 265n38; in general elections, 244n7; Loretta Sanchez against, 131; Lucid survey questions on, 227–28; name recognition of, 142; Obama versus, 140–43, *143*; racial attitudes toward, 146, *232, 233*, 265n38; research design for, 136–37; South Asians' pride in, 144, *145*, 230–31, *232*; Trump criticizing, 134, 135; vice presidential campaign by, 131–32; white male Democratic vice presidential nominees contrasted with, 136, 139–40, *141*; women's pride in, 144, *145*, 230–31, *232*
Harrison, Jaime, 210
Harshbarger, Scott, 24, 206

Healey, Kerry, 6, 42–43, 57–58; crime attacks emphasized by, 47, 74; Patrick contrasted with, 6, *81, 83, 114, 212, 214, 215*; Republican vote intention for, 78–79, *79*; Tim Murray criticizing, 215
Helmke, Paul, 206
Hersh, Eitan, 45
Hicks, Heather, 186
high-level statewide candidates, Black, 4–5; history of modern, 19–21; race influencing, 187–88; racial attacks faced by, 97–98
high-level statewide offices: Asian American candidates for, 200–201; Black candidates for, 1–2, 7, 71; Latino candidates for, 200–201
high-racial-resentment whites, 267n22, 271n34; A. Brown left by, 123–24, *125*; *justify + racial* rebuttals influencing, 194–95; racial attacks influencing, 170; rebuttals not affecting, 86–87, 116–17
Hoekstra, Pete, 209, 210
Hogan, Larry: A. Brown attacked by, 13, 99, 215; Republican vote intention for, 122–23, *123, 124*; taxes attacks by, 44, 50, 120, 121, *126*, 126–27, 213
Hollywood attacks, against Booker: effects of, *154*; racial resentment influenced by, 156, *234, 235*; wording of, 153
Hood, Jim, 208
Hoogendyk, Jack, 209, 210
Hopkins, Daniel, 27–28
Horton, Willie, 2, 6, 37, 74, 158, 173
Huckabee, Mike, 175–77
Hunt, Bootie, 205
Hutto, Brad, 208, 210

ideology, 27, 89; Lucid survey questions on, 222, 227; measurement of, 267n9; partisanship contrasted with racial resentment and, 78–79, *79*, 90, *103, 105*, 105–6, 122–23, *123, 124*; vote choice shaped by, 124–25

ignore rebuttals, 56
income (variable), Lucid survey questions on, 220–21, 222, 226–27, 258n23
incumbent races, open-seat races contrasted with, 26–27
incumbents, Black candidates as, 247n4
independents, 107–8, *108*

Jackson, Jesse, 95, 256n27
James, John, 198, *209*, *210*
James, Sharpe, 61
Jardina, Ashley, 200
Johnson, Constance, 208
Johnson, Gbemende, 188
Johnson, Ron, 1, 2
Johnston, Philip, 58
Jones, David, 231
justify + *racial* rebuttals, 169, *180*, 180–81, 183, *230*; Black candidates benefiting from, 184; description of, *176*; high-racial-resentment voters influenced by, 194–95; *justify* rebuttals contrasted with, 182; racially resentful whites influenced by, 183. *See also racial* rebuttals
justify rebuttals, 158, 175–77, *176*, *177*, *180*, 194–95; Abrams using, 63–64; Black candidates helped by, 180–81; description of, *176*; effects of, *236*, *239*, *240*; example of, *214*; information empowering, 168; *justify* + *racial* contrasted with, 182; B. Obama using, 169; Patrick using, 55, 58, 85, 160; racial resentment influenced by, 182; against *stripper* attacks, *159*, *162*, *235*; white candidates helped by, 180–81

Kaine, Tim, 139, *141*
Kantar Media/CMAG (research firm), 112–13
Kasich, John, *207*
Kean, Thomas, 254n32
Kelly, Gene, *205*
Kelly, Laura, 137
Kelly, Molly, 137

Kelso, Blanche, 248n6
Kemp, Brian, 130, 137, 191, *218*; Abrams criticizing, *212*; crime attacks by, 134; white Democratic women gubernatorial candidates compared with, 138
Kennedy, Edward M. "Ted," 57
Kennedy Townsend, Kathleen, 48–49, *208*, *209*
Kerry, John F., 57
Kilpatrick, Kwame, 173–74, 270n21
Kinder, Donald, 37, 38, 273n18
King, Gary, 25
Kirk, Ron, *205*
Krasno, Jonathan, 26

LaGuer, Benjamin, 74–75, *85*, *215*, 255n10
Land, Terri Lynn, *209*, *210*
Latino candidates, 200–201, 246n34, 254n32
Lautenberg, Frank, *208*
Laverty Jones, Jan, *206*
Lee, Lynsie, *212*
Leeper, Thomas, 73
Lewis, John, 191
Limbaugh, Rush, 135
local broadcast television, advertisements on, 261n18
Lonegan, Steve, 109, 163, *164*, 185, *212*; against Booker, 12–14, 39, 43, 99–101, *112*, 151, *153*, *234*, *235*, 266n3, 266n6; crime attacks by, 100–101; feeling thermometer ratings of, 267n21; racial attacks by, *105*, 118; Republican vote intention for, *103*, 216
Los Angeles Times/Bloomberg poll, 91, 96
Louisiana, 248n8
low-racial resentment whites, 259n31, 267n22, 271n34; in New Jersey, 261n19; Patrick supported by, 86–87; *racial* rebuttals influencing, 182
Lucid survey, 143–44; ANES compared with, 142; February 2021, 226–31; October 2020, 220–25; sexism measured by, 265n34

Lucid survey questions: on age, 221, 226, 257n14; on education, 221–23, 226–27, 257n14, 258n22, 260n12, 261n27; on feeling thermometer ratings, 221–22, 227; on gender, 229–30; on Harris, 227–28; on ideology, 222, 227; on income, 220–21, 222, 226–27, 258n23; on party identification, 221, 226; on race, 229–30; on racial resentment, 228–29; on sexism, 223–24, 229–30

Majette, Denise, 206
majority-minority electorates, diversity and, 199–201
margin of defeat, among all voters compared with white voters, 31
margin of victory, among all voters compared with white voters, 25–26, 211, 250n30
Martin, Jim, 206, 207
Martin, Trayvon, 195
Maryland, gubernatorial elections in, 99, 120–25, 126, 127
Maryland respondents, to surveys, 150, 162, 235, 236; attacks influencing, 154; New Jersey respondents contrasted with, 155; rebuttals influencing, 162
Massachusetts, gubernatorial elections in, 34, 47, 74, 81, 83, 257n9
McCain, John, 190, 272n4
McCall, H. Carl, 206
McClerking, Harwood, 171
McGraw, Kathleen, 160–61
Mechanical Turk (MTurk), 172, 269n14, 270n23
medium-racial resentment whites, 267n22, 271n34
Meek, Kendrick, 207
Memphis Commercial-Appeal (newspaper), 42, 88, 91, 92, 94, 95
Mendelberg, Tali, 36, 68–69, 158, 183
Menendez, Bob, 47, 208, 254n32
Metz, David, 44

Mihos, Christy, 79, 258n15
Mills, Janet, 137
Milne, Scott, 208
Mississippi, 148, 248n6, 251n41
Monmouth poll, 102–3, 104, 116
Morales, Victor, 205
"More Perfect Union, A" (B. Obama), 169, 195
Mourdock, Richard, 206
MTurk. *See* Mechanical Turk
Murphy, Patrick, 207
Murray, Tim, 214, 215
Musgrove, Ronnie, 205, 207
Myers, Woody, 209

NAACP, 95, 256n27
name recognition, 142, 265n36
National Institute on Money in State Politics (NIMSP), 26
Neal, Joe, 206
negative rebuttals, 85, 169–70, 177; Booker using, 157, 162–63; description of, 176; effects of, 236, 239, 240; example of, 214; by Ford, 95; by Kennedy, 57; B. Obama using, 55; to sex attacks, 59; *Twitter* attacks challenged with, 159, 162, 185, 193–94, 235
Nelson, Bill, 207
Nelson, Thomas, 171
Newark, New Jersey, Booker linked to, 60–61, 101, 151, 260n9
New Jersey: low-racial resentment whites in, 261n19; Newark in, 60–61, 101, 151, 260n9; without racial priming, 165; Senate elections in, 34, 99–101, 106–7, 112, 114, 118–19, 150–51, 266n3
New Jersey respondents, to surveys, 150, 162, 234, 236; attacks influencing, 154; Maryland respondents contrasted with, 155; rebuttals influencing, 162
news cycle, twenty-four-hour, 256n26
New York Times (newspaper), 246n28
NIMSP. *See* National Institute on Money in State Politics

nondiscrimination, white supremacy replaced by, 36–37
Noriega, Rick, 205
norms, against racial derogation, 184–85
Nunn, Michelle, 207, 210

Obama, Barack, 3, 22–23, 193, 195, 225; Biden associated with, 139–40; "birther" theory contested by, 190; Black candidates linked to, 152, 153; "chronic accessibility" and, 133, 165, 189–90; H. Clinton compared with, 273n18; *distract* rebuttals by, 170; in general elections, 244n7; Gingrich criticizing, 272n7; Harris versus, 140–43, 143; *justify* rebuttals utilized by, 169; Kilpatrick tied to, 173–74; *negative* rebuttals utilized by, 55; racial attacks faced by, 272n4; racial attitudes toward, 133, 202; racialization of, 134–35; as racialized cue, 39; racial prejudice and, 4; *racial* rebuttals used by, 55
Obama, Michelle, 143, 225, 265n36
Obama attacks, against Booker: *denial* rebuttals against, 159, 162, 235; effects of, 154; racial resentment influenced by, 156, 234, 235; wording of, 153
O'Brien, Shannon, 24, 206
Ocasio-Cortez, Alexandria, 1
OLS. *See* ordinary least squares
O'Malley, Martin, 44, 48, 120, 208, 209, 212
Omar, Ilhan, 1
open-seat races, 26–27, 247n5
Oppenheimer, Bruce, 188
ordinary least squares (OLS) regression, 30
O'Reilly, Bill, 38
"Oscars So White" controversy, 9
Ossoff, Jon, 210

pairwise comparisons, FDR for, 179
Palin, Sarah, 272n4
Parker, Susan, 206, 207
"parking-lot rape" ad, 6

partisanship, 104, 216; measurement of, 267n9; party advantage and, 251n42; racial resentment and ideology contrasted with, 78–79, 79, 90, 103, 105, 105–6, 122–23, 123, 124, 260n15; of state, 27–28
party advantage, partisanship and, 251n42
party identification, Lucid survey questions on, 221–22, 226
Patrick, Deval, 7–8, 11, 34, 36, 43, 47; advertisements against, 34, 36; *apology* rebuttals by, 255n10; Booker compared with, 117; A. Brown compared with, 127; campaign by, 74–85; *counterattack* rebuttals used by, 56–58; *counterimaging* rebuttals used by, 170; crime attacks challenged by, 54, 57, 75–76; Ford compared with, 12, 71, 94–95; Healey contrasted with, 6, 81, 83, 114, 212, 214, 215; *justify* rebuttals used by, 55, 58, 85, 160; LaGuer corresponding with, 74–75, 85; low-racial resentment whites supporting, 86–87; racial priming against, 76–80; *racial* rebuttals not used by, 58; toward racial resentment, 86, 86–87; rebuttals utilized by, 12, 58, 80–84, 81, 83; taxes attacks responded to by, 57–58; volume of, 81, 81–84, 83; white candidates compared with, 24, 206; white opinion influenced by, 80–84; white voters influenced by, 82, 85, 97
patriotism attacks, against Booker: effects of, 154; racial resentment influenced by, 156, 234, 235; wording of, 153
Peabody, Endicott, 19
Pinchback, P. B. S., 248n8
Pipkin, E. J., 207
police, Black Americans killed by, 193
population, Black. *See* Black population
primary elections: Black candidates underrepresented by, 188–89; in California, 24–25; 2010 and 2020, 18
Princeton Survey Research Center's Mercer County panel, 269n14

quality, of candidate (confounder), 26, 29–30
questions, Lucid survey. *See* Lucid survey questions

race, of candidates: Black candidates affected by, 21–23, 28–31, *31*; Black women candidates affected by, 130–31, 148; campaigns teaching about, 194; gender contrasted with, 147, 197; high-level statewide candidates affected by, 187–88; Lucid survey questions on, 229–30; outcomes affected by, *211*; racial attitude not activated by, 190; rebuttals influenced by, 170–72

racial activation, racial attacks and, 164–65

racial activation hypothesis, 135, 138, 139, 143, 146–47

racial animus, decline in, 249n22

racial appeals, 37, 134, 149; Black candidates combating, 186; *negative* rebuttals contrasted with positive, 169; white voters influenced by, 3

racial attacks, 34, 40–41, 189–91, 261n20; Black candidates facing, 11–12, 46, 53, 65–66, 128, 188, 203, *241*; Booker affected by, 100–101, *108*; A. Brown not challenging, 127; evocative imagery included in, 166; expected effects of, 72; high-level statewide candidates facing, 97–98; high-racial-resentment whites influenced by, 170; by Lonegan, *105*, 118; B. Obama facing, 271n4; racial activation and, 164–65; racialization without, 202; racial priming through, 110; racial resentment affected by, *103*, *105*, *178*, *216*; rebuttals to, 8, *103*, *112*; Trump embracing, 190–91

racial attitudes: Black women candidates affected by, 132; toward Harris, *146*, *232*, *233*, 265n38; toward B. Obama, 133, 202; political dynamics of, 10; race not activating, 190; taxation linked with, 121; vote choice influencing, 2, 22, 137, 189

racial bias, 32–34; approach to testing, 23–25; against Black candidates, 16–17; confounders for, 26–28; data on, 23–25; outcome measures for, 25–26

racial constituency, Black candidates associated with, 151, *153*

racial derogation, norms against, 184–85

racial distancing, by Black Republican candidates, 199

racial identity, whites' growing, 148–49

racial inequality, Black elected officials contrasted with, 196

racialization, 52; attacks causing, 189; of Black candidates, 46–51, *48*, *49*, *50*, *51*, 67; of Booker, 165; defining, 36–41; measuring, 41–44; of B. Obama, 134–35; without racial attacks, 202; rebuttals counteracted by, 119

racialized framing, rebuttals to, 67

racialized rhetoric, viability contrasted with, 45–46

racially resentful whites, 39, 74, 103; *justify + racial* rebuttals influencing, 183; racially sympathetic whites compared with, 123, 143, 154–55; rebuttals and, 160, 185, 201. *See also* high-racial-resentment whites

racially sympathetic whites, 74, 103; Ford losing, 192–93; racially resentful whites compared with, 123, 143, 154–55; rebuttals influencing, 163, 192–93; surrogates influencing, 186. *See also* low-racial resentment whites

racial prejudice, B. Obama and, 4

racial priming, 74, 104, 109, 126, 128; analysis of, 262n29; Booker deactivating, 115–16; against A. Brown, 121–25, *123*, *124*, *125*; during Ford campaign, 88–90, *89*, *90*; New Jersey without, 165; during Patrick campaign, 76–80; through racial attacks, 110; *racial* rebuttals affecting, 158–60, 166; racial resentment and, *217*; during Senate elections, 106–7; in statewide campaigns, 118–19

racial rebuttals, 157, 175, *176*, 177, 180, 195; Black candidates avoiding, 68–69;

deracialization contrasted with, 160; description of, *176*; effects of, *236*, *239*, *240*; example of, *214*; Gillum using, 62–63; low-racial resentment voters influenced by, 182; norms empowering, 168; B. Obama using, 55; Patrick not using, 58; racial priming affected by, 158–60, 166; surrogates using, 59–60, 95, 256n27; white candidates not helped by, 183

racial resentment, 104, 110, 115–18, *124*, *125*; advertisements affecting, 178; alternative explanations for, 107–10; attacks influencing, *234*, *235*; battery for, 88, 102, 122, 138, 221, 223, 228–29, 264n26, 270n20; *black hole* attacks influencing, *156*, *234*, *235*; toward Booker, 155, *156*; candidate evaluations contrasted with, 269n4; CCES predicting, 77–78; crime attacks influencing, 78–79, *79*, 155–56, *156*; against Ford, *96*, 96–97; *Hollywood* attacks influencing, *156*, *234*, *235*; *justify* rebuttals influencing, 182; Lucid survey questions on, 228–29; measurement of, 138; *Obama* attacks influencing, *156*, *234*, *235*; partisanship and ideology contrasted with, 78–79, *79*, 90, *103*, *105*, 122–23, *123*, *124*, 260n15; toward Patrick, *86*, 86–87; *patriotism* attacks influencing, *156*, *234*, *235*; racial attacks influencing, *103*, *105*, 178, 216; racial priming and, *217*; rebuttals influencing, *116*, *117*, 163, *164*, 170, *183*; Republican vote intention compared with, *139*; *results* attacks influencing, *156*, *234*, *235*; sex attacks and, 89; sexism contrasted with, 140, *141*, *143*, *218*; *stripper* attacks influencing, *156*, *234*, *235*; taxes attacks influencing, 122–23, *123*; *Twitter* attacks influencing, *156*, *234*, *235*; validation of predicted, 107; vote choice linked with, 78, 88–90, *105*, 128; white candidates and, 271n29. *See also* high-racial resentment whites; low-racial resentment whites

racism, 113, *225*; Black candidates affected by, 5; representation shaped by, 8; white candidates challenging, 193

Radnofsky, Barbara Ann, *205*

Rapaport, Paul, *207*

rebuttals, 72, 150, 157, *173*, 271n27; by Abrams, 63–65, *64*; *apology*, 84, 255n10; attacks contrasted with, 113, 158, *159*, 166–68, 193–94; by Black candidates, *180*, 180–82; by Booker, 60–61, *61*, 111–13, *112*, *113*, *114*, *115*, 163; by A. Brown, 61–62, *62*, 125–28, *126*, *127*; characteristics and expected effects of, 72; content of, 129, 149; crime attacks in proportion to, 82–83; descriptive observational analysis of, 257n1; effects of, *236*, *239*, *240*; election outcomes and, 71; examples of types of, 214–15; by Ford, 58–59, *59*, 91–94, *92*, *93*; frequency of, 57–65; high-racial-resentment whites not affected by, 86–87, 116–17; *ignore*, 56; Maryland respondents influenced by, *162*; New Jersey respondents influenced by, *162*; overall levels of, 65–68; Patrick using, 12, *58*, 80–84, *81*, *83*; race influencing, 170–72; to racial attacks, 8, *103*, *112*; racialization counteracting, 119; to racialized framing, 67; racially resentful whites and, 160, 185, 201; racially sympathetic whites affected by, 163, 192–93; racial resentment influenced by, *116*, *117*, 163, *164*, 170, *183*; to sex attacks, *95*; silence contrasted with, 192; subgroups affected by, 74; surrogates delegated, 69, 73, 84, 193; timing of, 73, 84, 94–95, 113–15; types of, 54–57, 73–74, 84, 95, 115; vote choice influenced by, 71; by white candidates, *180*; white voters influenced by, 83, 93, 114, *127*, *127*. *See also counterattack* rebuttals; *counterimaging* rebuttals; *denial* rebuttals; *distract* rebuttals; *justify + racial* rebuttals; *justify* rebuttals; *negative* rebuttals; *racial* rebuttals; volume

Reid, Rory, 206
representation, racism shaping, 8
Republican National Committee (RNC), 6, 87
Republican Party, 190, 191, 202
Republicans, 107–8, *108*, 198–99, 274n28
Republican vote intention, 102–3, *104*; for Corker, 89, *90*; in gubernatorial elections, *218*; for Healey, 78–79, *79*; for Hogan, 122–23, *123*, *124*; for Lonegan, *103*, *216*; racial resentment compared with, *139*; sexism compared with, *139*
Republican voters, "return home" by, 107–8, *108*
resentment, racial. *See* racial resentment
results attacks, against Booker: *denial* rebuttals against, *159*, *162*, *235*; effects of, *154*; racial resentment influenced by, *156*, *234*, *235*; wording of, *153*
Revels, Hiram, 248n6
Ridge, Tom, 207
Rippere, Paulina, 161
RNC. *See* Republican National Committee
Robinson, Jack, 205
Rogers, Jim, 208
Romney, Mitt, 38, 58, 205, 272n7
Rubin, Doug, 57
Rubio, Marco, 2
Rutgers-Eagleton poll, 102–3, *104*, *106*, 107, 116

Sanbonmatsu, Kira, 171
Sanchez, Loretta, 131, 262n4
Sanders, Bernie, 137
Sanders, Lynn, 38
Santorum, Rick, 272n7
Schaffer, Bob, 208
Scott, Marvin, 206
Scott, Phil, 208
Scott, Tim, 244n7, 249n24
Sears, David, 22, 38, 121, 165, 189, 264n20
Selin, Jennifer, 188
Senate campaigns, experiments simulating, 172, 237–38
Senate elections, *174*, *175*; advertisements in, 172; Black Americans in, 19–20; Black candidates in, *18*, *20*; in California, 131; economies shaping, 27; in Georgia, 131; in New Jersey, 34, 99–101, 106–7, *112*, *114*, 118–19, 150–51; racial priming during, 106–7; in Tennessee, 34, 87, *92*, *93*, 128. *See also* Booker, Cory; Ford, Harold, Jr.; Patrick, Deval
senators, from Mississippi, 248n6
sex (variable), 257n14
sex attacks, 35–36, 43, 93, 100–101, 152, *153*; Black candidates facing, *49*, *51*; examples and nonexamples of, 212–13, *212–13*, 253n24; against Ford, 87–88, 91–92; *negative* rebuttals to, 59; racial resentment and, 89; rebuttals to, 95; white voters influenced by, 92
sexism, 225, 265n31; ANES measuring, 218–20; ASI measuring, 138; battery for, 223–24, 229–30; CCES not measuring, 262nn4–5; H. Clinton and, 149, 264n20; toward Democratic vice presidential candidates, 141; Lucid survey measuring, 265n34; Lucid survey questions on, 223–24, 229–30; racial resentment contrasted with, 140, *141*, *143*, *218*; Republican vote intention compared with, *139*
sexual misbehavior, Corker emphasizing, 48
Shaftan, Bill, 101
"Shaky" (ad), 87–88
Silverstein, Matt, 208
Sink, Alex, 209
Sniderman, Paul M., 65
sniper attacks, Washington, DC affected by, 48–49
social groups, voter behavior affected by, 133
Songer, Carl Ray, 75
South Asians, Harris pride in, *145*, 230–31, 232
southern states, Black population in, 247n2
Sowell, Wayne, 206
Spitzer, Eliot, 206

SSI. *See* Survey Sampling International
stabilization phase, *vs.* decline phase, *115*
Star-Ledger (newspaper), 42
statewide campaigns, racial priming in, 118–19
Steele, Michael, *207*
Stephens-Dougan, LaFleur, 199
stereotypes, anti-Black, 229
Stout, Christopher, 169
stripper attacks, against Booker: effects of, *154*; *justify* rebuttals against, *159*, *162*, *235*; racial resentment influenced by, *156*, *234*, *235*; wording of, *153*
Study 1: Abrams examined in, 137–39; CCES used in, 136; sexism researched in, 265n34
Study 2: ANES used in, 136; Harris examined in, 139–40; racial activation hypothesis supported by, 143; sexism measured in, 218–20, 265n34
Study 3: Harris examined in, 140–43; Lucid survey used in, 136; question wording from, 220–25
Study 4, 144–47, *145*, *146*
Suddith, Clayton, *206*
surrogates, for Black candidates, 43, 54–55, *58*, *59*, *60*, 113–15; "call me" ad responded to by, 94–95; Ford and, *95*; racially sympathetic whites influenced by, 186; *racial* rebuttals used by, 59–60, *95*, 256n27; rebuttals delegated to, 69, 73, 84, 193
surveys, average error of, 249n27
Survey Sampling International (SSI), 150, 172
SurveyUSA poll, 77, 78, 80, 259n27
Swann, Lynn, *207*
Szeliga, Kathy, *209*

Taft, Bob, *207*
Talking Points Memo (news site), 101
Tampa Bay Times (newspaper), 42
Tate, Katherine, 44
taxation, racial attitudes linked with, 121

taxes attacks, 49, 61–62, 101, *153*; Black candidates facing, *50*, *51*; A. Brown not challenging, 120; *distract* rebuttals responding to, 64–65; economic dependency and, 37–38; examples and nonexamples of, 212–13, *212–13*, 253n24; Hogan emphasizing, 44, 50, 120, 121, *126*, 126–27, *213*; Patrick responding to, 57–58; as racialized issue, 39–40; racial resentment influenced by, 122–23, *123*; white voters influenced by, *126*. *See also* *black hole* attacks
"tax revolt," in California, 38, 121
Taylor, Mark, 47, *209*, 254n31
television, local broadcast, 261n18
Tenenbaum, Inez, *208*, *210*
Tennessee, 59–60, 259n26; CCES in, 259n26; Senate elections in, 34, 87, *92*, *93*, 128; SurveyUSA poll in, 259n27
Tennesseeans for Truth (group), 59–60
Tesler, Michael, 39, 139, 165, 189, 202, 264n20
Theriault, Sean M., 65
thermometer ratings, feeling. *See* feeling thermometer ratings
Thompson, Jill, *209*
Thurmond, Mike, *207*
timing, of rebuttals, 73, 84, 94–95, 113–15
Titus, Dina, *206*
Tlaib, Rashida, 1
Trump, Donald, 3, 142, 185–86; Gillum criticized by, 3; Harris criticized by, 134, 135; racial attacks embraced by, 190–91; Republican Party influenced by, 202
Tuke, Bob, 47, *206*, *210*, 254n31
Twitter attacks, against Booker, 101, 157, 185; effects of, *154*; *negative* rebuttals challenging, *159*, *162*, 185, 193–94, *235*; racial resentment influenced by, *156*, *234*, *235*; wording of, *153*

urban (variable), 258n23
USA Today/Gallup poll, 91, 96

Vallone, Peter, 206
viability, 254n29; of Black candidates, 35, 44–45; definition of, 44–45, 246n28; racialized rhetoric contrasted with, 45–46; of white candidates, 254n31
vice presidential campaign, by Harris, 131–32
vice presidential candidates, Democratic, 141
vice presidential nominees, white male Democratic, 136
volume, of rebuttals, 72–73; Black candidates helped with, 70; of Booker, 111–13, *112*, *113*; of Ford, 91–94, *92*, *93*; of Patrick, *81*, 81–84, *83*
vote choice, of white voters: attacks affecting, 77–78; gender attitudes and, 135, 137; ideology shaping, 124–25; racial attitudes influencing, 2, 22, 137, 189; racial resentment linked with, 78, 88–90, 105, 128; rebuttals influencing, 71. *See also* Republican vote intention
vote intention, Republican. *See* Republican vote intention
voter behavior, social groups affecting, 133
voting rights court cases, EI utilized by, 250n29

Wagner, Scott, 207
Wargotz, Eric, 207, 209
Warnock, Raphael, 210
Warren, Elizabeth, 142
Washington, DC, sniper attacks affecting, 48–49
Washington Post poll, 124, 125–26
Weld, William, 205
welfare, 151
white candidates: Abrams compared with, 209; Black candidates compared with, 29, 30, *31*, 32–33, *33*, 41, *48*, *49*, *50*, *51*, 168, 171, *174*, 174–75, 178, *183*, 205–10, *239*, *240*, 249n25; Booker compared with, 208, 254n33; A. Brown compared with, 208; Democratic women gubernatorial, 138; Ford compared with, 206; Gillum compared with, 209; *justify* rebuttals helping, 180–81; Patrick compared with, 24, 206; *racial* rebuttals not helping, 183; racial resentment and, 271n29; racism challenged by, 193; rebuttals by, *180*; viability of, 254n31
white Democratic women gubernatorial candidates, Kemp compared with, 138
white identity, 200
white male Democratic vice presidential nominees, Harris contrasted with, 136, 139–40, *141*
white opinion, 262n29; of Booker, 111–13, *112*, *113*; of A. Brown, 125–28, *126*, *127*; of Ford, 91–94, *92*, *93*; Patrick influencing, 80–84
white supremacy, nondiscrimination replacing, 36–37
white voters, 14; Black candidates penalized by, 11, 15–17, 21–23, 31, 34, 130; A. Brown losing, 8; crime attacks influencing, 81; general elections dominated by, 5; margin of defeat among all voters compared with, *31*; margin of victory among all voters compared with, 25–26, *211*; opposition to Black candidates, 246n34; Patrick influencing, 82, 85, 97; racial appeals influencing, 3; rebuttals influencing, *83*, *93*, *114*, *127*, *127*, 150; sex attacks influencing, *92*; taxes attacks influencing, *126*. *See also* high-racial-resentment whites; low-racial-resentment whites; racially resentful whites; racially sympathetic whites; vote choice
Whitmer, Gretchen, 137
Wilder, L. Douglas, 20
Willie Horton ads, 2, 6, 37, 74, 173
Wisconsin Advertising Project, 258n15
women: as Black Democratic candidates, 130–32, 148, 196–97; Harris pride in among, 144, *145*, 230–31, *232*; as white Democratic gubernatorial candidates, 138
Workman, Mike, 208
Wright, Jeremiah, 169, 185, 195

Yang, Andrew, 193

Printed and bound by CPI Group (UK) Ltd, Croydon, CR0 4YY
25/03/2024

14475399-0003